# Privacy on the Line

The right of the people to be secure in their persons, houses, papers and effects against unreasonable searches and seizures shall not be violated, and no Warrants shall issue but upon probable cause, supported by Oath or affirmation, and particularly describing the place to be searched, and the persons or things to be seized.

**Fourth Amendment**
**United States Constitution**

The evil incident to invasion of privacy of the telephone is far greater than that involved in tampering with the mails. Whenever a telephone line is tapped, the privacy of persons at both ends of the line is invaded, and all conversations between them upon any subject, and although proper, confidential and privileged, may be overheard. Moreover, the tapping of one man's telephone line involves the tapping of the telephone of every other person whom he may call or who may call him. As a means of espionage, writs of assistance and general warrants are but puny instruments of tyranny and oppression when compared with wire-tapping.

**Justice Louis Brandeis**
dissenting opinion in
*Olmstead v. United States*
(277 U.S. 438, 1928, pp. 475–476)

Senator Herman Talmadge: Do you remember when we were in law school, we studied a famous principle of law that came from England and also is well known in this country, that no matter how humble a man's cottage is, that even the King of England cannot enter without his consent.

Witness John Ehrlichman: I am afraid that has been considerably eroded over the years, has it not?

Senator Talmadge: Down in my country we still think of it as a pretty legitimate piece of law.

**United States Senate**
Select Committee on Presidential
Campaign Activities, Hearings,
Phase 1: Watergate Investigation,
Ninety-Third Congress, First
Session, 1973, p. 2601

# Privacy on the Line

## The Politics of Wiretapping and Encryption

Whitfield Diffie
Susan Landau

The MIT Press
Cambridge, Massachusetts
London, England

First MIT Press paperback edition, 1999
© 1998 Massachusetts Institute of Technology

Composed in LATEX $2_\varepsilon$ by the authors.
Set in Sabon by Loyola Graphics of San Bruno, California.
Printed and bound in the United States of America.

**Library of Congress Cataloging-in-Publication Data**

Diffie, Whitfield.
   Privacy on the line : the politics of wiretapping and encryption / Whitfield
Diffie, Susan Landau.
      p.   cm.
   Includes bibliographical references and index.
   ISBN 0-262-04167-7 (hc : alk. paper), 0-262-54100-9 (pb)
   1. Wiretapping—United States. 2. Data encryption (Computer science)—Law
and legislation—United States. 3. Privacy, Right of—United States. I. Landau,
Susan. II. Title.
KF9670.D54   1998
342.73'0858—dc21                                                97-42347
                                                                   CIP

# Contents

# Preface

In the spring of 1993, the White House announced an unprecedented plan for both promoting and controlling the use of secret codes to keep communications private. The plan, formally called *key escrow* but popularly known as "Clipper" after its star component, the Clipper chip, was to adopt a new federal standard for encryption, a standard that would ensure that the government could always read encrypted messages if it chose.

The Clipper proposal was met by a storm of protest. It was criticized by some as an outrageous violation of civil liberties, by some because the standard could only be implemented in hardware, and by still others on a wide variety of grounds. Despite the opposition, Clipper seemed, in a sense, to have won. After a mandatory public comment period, which produced two letters in favor and 300 against, the standard was adopted. In a more fundamental sense, however, the Clipper program seemed to have lost. Aside from the 9000 telephone security devices that the FBI purchased in an attempt to seed the market, very little Clipper-based equipment has been built.

The Clipper debate proved to be the opening engagement in an ongoing battle about the right to use encryption. Having tried to use its buying power and standards-making authority to impose key escrow, the government turned to the only other non-legislative tool available: export control.

The United States has approximately 5% of the world's population. In light of this, it is not surprising that, although the country's share of the world economy is way out of proportion to its population, most major US corporations sell more than half their products in other countries. This makes the larger part of their markets subject to export-control laws.

It is also true that a key competitive strategy in modern business is to eliminate unnecessary versions of products. Duplication can be particularly costly in high-technology products such as computer software. If US corporations are unable to export the same versions of their products that they sell at home, the effect is a significant increase in costs. The government's subsequent attempts to achieve key escrow have turned on this fact.

In January 1997, the administration began to permit the export of some unescrowed encryption products for 2 years to companies that submit detailed plans for developing escrowed products within that time.

Why is all this important? Why should anyone who is not in the cryptography business be concerned about regulation of the export of cryptographic equipment? The answer lies in the rush to put society online.

For most of human history, most communication between individuals was conducted face to face. For a few thousand years some has been conducted in writing, but this is in many respects a poor substitute. Letters took weeks, months, or even years to travel long distances. The fact that a letter might be opened en route and thus was less private than a whisper was just one of many limitations.

For a little more than 100 years, some human communication has been carried by electronic media, particularly the telephone. This has brought to remote communication an immediacy that approximates face-to-face contact. The quality of telecommunication continues to improve, and the portion of relationships in which telecommunication is the primary mode of communication continues to increase. We are moving the fabric of our society into electronic channels as quickly as we can.

When telecommunication was merely an adjunct to physical communication, it was possible to hedge about privacy. When two people meet frequently as well as talking regularly by telephone, they can reserve indiscreet remarks for their face-to-face meetings. But as telecommunication becomes more the rule than the exception, this becomes less feasible. In a future society (which may not be far off) in which most communication is telecommunication and many close relationships are between people who never meet in person, it becomes impossible. If people are to enjoy the same effortless privacy in the future that they enjoyed in the past, the means to protect that privacy must be built into their communication systems.

Were the discussion to stop here, the conclusion would be self-evident: we should design all our communication systems to guarantee confidentiality. Personal privacy, however, is not everyone's paramount concern. There are powerful elements of society—police and military organizations—that make use of intercepted communications in what they consider the protection of public safety. These groups view the ready availability of strong cryptography as threatening their ability to perform their functions. Moreover, these once-distinct government activities are drawing closer together in response to the perceived threat of international terrorism. Not surprisingly, this emerging coalition sees individual access to cryptography more as a curse than a blessing.

We see no simple resolution of this conflict. The debate so far has been largely an argument among partisans, all anxious to bias the evidence in their own favor. This is also a field with an extraordinary number of secrets. Neither the police and the spies, who oppose widespread cryptography, nor the big corporations, which support it, are the most open and forthcoming of society's institutions.

In this book, we attempt to lift enough veils to permit the reader to develop an informed opinion on the subject. We examine the social function of privacy: how it underlies other aspects of a free and democratic society and what happens when it is lost. We explore how intelligence and law-enforcement organizations intercept communications, what use they make of them, and what problems cryptography might create. We also describe how cryptography works and how it can be used to protect the secrets of both individuals and organizations.

If we have succeeded, the reader will come away from our book with a new understanding of an issue that, despite the publicity it has received in the past few years, has seemed mysterious and confusing.

# Preface to the Paperback Edition

The authors last modified the text of the first edition on 30 October 1997. As we write this, almost exactly a year later, we look back on a year that has been eventful without being decisive in the battle to protect communications privacy.

In January 1998 it was revealed that former White House intern Monica Lewinsky had described a sexual relationship with the President of the United States in phone calls to her friend Linda Tripp. Tripp had recorded the conversations and turned them over to Kenneth Starr, an independent prosecutor who had — up till that moment — been investigating quite different allegations of Presidential impropriety. Although the recordings violate the Maryland wiretap law — which requires two-party consent for the taping of a phone call[1]— they clearly exhibit a privacy problem that cryptography could only have made worse. Had Lewinsky been worried that her intimate revelations would be recorded and exploited by third parties tapping into and recording her calls, cryptography would have been an appropriate precaution but cryptography, even had she been using it, could have done nothing to protect her from betrayal by her confidant. She would, if anything, have talked more freely on a secure line than an unsecured one.

The incident, which illustrates both the importance and the difficulty of communications privacy, has set in motion events that promise to keep privacy on the public mind for some time to come.

The current public debate on encryption began in May 1993 with the *Clipper* proposal to build *key escrow* — spare keys for law-enforcement purposes — into secure telephones. Central to the Clipper program was a tamper-resistant chip containing a classified encryption algorithm called Skipjack. The demand that citizens should trust their privacy to products employing classified technology was one of the main objections to Clipper, voiced by businesses and civil liberties groups alike. The demand that Clipper be declassified so that it could be publicly evaluated was met with flat rejection and the assertion that Clipper would never be declassified. Now, it has been. The reason appears to be NSA's desire to save money by employing software for use in protecting the Military Message System.

To those of us who had hoped for cooperation rather than conflict with the government in securing communications, this represents a sadly missed opportunity. Had Skipjack been available for public scrutiny, the algorithm might have been seen as an appropriate replacement for DES. Had Skipjack been based on public technology (as all the contemporary proposals to replace DES are) key escrow might even have achieved public acceptance. As it stands, there is no sign of industry interest in embracing an algorithm that (like DES) is viewed as only marginally strong enough and likely to require replacement in another decade or two. Instead, another government action suggests its acceptance of the inevitability of very strong cryptographic algorithms in commercial communications.

The National Institute of Standards and Technology's plans for an Advanced Encryption Standard (AES) to replace DES by a cipher with blocks twice as long and a key nearly five times larger made dramatic progress in 1998. Fifteen designs were accepted for first-round evaluation from those submitted by the June 15, 1998 deadline. These were presented at the first of a series of evaluation conferences scheduled to extend over two years or more. In sharp contrast to the procedure by which DES was selected, the project has been gratifyingly open. Full details of the accepted algorithms have been published on the Web (http://csrc.nist.gov/encryption/aes/aes_home.htm) and on CD-ROM. The open process has also been a hit with the cryptographic community, attracting designs from many of the best known names in the field.

In the summer of 1996, the National Research Council's cryptography study panel recommended a relaxation of cryptographic export controls and proposed that products with encryption capabilities equivalent to those of DES be made easily exportable (Dam and Lin (1996), pp. 8–9). Acceptance took more than two years, but in September 1998 the

White House announced streamlined export of products containing DES. The government also added several new sectors (insurance companies, subsidiaries of US companies, and health and medical organizations) to the list of foreign-based organizations permitted to obtain US products containing strong (128-bit key) non-escrowed encryption (White House (1998)). Whether the relaxed export controls will allow US companies to compete with foreign ones in the security arena is doubtful, however. The very incident that precipitated the government's action cut it off at the knees.

In an event noteworthy for its neatly orchestrated publicity, the Electronic Frontier Foundation revealed that it had built the often designed *DES cracker* — a specialized computer capable of producing DES keys from cipher text in (at worst) just over a week.[2] The announcement had been held off for over a month waiting for RSA Data Security to issue the third of its DES challenge problems. The problem appeared on July 13th and by good luck was solved in 56 hours. (Markoff 1998) The machine cost approximately a quarter of a million dollars — right in line with the designers' predictions. The days of arguing that DES provided adequate commercial security were over.

Since Communications Assistance for Law Enforcement Act (CALEA) passed in 1994, it has been a battleground between telephone company concern about costs and FBI intransigence. Even Attorney General Janet Reno admitted that the FBI had been part of the problem ("As I indicated ... I think that we were perhaps a little too rigid in the beginning as we tried to address the FBI's requirements" (USHR 1998)). 1998 was to be the year in which the phone companies and the FBI came together to make peace, with the former providing the surveillance capabilities required by the law. There was not even a ceasefire. Although the cellular industry agreed to provide the capability to track the location of cellular users (a surveillance requirement explicitly omitted from the CALEA bill), and the telephone companies agreed to FBI requests that "packet switching" protocols provide full content of customer communications to the government even when investigators had court approval only for address data, industry refused to agree to all the FBI sought (similar disputes had been the reason for CALEA). The FBI wanted to monitor conference calls even *after* the subject of a wiretap order had left the call, and it wanted the telephone companies to provide detailed identifying information on each call participant (including those not yet under investigation). The FBI approached both the Federal Communications Commission, the regulatory body appointed to adjudicate on CALEA, and Congress, in an attempt to get these.

The telephone companies for their part sued the FBI Director and the Attorney General in US District Court over the implementation of CALEA, arguing that the proposed simultaneous surveillance standards set by the FBI were "arbitrary" and "capricious" (*United States Telephone Association v. FBI; Freeh; US Department of Justice; Reno*). Meanwhile in September the FCC ruled that the four years that had passed since CALEA were insufficient, and that telephone companies should be given until June 30, 2000 to comply with the law (FCC 1998a). In October the FCC tentatively ruled that location information should be provided to law enforcement when it is "reasonably available" to the carrier, but at this time it was inappropriate to have requirements on packet-switching information (FCC (1998b)).

The year has seen little legislative movement on cryptography. Bills liberalizing export of cryptography (beyond the most recent regulatory changes) went nowhere but neither did the FBI's attempt to impose restrictions on domestic use of encryption, which had the support of critical committee chairs. In a surprising flip-flop, however, only a year after the full House voted against permitting *roving wiretaps* (wiretaps placed on phones that law enforcement has "probable cause" to believe are used by the person being tapped, regardless of whose phones they are), Congress approved the measure. This represents a fundamental expansion of wire-tapping authority as compared to the maintenance of capability that the FBI has for several years asserted was its only goal.

The most disturbing aspect of the roving wiretaps measure is the way in which it was passed. It was inserted into an authorization bill (H.R. 3694, the Intelligence Authorization Conference Report) in a closed committee meeting. In order to oppose it on the floor, a member would have to vote against continued funding for the intelligence community, a decision that would take both courage and specific concern with the issues. The effect is not only to prevent public input into the legislative process but to eviscerate the voting power of the members of Congress.

Most recently, the House of Representatives has undertaken to determine whether William Jefferson Clinton's injudicious sexual behavior and clumsy attempts to cover it up are "high crimes and misdemeanors" as defined by the Constitution, and thus whether he should be impeached. The weeks and months of public hearings to follow promise to raise new issues of the privacy of all involved. Perhaps they will serve to show an administration that has had little concern for the privacy of the citizens the error of its ways.

# Acknowledgements

We would like to thank Marc Rotenberg, David Sobel, and David Banisar of the Electronic Privacy Information Center for their much-seeing eye on developments in Washington, for uncovering mountains of useful information through their Freedom of Information Act suits, and their willingness to answer the innumerable questions of a pair of legal novices; Lynn McNulty for explaining what really happened at the National Institutes of Standards and Technology; Elizabeth Rindskopf, former general counsel at the National Security Agency, for her straightforward attempts to explain the views of that inscrutable organization; David Burnham, for sharing an investigative reporter's sensibility on how to discuss these matters; Andrew Grosso for giving us a taste of the prosecutor's viewpoint and a lot of his expertise; and the government-documents librarians at the University of Massachusetts in Amherst, Bill Thompson, Len Adams, and Terrie Billel, for their ability to turn wild-goose chases into careful hunts that yielded ripe, rich fowl.

# Privacy on the Line

# 1

## Introduction

In the early nineteenth century it took six weeks for the British government to send a message from London to its representative in Delhi. In the late nineteenth century, the telegraph cut this time—first to days, then to hours. Today, on the eve of the twenty-first century, the time has been cut to a fraction of a second and the service is available not just to the government but to most of the citizens. In a century and a half, we have gone from a world in which people separated by distance could communicate only through the slow process of sending letters to one in which they can communicate quickly, directly, and interactively—almost as though they were standing face to face.

The result is that we now conduct more and more of our communications, whether personal, business, or civic, via electronic channels. The availability of telecommunication has transformed government, giving administrators real-time access to their employees and representatives in remote parts of the world. It has transformed commerce, facilitating worldwide enterprises and beginning the internationalization of business that is the byword of the present decade. It has transformed warfare, giving generals the ability to operate from the safety of rear areas and admirals the capacity to control fleets scattered across oceans. It has transformed personal relationships, allowing friends and family to converse daily even though they live thousands of miles apart.

These developments in technology have also had a profound impact on privacy. To attempt to function in modern society without employing telecommunication is to be eccentric. Most people use the telephone daily, and many make equally frequent use of fax machines and electronic mail. These communications are by their essential nature interceptable. A typical telephone call travels over many miles of wire, of which only a few feet are under the control of the people talking. For most of its journey the signal is in the hands of one or more telephone companies, who will give it a reasonable degree of protection, but who can readily listen to it or record it and will from time to time do so. Many a call travels by radio for some part of its journey. The radio link may be at an end, in the form of a cordless, or cellular telephone, or it may be in the middle, in the form of a microwave link or a satellite hop. In either case, the call's vulnerability to interception is increased, and many people, using many kinds of radio equipment, will have the ability to listen in.

The vulnerability of long-distance communication is nothing new; remote communication has always been subject to interception. Couriers have been waylaid, seals have been broken, and letters have been read. But before the electronic era conversing in complete privacy required neither special equipment nor advanced planning. Walking a short distance away from other people and looking around to be sure that no one was hiding nearby was sufficient. Before tape recorders, parabolic microphones, and laser interferometers, it was not possible to intercept a conversation held out of sight and earshot of other people. No matter how much George III might have wanted to learn the contents of Hancock's private conversations with Adams, he had no hope of doing so unless he could induce one or the other to defect to the Crown.

Achieving comparable assurance of privacy in today's world—a world in which many of the most personal and sensitive conversations are carried on by people thousands of miles apart—requires both advanced planning and complex equipment. Most important, privacy in long-distance communication is not something the conversants can achieve on their own. A secure telephone is a complicated device combining a voice digitizer, cryptography, and a modem. Building one is as much beyond the abilities of most potential users as building a television set is beyond the abilities of most viewers. In general, secure communication facilities are complex and require numerous people, many of whom must be trusted, for their construction and maintenance.

The vulnerability of telephone calls is the vulnerability of something that did not exist before the late 1800s. Unfortunately, holding a conversation face to face is not the guarantee of privacy it once was. The same electronic technologies that have made telecommunication possible have also given us a wide range of listening devices that make finding a private place to talk difficult indeed. Technology has changed the rules for the old game as well as for the new.

Telecommunication and to a lesser extent face-to-face communication suffer from another vulnerability that did not exist when the United States was founded: the possibility that one party to a conversation is recording it without the consent of the others. Before the development of sound recording, even one of the parties to a conversation had limited ability to reveal what had been said. Notes, an outline, or even a transcript would typically be only one person's word against another's. Audio recordings and video tapes have changed the standards of evidence and opened the way for the repetition—sometimes to a very broad audience—of remarks that the utterer did not expect to be repeated.

The result is that privacy of conversation is no longer, as it was 200 years ago, a fact of life. It is now something over which society has a large and ever-increasing measure of control—a privilege that governments can grant or deny rather than a rule of nature over which they have no influence.

Society's response to these developments has been both to exploit them for various ends and to regulate them. It has tried to replace the fact of inviolably private communications with a "right to communicate privately." In the process, however, society has stopped short of creating an absolute right comparable to the reality of a former day. Society has placed controls on the use of technology to violate privacy by either the government or the citizens, but has also allowed it under many circumstances. Police employ wiretapping in criminal investigations, and intelligence agencies intercept foreign, and occasionally domestic, communications on a grand scale. Both regard their activities as a natural prerogative of the state, necessary for an orderly society. Many who are not spies or police have a different perception of electronic surveillance. They see wiretapping not as a tool for law and order but as an instrument of the police state.

The ill ease that many people (including a number who were members of Congress at the time the federal wiretapping law was passed) feel when contemplating police use of wiretaps is rooted in awareness of the abuses to which wiretapping can be put. Unlike a search, the fact of whose occurrence is usually obvious, a wiretap is intrusive precisely because its invisibility to its victim undermines accountability. Totalitarian regimes have given us abundant evidence that the use of wiretaps and even the fear of their use can stifle free speech. Nor is the political use of electronic surveillance a particularly remote problem—the Watergate scandal is only the most recent example in contemporary American history for its use by the party in power in its attempts to stay in power.[1]

The fundamental similarity between the government's power to intercept communications and its ability to search physical premises has long been recognized. The Fourth Amendment to the US Constitution takes this ability for granted and places controls on the government's power of search. Similar controls have subsequently been placed by law on the use of wiretaps. There is, however, no suggestion in the Fourth Amendment to the US Constitution of a guarantee that government searchers will find what they seek. Just as people have always been free to protect the things they consider private by hiding them or storing them with friends, they have been free to protect their conversations from being overheard.

Today, a new development in communication technology promises—or threatens, depending on your point of view—to restore some of the privacy lost to earlier technical advances. This development is electronic cryptography, a collection of practical and inexpensive techniques for encoding communications so that they can be understood only by their intended recipients. Technology rarely exists in a vacuum, however. The rise of cryptography has been accompanied, and often driven, by a host of other phenomena.

Ease of communication, electronic as well as physical, has ushered in an era of international markets and multinational corporations. Today's business is characterized by an unprecedented freedom of movement for both people and goods. More than one-fourth of the gross national product of the United States, for example, comes from either foreign trade or return on foreign investment (Dam and Lin 1996, p. 28). When foreign sales rival or exceed domestic ones, corporations open new divisions in proximity to markets, materials, or labor.

Security of electronic communication is as essential in this environment as security of transportation and storage have been to businesses throughout history. The communication system must ensure that orders for goods and services are genuine, guarantee that payments are credited to the proper accounts, and protect the privacy of business plans and personal information. These needs are all the more pressing today because, as governments have come to view the economic battlefield as an extension of the military one, industry has become a direct target of foreign espionage (Dam and Lin 1996, p. 33; Schweizer 1993, pp. 15–20; Williams 1992).

The rising importance of intellectual property has expanded the role of electronic communications in business. The communication systems with which we have been familiar all our lives—the telephone and the mail on one hand, ships, trains, trucks, and airplanes on the other—serve quite different sorts of business needs. The business function of the former has lain primarily in negotiation of commercial transactions, that of the latter in delivery of goods and services.[2] Today these distinctions are blurring. A larger and larger fraction of our commerce is commerce in information, so delivery of goods and services by electronic media is becoming more and more common. To support this delivery, the media themselves are becoming more unified. These phenomena are commonly referred to as the development of a "Global Information Infrastructure."

Both the negotiation and the delivery aspects of commercial communications have long required security. In the pre-electronic world, the validity of letters was established by seals, letterheads, and signatures; that of negotiators was established by personal recognition or letters of reference. Goods were typically protected by less subtle mechanisms. In past centuries, merchant ships carried cannon, and port cities were fortified. Today, warehouses are locked, airports are guarded, and roads are patrolled.

The growth of an information economy merges the channels used for business negotiation with those used to deliver goods and services. Much of what is now bought and sold is information, such as computer programs and surveys of consumers' buying habits. The security of information has become an end in itself rather than just a means for ensuring the security of people and property.

In parallel with the growth of a commerce in information, there is a development that makes security harder to achieve: the rising demand for mobility in communication. Traveling executives sit down at work-stations they have never seen before and expect the same environment that is on the desks in their offices. They carry cellular telephones and communicate constantly by radio. They haul out laptop computers and dial their home computers from locations around the globe. With each such action they expose their information to threats of eavesdropping and falsification barely known a decade ago. It is the lack of security for these increasingly common activities that we encounter when we hear that most cellular telephone calls in major metropolitan areas are overheard or even recorded by eavesdroppers with scanners, that a new virus is destroying data on the disks of personal computers, or that industrial spies have broken into a database half a world away.

The growing awareness of security, particularly in regard to Internet communications, has given rise to an explosion in the market for cryptography and in the development of products to satisfy that market. Software examples include Lotus Notes, the Netscape browser, and the seamless encryption interface in the popular Eudora email program. Hardware encryption is used in satellite TV decoders, in automatic teller machines, in point-of-sale terminals, and in smart cards. One researcher estimates that the commercial market for cryptography—still in its infancy—has already outstripped the military market.[3]

Cryptography's good fortune has not been to everybody's liking. Its detractors see its potential use by criminals, terrorists, and unfriendly foreign countries as outweighing its benefits to commerce and privacy. Two groups in particular have emerged in opposition to the easy availability of strong cryptography: the national-security community and the law-enforcement community.

The Allies' ability to understand German and Japanese communications, even when they were encoded with the enemies' best cryptographic systems, is widely seen as having been crucial to the course of World War II. Since that time, the practice of communications intelligence has grown steadily. Today it accounts for one of the largest slices of the US intelligence budget.[4]

The availability of wiretaps—legal or otherwise—for more than a lifetime has given us generations of police who cannot imagine a world without them. Confronted with even the suggestion of losing this tool, they respond in the same way one would expect of a modern doctor faced with the prospect of returning to a world without x-rays, blood panels, and the numerous other diagnostic tests that characterize modern medicine.

The US government's response has been a series of programs designed to maintain its eavesdropping capabilities. The centerpiece of these efforts, initially called *key escrow* and recently reincarnated as *key recovery*, is a scheme that provides the users of cryptographic equipment with protection against most intruders but guarantees that the government is always in possession of a set of "spare keys" with which it can read the communications if it wishes. The effect is very much like that of the little keyhole in the back of the combination locks used on the lockers of schoolchildren. The children open the locks with the combinations, which is supposed to keep the other children out, but the teachers can always look in the lockers by using the key.

The first of these "spare keys" was the Clipper program, which made the term Clipper virtually synonymous with key escrow. The program was made public on Friday, April 16, 1993, on the front page of the *New York Times* and in press releases from the White House and other organizations. The proposal was to adopt a new federal standard for protecting communications. It called for the use of a cryptographic system embodying a "back door" that would allow the government to decrypt messages for law-enforcement and national-security purposes. Subsequently adopted over virtually unanimous opposition, the "Escrowed Encryption Standard" has not proved popular; most of the equipment implementing it has been bought by the government in an unsuccessful attempt to seed the market.

Business objected to the Clipper scheme on every possible ground. First of all, its workings were secret. This meant that the algorithm had to be implemented in tamper-resistant hardware, which was unappealing not only to the software industry but also to hardware manufacturers. Because of the secrecy and the tamper resistance, the Clipper chip's functions could not readily be integrated into other chips. And the scheme entailed the cost of adding a chip to each product—typically several times the cost of the chip itself.

Perhaps most important was the fact that Clipper's back door was accessible to the US government and only to the US government. This made it unlikely that Clipper products would appeal to foreign customers and undercut one of its major selling points. The Clipper chip, unlike most cryptographic equipment, was supposed to be exportable.

The White House saw the objections, which came from almost every quarter, as falling into two classes: those concerned with privacy and civil liberties and those concerned with business. In subsequent proposals, it has attempted to address the business objections while flatly rejecting the civil-liberties position and maintaining the view that the government has the right not only to intercept citizens' communications but also to ensure that it will be able to understand the intercepted material. In all these proposals the executive branch has attempted to use export controls—the only significant controls it has over cryptography under current law—to pressure industry to accommodate its desires.

The explosion in cryptography and the US government's attempts to control it have given rise to a debate between those who hail the new technology's contribution to privacy, business, and security and those who fear both its interference with the work of police and its adverse effect on the collection of intelligence. Positions have often been extreme. The advocates of unfettered cryptography maintain that a free society depends on privacy to protect freedom of association, artistic creativity, and political discussion. The advocates of control hold that there will be no freedom at all unless we can protect ourselves from criminals, terrorists, and foreign threats. Many have tried to present themselves as seeking to maintain or restore the status quo. For the police, the status quo is the continued ability to wiretap. For civil libertarians, it is the ready availability of conversational privacy that prevailed at the time of the country's founding. The fact that if cryptography has the potential to interfere with police investigations it also has the potential to prevent crimes and thus make society more secure has often been overlooked.

Had telecommunication merely given us a new option, the fact that the new medium lacked privacy would be at most regrettable—similar, perhaps, to the fact that telecommunication cannot provide physical contact, either friendly or hostile.[5] The problem arises from the fact that telecommunication has transformed society. It has made possible long-distance relationships between people who rarely or never meet in person.

Without secure telecommunication, these people are effectively denied the possibility of private conversation.

The issues are not cut and dried, and no amount of calling a tail a leg will make telecommunication equivalent to face-to-face communication. Any attempt to force such an equivalence and establish an absolute right of private conversation is doomed to failure. The interceptability of communications is as much a fact of life in the electronic era as the inviolability of private conversation was in the pre-electronic. On the other hand, if we deny the fact that telecommunication, whatever its new properties, is rooted in face-to-face conversation and shares much of its social function, we will doom ourselves to a world in which truly private conversation is a rarity—a perquisite belonging exclusively to the well-traveled rich.

Ultimately, to make good policy we must consider the sort of world in which we want to live and what effects our actions will, indeed can, have in bringing about such a world. Such consideration depends on awareness of many factors, including the technology of cryptography and electronic surveillance, the aims and practices of intelligence and law enforcement, and the history of society's attempts to deal with similar problems over more than a century.

# 2

# Cryptography

## The Basics

What does it mean to say that communication is secure? In most circumstances, it means that the communication is free from eavesdropping—that the information exchanged is kept private or confidential and does not, in the course of communication, become known to anyone other than the sender and the receiver. The techniques required to achieve this vary substantially, depending on whether the medium of communication is sound, writing, pictures, or some other form of data.

Security can be obtained in a variety of ways. The most common form of secure communication is the private conversation. Although it has become more difficult, in the age of electronics, to be sure of conversational privacy, it is still easier to have privacy in a face-to-face conversation than in any other sort. For a telephone conversation to be private, the speakers must at least have privacy at their respective ends of the line.

The security of conventional handwritten letters is a bit different. It is harder to remain unobserved while reading over the shoulder of someone writing a letter than it is to remain unobserved while listening to someone talk. Unless two people are communicating by passing notes back and forth while sitting in the same room (something people rarely do unless they suspect they are being spied upon), the easiest way to discover what they have written is to intercept the message as it travels from one to the other. In the case of messages written on paper, the primary means of protection is using a trusted means of transport, whether this is a private courier or a state-run mail system. Within this trusted transport medium, the message is further protected by an envelope, whose function is not so much to prevent entry as to ensure that entry will not go undetected. As we shall see, in the case of electronic messages there is no satisfactory analog to the envelope.

Physical protection is also used to guard electronic messages. A message traveling through copper wires is less vulnerable to interception than one carried by radio. A message traveling through optical fiber is less vulnerable still. Even a message that is sent by radio may be protected by an appropriate choice of frequencies and routes.[1]

There is, however, another possibility. A message may be put at risk of falling into the hands of opponents but may be disguised in such a way that even if unintended parties are able to intercept the message they will not be able to understand it. This is the domain of cryptography.

Less well known than the problem of keeping messages private is the problem of guaranteeing that messages are genuine—of being sure that they really come from the people from whom they appear to have come and that no one has altered them along the way. These properties of communication, called *authenticity* and *integrity*, are arguably more important than privacy. Nonetheless, we will devote more attention to privacy than to authenticity, for several reasons. Although privacy is of limited use in a conversation with someone you do not know,[2] it is generally more difficult to falsify communications than merely to intercept them. Sending a message exposes the sender to discovery in a way that receiving a message does not, because the message invariably exists as evidence of the fact that it was sent. This makes violations of authenticity difficult to achieve under circumstances in which violations of privacy are easy. The foremost reason we focus on privacy, however, is that the right to use cryptography for authentication is not in question; the right to use it for privacy is.

Encrypting a message is often described, by analogy with written messages, as placing it in an envelope, but the analogy is not entirely adequate. A well-encrypted message is far harder to open than one surrounded by paper; however, if the encryption is broken, the break leaves no traces. It is this difference between the functioning of cryptography and the functioning of physical protection mechanisms that gives rise to the issues of policy that have been so prominent in discussions of cryptography in the past several years.

We shall describe cryptography for the moment only by what it does: a transformation of a message that makes the message incomprehensible to anyone who is not in possession of secret information that is needed to restore the message to its normal *plaintext* or *cleartext* form. The secret information is called the *key*, and its function is very similar to the function of a door key in a lock: it unlocks the message so that the recipient can read it.

The analogy with locks and keys is particularly apt in another respect. The lock and the key are distinct components of a system that controls the use of doors, cabinets, cars, and other things. The lock is a moderately complex mechanical device with numerous moving parts—about two dozen in the case of a normal door lock. The key is a single piece of metal. There are, on the other hand, far fewer types of locks than cuts of keys. Most doors use one of a dozen popular brands of locks, each of which can be keyed to accept one of a million different possible keys. A lock is typically far more expensive than its key, and more expensive to replace, particularly with a lock of a different kind. Perhaps the most important distinction between locks and keys is that locks are not, in principle, secret. Locks are easily recognizable even if they do not display their brand names, and there is no reason to be concerned that people know what type of lock you use on your front door. The cut of the key, on the other hand, is a secret, and any locksmith or burglar who knows it can make a duplicate that will open the door.

In exactly the same way, cryptographic systems are divided into the so-called *general system* (or just *system*) and the *specific key* (or *key*). It has been a principle of cryptography for more than a century (Kerckhoffs 1883) that the general system should not be regarded as secret.[3] The keys, in contrast, must be kept secret, because anyone who is in possession of them will be able to read encrypted messages, just as anyone who is in possession of a door key can open the door.

There is a distinction that is particularly prominent in the older literature between codes and ciphers. *Codes* in this terminology are transformations that replace the words and phrases in a human language with alphabetic or numeric *code groups*. *Ciphers* are transformations that operate on smaller components of a message, such as bits, bytes, characters, and groups of characters. The distinction is not always entirely clear.[4] Most of the systems we discuss are cipher systems, but codes appear from time to time in historical discussions.

## Cryptography in the Small

In using cryptography to achieve secure communication, scale is everything. Two people who meet occasionally and usually communicate by postcard can make use of their infrequent contacts to exchange the secret keys that they will later use to encrypt what they write on their cards. This basic case, in which a small number of correspondents exchange messages of small size, is worth examining in some detail.

Suppose that, as you are about to embark on a journey, a reporter friend asks you for help. Within the next few months there is going to be a demonstration in the city you will be visiting. Your friend has great respect for your powers of investigation and is sure you can learn the time and place of the demonstration. There is one problem. The police are trying to learn just the same information so that they can stop the demonstration. If you call your friend and mention what you have learned, the police will surely overhear since they are tapping all the telephones. What should you do?

Clearly you must encrypt your conversation—encode it in such a way that no one who receives it (except your friend) will be able to understand it. Your friend has told you, however, that the police have all the government's resources available to them. You must, therefore, encrypt your conversation well to keep the police from reading it.

Cryptography on this scale is both theoretically and practically easy. Suppose, for simplicity's sake, that the city you are visiting has a very regular structure with numbered avenues running north-south and numbered streets running east-west. Any address in the city can therefore be given as a pair of numbers, the first representing the avenue and the second representing the street. The time, of course, can be represented by the year, month, day, hour, and minute. (The demonstration is expected to be brief but effective.) Your message will therefore have the form year month day hour minute avenue street,

where each of these elements is a two-digit number. Perhaps

19 99 12 30 15 25 01 44

means that the demonstration will take place at 3:25 PM on December 30, 1999, on the corner of 1st Avenue and 44th Street. Note that every digit in this message is significant. For example, were the demonstration to be only a few days later, four of the digits would change and the value of the year would be 2000 rather than 1999. The digits in some positions, however, are limited in their values. For example, the first digit of the day of the month can only be 0, 1, 2, or 3, and the first digit of the minute can never be more than 5.

In order to encrypt a message of this sort, you and your friend need only agree on a key that will transform the string of 14 digits into some other string of 14 digits. This key must be selected before your departure, and you must carry it with you and keep it secret.

In order to carry out the transformation you will add the digits of the message one at a time to the digits of the key, without carrying.

Suppose that the key is

64 25 83 09 76 23 55 72

and you add the message

19 99 12 30 15 25 01 44.

You will get

73 14 95 39 81 48 56 16

as the cryptogram. Note that in some cases the addition produced a number greater than 10. In the third place, for example, the sum is 11. In such cases the 1 in the tens place is simply thrown away, rather than "carried" into the next place as in ordinary arithmetic.

Once you have learned the time and place of the demonstration, you convey your message by calling and reading the encrypted version over the phone.[5]

To decrypt the received string of numbers, your reporter friend will take the cryptogram

73 14 95 39 81 48 56 16

and subtract (without "borrowing") exactly the same numbers you added:

64 25 83 09 76 23 55 72.

This will yield the original message:

19 99 12 30 15 25 01 44.

Assume that the police have intercepted your phone call. No matter what computers or codebreaking skills they may possess, they have no hope of recovering the underlying message; there simply is not enough information in what they have received. The fact that the key was chosen entirely at random means that for any possible message there is a key that would produce any observed cryptogram. For example, if the time and place of the demonstration had instead been January 11, 2000 at 5th Avenue and 23rd Street

20 00 01 11 10 45 05 23

and the key had been:

53 14 94 28 71 03 51 93

the cryptogram would have come out exactly the same.

A cryptosystem of this kind is called a *one-time* system because it is perfectly secure if used only once. If it is used even twice, the results are likely to be disastrous.

Suppose that, in your travels, you learned about not one demonstration but two. Since you have brought only one key along on your trip, you use it for both messages. Unfortunately for the second demonstration, the police cryptanalysts figure out what is happening. When the first demonstration occurs and, despite the secrecy of its planning, gets mysteriously good coverage in the foreign press, they consider the demonstration in light of your two telephone calls. By combining your first message with the date of the first demonstration, they extract what they presume to be a key. When they decrypt your second message with the same key, they get another place and time;[6] with that information, they can prevent the second demonstration before it begins.

If you follow sound procedures, this sort of error will never occur. You might perhaps carry only one copy of the key, written on the paper of a cigarette. Once the message has been sent, you can light the cigarette in the lee of the telephone booth and stroll off down the street, feeling like a real spy.

Cryptography is, of course, not limited to the occasional exchange of short messages between friends. It may require millions of bits of information to be encrypted in order to protect a first-run movie or a semiconductor mask file.[7] It may require the exchange of messages among hundreds or thousands of people to protect the communications of a large corporation. Often it requires both. As cryptography grows in each of these directions, it rapidly becomes more complex.

### One-Time Systems on a Larger Scale

The scenario that has just been described is entirely practical. In fact, the same procedure can be used and has been used on a much larger scale. It was a mainstay of Soviet diplomatic communications from the late 1920s until at least the early 1950s. Since their messages did not always have the convenient numerical character of those presented in our example, the Soviets first had to convert them into numerical form. This was done with *one-part codes*[8] similar to the following:

| | |
|---|---|
| abovementioned | 0000 |
| academician | 0001 |
| acknowledge receipt | 0002 |
| arrange meeting | 0003 |
| avoid contact | 0004 |
| . . . | . . . |

These four-digit code groups were then added to four digit key groups in the same digit-by-digit fashion employed in our example above.

Using one-time systems in a large network creates a number of serious problems. First, although it is trivial to produce a few dozen or a few hundred random digits by throwing 20-sided dice (figure 2.1) from a fantasy games shop, it is quite another thing to manufacture millions upon

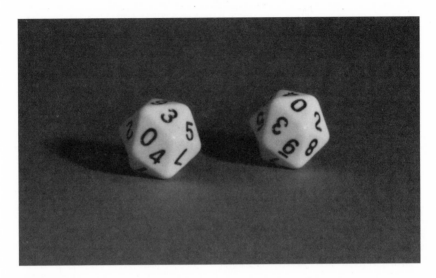

**Figure 2.1**
Twenty-sided dice. (Photograph by Eric Neilsen.)

millions, type them up onto sheets, and produce precisely two copies of each sheet.

Before we go further, a word about the terminology of modern cryptography is in order. In many papers, the participants in encrypted communication are personified, whether they are people, pieces of equipment, or computer processes. If there are two parties involved, they are called Alice and Bob. If more are required, they are drawn from a cast of supporting characters that includes the couple's friends Carol and Ted, along with Eve, the eavesdropper.

In a network with more than two correspondents, there is difficulty in coordinating the keys used. If three people share a body of one-time keys and Alice uses some in sending a message to Bob, she must inform Carol of what she has done. If Carol does not know this, she will at some time use the same key to send a message of her own and thereby create an insecurity. The feasibility of such coordination among three people is clear; for a thousand, it is not.

The way the Soviets dealt with this problem was by having all communications go through Moscow. Every embassy could communicate securely with Moscow using keys that it shared only with Moscow. If the Soviet embassy in the United States needed to communicate securely with the Soviet embassy in Mexico, it was required to send its message to Moscow and have it relayed to Mexico City. Such an arrangement makes a network less flexible and requires twice as much keying material to be expended in sending each message.

Despite the centralized approach, the Soviets got into trouble. For reasons that are still unclear, a serious mistake was made in the early months of 1942. Rather than making exactly two copies of the key sheets, they made four. These excess keys then entered the inventory and remained in use for several years. Western intelligence noted and exploited the multiple use of the keys, with disastrous results for Soviet security. Under the code name Venona, cryptanalytic study of the reused "one-time" keys went on for decades. The system was used for the most sensitive Soviet information, and the Americans and the British studied it in hopes of identifying Soviet "moles" thought to be operating at the highest levels of their intelligence establishments.[9]

One-time systems are not the only form of highly secure cryptography, and they are by no means the dominant form today. In order to avoid having to ship the titanic amounts of keying material that are required in one-time systems, most enciphering today is done by *cipher machines*: mechanical or electrical or computer devices that encode messages. One-time systems have the advantage of simplicity but the disadvantage of failing completely if used to encrypt an amount of text exceeding the size of the key. The functioning of cipher machines is more complex than that of one-time systems. This complexity is the price of a system that can protect quantities of traffic far greater than the size of the key.

## A Brief History of Cryptographic Systems

Despite the vast progress of cryptography during the twentieth century, there is a remarkable continuity with systems that have been known since the Renaissance.

Cryptography is always a matter of substituting one thing for another. The earliest cryptographic systems substituted one letter of the alphabet for another in an unchanging fashion, a technique called a *simple* or *monoliteral* substitution. Simple substitutions are easy to perform, even when the computational resources are limited to pencil and paper. There are also plenty of them: some $2^{90}$ for a 26-character alphabet. In other words, a simple substitution cipher has a 90-bit key—far larger than anyone could have needed before the computer age. Despite these virtues, simple substitution ciphers are quite easy to break. This is because they leave many characteristics of the message, such as letter frequency and letter patterns, unchanged.

The best-known approach to solving simple substitution ciphers is to compute the frequencies of the various letters. In English, the letters of the alphabet have widely varying rates of occurrence. The letters E and T, for example, occur quite frequently, accounting for 13% and 9% of typical text, whereas J and Z account for only 2% and 1% of such text. These characteristics frequencies permit a cryptanalyst to recognize the identities of the letters despite the substitution. Analysts also make use of the preservation of letter patterns. Figure 2.2 shows that the exceptional structure of the word 'bookkeeper' remains visible when it is encrypted under a variety of cipher alphabets. Notice that in each case the resulting cryptogram shows the letter pattern 1223344536—that is the cryptogram contains three consecutive pairs of repeated letters in the middle. Admittedly, this is a word chosen for its exceptional pattern of repeated letters (it is the only English word with three pairs of repeated letters in a row); however, it is only an extreme case of a very common phenomenon that occurs in such words as 'pepper', 'papa', and 'noon'. Repetition patterns allow a skilled cryptanalyst to read words of this sort directly from the ciphertext.

The cure for the shortcomings of monoalphabetic substitution—discovered some 500 years ago and still in use today—is to change the cipher alphabet from one letter to the next. *Polyalphabetic encryption*, as this is called, is the creation of three Renaissance scholars, Alberti, Belaso, and Trithemius (see Kahn 1967), but is commonly known by the name of another, Blaise de Vigenère—an error too deeply embedded in cryptographic terminology to admit of historical correction at this date.

The simplest form of polyalphabetic cipher employs a sequence of alphabets. The first alphabet is used to encrypt the first letter of the message,

```
b   o   o   k   k   e   e   p   e   r

g  a  a  o  o  b  b  t  b  w
z  e  e  w  w  i  i  a  i  k
o  z  z  e  e  j  j  s  j  y
n  s  s  i  i  r  r  o  r  q
```

**Figure 2.2**
The characteristic letter pattern of the word 'bookkeeper'.

the second alphabet to encrypt the second letter, and so on. Once the supply of alphabets has been exhausted, the encipherer starts over again with the first. The cipher alphabets may either be unrelated, as in figure 2.3,[10] or may be generated by simple transformations from a single alphabet. The more distinct alphabets are used, the more secure the system, but the more it suffers from the problems of a one-time system—the amount of keying material becomes excessive.

The general form of the Vigenère system employs a number of independent cipher alphabets, as in figure 2.3, and employs some subset of them sequentially in a pattern that may or may not repeat and may or may not use all of the alphabets. Note that each alphabet is labeled at the left with a letter of the alphabet. This allows a *key word* or *key phrase* to represent a sequence of alphabets, as in figure 2.3.

Polyalphabetic ciphers call on three basic processes to achieve security: they employ a set of unrelated cipher alphabets, they derive a number of secondary alphabets from each of these primary alphabets, and they vary the use of the secondary alphabets in a more or less complex pattern. These three processes can be traded off against each other. The more complex the pattern in which the alphabets are used, the smaller the number of distinct alphabets that are needed. Of the innumerable variations of polyalphabetic ciphers that are possible, we will examine a small number of examples illustrative of the development of cryptography from the Renaissance to the twentieth century.

The simplest form of Vigenère cipher uses *direct standard alphabets*—that is to say, the ordinary alphabet (standard) in its usual order (direct).[11]

The difficulty of solving a Vigenère system is entirely dependent upon the relationship between the length of the key and the length of the

## Vigenère table

```
   | A B C D E F G H I J K L M N O P Q R S T U V W X Y Z
 A | Q F A L H I M Z E T Y N B O U D X P C S K G R J V W
 B | Y L K O R U C J X P A S V H B D Q G M I T E Z J W N
 C | J O A M S I T Y R D N H X E W P F V Z B L G K Q U C
 ⋮ |              ·      ·      ·
```

Plain:    d   o   d   e   c   a   h   e   d   r   o   n

Key:    B   A   F   F   L   E   D   B   A   F   F   L
         ↓   ↓   ↓   ↓   ↓   ↓   ↓   ↓   ↓   ↓   ↓   ↓

Cipher:  O   U   A   S   M   O   P   R   L   U   Q   Y

"d" is carried to "O" under the "B" alphabet;
"o" is carried to "U" under the "A" alphabet;
"d" is carried to "A" under the "F" alphabet; etc.

**Figure 2.3**
Action of a Vigenère system.

message to be encrypted. After a certain point (called the *period*) in the encryption, a new sequence of message characters will be encrypted with the same sequence of key characters. The number of times this occurs is referred to as the *depth* of the message with respect to the key. The greater the depth, the easier the message is to break.

Despite the fact that Vigenère systems with short periods are not secure, they are often used. One example is the CAVE cipher used to protect digital cellular telephone calls in the United States  (Electronic Industries Association 1992).

A little examination will show that the short "time and place" message with which we began was encrypted in a Vigenère system using numbers instead of letters. A central theme in cryptography has been to produce systems with long periods without having to transport the large amounts of keying material required by the one-time systems. One way of solving the problem of short periods is to encrypt the message more than once—a *multiple Vigenère system* (figure 2.4).

Although encrypting two, three, or more times makes for a vast improvement in the security of messages, it was not actually feasible when enciphering was done by hand. In practice, errors by the code clerks—

```
Plain:      HENRY IS HUNGRY ...
Key-1:      PAPAD UM PAPADU ...
Cipher-1:   WECRB CE WUCGUS ...
Key-2:      HIPSH IP SHIPSH ...
Cipher-2:   DMRJI KT OBKVMZ ...
```

**Figure 2.4**
Double Vigenère system.

Stepping Mechanism

**Figure 2.5**
Rotor machine.

possibly in both the enciphering and the deciphering—made many messages unreadable. The wide use of such complex encryption techniques only appeared in the twentieth century, with the development of electromechanical enciphering equipment. The first of these was the *rotor machine*, a device that was to dominate cryptography for half a century.

The central component of a rotor machine is the *rotor*, a disk about the size of a hockey puck that serves to implement a cipher alphabet. On each face of the disk there are a number of electrical contacts corresponding to the letters of the alphabet. Each contact on the front face is wired to exactly one contact on the rear face. As an electrical signal passes through the rotor, the signal is carried to a new alphabetic position, just as a letter looked up in a cipher alphabet changes to another letter.

Rotor machines have had from three to more than ten rotors. Every rotor through which a "letter" passes represents an additional layer of encryption. Thus, the simplest rotor machines correspond to triple Vigenère systems, and the more elaborate ones may be several times as complex.

With the appearance of digital electronics after World War II, the dominance of rotor machines gave way to that of *shift registers*. A shift register is an electronic device made up of a number of *cells* or *stages*, each of

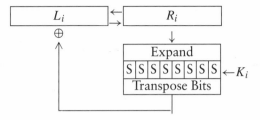

**Figure 2.6**
DES as a shift register.

which holds a single 0 or 1 of information. As the shift register operates, the data shift one or more places along the register at each tick of the clock. In addition to moving left or right, some of the bits are modified by being combined with other bits. In the more modern *nonlinear* shift registers, some of the bits are looked up in tables[12] and then used to change other bits of the register, under control of a key. This process is repeated over and over until every bit has changed in a way that is a complex function of every other bit and of every bit of the key. In other words, if a single bit of either the input or the key is modified, approximately half of the output bits will change.

Typical of modern cryptographic systems is the US Data Encryption Standard (USDoC 1977). DES, as it is generally known, is a *block cipher* or *electronic code book*. It takes 64 bits (8 bytes) of information as input, and, under the control of a slightly smaller (56-bit) key, produces 64 bits of output. DES is rarely operated in the basic mode in which it is described in the standard. It is intended as a primitive for building more complex modes of operation suitable for use in encrypting common data formats (USDoC 1980).

DES is a shift-register system in a modern style. In each of its 16 rounds it performs a complex operation on half of the 64 bits in its register and uses the result to alter the other half of its bits. Each round is controlled by a distinct 48-bit subset of the key.

DES expands the right-hand side of its register from 32 to 48 bits and exclusive-ors these with 48 bits selected from the key. It then contracts the 48 bits back to 32 by making eight substitutions, using six-bit-to-four-bit tables. These tables, called *S-boxes* (for *selection boxes*), are the heart of the algorithm; along with the key size, they have been sources of controversy (Bayh 1978). Finally the bits are rearranged (*transposed*) before the result is exclusive-ored with the left side of the register.

Just as rotor machines look at first to be quite different from Vigenère encipherment, shift registers look superficially quite different from rotor machines. There is, however, a deep similarity. All these systems combine a process of looking things up in tables with one of "adding" them together using some sort of arithmetic operation. In shift registers, the message and the key are more thoroughly mixed together, rather as though the positions of rotors in a rotor machine were affected by the letters passing through them.

## Strengths of Cryptosystems

Before we go further into the use of mechanical cryptosystems, a word about the strengths of ciphers is in order. A cryptosystem is considered secure when an opponent cannot break it under reasonable circumstances, in a reasonable amount of time, at a reasonable cost. The term "reasonable" is perforce vague. Despite being the most important problem in cryptography, the evaluation of cryptographic systems is the least understood. An adequate mathematical theory of cryptography has eluded cryptographers for centuries.[13]

The issue of what constitutes *reasonable* conditions for an attack on a cryptosystem is better understood than others. An opponent must, of course, be in possession of ciphertext to have any hope of discovering the underlying plaintext. If this is all that is available, we say that the cryptanalyst mounts a *ciphertext-only attack*.[14] Typically, however, the opponent knows some information about the plaintext before starting to work on the problem. A message from Alice to Bob, for example, is likely to begin "Dear Bob" and to be signed "Love, Alice." Although knowledge of such *probable words* or *cribs* is difficult to prevent, the situation may go much farther than this. Many messages, such as product announcements, are secret until a certain date and then become public. Under these circumstances an opponent has the corresponding plain text and cipher text of one message and can make use of this in attacking other messages sent using the same key. If this is the case, we say that the opponent is in a position to mount a *known-plaintext* attack.

At the time of World War II, the belligerents, not trusting their cryptosystems to resist known-plaintext attacks, imposed such *signaling rules* as "No message transmitted in cipher may ever be sent in clear." In fact a message sent in cipher could never be declassified without being *paraphrased* to reduce its cryptanalytic utility. This problem appears to have been solved for US government cryptosystems by the 1960s, permitting formerly encrypted messages to be declassified on the basis of content alone.

The sort of signaling rules formerly used by the military are entirely infeasible in a commercial environment. Fortunately, trust in modern electronic cryptosystems is sufficient that the availability of plaintext to an opponent makes no difference. In fact, we presume that the opponent can send an arbitrary number of text messages and will receive our cooperation in enciphering them or deciphering them before beginning to attack the actual message of interest. This is called the *chosen-plaintext* assumption.[15]

### Workfactors

Time is the essential element in measuring computation. The question is "How much will it cost me to get the answer when I need it?" It is a rule of thumb that computing power doubles every 18 months;[16] thus a personal computer purchased for $1000 today will have twice the computing power of one purchased less than 2 years ago.[17] These improvements in speed have profound implications for cryptographic systems.

The number of operations required to break a cryptographic system is called its *workfactor*. The form or complexity of the operations is not precisely stated. They might be encryptions, as they are when the analytic process is one of searching through the keys, or they might be something entirely different. In a spirit of oversimplification, we will assume that operations are always entirely parallelizable. If two processors can do a million operations in 5 seconds, then ten processors can do the same number of operations in 1 second. For our purposes, this assumption is conservative in the sense that if it is false the problem merely becomes somewhat harder.

If a system has a workfactor of $2^{30}$, it can be broken by a billion operations. These may not be elementary computer instructions; they may be complex operations requiring hundreds of instructions each. Even so, many desktop computers today can do a billion instructions in 5 seconds. If such a cryptosystem requires several hundred instructions per encryption, it can be searched in under an hour. In short, breaking a system with a workfactor of $2^{30}$ is trivial.

A workfactor of $2^{60}$ means that a million processors, each doing a million operations a second, can solve the problem in a million seconds (between 11 and 12 days). It is clear that a system with a workfactor of $2^{60}$ can be broken today if the analytic operations are such that processors capable of executing them are worth building or already available. If the operations are encryptions, the processors might be built from available encryption processors.

On this path, systems with workfactors of $2^{90}$ are the first that seem beyond reach for the foreseeable future. A billion processors in parallel can certainly be imagined. A billion operations a second, even operations as complex as DES encryptions, have been achieved (Eberle 1992). A billion seconds, however, is 30 years—long enough to count as secure for most applications.[18]

Workfactors of $2^{120}$ seem beyond reach for the indefinite future. A trillionth of a second is less than one gate delay in the fastest experimental technologies; a trillion processors operating in parallel is beyond reach; and a trillion seconds is 30,000 years.

Estimating the cost of searching through keys and validating the estimates by actually doing it have become sports in the cryptographic community. In the fall of 1995 a group of cryptographers met and prepared an estimate of search costs, concluding that 40-bit keys (the largest that could be readily exported) could easily be searched and that keys at least 70 to 90 bits long were needed to provide security for commercial applications (Blaze et al. 1996). The previous August, students at the Ecôle Polytechnique in Paris had searched out a 40-bit key. The following January, students at MIT repeated the feat using an $83,000 graphics computer. This amounted to a cost of $584 per key. At its annual conference in January 1997, RSA Data Security offered prizes for searching keyspaces of various sizes. The 40-bit prize was claimed before the conference ended and the 48-bit prize was claimed a week later. The 56-bit DES challenge lasted for only 5 months.

The US Data Encryption Standard uses a 56-bit key and thus falls within the range we have described as clearly possible. The standard is used extensively throughout the commercial world—particularly by banks, which commonly engage in billion-dollar electronic funds transfers. In such applications, the inadequacy of any algorithm with a 56-bit key is becoming apparent. Because the National Institute of Standards and Technology (NIST) has yet to issue a replacement standard,[19] *triple-DES*—a block cipher employing DES three times in a row with three different keys[20]—has arisen as a de facto standard and is being considered for formal adoption by the Banking Security Standards Committee (ANSI X9F) of the American National Standards Institute.

### Lifetimes of Cryptosystems

In designing a cryptographic system, there are two important lifetime issues to consider: how long the system will be in use and how long the messages it encrypts will remain secret.

Cryptographic systems and cryptographic equipment often have very long lifetimes. The Sigaba system, introduced before World War II, was in use until the early 1960s. The KL-7, a later rotor machine, served from the 1950s to the 1980s. DES has been a US standard for more than 20 years.[21] Other systems that are neither formal standards nor under the tight control of organizations such as the American military probably have longer lifetimes still.[22]

Secrets can also have very long lifetimes. The Venona messages were studied for nearly 40 years in hopes that they would reveal the identities of spies who had been young men in the 1930s and who might have been the senior intelligence officers of the 1970s. The principles of the Sigaba system were discovered in the mid 1930s and were not made public until 1996. Much of the "H-bomb secret" has been kept since its discovery in 1950, and the trade secrets of many industrial processes are much older. In the United States, census data, income tax returns, medical records, and other personal information are supposed to be kept secret for a lifetime.

If we set out to develop a piece of cryptographic equipment today, we might reasonably plan to have it in widespread use by the year 2000. We might also reasonably plan for the system to be in use for 20 or 25 years. No individual piece of equipment is likely to last that long; however, if the product is successful, the standards it implements will. If the equipment is intended for the protection of a broad range of business communications, some of the messages it encrypts may be intended to remain secret for decades. A cryptosystem designed today might thus encrypt its last message in 2025, and that message might be expected to remain secret 25 years later. It must therefore withstand attack by a cryptanalyst—whose mathematical and computing resources we have no way of predicting—in the year 2050. The prospect is daunting.

**Key Management**

*Key management*—the production, shipment, inventorying, auditing, and destruction of cryptographic keys—is an indispensable component of secure communication systems. Cipher machines make a spectacular reduction in the amount of keying material that users must ship around. This diminishes the problem of key distribution; however, it does not eliminate it, since the difficulty of distributing keys is typically more a function of how many people are involved than of whether each one has to get a large codebook or a short message.

The production of keys is the most sensitive operation in cryptography. Cryptographic keys must be kept secret and must be impossible for an opponent to predict. If they do not achieve these objectives, the results will be disastrous, regardless of how cleverly designed the cryptographic systems in which they are used. The failure of Soviet key production that led to the breaking of the Venona intercepts is one example of this. A far more recent example is the penetration of the Netscape Secure Socket Layer (SSL) protocol, which is used to secure Internet transactions by encrypting such sensitive information as credit card numbers. In the summer of 1995, a group of graduate students at the University of California at Berkeley discovered that the SSL protocol generated session keys by consulting the clock on the client machine (typically a personal computer). The time on the client machine's clock could be inferred quite accurately from other aspects of the protocol, and thus the key could be discovered easily.

In conventional cryptographic practice, reliability in key production is achieved by centralization. If all communications go to and from a central site, as in the Soviet diplomatic network, it is natural to manufacture keys at the center and ship them to the far-flung sites. The same procedure is typically followed even in cases where messages can flow directly from one field organization to another.

In US parlance, the organization that manufactures keys is called the *central facility*. The production process goes to great lengths to guarantee that the keys produced are completely random and are kept completely secret. From the central facility, keys are shipped to installations around the world through a special administrative structure called the COMSEC *materials control system*, which uses such elaborate security procedures as *two-person control*.[23] Keying material is stored by COMSEC *custodians* and constantly tracked by an elaborate system of receipts.

At one time, keys took the form of codebooks. Originally, these were produced by writing the words and phrases of the plain text on a set of index cards and shuffling the cards by hand. In the 1930s, handwritten or typed index cards were replaced by punched cards, and the shuffling was accomplished by using card sorters to sort cards at random. Later cryptographic systems used wired rotors, key lists, plugboards, and paper tape. The most recent have keys packaged in entirely electronic form.

Because keys are secret, they must have names to provide the users with a way of "talking" about which ones to use. A message sometimes contains the name of the key that is to be used in decrypting it. At other times the key is a function of the message's origin or subject matter. Thus an embassy might have one system for diplomatic messages, another for messages dealing with trade, and yet a third for the messages of the military attaché. A ship at sea might have one set of keys for communicating with shore-based facilities and another for communicating with each of the fleets with which it was likely to come in contact.

The distribution of keys follows the structure of the organization that employs them. Keys, however, usually change more often than organizational structures, and it would be confusing to ask a code clerk to remember an entirely new key name when the key was used in exactly the same way. The solution is to keep the name constant but to label each new key as to its *edition* (a term that dates from the era of codebooks but is still used today in naming purely electronic keys).[24]

The management of keys is a constant tug of war between the need for flexibility in communication and the need to maintain security by limiting keys. Typical of military communications is the US Navy's Fleet Broadcast System, which transmits constantly to American ships all over the world. The keys used by the Fleet Broadcast System are changed every day, but on any given day they are the same for every ship. This arrangement favors flexibility over security and has had its costs. In the late 1980s, a Navy chief petty officer named Jerry Whitworth sold keys from the Alameda Naval Air Station to Soviet intelligence officers. Because of the widespread distribution of those keys, the USSR was potentially able to decipher many US Navy communications. At the other extreme, keys may be issued for a communication network with only two members. The result is more secure but less flexible. If keys are distributed physically, the endpoints of the circuit must anticipate the need to communicate far enough in advance to order their keys—a process that may take days or weeks. In many circumstances (for example a secure phone system), this is an unacceptable burden and some less cumbersome solution must be found.

**Dynamic Key Distribution**

Suppose, in the traditional terminology of the modern cryptographic literature, that Bob wants to communicate with Alice. Bob may not know Alice; he may simply know that she is a lawyer, an investigator, or a doctor whose expertise and confidential collaboration he requires. If the proper arrangements have been made in advance, Bob and Alice can be "introduced" to each other in real time.

The mechanism that makes the introduction is called a *key management facility* (KMF).[25] It is a network resource, similar in function to a directory server, that shares a key with every member of the network.[26] In the description that follows, we will assume that Bob is using a cryptographically secure telephone to call Alice, and to simplify the description we will blur the distinction between the people and the instruments.

If Bob and Alice belong to the same community and rely on the same KMF, the process goes as follows:

- Bob calls the KMF and informs it that he wants to communicate with Alice. This call is encrypted in a key that Bob shares with the KMF.

- If the KMF finds that it "knows" Alice (i.e., that it shares a key with her), it manufactures a new key for the exclusive use of Bob and Alice and sends it to each party. In the particular case of telephones, which can have only one call in progress at a time, this is done by sending Bob a two-part message. Both halves of the message contain the same key, but the first half of the message is encrypted so that Bob can read it and the second half so that Alice can read it (Needham 1978; Rosenblum 1980).

- With the key now in hand, Bob calls Alice. The portion of the key that was encrypted so that only Alice can read it functions as a letter of introduction; Bob's phone sends it to Alice's phone at the beginning of the call.

- Bob's telephone and Alice's telephone now *hold* a key in common and can use it to make their secure phone call.

The *long-term* keys that Bob and Alice share with the KMF may reasonably be called *subscriber keys*; the ones they use for particular messages or conversations are called *session keys* or *traffic keys*. Because of the extra phone call required for Bob and Alice to acquire a common key, systems of this sort typically *cache* keys for some period of time. This allows the users to make repeated calls without the overhead of the KMF call.

This approach to keying secure phone calls is far from ideal. For one thing, if communication between any two members of a community requires the services of the KMF, it will be a busy facility indeed.[27] A far more serious problem, peculiar to security, is that Bob and Alice must place too much trust in the KMF.

**Strengths and Weaknesses of Cryptography**

Cryptography is the only technique capable of providing security to messages transmitted over channels entirely out of the control of either the sender or the receiver. To put this another way: the cost and applicability of cryptography depend very little on either the length or the "shape" of the path the encrypted message must follow.

Cryptography is not always the most appropriate security technique. In designing a system for securing the communications within a building, a campus, or a military base, it is appropriate to protect the signals physically by running them through shielded conduits or optical fibers. On the other hand, if the trunks of a network span great distances, cryptography is usually the most economical security mechanism and in some cases the only possible one. Physical protection techniques that are perfectly suitable for a network spanning distances of a few hundred yards will be prohibitively expensive if used to connect cities as far apart as Paris, Los Angeles, Hong Kong, and Sydney. If cryptography is used to provide security, however, the cost will be independent of the distance. Mobile and satellite communications represent an extreme case in which cryptography appears to be the only possible means of protection.

From a managerial viewpoint, security obtained through the use of physical means of protection must be bought at the cost of constant auditing of the signal path. If land lines are being leased, the customer must be constantly vigilant to the danger that the service provider will accidentally misroute the calls through a microwave or satellite channel. Ground routing is often more expensive than satellite routing and might thus be reserved for more sensitive messages. In the past, a similar phenomenon took the form of a choice between a faster route (telephone or telegraph) and a more secure one (physical shipment). If, however, a message has been properly encrypted, the communication network is free to send it any distance, via any channel, without fear of compromise.

One special case of this is particularly important: the freedom to pass an encrypted message through the hands of a potential opponent or competitor. Telecommunications suppliers, for example, often find themselves bidding against the local telephone system to provide equipment or services. In the process of bidding on these contracts, they often have no choice but to employ the services of the communications suppliers with whom they are competing.

Modern security protocols make special use of the ability to pass a message through the hands of a potential enemy. A party to communications is often asked to present cryptographically protected *credentials*. If the credentials can be deciphered correctly, the challenger who receives, deciphers, and judges them need not worry about having received them from a previously untrusted party. This is analogous to the procedure commonly employed to control international travel. When the border guards judge the traveler on the basis of a passport received from the traveler's own hands, they are placing their trust in the tamper resistance of the passport. If the passport appears intact and the picture resembles the traveler, they will not generally feel the need to conduct any further investigation into the traveler's identity.

In the world of paper documents, this mechanism is not considered adequate for all purposes. A visitor attending a secret briefing at a military installation, for example, must typically be preceded by a letter of authorization. The corresponding cryptographic process, however, is considered reliable enough to be used for the most sensitive applications.

Cryptography can best be thought of as a mechanism for extending the confidentiality and authenticity of one piece of information (the key) to another (the message). The protection of the key, which is typically small and can be handled very carefully, is extended to the message, which can then be handled much less carefully—routed through the least expensive communication channel, for example. As a consequence of this extension of security from the key to the message, the compromise of the key will likewise be extended to the message. The consequences of this compromise, however, differ markedly, depending on whether the compromised key is being used to protect privacy or authenticity.

In regard to authentication, compromise of a cryptographic key is similar to the compromise of other sorts of identifying information, such as passwords or credit cards. Suppose that on Wednesday morning the security officer of a bank learns that an authentication key in use since Monday has been stolen, but also knows that no messages have been received and authenticated with the key since the day before, when the key was known to be safe. The key will be changed immediately and no actual compromise will occur. The thieves cannot make use of a key acquired on Tuesday night to go back and initiate a wire transfer on Monday or Tuesday. If the key is used to protect the privacy of information, however, things are quite different. Even if the compromise of a key is discovered immediately, all messages ever sent in that key must be regarded as compromised. This is because no one can be sure that they were not intercepted and recorded by the same parties who later acquired the key. As soon as the compromise is discovered, the key will of course be changed, but this does far less to repair the damage than the change of an authentication key. The thieves can still read traffic they intercepted while the compromised key was in use. This gives breaches of cryptographic security the power to reach back in time and compromise the secrecy of messages sent earlier.[28] Changing the key will only prevent future messages from being read.

This vulnerability becomes especially critical in systems, like Alice and Bob's secure telephone in the previous section, that transmit some cryptographic keys encrypted under others. Although session keys in these systems typically last for only the duration of one phone call, session, or transaction, the subscriber keys may stay the same for weeks or months. If one of these is compromised at any time during its life, all the messages ever sent using session keys that were themselves sent enciphered under the subscriber key will likewise be compromised. Worse yet, if the key distribution center is compromised, the messages of every subscriber will be compromised.

Cryptography as we have described it so far has a very centralized character. If keys are distributed physically from a central facility, the center has the power to decide which elements of the network can communicate with which others. If the keys are distributed electronically and in real time, as described for secure phones, the key distribution center acquires control over communication on a virtually call-by-call basis. Implicit in this centralization is the phenomenon that is now called key escrow. The users of a cryptocommunication system may trust it to protect them against external opponents, but they can never be confident that they are protected against the system managers. There is always the possibility that the central facility will be employed to supply additional sets of keys for eavesdropping on the users.

The unique vulnerabilities of conventional cryptography and its centralization are intimately connected. In order to eliminate the former, we must also eliminate the latter.

## Public-Key Cryptography

All the cryptographic systems discussed thus far—one-time systems, Vigenère systems, rotor machines, and shift registers—are *symmetric* cryptosystems: the ability to encrypt messages is inseparably linked to the ability to decrypt messages. The course of cryptography for the past 20 years has been dominated by *asymmetric* or *public-key* cryptosystems.

In a public-key cryptosystem, every message is operated on by two keys, one used to encipher the message and other to decipher it (Diffie and Hellman 1976). The keys are inverses in that anything encrypted by one can be decrypted by the other. However, given access to one of these keys, it is computationally infeasible to discover the other one. This makes possible the practice that gives public-key cryptography its name: one of the two keys can be made public without endangering the security of the other. There are two possibilities:

- If the secret key is used for deciphering, anyone with access to the public key will be able to encipher a message so that only the person with the corresponding secret key can decrypt it.

- If the secret key is used for enciphering, its holder can produce a message that anyone with access to the public key can read but only the holder of the secret key could have produced.

The latter property is what characterizes a signed message, and a public-key cryptosystem used in this way is said to provide a *digital signature*.[29]

### Using Public-Key Cryptography

In a network using public-key cryptography, the secret key that each subscriber shares with the key management facility in a conventional network is replaced by a pair containing a public key and a private key. The function of the KMF is now merely to hand out public keys. Since these keys are not secret, they are not subject to compromise.

One problem remains, however: a subscriber who receives another subscriber's public key from the KMF must have a way of verifying its authenticity. This problem is solved by providing the KMF with a private signing key and providing every subscriber of the network with a copy of the corresponding public key. This enables the KMF to sign the keys it distributes, and it enables any subscriber to verify the KMF's signature.

Public-key cryptography vastly diminishes the vulnerability of the KMF. If the KMF is compromised, that compromise is the compromise of an authentication key (the KMF's signing key, the only piece of secret information the KMF knows) rather that the compromise of any key used to protect secrecy. If the signing key of the KMF is found to be compromised, that key can be changed. The network's subscribers will have to be informed of the KMF's new public key and warned not to accept any key distribution messages signed with the old one. Such reinitialization of the network may be costly, but it does not expose past network traffic to disclosure.

This use of public-key cryptosystems also has the practical benefit of reducing the load on the key distribution center. Instead of requiring the subscribers to call the KMF on the occasion of any conversation, they can be provided with a form of credentials called *certificates*. A certificate is a signed and dated message from the KMF to a subscriber containing that subscriber's public key, together with such identifying information as name and address. When two subscribers begin a call, they exchange these credentials. Each one verifies the KMF's signature on the received certificate and extracts the enclosed public key.

Although public-key cryptography as described above does much to diminish the vulnerability of the network as a whole, it does nothing to reduce the vulnerability of individual subscriber's private keys. If a subscriber's private key is compromised, it is possible that any message ever sent in the corresponding public key will be read.

For non-interactive communications, such as electronic mail, there does not appear to be any way around this problem. The person who looks up a public key in a directory and encrypts a message with it is sending the message to the holder of the corresponding private key. Possession of the correct private key is the only thing that distinguishes the receiver, and anyone who has it will be able to read the letter.

For interactive communication, however, the problem can be solved by means of another form of public-key cryptography: *Diffie-Hellman key exchange*,[30] which allows communicating parties to produce a shared secret piece of information despite the fact that all messages they exchange can be intercepted (Diffie and Hellman 1976). Alice produces a secret piece of information that she never reveals to anyone, and derives a corresponding public piece from it. She sends the public piece to Bob and receives from him a piece of public information formed in the same way. By combining their own secret information with the other's public information, Alice and Bob each arrive at a common shared piece of information that they can use as a cryptographic key. The process is analogous to a perfect strategy for bridge bidding in which the North-South partners (each of whom knows his own hand) agree on a secret but the East-West partners (who do not know either North or South's hand) remain completely ignorant of what North and South have concluded even though they have heard their opponents' every bid and response.

Alice and Bob use the key they have negotiated to encrypt all subsequent messages, but being engaged in encrypted communication is not a sufficient condition for secure communication. Not only does neither Alice nor Bob yet have secure knowledge of the other's identity; they cannot even be sure that an intruder who has performed a key exchange with each of them is not sitting in the middle, translating between keys and recording the plain text of their conversation.

The second step, therefore, is to exchange certificates: Alice sends Bob hers, and he sends her his. Verifying the KMF's signature on the received certificates allows the receiver to be sure that the certificate is authentic but does not guarantee the authenticity of the person who sent the certificate. It remains, therefore, for Alice (for example) to verify that the person with whom she is in contact is actually the legitimate holder of Bob's certificate—the person who knows the secret key corresponding to the public one it contains. This final step is done by a process called *challenge and response* in which the challenger sends a test message and judges the legitimacy of the responder by verifying the signature on the response. In this case, it is best to use as the challenge the piece of public information from the exponential key exchange, since so doing gives assurance that the encryption is actually being performed by the same entity that engaged in the authentication process.

**Communication Security**

The indispensable application of cryptography is the protection of communication. How this is accomplished depends on the form of the communication network and on whether the protection is being applied by the network's owners, by the subscribers, or by communication providers who supply the network with particular communication resources (such as satellite channels).

There are three basic ways in which encryption can be applied to network communication:

- *Net keying.* Every element in the network uses the same key, which is changed at regular intervals (often daily). This is the key-management technique employed by the US Navy's Fleet Broadcast System and many other government networks.

- *Link keying.* Messages are encrypted as they go from switching centers onto communication channels and decrypted as they go back into switching centers. A message is thus encrypted and decrypted several times as it goes from sender to receiver. This technique permits addressing information as well as message contents to be encrypted and makes the traffic particularly inscrutable to anyone outside the network.

- *End-to-end keying.* Each message is encrypted as it leaves the sender and cannot be decrypted by anyone other than the receiver. This is the typical behavior of secure telephones and secure email.

The results achieved by applying cryptography to secure communication networks depend dramatically on where it is applied. The most effective way for two individuals or two organizations to communicate securely over a network they do not control is to encrypt their communications using end-to-end keying. Relying on measures applied by network management may protect them from most opponents but will always leave them vulnerable to a foe with the resources to seek out a weak point along their communication path and exploit it. On the other hand, network keying and link keying allow the network to provide the users with security services they cannot provide for themselves.

**Transmission Security and Covert Communication**

Through a technique known as *traffic analysis*—the study of the patterns of communication—an opponent can learn a great deal about the activities of an organization without being able to understand any individual message. The counter to traffic analysis, *transmission security* or *communications cover*—which always amounts to sending dummy traffic to conceal the pattern of real traffic (Kent 1977)—is difficult and expensive to implement on an end-to-end basis and is best left to the network infrastructure.

The most extreme form of transmission security is to conceal the existence of communication altogether. This is often done by using *frequency-hopping radios*, whose frequencies change many times a second in an unpredictable pattern. When concealment of the existence of communication is the primary objective, we speak of *covert communication*. This is the dominant concern in the communications of criminals and spies.

### Supporting Technologies

In order to be effective in network security, cryptography must not only be employed for the right purposes, it must also be implemented correctly. Several *supporting technologies* play important roles in this respect.

*Reliability* is critical in secure communication. Failures of either cryptographic equipment or its human operators, called *busts*, are typically the most lucrative sources of cryptanalytic successes (Welchman 1982). Automation has made a major contribution to the ease of use of cryptoequipment, making human errors less likely, but rising data rates have made reliability of the equipment vastly more significant. Performing a *security failure analysis* to trace the effects of all likely failures and including self-check and failure-monitoring circuitry in essential in designing cryptographic equipment.

*Secure computing* practices are integral to the construction of reliable communication-security (COMSEC) equipment whose functioning can be trusted under adverse conditions. A particularly difficult aspect of the logical analysis is the detection of malicious hidden functions, and no good solution to this problem is known for equipment acquired from untrusted suppliers.

*Electromagnetic shielding* is essential to prevent cryptographic channels from being bypassed by radiative or conductive emissions or by accidental modulation of a ciphertext signal with a plaintext signal. The military term for this particular form of protection is Tempest.[31]

The most interesting and difficult Tempest problem is the contamination of ciphertext by plaintext. In the United States, this problem first seems to have been observed in the late 1940s or the early 1950s in an online version of a one-time-tape system called SIGTOT (Martin 1980, pp.

74–75). What they observed was probably a form of amplitude modulation in which combining a 0 in the key with a 1 in the plaintext produces a waveform that is distinguishable from the waveform produced by combining a 1 in the key with a 0 in the plaintext, even though the results are supposed to be identical. If this occurs, opponents with the right equipment can read both the plaintext and the keystream from the ciphertext signal. The effect as described is unlikely to occur in modern digital cryptosystems, but amplitude modulation is only the simplest form of plaintext contamination. Frequency and timing modulation present subtler pitfalls for the designer.

*Tamper resistance* guarantees that COMSEC equipment will not be altered to defeat its functioning without requiring the expensive practice of guarding it constantly or locking it in safes when not in use. Tamper resistance dramatically reduces the level of trust that must be placed in personnel permitted to operate COMSEC equipment and has become a mainstay of US military cryptography.

## The Operation of Secure Communications

A secure communication system must not only be designed and built correctly; it must be operated correctly over its entire lifetime. The threat posed by opponents must be assessed, not once when a system is developed, but continually. The vulnerability must be judged against advancing technology. This should include continuing cryptanalytic study of the cryptosystems, other sorts of penetration studies, and continuing reevaluation of who the opponents are and what their resources are.

Equipment that worked securely when it was new may not continue to work securely. Ongoing assessment of the functioning of installed equipment must be accompanied by a careful program of maintenance.

A vital element of a secure communication posture that is operational rather than architectural is *communication security monitoring*. This is the practice of intercepting friendly communications to monitor the effectiveness of COMSEC practices. COMSEC monitoring is a difficult and sensitive task that is rarely undertaken by non-governmental organizations.

### Cryptographic Needs of Business

Many large American firms have manufacturing plants around the world and need to communicate product-design information, marketing plans, bidding data, costs and prices of parts and services, strategic plans, and orders to them. Much of this information, which is often communicated electronically, must be kept secret from competitors.[32]

In the current banking system, the transfer of currency is the transfer of electronic bits, and it could not be undertaken without adequate security. Cryptography is simply the latest manifestation of the security upon which the banking industry has always relied. Internationalization of banking complicates the security problem while exacerbating the need for security.

Except to the extent that loss of confidentiality threatens security by exposing access controls, authentication is more important in banking than data confidentiality.[33] In part, this is because exposure of one person's data typically harms only that individual, whereas failures of authentication can result in loss of assets. In part, it is because there is already substantial government monitoring of financial transactions.[34]

Electronic funds transfer is already several decades old, but bankers now face the complex security issues posed by opening the transfer mechanisms to a wider audience. Indeed, despite stringent security procedures, Citicorp has already been the victim of such a scam, losing $400,000 in a theft that occurred over several months and involved three continents.[35] After this electronic theft became public, six of Citicorp's competitors went after its largest accounts, claiming they could provide better security than Citicorp (Carley 1995; Hansell 1995).

Although banking is a highly regulated industry, that does not mean that the government and banks see eye to eye on cryptography. In the 1980s, the National Security Agency proposed replacing the Data Encryption Standard with a classified algorithm. Bankers, having invested heavily in designing protocols based on DES, protested, and the NSA plan was dropped. Bankers also objected to the Clipper Chip.

In the oil industry seismic data and other geographic information can be worth a small fortune. Even before they came to rely on electronic communications, oil companies were targets of electronic eavesdropping.[36] Oil companies often operate in politically unstable regions, and criminal actions against employees, including kidnappings, are not unknown. Thus, in order to minimize knowledge about their whereabouts, employees' communications must be secured (Dam and Lin 1996, p. 464).

Other businesses face different requirements. In contrast to banking, the health-care industry emphasizes confidentiality. Medicine's heavily integrated systems of insurance records, hospital files, and doctors' records require a system that preserves patient confidentiality while allowing access by a large set of users (NRC 1997). The entertainment industry, whose product is increasingly digitized, will need cryptographic techniques for protecting copyright. Digital signatures can also provide a guarantee that movies, recordings, and other works of art have not been modified. Various knowledge-based industries seek to guard their heavy investments in intangible goods, and cryptography will be one aspect of that security.

Economic espionage is not solely the province of competing companies; it is also done by governments. One of the top priorities of the French intelligence service is industrial spying. Pierre Marion, a former director of the Direction Générale de la Sécurité Extérieure, the French Intelligence Service, told NBC News that he had initiated an espionage program against US businessmen to keep France economically competitive.[37] Another French spy, Henri de Marenches, the director of the French secret service from 1970 to 1981, observed that economic spying was very profitable: "It enables the Intelligence Services to discover a process used in another country, which might have taken years and possibly millions of francs to invent or perfect." (Schweizer 1993, p. 13) The British wiretap law includes protecting the economic well-being of the country as one of the reasons to permit wiretapping.[38] The Japanese invest heavily in industrial espionage, sending hundreds of businessmen abroad to discover in detail what the competition is doing, hiring many foreign consultants to further the contacts, and electronically eavesdropping on foreign businessmen in Japan (ibid., pp. 74–82 and 84).

In many countries, telecommunications are run by the national government. This makes electronic eavesdropping particularly simple. In one case, an American businessman working for a multinational firm reported that his laptop computer was taken by customs officials of an unnamed country and returned to him three days later; as he attempted to negotiate his business deals, it became clear that his sensitive files had been copied during those three days (Dam and Lin 1996, p. 471). The Chinese office of a multinational company experienced a theft in which unencrypted computer files were copied (ibid., p. 471). The governments of Japan and France are notorious for eavesdropping on the communications of US businessmen (Schweizer 1993, pp. 16 and 84). It is alleged that the Bundesnachrichtendienst, the German intelligence service, regularly wiretaps transatlantic business communications (ibid., p. 17).

Similar charges have been raised against the US government. There was suspicion in Britain for some time that the NSA establishment at Menwith Hill was being used as much to spy on the British as on the Eastern Europeans (Bamford 1982, p. 332). During the Cold War such espionage was limited out of concern for not alienating allies, but now these considerations are of less importance. In 1990 FBI Director William Sessions said that the FBI would devote greater investigative energies to the intelligence activities of "friendly" nations (Schweizer 1993, p. 4). Of course, greater protection of the goods to begin with would decrease the need to investigate thefts after they had occurred—a point that is surely not lost on the FBI.

It has been claimed that a system like public key, in which the private key is stored with a single user, will not provide the data-recovery features that corporations require. In fact, the danger posed to corporations by this lack of data recovery for communications is minimal. With the exception of the financial industry, few businesses currently record telephone communications. Those that do can continue to do so even if the telecommunications are encrypted. Because the ends of the conversation will be unencrypted, and the recording can be done at that point, the choice of encryption—whether public key or some form of escrow—will not affect data recovery. Encrypted communications will provide corporations with at least as much security as they have now; they will not be losing information, for *they do not have such information in the first place.*

Because they rely on "written" records rather than recordings of conversations, businesses are in the same position as law-enforcement agencies. Conversations are transient whereas records endure, and wiretaps are used in far fewer criminal cases than seized records (Dam and Lin 1996, p. 84).

Today, talk of a global information infrastructure, an information superhighway, and Internet commerce is everywhere. The underlying notion is that we are moving a lot of our culture into digital channels of communication. If this is to be a success, we will to have to find digital replacements for a lot of everyday physical practices. In the area of security, many of the new practices will be cryptographic.

In some cases, the correspondences are obvious. In the physical world, we close doors, or stroll off somewhere by ourselves, or whisper in order to have privacy. In the digital world, we encrypt. In other cases, the correspondence is not so obvious. In the physical world, we place written signatures on contracts, letters and checks. In the digital world, we add digital signatures and rejoice in the degree of similarity. Some of the correspondences leave us completely puzzled. A copying machine may reproduce a readable copy of a bestseller, but for most purposes the copy is a poor imitation of the original. In the digital world, if you can get your hands on a document you can copy it exactly. Cryptography does not seem to be of much help.

Digital equivalents have been found for a surprising range of human interactions, including:

> The delivery of a registered letter. (You get the letter if and only if the deliverer gets a signature on the receipt.)

> The signing of a contract. (The contract is valid only if both signatures are on both copies and neither party can get a final copy while denying one to the other.)

> Sharing of authority. (The president of the company can sign a million dollar check, but it takes two vice presidents.)

> Power of attorney. (My lawyers have access to the contents of my safe deposit box because they are working for me.)

> Issuing of credentials. (A passport certifies that the secretary of state vouches for the bearer.)

### Why Has Cryptography Taken So Long to Become a Business Success?

If cryptography is so valuable, why has it taken so long to become a business success? One answer lies in the truly remarkable qualities of communications intelligence. Unlike installing an infiltrator, breaking and entering, or going around asking questions, interception of communications is very hard to detect. People may suspect that their communications are being spied on, but they are rarely able to prove it or to convince themselves with certainty that that is happening. Even an intelligence agency typically has difficulty discovering that it is being spied on and how. During the 1960s and the 1970s, the British and American intelligence establishments were convinced that they had been penetrated by the Soviets and spent an excessive amount of their time trying to discover who the turncoats were (Wright 1987). Despite their efforts, the investigations were inconclusive.

For an organization that is not an intelligence agency, such *counterintelligence* is much harder. Merely discovering that information has been leaking is very difficult. Discovering how or to whom is far more difficult. It may even require an intelligence agency to uncover the fact of the eavesdropping; this has happened several times for American companies.[39] Selling secure communications has often been likened to selling insurance, in that the customer must pay up front for protection against something that may occur in the future. The fire, auto, and medical insurance salesmen have an advantage, however. Everyone has seen houses burn down, cars crash, and friends get seriously ill. Almost no one has seen information taken by eavesdroppers and used to bankrupt an otherwise profitable business. Indeed, admitting to break-ins has its own costs: competitors may use the seeming lack of security to woo customers.

### The Problem of Standards

Cryptography also suffers from a serious standards problem. In a sense, security equipment exists to amplify minor incompatibilities into absolute non-interoperability. If a radio is not tuned to quite the right frequency, reception will suffer but communication may still be possible. If a cryptographic key is off by even one bit, communication is impossible. By themselves standards problems probably would not account for cryptography's slow start, but in combination with other factors they have played a major role. In particular, the lack of standards has contributed directly to the lack of "critical mass." A single secure telephone, just like a single telephone, is a useless piece of hardware, and even a pair has only limited applicability. Only when there is a proliferation of such devices does their value increase to the point that purchasing a security device for one's telephone is as common as purchasing a lock when buying a bicycle.

Similarly, the lack of a supporting infrastructure has slowed the adoption of secure communications. Without a national key management facility, the exchange of keys is a remarkably cumbersome process, and encrypted communications are unlikely to be used by any but the most committed of participants. The government is well aware of this, and indeed it tailors its export-control policy accordingly; it does not dispute that strong cryptography is currently available outside the United States, but it observes that outside the United States strong cryptography is not integrated into shrink-wrapped software (Dam and Lin 1996, p. 73). Thus, the national-security establishment claims the current availability of strong cryptography outside the United States does not yet pose a serious problem, since encryption is not available to the mass market.

### The Adverse Effect of Government Opposition

In the United States, cryptography has been hurt by the ambivalent attitude of the federal government. Despite the controversy that surrounded the adoption of the Data Encryption Standard in 1977, this standard and the others that accompanied it have made a major contribution to the deployment of cryptography both in the US and abroad. This latter aspect made the government wonder whether it had done the right thing, and in the 1980s it became an antagonist rather than a proponent of cryptographic standards.

### The Effect of the Internet

Since 1995, the market for cryptography has exploded. What has changed? Most conspicuously, the Internet.

The Internet has made the prospect of global electronic commerce appear real to a large number of people.[40] And commerce, on a large scale, can prosper only when people can deal confidently with people they have never met and have no reason to trust. The problem is made worse by the Internet's internationality. No uniform system of law or policing can patrol it. The merchants, like the cannon-carrying merchant ships of two centuries ago, must provide security themselves. The more secure people can be in their transactions, the larger those transactions will be and the more profitable the Internet will be as a business medium.

### What Is Cryptography's Commercial Future?

In light of the sudden growth of cryptography, it is natural to ask how big a business it will become. In order to find the answer, we might look at an existing business.

Locksmithing is not a large fraction of the building trades. If you own a $500,000 house you are unlikely to have $500 worth of locks on it. Even if, like Oliver North, you have a fancy electronic security system, its total value probably doesn't exceed a few percent of the house's value. On the other hand, no one would argue that locks are not essential to the functioning of society. The modern suburb, in which most members of most families are gone for most of the day, would not function without them.

# 3
# Cryptography and Public Policy

## The Legacy of World War I

Histories of cryptography usually begin by observing that cryptography is of ancient lineage, having been used by Caesar and recommended as one of the feminine arts in the Kama Sutra. As we saw in the last chapter, there is a remarkable degree of continuity in the basics of cryptographic technology over the past several centuries, and new ideas often turn out to have old roots.[1] Be this as it may, the field we know today is a creature of the twentieth century.

World War I was the first war to be fought in the era of radio. In the early years of the century, the military (particularly navies) saw the potential of the new medium of communication and adopted it wholesale. Before the advent of radio, Britain's First Sea Lord sent an admiral off with a fleet and expected to hear news in weeks or months. With radio, ships at sea were brought under much closer control by shore-based headquarters. Radio also had the advantage of being able to carry human voice, which undersea cable systems of the time could not do. Radio, however, had a serious disadvantage: anyone could listen in. Sometimes an unintended listener even got better reception than the intended recipient.

## The Mechanization of Cryptography
The solution to the ubiquity of radio reception was, of course, to use cryptography. Messages were enciphered before being transmitted, and were deciphered upon reception. Radio was much more vulnerable to interception than any communication channel that had been in use before, with the result that a much larger fraction of the messages required encryption. The methods in use, codes and some hand cipher systems,

had grown up over centuries of written communication in which they were usually reserved for the most sensitive traffic. In consequence, there was a crushing burden on the cipher clerks, and often a glut of traffic waiting to be deciphered.

In the years immediately after the war, inventors turned their attention to the problem of mechanizing encryption and embarked on the path that has led us to the automatic cryptography of today. As described in the previous chapter, the technique was a form of multiple-Vigenère cipher in which letters were looked up in tables by electric currents passing through wires rather than by cipher clerks.

Rotor machines arose simultaneously on both sides of the Atlantic. The inventions of Edward Hebern of Oakland, California emerged as the backbone of US cryptography in World War II. Those of Arthur Scherbius and Arvid Gerhard Damm played a similar role in Europe and gave rise to the most widely used of all rotor principles: that of the German Enigma machine (Kahn 1967, pp. 420–422).

At the time of World War I, cryptography was more an esoteric than a secret field. It was not widely understood, and codebreakers kept their intrusions into opponents' codes secret. Yet the whole culture of military secrecy, rampant today, was in its infancy, and military secrets did not belong to governments in the way they do now. Works on cryptography reasonably representative of the state of the art were published and enjoyed a status similar to that of other technical treatises. Indeed, during the war, William Frederick Friedman, the intellectual founder of the organization that eventually grew to become the National Security Agency, published groundbreaking new cryptographic discoveries as technical reports of the private Riverbank Laboratories.

The inventors of the rotor machine all took out patents, intending to sell their machines commercially. In the United States and in Europe the granting of a patent is a very public process and the publication of patents is regulated by treaty. Both earlier and later laws made it possible for the US government to declare a patent application secret and delay the granting indefinitely, but in 1919 this was not the case.

The issuing of the patents turned out to be one of the last public things about rotor machines. The commercial market for cryptographic equipment proved not to be as good as the inventors expected, and Hebern

**Figure 3.1**
Simplified Sigaba.

tried to sell his invention to the government. As designed, Hebern's machine was not secure, and it was broken by Friedman in 1921 (Deavours and Kruh 1985, pp. 46–47). Although attacks on the machine Friedman broke can be found in the contemporary public literature, Friedman's 1925 paper on the subject is still secret.

The government bought only sample quantities of Hebern's device. The weaknesses Friedman discovered were correctable, but the Army did not share its design changes with Hebern. It developed and employed his invention without compensating him, under cover of cryptography's growing secrecy. Only in the 1950s did Hebern's heirs succeed, through a lawsuit, in recovering some of what Hebern was owed (Kahn 1967, p. 420). In the United States, development of cryptographic systems became a secret enterprise of small groups in the Army and the Navy.

Hebern's simple three-wheel machine and regular pattern of wheel movement led to Sigaba, the most secure rotor machine of World War II. In the mid 1930s Friedman designed a rotor machine, designated M-134a, whose five wheels moved under the control of a paper tape. In retrospect this can be seen to be merely an overly complicated way of achieving a one-time cryptosystem, but at the time the additional complexity must have seemed an advantage. Unfortunately, the M-134a had the same problem that goes with any one-time system: it needed lots of keying material. A young cryptanalyst named Frank Rowlett was given the task of producing matching pairs of key tapes—a task made tedious by the fact that any error in the tapes would produce not only an error in the plain text but also a disastrous loss of synchronization between the sending and receiving machines. Rowlett conceived of using one rotor machine to manufacture the pattern of rotor motions for the other, an idea that was to remain officially secret for 60 years.

### The Growth of US Signals Intelligence

After World War I, the United States maintained and developed its capacity for signals intelligence (SIGINT), something unprecedented in peacetime. Equally important, the responsibility for signals intelligence was merged with the responsibility for developing codes to protect US military communications.[2] Both intelligence and security prospered under this arrangement. By making good use of signals intelligence during arms negotiations with Japan in 1921, the US pushed the Japanese all the way to their planned best offer (Kahn 1967, pp. 357–359; Yardley 1931).

The role secrecy plays in intelligence is quite different from the role it plays in security. Cryptography relies on the secrecy of cryptographic keys, just as safes rely on the secrecy of their combinations. It may also profit from the secrecy of cryptographic systems. It could hardly be easier to break a cryptosystem whose workings are not known than to break one whose workings are known. On the other hand, such secrecy has costs that usually outweigh its benefits. The workings of ordinary pin-tumbler door locks and those of the combination locks that guard bank vaults are familiar to locksmiths and burglars alike, yet both are widespread and successful security devices. It is essentially impossible, on the other hand, to practice intelligence without secrecy. If you reveal the fact that you are spying on people or, worse yet, precisely how you are doing it, it is almost certain that, if those people care at all about security, they will change their communication practices in order to make your task more difficult.

A celebrated example of this occurred in Britain in 1927. The Security Service (MI5) raided the London office of the All-Russian Cooperative Society (ARCOS), whose trade activities were a key element of Soviet spying on British industry. Parliament imprudently demanded to know what had led MI5 to such an action and publicly extracted the fact that Britain had been reading Soviet messages for years. In the words of R.V.

Jones, Britain's head of scientific intelligence during World War II, that incident showed the Soviets the weakness of "their diplomatic codes, which were changed a fortnight later and were not since readable, at least up to the time that I left MI6 in 1946" (Corson et al. 1985, pp. 286 and 440).

The integration of communications intelligence (a field in which it is advantageous to keep even the basic techniques secret) and communication security (a field whose need for secrecy is far narrower) is the apparent cause of the general increase in the secrecy of cryptography that occurred from the 1920s through the 1960s.

## World War II

World War II was a triumph for America's codemakers and codebreakers. On the defensive side, American high-grade cryptosystems, Sigaba in particular, survived the war, apparently unread by our opponents. On the offensive side, communications intelligence contributed decisively to victory in both the Atlantic and the Pacific. The United States routinely read high-level Japanese traffic in both military and diplomatic systems, and collaborated extensively with Great Britain in reading German communications.

Cryptography and signals intelligence during World War II have been written about extensively, but a little-known project undertaken during the same period presaged much of what has happened since: the development of the first secure telephone.

Voice scramblers of various sorts had been in existence since the early years of the twentieth century, but none of these systems was in any real sense secure. Scrambling systems were adequate to thwart casual listeners; however, most of them were vulnerable to being unraveled by talented ears—particularly after the development of recording, which permitted the signal to be listened to more than once. The existing scramblers were inadequate to protect high-level traffic, and the US military started development on Sigsaly, the first digital secure telephone.

Sigsaly was in some ways like and in some ways preposterously unlike a contemporary secure phone. Sigsaly was a digital telephone. It used a vocoder developed at Bell Laboratories to convert the speaker's voice into a 2400-bit-per-second stream.[3] The digitized voice was then encrypted with one-time keys stored on phonograph records. The records were shattered after each use to ensure that they could not be reused. Although modern secure phones do not normally use one-time keys, there is nothing bizarre about the practice. Especially remarkable were Sigsaly's size (30 equipment racks, each 7 feet tall) and cost (so high that only two people in the world could afford such installations: Franklin Roosevelt and Winston Churchill — later a few more were installed in high level military headquarters).

The successes of the American signals intelligence establishment during the war set the stage for further expansion and consolidation.

### The Cold War

The late 1940s brought the explosion in technology that has dominated the lives of the baby-boom generation. Some technologies, most conspicuously atomic energy and radar, were developed as consequences of World War II. Others, including television, had been put on hold by the war and now profited from the overall growth of the electronics industry that the war had produced. In the world of cryptography, it was a great period of conversion from mechanical and electro-mechanical cryptosystems to purely electronic cryptosystems.

Inappropriate as Sigsaly was for any normal military or civilian communication requirement, it showed the possibility of genuinely secure voice communication. However, there were many hurdles to jump. The highest of these was the problem of digitizing the voice. Decades would pass before secure voice equipment at the low data rates of Sigsaly would be widely available. In the meantime, it was necessary to simplify the problem by sending voice at between 6000 and 50,000 bits per second. This created a new cryptographic problem.

Sigsaly had achieved 2400-bit-per-second encryption by using a one-time system to protect its signal. Like all one-time systems, it suffered from inflexibility of key management. This was of little concern when the supply of instruments numbered two, but it would be a limiting factor in wider deployment. What was required was a cryptographic machine capable of operating at voice speeds. Unfortunately, rotor machines, which

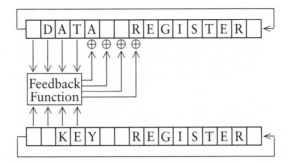

**Figure 3.2**
Nonlinear shift register.

operated at 10 characters per second, could not come close to keeping up with Sigsaly's 2400 bits (240 characters) per second.[4] The result was the development of shift-register cryptography, which accounts for most of the encrypted bits transmitted today.

During and before World War II, intelligence in general and communications intelligence in particular was attached to military commands. After the war, there was a move to improve the quality of US intelligence by centralizing authority and coordinating the activities of various groups. The year 1947 saw passage of the Central Intelligence Act, which created the Central Intelligence Agency and the position of Director of Central Intelligence (who, at least in principle, coordinated the efforts of the whole US intelligence community). The centralization of signals intelligence took longer and was far less public, but in 1952, after some 5 years of study and reorganization, President Harry Truman signed a secret presidential order creating the National Security Agency. From its creation the new organization sought to capture control of all cryptographic and cryptanalytic work within the United States. Overall, this effort was remarkably successful.

In 1948, Claude Shannon, a professor of electrical engineering at MIT, published a paper entitled "The Communication Theory of Secrecy Systems" in the *Bell System Technical Journal*. In 1967, David Kahn, a journalist who had been interested in cryptography since childhood, published a massive history of cryptography called *The Codebreakers*. In between, no overtly cryptographic work of any significance saw public print in the United States,[5] though various papers whose cryptographic significance is not immediately apparent did.[6]

NSA successfully suppressed cryptographic work in other parts of the US government. Probably as a result of this, application of cryptography to the nuclear command and control system did not get underway until directly ordered by President John Kennedy in the early 1960s.[7]

### Horst Feistel's Group at the AFCRC

There was, however, one very significant failure of NSA's territorial ambitions.

Cryptography can play a number of roles that are not explicitly parts of communication. One of these is distinguishing between friends and enemies. During World War II, US warplanes began to carry *Identification Friend or Foe* (IFF) devices to reduce the chance that they would be shot down by "friendly fire." Early IFF devices were analog and were not very secure against replication by opponents seeking to impersonate US forces. IFF without cryptography eventually evolved into a system called the Mark X, which is now an essential component of air traffic control and is used by civilian aircraft, and many military ones, all over the world.

In the early 1950s, the US Air Force recognized the need to improve its IFF equipment and turned to the established cryptographic authorities for help. The Armed Forces Security Agency, NSA's immediate predecessor, had little interest in the problem, and so the Air Force set out on its own. A prototype cryptographic IFF device was built at the Air Force Cambridge Research Center (AFCRC) using the recently developed transistor. Central among this project's objectives was to show that the equipment could be made small enough to fit in a fighter's nose. At this point, the project crossed the path of a man whose role in modern cryptography has been widely underappreciated, despite the fact that he is recognized as the "father of the Data Encryption Standard."

In 1934, the 20-year-old Horst Feistel moved to the United States from Germany. Seven years later, the Japanese attacked Pearl Harbor, the US declared war on Japan, and Germany, in an act of bravado, declared war on the US. Feistel, on the verge of becoming a US citizen, was put under "house arrest"—he could move freely around Boston, where he lived, but was required to report his movements if he went to visit his mother in New York. On January 31, 1944, the restraints were suddenly lifted and Feistel became a US citizen. The following day he was given a security clearance and began a job at the AFCRC.[8]

Feistel, who says that cryptography had interested him since he was in his teens, recalls that when he mentioned his interests shortly after arriving at his new job, he was told that it was not the time for a German to be talking about cryptography. His career in cryptography had to wait until after the hot war against Germany was over and the Cold War against the Soviet Union was underway.

Several years later, Feistel, who had by now built a research group in cryptography at the AFCRC, discovered that the Air Force's cryptographic IFF system was on its way to being put into service without what he considered adequate evaluation. He put his team of young mathematicians, supported by a number of academic consultants, to work analyzing the new system. The group alternately found weaknesses in the original design and discovered how to fix them. Over a period of several years it made a major contribution to modern cryptography, developing the first practical block ciphers.[9]

Although Feistel's group at the AFCRC was in steady communication with NSA and seems thereby to have exerted a profound influence on cryptographic design in that organization, NSA appears eventually to have succeeded in shutting down the Air Force work. In the late 1950s, the group dissolved. Horst Feistel moved, first to MIT's Lincoln Laboratory and then to its spinoff, the Mitre Corporation. In the mid 1960s, Feistel, who devoted himself to one problem throughout his career, attempted to set up a new cryptographic development group at Mitre. He was forced to abandon the project as a result of what was perceived at Mitre as NSA pressure.[10] At this point, Feistel found a new champion, IBM, and moved to the Watson Laboratory in Yorktown Heights, New York.

## The 1960s

In 1965, Representative Jack Brooks of Texas authored a thoroughly non-controversial law providing for the purchase and leasing of computer equipment (Brooks Act 1965, 89-306(f)). The law decreed that the Secretary of Commerce was authorized to "make appropriate recommendations to the President relating to the establishment of uniform Federal automatic data processing standards" (ibid., 89-306(f)). Thus the responsibility for setting civilian computer standards fell to the National Bureau of Standards (NBS), which already determined everything from standard US time (based on an atomic clock in Boulder, Colorado) to methods for testing the flammability of fabrics. The new series were called Federal Information Processing Standards; their purpose is to provide incentives for industry to manufacture what the US government needs. Although FIPS are only binding on government organizations, the enormous purchasing power the government brings to bear causes most FIPS to become de facto commercial standards.[11] This assignment of responsibility to NBS was later to prove difficult for the Department of Defense, but there were no objections when the Brooks Act was passed.

In 1967, a non-technical phenomenon had a profound effect on the course of cryptographic technology. Despite NSA's efforts, David Kahn's book *The Codebreakers* was published. Kahn was neither a mathematician nor an engineer, but a historian, and his book focuses far more on the military and diplomatic impact of codebreaking than on its technique. Nonetheless, Kahn explained everything he knew about cryptography and cryptanalysis. All of a sudden, there was a book in print that explained rotor machines and at least mentioned that they had been succeeded by purely electronic devices. Furthermore, what explanation of the technology the book did contain was wrapped in an extensive explanation of why the subject was important. The result was a wave of interest in cryptography that rippled through the engineering world.

IBM was also interested in cryptography in the late 1960s. The company had undertaken to provide automatic teller machines for Lloyds Bank in London. Lloyds, which planned to have several hundred of the machines scattered around London, had a scenario for disaster. It imagined a gang with a confederate inside the post office, which, in Britain, ran the telephone system. The members of the gang would drive around London visiting the teller machines at the start of a bank holiday weekend, when the machines had just been stocked with thousands of pounds of cash apiece. The post office confederate would call each machine in turn and tell it to hand out all its money. At the end of the evening the gang would be several million pounds richer. Nobody else would be likely to notice anything but the fact that some of the machines had run out of money till Tuesday morning, when the bank holiday weekend ended. By then the money would no doubt be sitting comfortably in a bank in Zurich, a city whose bankers had not taken the previous day off.

IBM hired Horst Feistel, who continued with his life's work. Colleagues recall that Feistel had been talking back in the 1950s about much larger systems than could be built at the time. Now, a quarter century later, electronics had caught up with Feistel's imagination. The work resulted in a number of cryptographic systems. One was used in the IBM2984 banking system and was commonly called Lucifer.[12]

## The 1970s

### The US Data Encryption Standard

In the early 1970s, some people at the National Security Agency and some at the National Bureau of Standards[13] recognized that the Privacy Act of 1974 and other federal laws, together with the increasing use of computers and digital communications by the federal government, would require that approved cryptography be available to government users other than NSA's traditional national-security clients.

NSA was reluctant to provide equipment of its own design to a wider range of users. Its reasoning is easy to imagine. Cryptographic secrecy was part of NSA's security philosophy. The designs of NSA cryptographic systems were uniformly classified SECRET NOFORN,[14] and the equipment in which they were implemented was classified CONFIDENTIAL. The tamper-resistance technology being used today to put SECRET algorithms in UN-CLASSIFIED chips did not yet exist. Any equipment that was to be put in the hands of uncleared users would have to embody an unclassified cryptographic algorithm. NSA was afraid, however, that, by making public an algorithm it had designed itself, it would reveal information about its design philosophy and potentially compromise other equipment. A system that was made public would be widely available to attack. If it was broken, and if it resembled other NSA cryptosystems, the attack might work against those as well.

Following the FIPS process, NBS published a solicitation for a standard cryptographic system in the *Federal Register* (USDoC 1973). The process by which the Data Encryption Standard was selected has never been adequately explained, and the identity of the other contestants, if there were any, has not become public. On the face of it, IBM submitted the winning algorithm and NSA, acting as a consultant to the NBS, approved it. In fact it is generally agreed that NSA had a substantial hand in determining the algorithm's final form (Bayh 1978).

### Public-Key Cryptography

During the academic year 1974–1975, Whitfield Diffie and Martin Hellman, working at Stanford University, and Ralph Merkle, at the University of California at Berkeley, discovered a new concept in cryptography that was to have profound implications for policy as well as for technology.[15]

The idea was that the capacity to encrypt messages and the capacity to decrypt messages were not, as had always been taken for granted, inseparable. It was possible for one person to have a key that would encrypt messages in such a way that decrypting them required a different key, held by a different person. Diffie, Hellman, and Merkle called the new concept *public-key cryptography*.

Instead of having one key that could both encrypt and decrypt messages, like a conventional cryptosystem, a public-key system had two keys. What was essential was that with one key, called reasonably enough the *public key*, it was very hard to figure out the corresponding *private key* that could be used to decrypt a message encrypted with the public key. Exactly how hard? Just as hard as breaking a cryptogram produced by encrypting something with the public key.

Public-key cryptography has two implications: if I know your public key and want to send you a secret message, I can encrypt it with your public key, and, since only you know your private key, only you will be able to read the message. I don't need to share a secret with you in order to send you a secret message.

Not only did public-key cryptography make a major contribution to key management, it provided a *digital signature* that could be used on electronic documents. Suppose I receive a message from you encrypted with your private key. If I decrypt the message and find that it makes sense, I have evidence that, unless someone else knows your private key, the message must have come from you.

Although the research that led to this new field was carried on in academia, it grew out of two very practical considerations. Diffie had been trying for years to figure out how to build a system that would secure every telephone in the country. Getting away from the traditional need to distribute secret keys from a central facility brought this vision a step closer to reality. By what seems to be coincidence, Diffie had also been thinking about signatures for years. Around the time of Diffie's arrival at Stanford in late 1969, his new boss, John McCarthy, had given a paper on what we would now call Internet commerce, and Diffie had begun wondering what would play the role of the signed contract in the new environment.

In 1976, Diffie and Hellman published a paper entitled "New Directions in Cryptography," which contained a partial solution to the problem of creating a public-key cryptosystem. This system, commonly known as *Diffie-Hellman key exchange*,[16] provides an additional feature with policy implications that took years to be recognized: the creation of truly ephemeral keys.

In early 1977, Diffie and Hellman's paper was read by a team of three young faculty members at MIT, Ron Rivest, Adi Shamir, and Len Adleman. With a far better grasp of number theory than the three West Coast researchers, Rivest, Shamir, and Adleman quickly found a solution to the problem Diffie and Hellman had posed. They named the resulting system after their initials: RSA (Rivest et al. 1978).

### The Meyer Affair

Public-key cryptography created quite a splash. In August of 1977 it was described in Martin Gardner's column in *Scientific American*, and requests for the MIT technical report came from around the world. Rivest was scheduled to present the work at an Institute of Electrical and Electronics Engineers (IEEE) meeting in Ithaca, New York, in October. The IEEE received a letter from one "J. A. Meyer" warning that, because foreign nationals would be present, publication of the result was a potential violation of the US International Traffic in Arms Regulations.

This was the first that Rivest and his colleagues had heard of ITAR.

Aside from an address in Bethesda, Maryland, J. A. Meyer was unidentified. Nonetheless, the MIT scientists took the warning seriously and halted distribution of their paper. Then an enterprising *Science* journalist, Deborah Shapley, discovered that Meyer worked at the National Security Agency. NSA denied any connection with Meyer's letter, and the MIT scientists decided to resume distribution of the paper (Shapley and Kolata 1977). Rivest spoke on the results at the Ithaca conference, and for the moment the furor subsided.

But 1978 brought new problems. Two inventors filed for patents and found themselves subjected to secrecy orders under a little-known provision of US patent law that permits the federal government to order an inventor to keep secret not only the substance of the invention but the fact that the order has been issued. The first of these inventors was Carl Nicolai, a garage-shop entrepreneur in Seattle who had developed a telephone scrambler based on spread-spectrum technology. The second was George Davida, a professor of computer science at the University of Wisconsin. Davida's invention, more technical than Nicolai's, was a way of combining linear and nonlinear finite automata in a cryptosystem. Most patent secrecy orders are placed on inventions growing out of government-sponsored secret work. Almost all of the remainder are directed at patents filed by large corporations,[17] which have little motivation to argue with the government's decision.[18]

Fights about secrecy orders are rare. But, despite the aspect of the law that makes the order itself secret, both Nicolai and Davida chose to fight. Ultimately, both orders were overturned—Nicolai's ostensibly on the grounds that a mistake had been made and the invention should not have been declared secret in the first place; Davida's on the pretext that, since it had earlier appeared as a Computer Science Department technical report, it could not effectively be kept secret.

### Research Funding and Publication Rights

In the late 1970s action developed on another front: funding. Frederick Weingarten was a program officer at the National Science Foundation (NSF). One day in 1977 "two very grim men" walked into his office and informed him that he was "probably" breaking the law by funding cryptography research through the NSF (Weingarten 1997; Burnham 1980, pp. 139–140). He was not, but a new battle ensued.

Len Adleman submitted a research proposal to the NSF, whereupon the MIT scientist found himself in the midst of an inter-agency conflict regarding funding. Because Adleman had proposed research in cryptography, the NSF had sent the application to NSA for review. Now NSA wanted to support Adleman's work. Unwilling to accept funding from NSA for fear that the agency's requirement of prior review could lead to classification of his work, Adleman was caught in a bind: since he had an alternative source of support, the NSF—whose purpose is to support "non-mission-oriented" research—now refused to support him.

Adleman's concerns tied in with another issue that had disquieted the research community: in 1979, the director of NSA, Admiral Bobby Inman, warned that open publication of cryptography research was harmful to national security. Inman threatened that, unless academia and industry could come to a satisfactory compromise with his agency, NSA would seek laws limiting publication of cryptographic research.

Adleman's problem was resolved when it was decided that both NSF and NSA would fund cryptography research. While NSF would make applicants aware of the alternate source of grants, it would not require them to accept NSA support.

Inman's concerns led to the creation of an American Council on Education study panel consisting of mathematicians and computer scientists from industry and academia and two lawyers, including the representative from NSA. The panel recommended a two-year experiment in which NSA would conduct pre-publication reviews of all research in cryptography (ACE 1981). Submissions would be voluntary, reviews prompt. The academic community feared that this process would have a chilling effect on the emerging field, but the experiment proved successful. Concerns eased when relatively few authors were asked to modify their publications. There have been NSA requests that an author not publish, and the agency has made suggestions for "minor" changes in some papers (Landau 1988, p. 11), but the research community reports that such requests have been modest in number. In an ironic twist, there was even an incident in which NSA apparently aided in the publication of cryptography research that the Army had tried to silence.[19]

## The 1980s

The conflicts of the 1970s appeared to have abated. Behind the scenes, however, NSA's efforts to limit civilian research in cryptography continued. The result was a protracted delay in any widespread application of cryptography to civilian communications.

For example, in 1982 the NBS issued a *Federal Register* solicitation for algorithms for a public-key cryptography standard (USDoC 1982). RSA Data Security (the corporation formed by Rivest, Shamir, and Adleman) was interested in having the RSA algorithm become a federal standard, but the NSA was not. At the intelligence agency's request, NBS's plan to develop a federal standard for public-key cryptography was shelved (USGAO 1993b, p. 20).

### Commercial Comsec Endorsement Program

In the mid 1980s, NSA changed its approach to broadening cryptographic coverage of American communications. Even though the initial promises that DES would be exportable had been broken, NSA was distressed by the algorithm's widespread availability[20] and was looking for a way to put the lid back on the box. Aided by the development of tamper-resistant coatings for chips (Raber and Riley 1989), NSA embarked on a program to supply equipment whose functioning was secret to a much wider user base.

Not only did NSA intend its new Commercial Comsec Endorsement Program (CCEP) to secure a much wider range of American communications, including industrial communications, NSA intended the program to do it with industry money.[21] As announced, the program was open to companies that had SECRET facility clearances and were willing to contribute expertise and funding to the development of secure versions of their products.[22]

The most significant feature of the new program, however, was that it would provide a new category of equipment certified only for the protection of "unclassified sensitive information" but available without the tedious administrative controls that applied to equipment for protection of classified information. The traditional equipment was termed Type I,

| Type I (High Grade) | Type II (Medium Grade) | |
| --- | --- | --- |
| Winster | Edgeshot | Voice ($\leq$ 100 KB) |
| Tepache | Bulletproof | Data ($\leq$ 10 MB) |
| Forsee | Brushstroke | High speed ($\approx$ 100 MB) |

**Table 3.1**
CCEP cryptomodules.

the new equipment Type II. Thus NSA was sponsoring the production of equipment directly competitive with DES.

The new undertaking was essentially a marketing effort, and in this situation NSA acted the same way commercial organizations often do: it began to undercut its previous "product line." The agency announced that it would not support the recertification of DES at its next five-year review, due to take place in 1988, and told the banking community so in a letter to the chairman of X9E9, the security standards committee.

It didn't wash. The bankers and their DES suppliers, few of whom were members of CCEP, were furious at the attempt to scuttle efforts on which they had been pressed to spend money only a few years earlier. Banking, furthermore, was international and had successfully negotiated special export arrangements in acknowledgement of this fact; secret American technology would not satisfy its worldwide need for security. In the end, NBS showed some backbone; in 1988 it recertified DES over NSA's objections. NSA had second thoughts about the wide availability of Type II equipment and, citing the Computer Security Act of 1987, imposed restrictions on its availability arguably as onerous as those for Type I equipment.[23] As a result, Type II products never approached market success, and few were ever manufactured.

### The STU-III
Although technically not a part of CCEP,[24] the third-generation secure telephone unit, STU-III, shared a lot of its technical and administrative

approach. The project began in 1983 and, like CCEP, incorporated Type I and Type II devices. The first instruments were delivered in late 1987.[25] Unlike CCEP, they have been a dramatic success, with over 300,000 installed by the mid 1990s.[26]

With CCEP and STU-III, NSA began using public-key cryptography. The exact method, called Firefly, was kept secret[27] but appears to employ the same exponentiation operations used by commercial gear (AWST 1986).

## NSDD-145

In September 1984, President Ronald Reagan issued a National Security Decision Directive (NSDD-145) establishing a federal policy of safeguarding "sensitive, but unclassified" information in communications and computer systems—a directive with NSA's fingerprints all over it (Brooks 1992). In 1985 the president's Assistant for National Security Affairs, John Poindexter, sent out a directive implementing NSDD-145 by putting a Defense Department team in charge of safeguarding all federal executive-branch departments and agencies *and their contractors*.[28]

The Poindexter directive, as it came to be known, attracted a lot of attention. Federal executive-branch contractors included a fair number of civilian companies, many of which had little or nothing to do with secret work. Mead Data Central (a supplier of databases, including the Lexis and Nexis systems, which provide law cases and news and magazine stories respectively) was one of the companies affected. Jack Simpson, the president of Mead, told Congress: "We have had a number of visits to inquire about our system, how it works, who uses it, whether we would be amenable to controls or monitors, and whether the Soviets used it. On April 23, 1986, AFMAG, five people came; September 29, US Government Intelligence Committee, CIA, NSA represented; October 7, FBI; October 21, FBI. Cordial visits, but asking the same questions." (Simpson 1987, p. 328) Cordial though these visits may have been, their effect was chilling. The National Technical Information Service, a database of unclassified federal scientific and technical material, had been part of Mead's information systems. After the visits from representatives of federal agencies, Mead got rid of NTIS. "This may have removed Mead Data Central from concern under NSDD-145," Simpson told Congress.

"I guess I wonder about other information providers of NTIS." (ibid.) He got it right.

In 1986, Assistant Secretary of Defense Donald Latham said: "I am very concerned about what people are doing, and not just the Soviets. If that means putting a monitor on NEXIS-type systems, then I am for it." (Schrage 1986) The FBI visited various university libraries, attempting to discover what scientific information foreign students were accessing. Here the government agents ran into an unexpected obstruction: the librarians insisted on subpoenas before they would release information.

A committee of the House of Representatives examined NSDD-145. Legislators saw an inappropriate incursion of presidential authority into national policy, and a turf battle developed. "[T]he basement of the White House and the backrooms of the Pentagon are not places in which national policy should be developed," Representative Jack Brooks declaimed (Brooks 1987, p. 2).

NSA backpedaled. "NSDD-145 in no way sets NSA as a computer czar," Lieutenant General William Odom, NSA's director, told the representatives. "[O]ur role with the private sector is one of *encouraging, advising and assisting* them with regard to their security needs. We view our role, then, as one that is clearly *advisory* in nature...." (Odom 1987, p. 281)

Many in industry and academia beheld NSDD-145 in a different light. "[Latham] is talking about monitoring private computer systems, private information sources, and unclassified data, and we find that incredible," Jack Simpson said before the House Committee (Simpson 1987, p. 328). Cheryl Helsing, chair of the Data Security Committee of the American Bankers Association and a vice president of BankAmerica, told the committee: "NSA's new ... algorithms ... absolutely cannot be used by the banking industry. Those conditions might well be appropriate for national defense related security, but are clearly inappropriate for use in our industry." (Helsing 1987, p. 113) Indeed, NSA's encryption algorithms threatened years of development work by the banking industry. Eventually NSA decided to accept the use of old DES-based technology[29] in the financial industry, but in the interim "sixteen months ... elapsed while we worked to educate the NSA about our business," Helsing told Congress (ibid., p. 114).

Shortly after the congressional hearings on NSDD-145 began, the Poindexter directive was withdrawn.[30] "The policy was a good idea, in response to a real security threat," explained a senior Defense Department official. "The problem was that no one thought through all the implications." (Sanger 1987)

### The Computer Security Act

The experience with NSDD-145 and NSA's behind-the-scenes actions convinced some US representatives that legislation was needed to reestablish which agency was in charge of assessing the security of civilian computer systems. NSA tried hard to convince the representatives that it was the right agency for the job. "[W]e are beginning to see civil agencies study and understand the usefulness of mechanisms resulting from [NSA's] earlier work," NSA Director Odom testified.

NSA could lead the way; it had "talent": "The [NSA] National Computer Security Center has a staff of more than 300 people," Odom told Congress (Odom 1987, pp. 294–295). He reminded the legislators that NSA already had responsibility for providing security for defense computer systems: "My concern with [the Computer Security Act] in its current form, then, it would create a wasteful, redundant bureaucracy that would busy itself with finding solutions to problems in computer security for the civil and private sector, while another government entity would be busy seeking the same solutions for the defense sector" (ibid., p. 296).

Congress did not buy the NSA director's arguments. The National Bureau of Standards (soon to be renamed the National Institute of Standards and Technology—we will refer to the agency as NIST from here on) was put in charge of developing computer security standards for the civilian sector. The representatives observed that developing civilian standards was a very different game from developing military ones, and that NIST had 22 years' experience with it whereas NSA had none.[31] The report by the House Government Operations Committee described the concerns about giving such a charge to the intelligence agency: "NSA has made numerous efforts to either stop [work in cryptography] or to make sure it has control over the work by funding it, pre-publication reviews or other methods." (USHR 100b, p. 21)[32]

The House committee was explicit that NIST was to be in charge, although NIST was to consult with NSA in the development of computer security standards, including those for cryptography: "By putting NSA in charge of developing technical security guidelines (software, hardware, communications) ... [NIST], in effect, would on the surface be given the responsibility for the computer standards program with little to say about most of the program—the technical guidelines developed by NSA. This would jeopardize the entire Federal standards program." (USHR 100b, p. 26)

The Computer Security Act (Public Law 100-235) was written to ensure that NIST would have responsibility for developing standards for the protection of "sensitive, but unclassified, information." All that remained was to fund the NIST program.

### NSA's Response

NSA felt it had been had. A TOP SECRET NSA memo described what had transpired as follows:

- In 1982 NSA engineered a National Security Decision Directive, NSDD-145, through the Reagan Administration that gave responsibility for the security of all US information systems to the Director of NSA, eliminating NBS from this.

- This also stated that we would assist the private sector. This was viewed as Big Brother stepping in and generated an adverse reaction.

- Representative Jack Brooks, chairman of the House Government Operations Committee, personally set out to pass a law to reassert NBS's responsibility for Federal unclassified systems and to assist the private sector.

- By the time we fully recognized the implications of Brooks' bill, he had it orchestrated for a unanimous consent voice vote passage.

Clinton Brooks
Special Assistant to the
Director of the NSA
April 28, 1992

Congress legislates, but agencies implement; the ball game wasn't over. Under the Computer Security Act, NIST had been given additional responsibilities, but now it needed funds to go with the new responsibilities. NSA, the largest employer of mathematicians in the United States, had a vast operation working on issues of computer security and cryptography that dwarfed NIST's efforts. In 1987 NSA's *unclassified* computer security program had 300 employees and a budget of $40 million (USHR 102, p. 176); NIST's 1987 computer security operation had 16 employees and a budget of $1.1 million (USC-OTA 1994, p. 164). The Congressional Budget Office estimated that implementation of the Computer Security Act would cost NIST $4 million to $5 million dollars annually (USHR 100b, p. 43).[33] It was time for Congress to appropriate the funds, but circumstances conspired to make that difficult.

During the Reagan-Bush years, the White House favored funding the Defense Department over funding civilian agencies, and NIST, part of the federal regulatory apparatus, was very much out of favor with a number of Republicans, some of whom were even in favor of eliminating the Department of Commerce. The Gramm-Rudman-Hollings Act[34] severely constrained discretionary funding. Yet by 1990 NIST's operation had a staff of 33 and a budget of $1.9 million.[35]

After the passage of the Computer Security Act, NSA began negotiating with NIST over their respective responsibilities in the development of cryptography. NSA went directly to Raymond Kammer, the acting director of NIST, to discuss drafting a Memorandum of Understanding (MOU) delineating the two agencies' responsibilities under the Computer Security Act. Kammer, the son of two NSA employees, was deeply concerned about protecting national-security and law-enforcement interests in cryptography. His instincts were to defer to the intelligence agency on control over civilian cryptography standards.[36]

The debate surrounding the Computer Security Act, as well as the act itself, had made it clear that NIST was in charge of developing civilian computer security standards. The MOU between NIST and NSA mandated that NIST would "request the NSA's assistance on all matters related to cryptographic algorithms and cryptographic techniques" (USDoCDoD 1989, p. 2). A Technical Working Group (TWG), consisting of three members each from NIST and NSA, would review and analyze issues of mutual interest, including the security of technical systems, *prior to* public disclosure (USDoCDoD 1989, p. 3). The opportunity to vet proposed standards before any public airing put NSA in a controlling position in the development of civilian computer standards.

In making civilian computer security standards part of NIST's bailiwick, the Computer Security Act had placed decisions regarding the approval of these standards in the hands of the Secretary of Commerce. The MOU changed this so that, although appeals could still be made to the Secretary of Commerce, members of the Defense Department were free to appeal proposed NIST standards to the Secretary of Defense before any public airing. Appeals of TWG disagreements would go to the Secretary of Commerce *or* the Secretary of Defense, and from there to the president and the National Security Council (the same group that had promulgated NSDD-145).

The Government Accounting Office was appalled. Milton Socolar, a special assistant to the Comptroller General, told Congress: "At issue is the degree to which responsibilities vested in NIST under the [Computer Security] act are being subverted by the role assigned to NSA under the memorandum." (Socolar 1989, p. 36) Congress's research arm, the Office of Technology Assessment, described the MOU as "ced[ing] to NSA much more authority than the act itself had granted or envisioned, particularly through the joint NIST/NSA Technical Working Group" (USC-OTA 1987, p. 164). NIST Acting Director Raymond Kammer, who had signed the document, disagreed: "As I've heard people interpreting the ... memorandum of understanding, it occurs to me that many individuals doing the interpreting are perhaps starting from a perspective I don't share, namely that NSA has had some trouble accepting the act. My experience in the months that I have been negotiating and working with the current management of NSA is that they fully understand the act, and that their understanding and my understanding are very consistent. I have no reservations about their willingness to implement the act as written." (Kammer 1989)

Representatives Jack Brooks and Daniel Glickman viewed the Digital Signature Standard as a test of who was running the show on civilian computer standards;[37] they were proved right.

### The Digital Signature Standard

Many breaches of confidentiality are difficult to detect, and even when a breach is clear it is often not at all clear where the problem lies. In light of this, any attempt by a litigant to claim that the insecurity lies with bad cryptography and thus force the protection techniques into the open is likely to fail. On the other hand, digital signatures—as a consequence of their function of resolving disputes between users of electronic networks—are certain to give rise to litigation over the adequacy of the signature methods. This is all the more true because digital signatures are a novel idea in commerce, whereas the notion of protecting messages by encryption is well established even though the details of particular methods may be unfamiliar. It is therefore necessary to provide a public digital signature mechanism that is open to examination by cryptographic researchers and expert witnesses in order to foster the public confidence necessary to achieve acceptance of the new technology.

In the spring of 1989, representatives from NIST and NSA began meeting to develop a set of public-key-based standards. First on the agenda was a digital signature standard to be included in the FIPS series. NIST proposed the Rivest-Shamir-Adleman algorithm (USGAO 1993b, p. 20). During its very public twelve-year lifetime, no cryptanalytic attacks had succeeded in breaking that algorithm. It was an accepted industry standard for digital signatures, and several standards organizations had formally adopted it. But in Technical Working Group meetings the NSA representatives rejected RSA. Presumably they objected to its flexibility, which allowed it to be used for purposes of confidentiality as well as authenticity. Raymond Kammer concurred in the decision, arguing that the infrastructure needed for public-key management made RSA an unwieldy digital signature standard. Kammer ignored the fact that any digital signature standard adopted for widespread use would entail a key management facility.

Through 1989 and 1990 the Technical Working Group of NIST and NSA representatives met once a month, and each month no progress was made. "We went to a lot of meetings with our NSA counterparts, and we were allowed to write a lot of memos, but we on the technical side of NIST felt we were being slowrolled on the Digital Signature Standard," recalled Lynn McNulty, NIST's Associate Director of Computer Security,

"In retrospect it is clear that the real game plan that NSA had drawn up was the Capstone Chip and Fortezza card—with key escrow all locked up in silicon."[38]

A year after the meetings on digital signatures began, NSA presented its proposal: an algorithm it had developed itself. NSA's justification for its algorithm was a "document, classified TOP SECRET CODEWORD, [that] was a position paper which discussed reasons for the selection of the algorithms identified in the first document" (USDoC 1990b). According to NSA, the proposed algorithm was based on unpatented work done by Taher ElGamal when he was a graduate student at Stanford University under Martin Hellman (ElGamal 1985). Outside the agency even that was questioned. The algorithm had been developed by David Kravitz at NSA (Kravitz 1993), and the technique bore a strong resemblance to one developed by the German mathematician Claus Schnorr, who had patented his algorithm in the United States and in various European countries.[39] Concerned about potential patent conflicts, NIST officials went to negotiate with Schnorr over selling his rights, but the government did not want to pay his asking price (reputed to have been $2 million).

NIST proposed Kravitz's algorithm as the Digital Signature Standard (USDoC 1991b). The computer industry objected to this because the algorithm was not interoperable with digital signatures already in use. The proposed standard had a 512-bit key size, but Bell Labs scientists had already shown that the Kravitz algorithm was not particularly secure with a 512-bit key (LaMacchia and Odlyzko 1991; Beth et al. 1992). Furthermore, it was significantly slower than the RSA algorithm in signature verification, taking roughly 10 times as long on comparable processors.[40] In abandoning the RSA algorithm in favor of the proposed NSA algorithm, NIST had traveled a considerable distance from the Computer Security Act.

Critics saw the dark hand of NSA behind NIST's bumbles. When questioned by a congressional committee, NIST director John Lyons denied such pressure. "What's your response to charges that NSA, either directly or through the National Security Council, continues to control NIST's computer security program?" Representative Jack Brooks asked Lyons. "My response is that it's not true," said Lyons. "We're running our program. We consult with them, according to the 1987 legislation, but they know and we know that we make these decisions." (Lyons 1992, p. 176) The record, released after Freedom of Information Act litigation, told a different story. A January 1990 memo from the NIST members of the Technical Working Group said: "It's increasingly evident that it is difficult, if not impossible, to reconcile the requirements of NSA, NIST and the general public using the approach [of a Technical Working Group]." (USDoC 1990a) Completely contrary to Congress's wishes, NSA was making the decisions on civilian cryptography.[41]

In its report on the Computer Security Act, the House Government Operations Committee said "NSA is the wrong agency to be put in charge of this important program." (USHR 100b, p. 19) Congress concurred and passed the measure. It looked as if the intelligence agency had made an end run around Congress. Under the Computer Security Act, NIST was supposed to develop cryptography standards for the public sector, but the combination of the MOU and NSA's clout prevented such an outcome. Lynn McNulty later commented: "We bent a hell of a lot backwards to meet national security and law enforcement requirements, but we didn't do much to meet user requirements." Various government observers, including the Office of Technology Assessment and the General Accounting Office, concluded that the MOU had put NSA in the driver's seat.[42]

The proposal for a Digital Signature Standard was put forth in 1991. Public objections resulted in modifications, including a flexible key size (key sizes from 512 to 1024 bits are permitted, in jumps of 64 bits). On May 19, 1994, over strong protests from industry and from academia, the government adopted DSS as Federal Information Processing Standard 186, announcing that the "Department of Commerce is not aware of patents that would be infringed by this standard" (USDoC 1994c).[43]

### Ceding Even More Control

While Congress waited to see how NIST would handle implementing a digital signature standard, a transfer of power was occurring behind the scenes. In the drafting of the MOU, NSA had recommended that the FBI be part of the Technical Working Group; NIST staffers had objected, and this clause was dropped (USDoC 1989). But Kammer, the acting director of NIST, was concerned that his agency was not properly equipped to develop civilian cryptography, the job Congress had handed to it. He and

Clinton Brooks, advisor to NSA's director, shared their concern with the FBI.

Their initial reception was cool. "The first couple of times [we went there] they said, 'Why are you bothering us?'" recalled Kammer. "They kept giving inappropriate responses; the FBI didn't understand the issue. Cryptography is a somewhat peripheral issue to the FBI." Brooks and Kammer presented the dangers of encrypted telecommunications, but it took the FBI some time to understand. "Ray and I kept encountering lots of blank stares," Brooks said later. "What we were encountering was a lack of appreciation that digital communications was here. Wiretapping was just doing clips, or going to the phone office. But the phone companies had all gone digital. The next step [in understanding] was that encryption was going to exist on the digital lines."[44] To the FBI the cryptographic issues seemed futuristic.

There was a clash of understandings. "A successful FBI agent," Kammer explained, "kicks in the door, arrests the guy, and goes on to the next case." The issues NIST and NSA were raising were more subtle. "A successful NSA man ... well give him a hard problem and the first thing he'll do is sit down and think—sometimes for a very long time."[45] NSA had been thinking about strong cryptography for a long time, but the FBI did not have any experts remotely close to the area. The closest the Bureau had were agents working on defeating electronic locks and alarms.

After a number of visits to the FBI over several months, Brooks and Kammer encountered James Kallstrom, Chief of the Special Operations Branch of the New York Field Office. "It was obvious," Kallstrom recalls, "that encryption had been around a long time. What was new here was it had never been an issue before for the general public. Old encryption didn't work; it was too bulky, you sounded like Donald Duck. But in the late eighties we could see that it wouldn't be very long before cheap encryption would be around that would put us out of business."[46]

Kallstrom's tenure in New York undoubtedly shaped his viewpoint. Historically, New York State has relied heavily on electronic surveillance.[47] For example, over a third of the 1994 Title III electronic surveillances occurred in New York State.[48] California, whose big cities suffer similar problems of drugs and crime, had one-eighth as many.[49]

Kallstrom could not imagine law enforcement without wiretapping and did not want wiretapping to disappear from law enforcement's arsenal. He went to work: "From the standpoint of this becoming an issue in the government, from the standpoint of law enforcement, we were the user, the customer. An Interagency group was formed; the squeaky wheel was us. We went to both [NIST and NSA]. We have a long-standing relationship with NSA; we have a responsibility for counter-terrorism and intelligence." NSA was immediately part of an interagency group focusing on problems of domestic use of strong cryptography. NIST joined shortly afterwards. "It wasn't a function of official policy. We have always recognized NSA as a premier agency [in intelligence]. NIST was also at the table."[50]

By 1991 the FBI had formulated a policy that included shoring up its ability to perform electronic surveillance, particularly wiretaps, and preventing the establishment of unbreakable cryptography in the public sector. Efforts in support of this policy included the Digital Telephony Proposal and the concept of key escrow, which were introduced to the public in 1992 and 1993 respectively.

In negotiating the MOU, NSA had sought to include the FBI as a full-fledged member of the Technical Working Group (which would have meant that two-thirds of the participants came from either law enforcement or national security). After that effort was rebuffed by NIST scientists, Kammer and Brooks brought the FBI in by different means. The FBI's involvement in encryption issues buttressed NSA's position. With the end of the Cold War, law-enforcement issues were significantly closer to the public's heart than national-security concerns. By replacing national-security concerns over cryptography with law-enforcement concerns, the FBI succeeded in returning much of the control of civilian cryptography to NSA.

"The whole Digital Telephony [effort] came out of [our meetings]," Clinton Brooks said some time later.[51]

# 4

# National Security

In discussions of cryptographic policy, "national security" is usually short-hand for *communications intelligence*—spying on foreign communications. It is taken for granted that the United States depends on breaking foreign codes for much of its intelligence and that any decline in the success of this activity will make the country less secure. Intelligence, however, is only one of cryptography's roles in national security.

## The Concept of National Security

The notion of national security is a relative newcomer to American political iconography. Although the term dates to the early post-World War II era, it does not appear in Webster's Third International Dictionary, which was published in 1961 and which sought to capture an up-to-date picture of American English.

The essence of national security is, of course, the protection of the country against attack by foreign military forces. The term is broader than this, but not so broad as to encompass all of the national interest. Its focus is protection of the country, and in particular its government, against threats that are characteristically but not invariably foreign.

National security includes the following:

- Maintenance of military forces adequate to deter attacks on the United States, repel invaders, control domestic unrest, and undertake other military actions that may be in the national interest.

- Provision of intelligence on the capabilities and intentions of all powers, both friendly and hostile, sufficient to inform foreign policy and military action. Such powers are understood to be primarily, but not entirely, national states. They may, in addition, include organizations representing landless peoples, revolutionary movements, terrorist groups, organized crime, trans-national political movements, and multi-national corporations.

- Denying to foreign powers intelligence about the United States that would interfere with American diplomatic, military, or trade objectives.

- Enforcement of certain laws, in particular those governing espionage, terrorism, the integrity of the national-security community itself, and the movements of people and material across borders.

- Maintenance of an industrial base, a resource base, and an infrastructure adequate to support essential government activities, including military forces, intelligence, and relevant aspects of law enforcement.

The set of issues that define the national security is naturally neither free from debate nor immune to change. In the late 1960s and the 1970s, the idea that drug trafficking should be seen as a threat to the national security and approached with military resources and tactics gained substantial ground.[1] Since the end of the Cold War, a quite different constituency has argued for the inclusion of broader economic issues, such as education and competitiveness in the world marketplace.[2]

From the viewpoint of cryptographic policy, the relevance of the second and third points—intelligence and security against foreign intelligence— is most apparent. We will examine these first and in more detail, but issues of infrastructure, law enforcement, and offensive capability will also be considered.

### The Spectrum of Intelligence

When we speak of intelligence, we will usually mean national intelligence —information obtained by national governmental organizations. The intelligence activities of governments, however, have much in common with those of other organizations. Scholars, reporters, political parties, businesses, criminals, and police all practice intelligence in one form or another. The intelligence-gathering activities of nations are generally more ambitious and include things not accessible to organizations without state power (for example, launching spy satellites), but the similarities outweigh the differences.

The most familiar form of intelligence—so familiar that it is usually not recognized as intelligence—is *open-source intelligence*: information obtained from sources that are not attempting to conceal it. Open-source intelligence is almost the only form of intelligence practiced by scholars, reporters, and business people, but it also plays a major role in national intelligence. In the national case, typical open sources are newspapers, radio broadcasts,[3] foreign government publications, propaganda, maps, and phone books. In industrial intelligence, advertisements and product literature are major sources.

Older open sources have recently been joined by the Internet and the World Wide Web. Browsing the Web is practicing open-source intelligence.

*Operations intelligence* is information obtained by observing and recording a target's visible actions and inferring actions that are not visible. Although it is hardly limited to military affairs, a typical example of operations intelligence in a military context was widely touted during the 1991 Gulf War: a pizza parlor near the Pentagon told newsmen that it could always tell when something was about to happen because large numbers of people stayed late at the Pentagon and ordered pizza in the middle of the night.[4]

What most people think of when they think of "spying" is called *human intelligence* (HUMINT), which runs the gamut from interviewing travelers[5] to infiltrating illegal agents and sometimes extends to breaking and entering. In the most basic form of human intelligence, intelligence officers from one country, traveling under diplomatic or journalistic or commercial cover, recruit an agent who has access to secret information. The agent then passes information to the foreign handlers, usually either for ideological reasons or in exchange for money.

In the twentieth century, open-source intelligence, operations intelligence, and human intelligence have been joined by a host of new methods having only the barest antecedents. These developments originated in the use of new technologies to gather intelligence about societies that exercise tight control over the information they release to the outside world and over the movement of people across and within their borders. Their success has pushed back the frontiers of national sovereignty; by limiting the degree to which nations can keep their military preparations secret from each other, it has also become a fundamental stabilizing influence on international relations. For the United States, spurred on by the memory of Japan's surprise attack on Pearl Harbor, intelligence has become a national obsession.

The techniques of intelligence gathering have also been guided by adaptation to political reality. Throughout the twentieth century, improvements in communication and increases in interdependence have produced the "shrinking of the world" that has changed so much of modern life. This has increased peer pressure among nations, giving rise to the World Court, the United Nations, and other international institutions. In this environment, nations have become more concerned than ever with appearance.

Spying exists, and has perhaps always existed, in a sort of limbo. "Everyone" knows that "everyone" does it, yet it remains frowned upon, hidden, and, under the laws of the nation being spied on, illegal. Most if not all nations use their embassies and consular facilities for intelligence gathering. Some of the activities are aboveboard. Ambassadors, trade representatives, and military attachés all report on both their meetings with representatives of the host country and their observations of life, politics, industry, and military activity. Others are not. Embassy personnel often recruit spies from among the local population or undertake more technical forms of information gathering from the legally protected premises of the embassy (Frost 1994).

Often a host country is aware of the clandestine intelligence activities of foreign diplomatic and consular personnel but finds itself unable to interfere for fear of retaliation against its own diplomats. When an espionage case becomes public, the host country usually feels obliged to put on a show of public indignation, and a scandal ensues. Such was the case when Soviet Colonel Oleg Penkofsky was caught spying for the West in the 1960s, and more recently when CIA officer Aldrich Ames was caught spying for Russia. The embarrassment is most acute when the countries involved are supposed to be friends, as happened in the case of Jonathan Pollard, an American naval intelligence officer found to be spying for Israel. A desire to avoid embarrassments of this sort is one motivation for the development of a variety of new forms of intelligence that do not intrude on the territory of the target country.[6]

Another outgrowth of the "shrinking" is the relationship between the tactical and the strategic. The time-honored practice of climbing a hill to get a look at an opposing army—which, in the past, was of little use except during battle—has evolved into a new field of strategic reconnaissance.

No aspect of modern intelligence is more impressive or more important than *photographic intelligence* (PHOTINT): information from photographs at frequencies both in and out of the human visual range. Although photography dates from the nineteenth century, it did not become a distinctive tool of intelligence until aircraft and later spacecraft gave cameras secure platforms from which to operate—platforms that could observe an opponent's territory from a safe distance.

Today, the most important intelligence photographs are those taken from orbiting satellites. Paradoxically, despite the fact that photo-reconnaissance aircraft fly much closer to their targets than satellites (10–20 miles as opposed to several hundred), the larger cameras carried by satellites produce far more detailed pictures. Images of a Russian shipyard taken by an American KH-11 spy satellite appear to be from a distance of 500 feet rather than the actual 500 miles (Burrows 1987, pp. 166n–166o; Richelson 1990, p. 186).

Photographic intelligence provides high-resolution images of Earth's surface but is impeded by clouds, sandstorms, and vegetation. The passive form is therefore complemented by the use of radar-imaging satellites, such as the American Lacrosse, which produce lower-resolution images but are unaffected by night and fog and can penetrate trees and even buildings. Orbital lasers open yet other possibilities (AWST 1997b).

Besides cameras and radar, modern intelligence employs a broad range of sensors for *measurement and signatures intelligence* (MASINT), which seeks to characterize objects or events by their observable characteristics and to detect or analyze them by combining information from various sensors. In the late 1940s, the United States began collecting atmospheric samples and testing them for radioactive isotopes in an attempt to discover nuclear tests. It was this technique that made the US aware of the Soviet Union's successful test of a nuclear weapon before it was announced. At about the same time an Air Force activity named *Project Mogul* sought to listen for the sounds of nuclear explosions propagating along the boundaries between layers of the atmosphere.[7]

For decades, the Sound Surveillance Underwater System (SOSUS) has tracked the movements of submarines and other ships by means of arrays of microphones lying on the ocean floor. In the 1960s, a family of satellites called Vela-Hotel were put in orbit to watch the earth for nuclear explosions. These satellites exemplify the "signatures" aspect of intelligence, distinguishing nuclear events from other phenomena such as lightning flashes or meteor impacts by characteristics more subtle than the brightness of the flash.[8] More recent satellites called simply Defense Support Program (DSP) satellites also watch for the infrared signatures that characterize the exhaust plumes of rising ballistic missiles. Satellites were only one part of the wider Vela program for detecting nuclear explosions. Another important element was seismographic. An array of seismometers called NORway Seismic ARray (NORSAR) was placed at a location geologically coupled to the area in which the Soviets conducted their nuclear tests. Seismic measurements served to verify compliance with a treaty limiting the yields of underground nuclear explosions.

Measurement and signatures intelligence can be viewed as a refined form of operations intelligence. It seeks out one or more subtle but unavoidable consequences of an event and infers the occurrence and character of that event from the observed phenomena. Its efficacy depends not only on the sensors but on the computing required to draw useful inferences from the data they produce.

Another aspect of modern intelligence that leans heavily on inference may be called *technical intelligence*. As the term suggests, this is the study of an opponent's technology, but the emphasis in this case is on inferences drawn by simulating or duplicating technologies whose existence has been inferred from observations or from information provided by human sources. The British Office of Scientific intelligence made extensive use of such methods during World War II to improve its understanding of developing German weaponry. Accounts of its work convey a novel perspective in which the reports of human agents were essentially regarded as rumors to be confirmed or refuted by technical means (Jones 1978; Johnson 1978).

The various means of gathering intelligence are far from independent. This is true both in the sense that the boundaries are not sharp (it is sometimes difficult to pigeonhole something as photographic intelligence rather than imaging intelligence) and in the sense that frequently information obtained by one technique may be useful or even indispensable in acquiring information by another technique or in interpreting the information acquired by another technique.[9]

## Signals Intelligence and Communications Intelligence

We have surveyed a variety of forms of intelligence in an attempt to convey the breadth of modern intelligence work. No one intelligence method exists in a vacuum, and the intelligence analyst draws on information from a wide variety of sources. It is within this context that we now turn to the form of intelligence with which we are most concerned.

*Communications intelligence* (COMINT) is the practice of extracting information from an opponent's communications. Although, as we shall see, communications intelligence is quite broad, it is embedded within a yet broader category. *Signals Intelligence* (SIGINT) is the information obtained by analyzing signals emitted by a target. When signals intelligence is distinguished from communications intelligence, the broader category includes such electromagnetic phenomena as radar signals, which are not intended to convey information but rather to locate physical objects and measure their movements. The study of radar signals is at the heart of electronic warfare and is prerequisite to all efforts either to jam radars or to evade them by stealth.[10] The areas of signals intelligence other than communications intelligence are collectively called *electronic intelligence* (ELINT) and include radar intelligence (RADINT), *telemetry intelligence* (TELINT), and *emissions intelligence* (EMINT).

Although normally categorized as electronic intelligence, some aspects of emissions intelligence can be better regarded as communications intelligence. These include processing ciphertext to extract plaintext signals accidentally encoded "piggyback" and listening to the sounds of electromechanical cryptoequipment as an aid to cryptanalysis (Martin 1980, pp. 74–75; Wright 1987, p. 84; Agee 1975, pp. 474–476). Another aid to communications intelligence is *emitter identification*, the technique of distinguishing individual radio transmitters by minor variations in behavior too small to be eliminated by ordinary quality-control techniques.

One of the most disquieting techniques of emissions intelligence is Rafter, a technique for monitoring the behavior of radio receivers.[11] It is not surprising that it should be possible to exploit the signal of a radio transmitter. That a receiver should reveal the frequency it is listening to is both surprising and frightening. It can be used, for example, to determine who is listening to banned foreign radio broadcasts.

Despite the elaborate taxonomy, the distinctions are not always clear. Telemetry intelligence, for example, is the study of communications between moving platforms (usually aircraft, rockets, or satellites) and their controlling stations. Test firings of ballistic missiles are monitored via radio transmissions from the missile being tested, and interception of these signals permits an opponent to learn almost as much from the test as do the people conducting it.[12] Similarly, communication satellites, spy satellites, and others are controlled from the ground, and interception of the control channel can reveal information about a satellite's attitude, fuel supply, and activities.[13] It is clear that these examples of telemetry intelligence, though commonly classified as signals intelligence, are as much examples of communications intelligence.

In short, although the term SIGINT is sometimes used to distinguish interception of non-communications signals from communications signals, it is also used to encompass both activities. Communications intelligence so dominates signals intelligence that the term "SIGINT" is often used when the narrower term COMINT would do.

With the possible exception of human intelligence, communications intelligence exhibits unparalleled breadth and flexibility. Observation of the gross characteristics (often merely the occurrence) of messages can be used to monitor military, diplomatic, commercial, or criminal activity or to detect relationships between persons, organizations, or events that have, to public appearances, no connection.[14] On the other hand, the analysis of carefully selected messages can sometimes reveal the intentions of military or political leaders even more accurately than information obtained by recruiting members of their staffs.[15]

Because it relies primarily on radio reception, with only occasional recourse to transmission or physical taps, communications intelligence rarely results in diplomatic incidents; indeed, rarely is the target aware of being monitored.[16]

**Taxonomy of COMINT**

Cryptography is often considered, particularly by those primarily concerned with security, to be the only serious barrier to communications intelligence. Histories of the field have generally fostered this impression by painting a picture of war between codemakers and codebreakers. In practice, spying on communications is a multi-stage activity in which each stage plays an essential role. It is entirely possible that the cryptanalysis of a message, once the message has been identified and captured, may be less difficult than acquiring and filtering the traffic to locate it. On balance, the greatest problem in communications intelligence—as in most efforts to learn things—is sorting out the information you are after from the information you are not.

The *sine qua non* of communications intelligence is acquisition of signals. Without communications in the form of radio waves, electrical currents in wires, written materials, or copied disks and tapes, there can be no work for cryptographic or intelligence analysts. The interception of communications presents both a strategic and a tactical aspect.

Strategically, it is crucial to learn as much as one can about an opponent's communications infrastructure. The first step is to come up with the most precise possible description of the target—what the military call the *order of battle*. If the target is a country, it may have millions of residents who in turn make millions of phone calls every day. Most of these calls are not of interest; the people who make them do not work for the government or in critical industries and say little of intelligence value. Describing the target is one of the many areas where *collateral intelligence*—information from sources other than covert interception of communications—plays a vital role. Most of the information about a country and its government can be learned from open sources, such as phone books, newspapers, histories, and government manuals. Some, however, will come from covert sources such as spies, and some will come from communications intelligence itself.

Once the targets have been precisely identified, it is necessary to discover how they communicate with one another. Are their communications carried by high-frequency (HF) radio, by satellite, or by microwave? How accessible the communications are and how they can be acquired is a function of the means chosen. High-frequency radio and satellite transmissions are the most accessible. At the time of World War II, most radio communication and thus most of what was intercepted was HF. Such signals bounce back and forth between the ionosphere and the ground and can travel thousands of miles. This property makes intercontinental radio communication possible; at the same time, it makes it essentially impossible to keep HF signals out of the hands of opponents. Today a large fraction of radio communication is carried by satellite. Satellite downlinks typically have "footprints" thousands of miles across that spread over more than one country.[17] Terrestrial microwave communications are significantly harder to intercept. They travel between towers a few miles or tens of miles apart. Intercept facilities on the ground must generally be located within a few tens of miles of the microwave path and often require facilities in the target country. In the 1970s and the 1980s, there was a war of words between US and Soviet diplomats over Soviet microwave interception activities from a residence the Soviets maintained at Glen Cove, New York (Broad 1982).

As with the organizational structure, a target's communication practices can often be derived from open sources. Since national and international organizations cooperate in allocating the radio spectrum, it is easier to identify the frequencies used for military, police, or air traffic control communications by consulting regulations and standards than by direct spectrum monitoring.

The output of the strategic or *targeting* phase of communications intelligence is a map of the opponent's communications, which will guide the selection of locations, frequencies, and times of day at which monitoring is conducted. Interception can also be conducted from many sorts of platforms: ground stations, aircraft, ships, embassies, covert locations, and orbiting satellites.

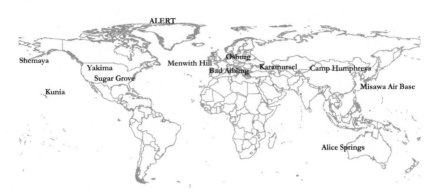

**Figure 4.1**
NSA installations around the world. (Illustration by Roland Silver.)

The United States has several major intercept facilities within its borders and a host of others abroad (figure 4.1). Despite attempts to keep these locations secret, many, including Menwith Hill in Britain, Alice Springs in Australia, ALERT in Canada, Osburg in Germany, Misawa in Japan, and Shemaya in the Aleutian Islands have been in the news at one time or another (Bamford 1982; Shane and Bowman 1995).

The Soviet Union made extensive use of small ships as collection platforms. Usually operating under very thin cover as fishing trawlers, these boats carried large antennas and were thought to be making their biggest catch in the electromagnetic spectrum. The United States has been less successful with this approach. In the 1960s it commissioned two ships described as research vessels, the *Liberty* and the *Pueblo*, for intercept duty. The *Liberty* was attacked by the Israelis, for no publicly apparent reason, while supposedly intercepting Arab communications in the Eastern Mediterranean during the Six Day War of 1967.[18] A year later, the *Pueblo* was captured by the North Koreans. It turned out to have been carrying many TOP-SECRET documents for which it had no apparent need, and most of these fell to its captors. As quietly as it had begun, the United States ceased using small ships as collection platforms.

Airborne collection, by comparison, has been an important component of US COMINT for decades. Boeing 707s, under the military designation

RC-135, are equipped with antennas and signal-processing equipment. These aircraft can loiter off foreign coasts for hours at a time. Flying at altitudes of 30,000 feet or higher, they can pick up radio transmissions from well inland.

The use of embassies to do intercept work exemplifies the twilight-zone character of intelligence. Despite widespread "knowledge" that many embassies are engaging in intelligence collection, such activity is a breach of diplomatic etiquette that could result in diplomats' being asked to leave the host country if discovered. All the equipment used must therefore be smuggled in or constructed on the spot and must be made from components small enough to fit inconspicuously in the "diplomatic bag"— a troublesome limitation on the sizes of antennas. Politics and public relations aside, if an embassy is not suspected of interception, it is likely to be more successful. Mike Frost, a Canadian intelligence officer who spent most of his career intercepting host-country communications from Canadian embassies, reported that the Chinese put up a building to block radio reception at the US embassy in Beijing but failed to protect themselves against the Canadian embassy because they did not realize that it too was engaged in interception (Frost 1994).

Interception can also be conducted from covert locations that do not enjoy the legal protection of diplomatic immunity. Britain operated a covert direction-finding facility in neutral Norway during World War I (Wright 1987, p. 9). In the early 1950s, the CIA established a group known as "Staff D" to carry out interception from covert locations.

One of the most ambitious undertakings in communications intelligence has been the development of intercept satellites, which did not arrive on the scene till roughly a decade after their camera-carrying cousins. Low-altitude satellites are not well suited to intercept work. They are relatively close to the transmitter, which is good, but they are moving quickly relative to the Earth, which is not. No sooner have they acquired a signal than they move on and lose it again, because the source has passed below the horizon. The comparison with communications satellites is interesting. The mainstay of satellite-mediated communications has been satellites in synchronous orbits, 22,500 miles up. Only recently have communications satellites been placed in low orbits. Tens of satellites are required so that as soon as one moves out of range of a transmitter on the ground, another comes close enough to take over. Systems of this kind have the advantage that the satellites and the transmitters are cooperating. A system in which the satellites were attempting continuous coverage of uncooperative targets would be far more complex, and to our knowledge, none has been attempted.

Because they are in very high orbits, intercept satellites must carry antennas tens or hundreds of feet across. It is difficult to make an antenna of this size light enough to be lifted into synchronous orbit. In addition, the antenna must be launched in a folded configuration, which adds complexity and detracts from reliability. In sum, communications intercept satellites are more complex and expensive than other types.

Because of its huge size and the low population density of much of its territory, the Soviet Union made more extensive use of radio communications than the United States or Western Europe. Most of the territory of the Soviet Union was far north and not conveniently served by synchronous satellites, so the Soviets developed a family of communication satellites, called Molniya, that move in polar orbits. A "Molniya orbit" passes over the Northern Hemisphere at very high altitude and thus moves quite slowly during this part of its journey. Its perigee, in contrast, is low over the Southern Hemisphere, and that part of the trip goes very quickly. The result is that most of the time the satellite "hangs" above the Northern Hemisphere, where it can be used for high-latitude communications. In order to spy on these communications, the US built satellites, called Jumpseat, that move in Molniya orbits. These satellites are in a position to listen to both radio transmissions from the ground and those from Molniya satellites.

Communications intelligence depends for its success on tactical as well as strategic elements. When an intercept station has been put in the right location, operates at the right time of the day, points its antenna in the right direction, and tunes its radio to the right frequencies, it is rewarded with a flood of traffic too large to record, let alone analyze. The process of examining intercepted traffic to determine what is to be retained and what is not may be as "simple" as detecting which channels within a trunk are active or as complex as recognizing the topic of a conversation. Typical selection processes include active channel detection, called and calling number identification, speaker identification, keyword spotting (in either text or voice), fax recognition, and semantic information processing.

The difficulty of locating and isolating just the right messages is an intrinsic consequence of the volume of traffic in modern communications. Communications intercept equipment must decide in a fraction of a second whether to record a message it has detected or to permit the message to escape. Often it must make the decision to record communications of which it has only one part. If, for example, the two directions of a telephone call are carried on separate facilities, an individual intercept point may have access to only one side of the conversation. Although the entire call may in fact be recorded, so that both sides of the conversation will ultimately be available to an analyst, it will be recorded by two devices acting independently. Should either fail to detect that the call is of interest, and therefore fail to record it, the utility of the other component will be vastly reduced.[19] The problem of identifying traffic of interest among all possible traffic is the problem of *search*.

Communications are organized at many levels. The entities communicating have addresses—in radio these are called *call signs* (commonly known in the case of commercial stations as *call letters*); in the case of telephones they are telephone numbers; in the case of computer networks, they are IP addresses, email addresses, URLs, etc. Messages follow *routes*, which in turn are made up of *links* or *hops* on *trunks*. Within an individual trunk, messages are *multiplexed* into channels, which make up the trunk much as lanes make up a road.[20]

At the lowest level, intercept equipment sits and looks through the space in which messages might be found. At each frequency, or time slot, or code pattern, it listens to see if there is any traffic at all. It may well be the case that most of the channels in a trunk are inactive most of the time.

When intercept equipment detects an active channel, it must decide whether to record what it finds there. This depends on *diagnosis*: characterization of the form and the significance of the signal that has been found. If the channel is a telephone channel, for example, the likely possibilities are voice, fax, and data. The intercept device must try to decide what it is hearing and may then discriminate more carefully depending on the category. The first step will usually be to listen for dial pulses or touch tones and attempt to determine what number is calling and what number is being called. If the call is voice, the device may attempt to determine what language is in use, or even listen for keywords. If the call is fax, it may try to determine whether the transmission is text or pictures. If the call carries data, it will attempt to determine what type of modem is in use and what codes (ASCII, Baudot, EBCDIC) or data formats are present. When text is detected, the equipment may go further and apply semantic processing to determine the subject of the message in much the same way that a search engine tries to locate a topic of interest on the World Wide Web.

One strategy followed by many pieces of intercept equipment should be a caution to anyone using cryptography: if an intercepted message is found to be encrypted, it is automatically recorded. This is possible because at present only a small fraction of the world's communications are encrypted. The first lesson to be drawn from this is that if you encrypt something you had better do it well; otherwise you will only succeed in drawing attention to yourself. The second is that as the use of cryptography increases, the privacy of everyone's traffic benefits.

Once traffic has been diagnosed as interesting, it will be recorded. This is not as simple as it sounds. Typically a signal can be recorded in several different formats, depending on how well it has been understood. It is always possible to make a recording of the waveform being received, but this may turn out to be much bulkier than the message it encodes. For example, recording a modem signal carrying 2400 bits per second of information (about 240 characters a second), without demodulating it, uses up the 48-kilobyte-per-second capacity of a digital audio tape. A direct recording of the signal is thus 20 times the size of the message it contains.

Neither diagnosis, nor recording, nor any form of analysis that may be done on an intercepted signal can be separated from *signal processing* —study of the signal by mathematical and computational means. Digital signal processing (one of the fastest-growing areas in computing) is revolutionizing communications. The availability of $100 modems is a consequence of the availability of signal-processing chips costing a few dollars apiece.

Demodulating modem signals (which accounts for most of the signal processing in data interception) is far harder for an intercept device than for the modems used by the sender and the receiver. Present-day modems go through a period of training at the beginning of a call during which they study the communications path and "discuss" how best to make use of it. Even if the intercept device is listening to this "conversation," it cannot transmit without revealing its presence, and thus it cannot engage in the negotiations. The signal quality available to the intercept device is therefore rarely as good as that available to the communicating modems.

Only after traffic has been located, demodulated, and recorded do we finally get to the most famous process in communications intelligence, the process of breaking codes: *cryptanalysis*. This book is not the place for a technical discussion of cryptanalysis; such discussions now abound in both the technical and the historical literature of cryptography.[21] It is, however, the place for a discussion of the process of cryptanalysis.

Most of the public literature, both technical and historical, is devoted to *research cryptanalysis*, the process of breaking codes for the first time. This is naturally an indispensable component of any production cryptanalytic organization, but does not account for most of its budget or most of its personnel.[22] The object of "codebreaking" is the development of *methods* that can be applied to intercepted traffic to produce plaintext. In modern cryptanalysis, this is often done entirely by computers, without human intervention.[23]

The process of converting ciphertext to plaintext is called *exploitation*. It follows a process of *diagnosis* closely related to the more general diagnosis of traffic discussed above.

The heart of a communications intelligence organization, however, is not cryptanalysis but *traffic analysis*—study of the overall characteristics (length, timing, addressing, frequencies, modulation, etc.) of communications.[24] Traffic analysis by itself provides a broad picture of the activities of communicating organizations (Wright 1987). Moreover, it is essential to assessing the signaling plan, the traffic patterns, and the relationships among communicating entities. Elaborate databases of observed traffic (Hersh 1986, pp. 258–259) underlie all COMINT activities.

A last operational point that bedevils communications intelligence is *retention*—the preservation of intercepted signals for short or long periods of time until they can be processed, cryptanalyzed, interpreted, or used. As we have noted, storing a signal that the holder is unable to restore to its original form typically takes far more memory than storing an understandable signal. This is justified because, enciphered messages can be of value even if they are first read only months or years after they were originally sent. During World War II, Allied cryptanalysts were sometimes weeks or even months behind on some classes of traffic (Welchman 1982). Some signals intercepted during the Cuban missile crisis of 1962 were not read until 2 years later (Hersh 1987). In what is probably the granddaddy of ciphertext longevity, Soviet messages sent in the 1940s were still being studied in the 1970s (Wright 1987). Managing the storage of intercepted material is thus a major problem in all signals intelligence activities.

After all of the technical processes characteristic of communications intelligence, the *product* enters into the part of the process common to information from all intelligence sources: interpretation, evaluation, dissemination. One process looms larger over COMINT than over perhaps any other intelligence material: *sanitization*—removal from the intelligence product of information that would reveal its source. Sanitization to greater or lesser degrees produces intelligence of varying levels of classification.[25]

## Secrecy in Communications Intelligence

It is impossible to exaggerate the importance of security to every phase of communications intelligence. In other areas of military activity, secrecy plays an important role but is rarely indispensable to success. A superior army often vanquishes its adversary despite lacking the element of surprise. Even in the area of nuclear weapons (where it abounds), secrecy serves primarily to prevent proliferation. If all of America's nuclear secrets were to be published tomorrow, nuclear weapons would remain just as destructive as they are today and almost as effective as weapons of war. In contrast, communications intelligence would be rendered significantly less effective by disclosure of its techniques and capabilities. Even a credible warning to an opponent that its communications are being intercepted and exploited can result in the opponent's taking action to restore the security of its communications and can destroy the results of many years of intelligence work.[26]

Once traffic has been identified and recorded, shipping it home for further analysis presents security problems of its own. If the intelligence is needed promptly, telecommunication channels must be used. The traffic is, of course, encrypted to conceal from the opponent the details of what is being recorded, if not the fact of interception itself. The circumstances, however, give the opponent a measure of control over what is transmitted on the channel and may provide the opportunity for a chosen-plaintext attack (see chapter 2) on the cryptography. Moreover, unless careful measures are taken to counter traffic flow analysis, correlation is likely to reveal much detail of the interceptors' activities to the opponent.[27]

### Current Status of the COMINT Product

Communications intelligence is enjoying a golden age.[28] The steady migration of communications from older, less accessible media—both physical and electronic—has been the dominant factor. The loss of information resulting from improvements in security has been consistently outweighed by the increased volume and quality of information available. As a result, COMINT has been improving for more than 50 years and has become a growth industry.

Even 50 years of success has not made the supporters of COMINT confident that the success will continue, however. From the beginnings of the multinational arms buildup that followed World War II, there have been repeated warnings that improvements in cryptography would bring about the demise of communications intelligence. Since the emergence of a public cryptographic technology in the late 1970s, these warnings have become especially shrill and have been joined by self-confident predictions from the academic and commercial cryptographers that they could produce unbreakable systems.[29]

It is often said that the intelligence agencies of the major powers can no longer break each other's high-grade systems and must subsist on reading the traffic of Third World countries (Simmons 1986). Although the intelligence community itself has done all it can to foster this view, the steady expansion of COMINT facilities[30] suggests it is too modest.

The status of cryptanalysis in the contemporary world is hard to determine, owing to pervasive secrecy. Oddly enough, although the "Russian Project" is the most secret of NSA's secrets, the fortunes of an activity this important are hard to conceal. What evidence there is makes it plausible that high-grade Russian traffic continued to be read at least until the early 1980s and may still be accessible today.

In its early years, the Soviet Union, like most of the world at that time, relied on secret codes to secure its military and diplomatic communications. This practice appears to have come to an end in 1927 with MI5's raid on the London offices of the All-Russian Cooperative Society and with the prime minister's admission in Parliament that Britain had been reading Soviet messages for years. It is presumably at that point that the Russians began the extensive reliance on one-time systems that was long characteristic of their operations. In the 1930s and the 1940s their use in Soviet diplomatic communications seems to have strained the facilities for key production to the breaking point, and they began to reuse keying material. Despite the subtle worldwide pattern of the reuse, it resulted in some of their most sensitive messages' being read (Wright 1987). Discovery of this fact after World War II must have led to a broad program to improve the security of Soviet communications.[31]

The Russians were undoubtedly aware of rotor machines and other mechanical cipher equipment as early as the 1920s, but they seem not to have made much use of this awareness before the end of World War II. With their capture of the eastern part of Germany and the acquisition of many of the papers of Pers Z (probably the best of the German cryptanalytic organizations; see Kahn 1967), the awareness must have been enhanced, and perhaps their interest was piqued.

In the late 1940s a cryptographic laboratory was established at Marfino, in the suburbs of Moscow. The focus of its efforts was secure telephones, of which it produced several, some analog and some digital.[32]

If developments in the Soviet Union followed a course similar to those in the West, rotor machines could comfortably operate at teletype speeds of 50–110 bits per second, but could not keep up with the 2400 bps and higher needed for digitized voice. This led to the development of purely electronic shift-register systems, although rotor machines remained in use for text traffic for many years thereafter.

In the late 1950s, according to Peter Wright (1987, p. 148), NSA and its British counterpart, the Government Communications Headquarters (GCHQ), jointly mounted an attack on a Russian machine they called "Albatross." Development cycles in cryptography are long, and at that date this was probably a rotor machine. Wright makes no concrete statement about the success or failure of the project, but the self-congratulatory tone in which he describes pushing the endeavor suggests success.

Traffic encrypted by Soviet cipher machines was also read by the Americans during the 1960s. The messages, encrypted in a Soviet cryptosystem which NSA code-named *Silver*, played a prominent role in a 25th-anniversary post mortem of the Cuban missile crisis, held at Harvard University, at which it was revealed that for several hours the Cubans had taken control of a Soviet military base and of some of the nuclear missiles. NSA was not able to read the traffic at the time it was sent; it only became aware of this critical new dimension of the crisis when the messages were first read in 1964.

In their analysis of a number of spy cases from the 1970s, Corson et al. (1989, pp. 94–95) refer to an "NSA intercept from the Soviet Embassy in Washington in April 1977." They go on to say: "The cable was sent by Ambassador Anatoly Dobrynin to the Foreign Ministry in Moscow. It referred to advice Henry Kissinger had given Dobrynin on how to deal with the new Carter administration in the ongoing SALT II negotiation." (ibid., 1989, pp. 94–95) It strains credulity to suppose that such a telegram would have been sent in clear. If the telegram was intercepted by NSA, it must have been cryptanalyzed. The process by which the authenticity of the cable was established lends further weight to this view. The CIA officers involved are quoted as saying that "the only way to confirm the authenticity of the cable was to go out to NSA, pull the transcripts of other cables sent from the Soviet Embassy, and compare the style, content, and timing." As a result, "the experts at NSA concluded that the cable was real and not a Soviet disinformation effort." (ibid., pp. 97–98) This information is all the more persuasive because the authors mention "intercepts" without appearing to have given any thought to cryptography. Their concern is entirely with the content of the cable and its implications about the propriety or impropriety of Kissinger's relationship with Dobrynin.

Evidence of still more recent US success in reading high-level Soviet traffic arises in connection with the September 1983 destruction of Korean Airlines 007. Seymour Hersh's book on the subject describes the interception of a call from Khabarovsk to Moscow placed via the Soviet Raduga satellite and intercepted by the US Jumpseat satellite—which had been placed in a similar orbit for just that purpose. Hersh (1986, p. 232) quotes an unnamed NSA official as saying that "the cipher signal snapped on and some long-precedence message was sent." He remarks that the "NSA officials would not say anything further about the message." Others were more forthcoming, including a senior US intelligence officer who "vividly recalled his reaction well after the shootdown of Flight 007, upon being shown a copy of the deputy commander's intercepted and decoded message to Sakhalin."

### Non-Cryptographic Impediments to Interception

If cryptography has not stopped communications intelligence, other developments must at least have slowed it down. During the past two decades, the loss of intelligence resulting from the use of cryptography to protect communications appears to have been eclipsed by losses due to other developments not intended primarily for security. These include optical fiber, high-speed modems, and dynamically routed communications.

Between World War II and the appearance of optical fiber, the major developments in transmission technology had the effect of rendering communications more vulnerable to interception. Microwave relays were more accessible than the copper wires they replaced, and satellite channels were more accessible still. Optical fiber, on the other hand, is directly competitive with these radio technologies in cost and bandwidth, and immeasurably more secure. Although undetectable taps on unprotected fiber circuits are possible, they always require physical contact, which is often infeasible. Owing to its economic advantages, optical fiber has been used to reduce the vulnerability of US communications and those of other nations around the world.[33]

A more interesting signal-acquisition problem has arisen out of improvements in modem technology. For decades, Telex and similar low-speed data-communication facilities were the backbone of both commercial and government communications in most of the world. Data rates increased gradually from 50 bits per second to 75 to 110 to 150, and finally to 300. Around 1980, the speeds of inexpensive modems jumped to 1200 bps. Today, they are 28,800 bps.[34] Since the older modems acted essentially independently, each using a phase-locked loop to interpret a set of data pulses in relation to a predictable timing pulse, an intercept modem had no difficulty in doing exactly the same thing.

The new modems not only indulge in initial training to optimize their use of particular communication circuits; they also employ auto-cancellation: both modems transmit simultaneously on the same set of frequencies, and each subtracts its own transmission from the signal it is receiving.[35] Even at 2400 bps, this presents serious difficulties for a passive intercept device attempting to separate the two halves of the signal. At 4800 bps, 9600 bps, and higher, the problem becomes progressively more difficult. Furthermore, it appears to be, in a sense, intrinsic. If the intruding modem can separate and interpret the two data streams, it is receiving information twice as fast as the "legitimate" modems. This suggests that a modem using the same techniques as the intercept device could operate twice as fast. In many cases, the development of the technology of communications and that of communications intelligence proceed independently or even synergistically. In the case of modems, improving technology works directly, if unintentionally, against interception.

The increasing difficulty of acquiring modem signals goes hand in hand with another trend in modern communications: better modems have led to an explosion in the use of dialed-up point-to-point connections to replace leased lines. Private networks often use the same circuits month after month or even year after year. Once such a network has been mapped and access points located, the same intercept facilities can be employed for long periods of time. Furthermore, the ownership of such a net typically determines much about the traffic it carries, which drastically reduces the need for further filtering. In contrast, dialed-up point-to-point connections must be identified within the larger traffic volume of a common carrier's network. This is complicated by *dynamic routing*.[36] Even after it has been determined that a high fraction of the traffic between two particular telephone numbers is worth targeting, it may be difficult to acquire this traffic because different circuits are established on different calls.

A related development in switching systems, common-channel signaling (the practice of sending signaling information out of band in a separate digital signaling channel), can be both a blessing and a curse to the interceptor. It is a blessing in that it gathers together in one place the calling number, the called number, and the way the call is to be handled and routed. It is a curse because the common channel can be routed more securely—through copper or fiber, or on an encrypted channel.[37] If this is done, the call itself carries no identifying information and becomes difficult for an opponent to locate. This characteristic makes it possible to upgrade an existing wire-line communication system to a radio-based system of a much higher capacity with little loss of security. All signaling is routed through the pre-existing (and more secure) wires to minimize the vulnerability of the radio circuits.

## The Impact of Encryption on Communications Intelligence

Although the spread of encryption technology is not at present the most serious cause of lost communications intelligence, its potential impact on intelligence activities should not be underestimated. Today's secure telephones require the users to secure the call as a distinct action from making the call. The process takes 10–20 seconds—long enough to be a deterrent to doing it at all. The digitized voice is of lower quality and may exaggerate other unpleasant phenomena, such as line noise. The callers are likely to say at least a few words to each other before initiating security. If the message is short enough and seems innocuous, they may not bother with security at all. All this leaves room for various sorts of information leakage.

The Integrated Services Digital Network (ISDN)—a set of telephone standards for direct digital telephone service—may alleviate the problems of present-day secure phones.[38] The time required to initiate a secure call drops to 1 or 2 seconds, and encryption has no effect on voice quality since the signal is digitized in any case. Should ISDN fulfill its promise to permit digital end-to-end negotiation before the called phone rings, the need to initiate security explicitly will be eliminated and the result will be a form of secure caller ID.

Extensive use of link encryption can also have devastating effects on intelligence gathering. When link encryption is applied to microwave beams and to satellite channels, it conceals everything passing over them; the intruder sees nothing but a steady flow of random data that does not even reveal whether real communication is taking place. Typically, however, link encryption cannot be applied by the users and must be supplied by the carrier. Link encryption will therefore provide users with protection against some spies but not others. In a world with an ever-growing number of interconnected and competing communications carriers, this opens numerous opportunities to couple communications intelligence with human intelligence and network penetration.

Despite the possibilities, the vast majority of the world's traffic is currently in plaintext.[39] This makes it feasible to sort traffic in real time to determine which messages are of interest and which are not. On circuits where the fraction of ciphertext is not too high, the fact of encryption itself provides a valuable clue to the potential significance of intercepted material.

Combined with the limited use of encryption is the diversity of cryptographic products in use throughout the world. The relatively small fraction of traffic that is encrypted today is encrypted in a wide variety of cryptographic systems. This enables interceptors to recognize traffic by identifying the encryption techniques or equipment used. This *diagnosis* of cryptosystems need not require cryptanalysis or cryptomathematical statistics. Distinct cryptosystems typically employ different data formats that can easily be distinguished, and it is desirable from the COMINT viewpoint to preserve those characteristics of communications that permit the filtering of traffic and the selection of messages. The rise of international encryption standards, even de facto standards, would make this task immeasurably more difficult.

One of the distinguishing characteristics of cryptography is that it is robust. Much cryptographic equipment is located close to its users and is likely to survive any attack that does not destroy the users themselves. Cables and optical fibers, like roads and railways, are vulnerable to attack all along their lengths.

The first British military action of World War I was the cutting of an undersea cable, which forced the Germans to use radio for messages to

North America and made their communications vulnerable to interception (Kahn 1967, p. 266). Similar scenarios were played out during the Normandy invasion in World War II[40] and at the start of the Gulf War.[41]

## Information Warfare

The meaning of the term "information warfare" is far from settled and the term is applied to subjects that range from modern, but established, military practice to complete science fiction. In one of its solider embodiments, information warfare is the management of information in warfare. In World War II, pilots would receive intelligence information in a pre-flight briefing; during the mission they would get no new information except for what they could see with their own eyes and an occasional radio message. Today, however, fighter and bomber pilots are assisted from takeoff to landing by the products of a real-time intelligence machine that integrates information from signals intelligence, satellites, surveillance aircraft, and other combatants. It will tell them whether the targets for which they set out have already been destroyed, whether interceptors have scrambled to meet them, or whether previously concealed anti-aircraft batteries have become active and present a threat. It is one of the major objectives of the modern military to close its information-processing loop, bringing observation, decision, and action closer together. The Gulf War was both a test bed for and a triumph of this approach, which is now solidly established in American military doctrine (Campen 1993a).

Where information processing is an essential military tool, it will naturally be subject to attack. Radar installations are now vulnerable to missiles that follow a radar beam and destroy its source,[42] and much recent military thinking has gone to improving strategies for attacking communication facilities and surveillance aircraft. The possibilities include frying computers with high-power microwaves and shorting them out with carbon fibers.[43] Some attacks on information resources are meant not to destroy them but merely to render them temporarily ineffective. This aspect of information warfare is an outgrowth of the established field of electronic warfare, in which radio and radar are pitted against jamming,[44] decoys, and chaff.

Discussions of this sort are real enough and genuinely high-tech, but in a sense unimaginative. The heart of information warfare today is the notion of attacking the enemy with information alone. This idea is not entirely new. In classical warfare it is called propaganda and disinformation. A less classical antecedent is the practice of communications deception: making use of the opponents' own signals intelligence activities to fool them.[45]

The present-day concept is rooted in the essential role of information not just in battle but in all aspects of society. An opponent who is critically dependent on information will be catastrophically vulnerable to corruption of that information. The notion has been enveloped in an apocalyptic aura by the development of *viruses* and *worms*[46]—malignant forms of software that reproduce within an opponent's computers and eventually cause them to malfunction. Computer viruses originated as a malicious prank and are now a widespread hazard of the computer world.[47] The military vision is that by the application of millions of dollars and hundreds of people far more subtle forms of viruses, suitable as weapons in military conflicts, can be developed.[48]

**Computer Intelligence**

One aspect of information warfare that is unquestionably real, though how much of it is going on is open to question, is the practice of obtaining information by active intrusion into a target's computers or networks. We shall call this field *computer intelligence*.

Both the strengths and the weaknesses of communications intelligence derive from the fact that it is passive. On one hand, its passive character means that communication spies are rarely caught. On the other, its passivity deprives it of the chance to go after particular pieces of information and restricts it to listening to what opponents decide to transmit. This raises the cost of interception by obliging the intercepters to winnow through vast quantities of traffic in order to find what they want to know. A passive eavesdropper must wait for some legitimate user to access the information and then record the result; an active one can go to a database and extract a particular piece of information.

Intrusions into American computers by a group in Germany with ties to the KGB are described in a 1989 book by Clifford Stoll. An operation in Tripoli by the Israeli Mossad provides an interesting example of the intersection between human intelligence and the low-tech end of network intelligence. Using a phone line that actually originated in Israel but appeared to originate in France,[49] and masquerading as French shipping insurers, the Mossad recruited the harbormaster in Tripoli, Libya, and "ran" him for more than 2 years (Ostrovsky 1990, chapter 16). With the worldwide linking of computers through the Internet, new techniques for extracting information by active penetration are at the frontier of intelligence research (Schweizer 1993, pp. 158–163) and are being developed all over the world.

At a recent meeting on information warfare at Stanford University, members of the President's Commission on Information Warfare and Critical Infrastructure Protection acknowledged that there has not yet been an example of information warfare in its pure form. No nation has attacked another nation's computers using information. Nor is it believed that a politically motivated attack on computers using information alone has been made by terrorists or other non-national groups. Nonetheless, information warfare is very real, and very alive as a subject of military speculation, planning, and development. Not a month passes without a conference, meeting, or war game devoted to the subject.

The relevance of information warfare to cryptographic policy is twofold and straightforward. The major worry of most pundits is that critical elements of national infrastructures such as transportation systems and power grids will be connected to control systems that communicate via the Internet. Much of the plausibility of this concern lies in the lack of authentication in current computer networks. Viruses might get in because new versions of programs are loaded over the Internet, and there is no way of telling a genuine program from an alternate one prepared by intruders. Furthermore, the information that opponents would need to mount an attack is available as a result of the general lack of security in communications. Widespread deployment of cryptography in the "command and control" of the civilian infrastructure would solve both problems.

## The Relationship of Security and Intelligence

In loose correspondence with the various categories of intelligence are security measures intended to counter them and limit their effectiveness. Thus, for example, human intelligence can be countered by limiting information access to vetted personnel, photographic intelligence can be countered by camouflage, and open-source intelligence can be countered by restricting public access to information or mixing false information with genuine.[50] Cryptography is the centerpiece of communication security, the countermeasure to communications intelligence.

As with the various aspects of intelligence, security measures are far from independent. For example, good personnel security is essential to communication security, and communication security can in turn make a major improvement in operations security.

## The Security of Communications in the United States

No nation in the world is more dependent on electronic communications than the United States. As a result, no nation is more vulnerable to subversion of its commerce, its money supply, and its civic functions by electronic intruders. Attempts to address this vulnerability take two forms:

- protecting American communications by government action in the same way that the country as a whole is protected by defense and law-enforcement agencies
- making the tools for protecting communications available to the private sector and encouraging their use, just as physical security is provided by locks and alarm systems in civil society.

In practice, any comprehensive solution must have elements of both.

In the 1970s, the US government made its first attempts to secure broad segments of American communication rather than narrow classes of military, diplomatic, and intelligence traffic. Some communications (in Washington, New York, San Francisco, and other areas that harbored Soviet diplomatic or consular facilities) were routed through underground cables rather than over microwave relays, analog and digital encryption devices were developed for the protection of telephone trunk lines,[51] the security of common-channel interoffice signaling was improved,[52] and telephone satellite channels were encrypted.

All efforts to date, however, fall far short of providing the degree of protection desired in a communications infrastructure that has become indispensable to American prosperity.

## Federal Policies and Programs

The challenge, from the national-security viewpoint, is to achieve a two-fold objective:

- Improve the security of communications and computing within the United States and for US government and commercial activities abroad.

- At the same time, attempt to minimize the impact both on US intelligence activities and on domestic security that could result from having the country's own technology used against it.

This objective is difficult, if not impossible, to achieve by a reactive strategy of permitting events to unfold as they will and responding to them piecemeal. Threats to American intelligence capacity, both domestic and foreign, can be anticipated, and policies can be developed to nullify them. Only a misplaced sense of fair play would demand that threats to American well-being should be allowed to develop freely when the means to control them are at hand.

## Export Controls

Most of the federal activities discussed so far do not affect the public directly. For one thing they are secret. When foreign policy is successful, people who give the subject some thought may attribute a share of the success to intelligence. When the United States is surprised by something —like the taking of the hostages in Iran or the Iraqi invasion of Kuwait —poor intelligence is likely to be blamed. Intelligence has, however, no visible day-to-day impact on the lives of most Americans.

There are, however, federal activities in support of intelligence that affect many people—usually, as those people see it, adversely. These are the export-control laws. Although the US Constitution prohibits export tariff, it does not prohibit an outright ban on exporting particular things to particular countries.

All exports from the United States are regulated under one of two laws: the Arms Export Control Act (22 U.S.C. 2571–2794) and the Export Administration Act (50 U.S.C. App. 2401–2420). The Arms Export Control Act takes precedence over the Export Administration Act and confers on the Department of State the authority to regulate the export of anything it deems to be a weapon of war (or, as the export laws term it, a *munition*). Items ruled to be munitions require individually approved export licenses designating the customer, the application, and often conditions for the handling or redeployment of the item.

Things that are not munitions but that may have military applications are called *dual-use items*. If the Department of State decides that something is a dual-use item, it transfers jurisdiction over its export to the Department of Commerce, which administers the Export Administration Act. Under the Export Administration Act, exporters can receive licenses to export to broad classes of customers in broad regions of the world. In the area of cryptography, for example, equipment that uses the Data Encryption Standard to authenticate bank-to-bank wire transactions can be exported to banks in most countries in the world. Under the Export Administration Act, furthermore, the Department of Commerce is obliged to take into account the foreign availability of equivalent products[53] in deciding whether to grant or deny an export permit—that is to say that it can block exports only where there is evidence that such action is actually likely to prevent a foreign customer from acquiring a product with equivalent capabilities. Under the Arms Export Control Act, no such test of foreign availability is required. All cryptographic devices that do not fall into certain narrow categories are regulated as munitions and require individually approved licenses.

Many of the actions of the export-control authorities seem ludicrous and have inspired widespread resentment. In 1994, Philip Karn, a security engineer at the cellular telephone maker Qualcomm, applied for a license to export a copy of Bruce Schneier's popular book *Applied Cryptography*. The license was granted, and the accompanying letter stated that the Department of State did not have authority over published material—a view commendably in accord with the First Amendment. Karn then applied for an export permit for a small part of Schneier's book—an appendix containing source code for cryptographic algorithms—transcribed onto a floppy disk, rather than on paper. That application was denied. This case, which is working its way through the federal courts, has made the export-control regime an object of ridicule, but the cryptographic export policies of the United States may appear less foolish and irrational when examined in light of communications intelligence practices.

One natural objective of cryptographic export control is to limit foreign availability of cryptographic systems of *strategic capability*, those capable of resisting concerted cryptanalysis by US intelligence agencies. Were this the only objective, export control in the cryptographic area would be much like export control in other areas—items that have only military uses or have been explicitly adapted to military applications would be treated as munitions, others would not.[54]

Probably the most important objective of the export-control regime in the area of cryptography is to slow the widespread deployment of cryptographic systems of sufficient strength to present a serious barrier to traffic selection. Rather than limiting the export of cryptosystems whose traffic would take weeks, months, or years to break, the objective is to prevent the export of cryptosystems that cannot be broken in real time by intercept equipment in the field. This is a far lower bar, and it precludes the export of any system that could reasonably be said to provide acceptable security for most commercial applications.[55]

It also appears to be an objective of export control—and, if so, one that has had remarkable success—to prevent widespread adoption of standard cryptographic systems. The development of standards would have two effects from an intelligence viewpoint. It would expand the use of cryptography, thereby complicating both traffic selection and exploitation. It could also result in a uniform appearance of broad categories of messages, making the problem of selection harder still.

A final objective of export control goes virtually unnoticed. It is to maintain an ongoing assessment of the quality, availability, and functioning of commercially supplied cryptographic equipment. Would-be exporters are required to disclose the details of their products to the government on a routine basis. Even if they are not obliged to modify their products in order to get export approval, this guarantees that NSA will have the details of each product's functioning on file. The process of acquiring information on how cryptographic products work is thereby separated from any actual occasion on which their traffic is being intercepted, thus contributing to security. From this point of view, a product exported under an export-control permit is entirely different from and far preferable to one exported without any permit or any reporting requirement.[56]

By limiting the strength of exportable cryptosystems to well below what the users feel they need, export control creates a direct conflict between the needs of the government and the needs of commercial and private cryptographic users. It is an oft-expressed opinion that commercial communications do not require the same level of protection as military communications. This is probably more a reflection of the fact that the military are aware of who their opponents are and of the level of effort that these opponents put into attacking them than a reflection of the value of the communications. The communications of commercial organizations are often worth hundreds of millions of dollars,[57] and many industrial secrets, along with much personal and personnel information, have long lifetimes. Air traffic control, power grid regulation, and control of communication networks are essential to the working of society; their disruption would expose participating corporations to immense liabilities and might cost lives as well as dollars.

Cryptographic keys are often held to be the most sensitive of all secrets, because anyone who has access to the keys can gain access to all other secrets (Clark 1986, p. 11-1313). In a similar way, controlling the export of cryptography is essential to controlling the export of any information. The increasing importance of intellectual property to modern commerce has already been noted. If smugglers have access to encrypted communications, the export of any form of information will become impossible to regulate and the United States will lose all control of its "electronic borders."

# 5

## Law Enforcement

### The Function of Law Enforcement: Solution versus Prevention

The purpose of law enforcement is to prevent, interdict, and investigate crimes and to prosecute criminals. There is a certain logic to the order in which these objectives are presented; it goes from the most anticipatory to the most reactive. The closest relationship is between investigation and prosecution, which are by and large the most visible and best known of law enforcement's functions. We will examine these first, then turn to prevention, of which a major component, deterrence, is closely related to the success of investigation and prosecution. Finally we will examine interdiction, which is the area that most often brings law enforcement into conflict with civil liberties.

If asked to name a crime, most people would pick a typical crime: murder or robbery or rape or fraud. Everybody agrees that these are crimes (although there is often disagreement about whether a particular event is an instance of the crime), and they are crimes in which the victims are identifiable. Except (of course) in the case of murder, police generally begin their investigation by questioning the victim to get a description of what has happened and to get "leads."

The investigation of crimes has not changed since the rise of the police in the mid nineteenth century, but the way in which they go about it has changed a great deal.

In the nineteenth century, police work was largely a matter of interpersonal relations. The policeman walking a beat depended as much on rapport with the people of the neighborhood as on a gun or a nightstick.

In the absence of a radio or even a call box, he did not have the option—the first resort of police today—of communicating with the station before taking action of any kind. If he encountered trouble, his choices were to deal with it himself or to turn and go for help. The actions of the police in investigating crimes reflected the same skills and resources they used on patrol. They relied less on forensic evidence, record keeping, and communications and more on talking to people and knowing the community. Police action after a crime would rely heavily on an expertise in community functioning acquired continually as the police developed informants or kept watch on markets known to include stolen goods among their wares.

Since then, the character of policing has changed dramatically, and today the police depend as heavily on technology as on their skill in dealing with people. Nowhere is this more apparent than in detective work. The invasion of technology began around 1900 with the development of fingerprinting[1] and forensics. Forensics, as popularized in the Sherlock Holmes stories, has become a mainstay of detective work, and today crime laboratories maintain vast files of common items (such as paper, automobile paint, and duct tape) that enable them to identify and track these items when they are found at crime scenes (Fisher 1995, pp. 159–193).

When police investigate the scene of a crime today, their first action is to seal off the scene and take numerous samples—fingerprints, cartridge cases, clothing fibers, and so on. In conjunction with the lab analysis of these samples, they will make extensive use of their records on people (suspects or witnesses) and on cars, guns, jewelry, and other objects that may have been involved.

The act of investigating a crime consists most conspicuously of attempting to discover who committed the crime, but it may also involve determining the nature and extent of the crime and whether there was a crime committed at all. If this process is successful, the next step is prosecution. Once a suspect has been identified, the police must supply the state's attorney with sufficient evidence to prove the suspect's guilt. Sometimes this process is barely distinguishable from investigation. The police may, for example, observe a suspect's movements until they have a persuasive case that he was in a position to commit the crime and was the only person in such a position. In other cases, particularly in crimes such as burglary or fraud that are likely to be repeated, the process of developing evidence takes on a life of its own and looks quite different. The police may watch someone, whom they suspect of committing a crime but against whom they lack sufficient proof, in hopes that the suspect will grant a repeat performance. They may go so far as to create attractive conditions for the commission of the crime and lie in wait for the suspect to take the bait.

The prevention of criminal activity relies on a combination of security and deterrence. Security measures, ranging from locks and fences to surveillance cameras and patrols, make it more difficult to get away with crimes. Deterrence is in part a result of security and in part a result of the investigation and prosecution of crimes. It persuades a would-be criminal that even success in committing a crime will not mean he has gotten away with it. Security and deterrence are not always easy to distinguish. Police walking beats or patrolling in cars convey the impression that a crime might be observed and stopped outright; they also serve to remind the citizens that the police are present and are likely to find and prosecute the perpetrators of crimes.

The important factor unifying security and deterrence is that neither is aimed at particular individuals. Both are intended to prevent the commission of crimes—to communicate to everyone that criminal efforts are unlikely to succeed and likely to be discovered and punished.

Interdiction of crimes has a different flavor. It is aimed not at everyone, but at particular people who have been detected in the process of planning or preparing to commit criminal acts. Unlike deterrence, it involves concentration of police attention and possibly police action on people who have yet to commit any crime. Any police program of interdiction must, therefore, involve watching people who, at least under US law, are entitled to a presumption of innocence.

## A Brief History of the Police

The police as we know them today—an armed force maintained by the state to perform the functions described in the previous section and paid a salary rather than a share of fines[2]—are a rather recent phenomenon.

Police appeared in France as one of the products of the revolution, but police in the United States stem more from the British tradition.

In 1829, Home Secretary Robert Peel established the Metropolitan Police in London. Initially this force was limited to uniformed patrolling, but in 1842 it was expanded to include the Criminal Investigation Division, responsible for detective work. London's salaried force became the organizational model for police throughout Britain and subsequently the United States. Police forces were formed in all major US cities during the latter half of the nineteenth century.

At the time of their founding, the fundamental mandate of the police was a combination of deterrence (through their visible presence on patrol) and investigation. Under earlier British law, there was less provision than there is today for discovering the perpetrators of a crime when their identities were not obvious; it was the responsibility of the injured parties to investigate and "solve" the crime. Over time, however, investigating and solving crimes has evolved into one of the most important functions of the police.

At the time of their founding, the police were viewed not as an outgrowth of the state's ability to make law but as a manifestation of its ability to use violence. As time went by, they gradually became essentially the only body entitled to employ violence in anything other than self-defense and narrowly construed instances of defense of property. They also came to be seen as the lower rungs of a ladder whose upper steps are the prosecutors and the courts.

In the original British conception, police powers of arrest were limited, and police were supposed to have little or no influence in whether cases were brought to trial. Over time, however, the influence of the police over such decisions has increased dramatically,[3] as has their influence over the making of laws.[4]

### The Use of Wiretaps in Law Enforcement

Both before and after the development of telecommunication, a central element of police work has been the acquisition of information about criminals' plans and conversations without their knowledge or cooperation. There are two fundamental ways in which this can take place:

- through conversations in which a criminal is talking to someone who, usually unbeknownst to the criminal, is an undercover police officer or is providing information to the police

- through conversations between criminals being overheard by the police or by their agents.

The development of telecommunication has had an impact on both of these scenarios, but it has affected the latter far more than the former.

Our first scenario occurs widely in traditional police work—for example, when a victim of extortion or blackmail relates the threats he or she has received to the police, or when the police employ a stool pigeon. Telecommunication has left many of these practices unaffected while opening new opportunities for others. Demands by kidnappers and blackmailers are often delivered by phone and may readily be taped at the victim's end for use as evidence or for other investigative purposes. Such taping, legally and practically distinct from a wiretap, is called a *consensual overhear*.

Our second scenario is the home territory of electronic surveillance.

The crimes we have called typical are investigated largely at the interface between the criminal and non-criminal worlds. But neither the typical crimes nor the broader class of acts generally accepted as crimes and having identifiable victims exhaust the criminal repertoire. Many activities that are criminal under law do not have readily identifiable victims. Not coincidentally, the criminal status of such activities—which include such classic activities of organized crime as prostitution, gambling, and drugs—is often controversial.

Under these circumstances, the police cannot proceed from questioning an aggrieved victim to investigating and prosecuting an offender. They must instead attempt to infiltrate the criminal activity—to intrude on the interactions of a group of people who are, by and large, either satisfied purveyors or satisfied customers in the illegal trade.

For many crimes, including conspiracies to fix prices, bribe government officials, or commit terrorist acts, such infiltration is a difficult procedure. The participants are wary of newcomers, and normal routes of investigation are sealed; it may even be hard to determine what crimes are occurring. It is in such environments that electronic surveillance comes into its own, providing information about the crime being committed and insight into the structure of the criminal organization.

Rarely is it possible to develop or plant an informer high in a syndicate. Information from surveillance enables law enforcement to develop a coherent view of a conspiracy. In the Illwind investigation of corruption in the procurement of weapons for the US military, FBI agents were afraid to run credit checks on suspects for fear of alerting them. Instead they used wiretaps and electronic bugs (which were even more productive) to assemble a picture of the conspiracy. Hundreds of agents were involved in the surveillance (Pasztor 1995, p. 190–191). Wiretaps can also provide mundane details—the suspect's daily schedule (Weiner et al. 1995, p. 223), or the personal relationship between the suspect and his co-conspirators—that can vastly simplify an investigation.

Though equivalent to electronic bugs from a legal viewpoint, wiretaps are generally easier and less dangerous to install. They usually do not provide the same quality of information, however. Criminals are typically considerably less forthcoming over wiretapped telephones than in bugged rooms.[5] Microphone rather than wiretap evidence was responsible for convicting John Gotti, head of the Gambino crime syndicate; information obtained by means of a bug in a Gotti hideaway convinced underboss Sammy Gravano to testify against Gotti.[6] Electronic bugs were also responsible for the conviction of John Stanfa, a Philadelphia crime boss (Anastasia 1994; Hinds 1994).

Even when wiretaps do not directly provide evidence, they can be useful. Wiretaps informed US agents about meetings between the spy Aldrich Ames and his Soviet handlers (Weiner et al. 1995, p. 246).[7] Wiretaps also apprised agents of the fact that Ames's wife had aided him in his illegal activities. Investigators used this knowledge to extract a more detailed confession from Ames in exchange for a reduced sentence for his wife (ibid., pp. 261–262 and 288).

In general, wiretaps appear to be of greater value in gathering intelligence than in developing evidence. They can expose the connections within an organization, and they may reveal events before they occur. Not to be undervalued is the fact that knowledge of the possibility of wiretapping renders the telephone far less useful to criminals.

## Wiretaps and Their Relatives

### How Wiretaps work

Words spoken into a telephone begin their journey at the microphone of the handset, which may be connected to the phone by wire or (in the case of a cordless phone) by radio. From the phone, the signal is passed down a line cord to a wall socket. If the phone is in an office building, its next stop is typically a phone closet where the wires from many phones on the same floor come together. If the phone is in a private home, the signal generally goes directly to a junction box on an outside wall and then by wire to a pole; it is likely to run on poles for only a short distance before it joins wires from other houses in a junction box (similar to the office phone closet) and is routed underground. At this point, the signal takes a fairly long hop and makes its way to the local telephone exchange, where it is received on a frame.

By comparison with the previous elements, the frame plays a more profound role in the call's progress. Up to that point, phone lines were arranged in a basically geographical way, lines coming from nearby houses being routed close together. The frame rearranges the lines to put them in numerical order by phone number. From the frame the lines go into a telephone switch, the formerly mechanical and now electrical equipment that routes calls from one telephone to another. From this point on, no path is permanently bound to any particular phone.

From the viewpoint of security, a phone call is vulnerable to wiretapping at every point along its path. A wiretap may be placed in or close to the phone.[8] It may be placed in a phone closet or in a junction box. It may be placed on the frame or inside the telephone switch. From the viewpoint of an intruder, however, things look entirely different and each of the possible opportunities for wiretapping has serious disadvantages.[9] If he tries to put the tap in the phone, he may get caught in the act of planting the device.[10]

Tapping intermediate junction boxes, whether in phone closets, on poles, or elsewhere, presents both the danger that the installation will be observed and the danger that the tap will later be found by maintenance personnel. Precisely because a junction box serves a number of different clients, it is subject to unpredictable visits by installers and repairmen connecting, disconnecting, or troubleshooting the phones of subscribers other than the target. Any of these maintenance personnel may mistake the tap for a wiring error and disconnect it or take some action that will reveal the tap to its target.

One traditional point for attaching wiretaps was the frame, where an incoming line can readily be connected to an outgoing one in such a way as to make the call accessible at an additional external location. Occasionally this is done for quality-control purposes in the normal course of telephone operations. Like a junction box, however, a frame is tended by numerous people from whom the tappers are trying to keep the tap concealed.

Until the advent of digital telephone switches, the phone, the junction boxes, and the frame were essentially the only points at which a tap targeting an individual line could be placed. It was within the ability of intelligence agencies to target multiplexed flows of traffic further removed from the targets, but only because they had both the budget and the legal mandate to listen to whatever they could find that was of value. Police wiretapping, by comparison, was targeted at individuals and had to be conducted on a limited budget with limited cooperation from the telephone companies.

Digital telephone switches, such as AT&T's ESS series and Northern Telecom's DMS-100, introduce a new (and, from the police viewpoint, far superior) way of wiretapping. The new technique is to make use of the switch's ability to create conference calls. (A tapped call is, after all, simply a conference call with a silent and invisible third party.) Conference calling, however, was not designed with the wiretapper in mind. The technology was intended primarily for creating conference calls in which all connected phones were active and cooperating participants. The new switches had secondary applications to debugging and quality-control monitoring that were closer to the tapper's desires, but a switch's capacity to provide these services was typically limited to a few lines at a time. Although this was generally sufficient for law-enforcement use in the past, law-enforcement agencies have recently begun pushing for vastly expanded wiretapping facilities.

**Pen Register and Trap and Trace**

As we noted in the previous chapter, the backbone of a communications intelligence organization is not its ability to read individual messages, valuable as that is, but its ability to keep track of a broad spectrum of communications through traffic analysis. Although this is less true of law-enforcement intercepts, a sort of traffic analysis, generally targeted at individual lines, plays an important role here.

A log of the numbers of all phones called by one particular phone is called a *pen register*.[11] In the United States the ability to record called numbers has been an essential component of billing for a long time and thus has been built into telephone equipment for a long time.[12] Call logging can also be carried out by equipment on a subscriber's premises (Jupp 1989).

The inverse activity—taking note of the numbers of all phones that call a particular phone—is called *trap and trace*. Unlike logging the numbers of outgoing calls, this was very difficult before the changes made during the past two decades in telephone signaling.[13] In the era of electro-mechanical telephone switching, call tracing took many minutes, during which the caller had to be kept on the line.[14] With digital switching, however, tracing information is almost always available until at least the last switch through which the call passes, and it is often available to the receiving telephone in the form of Caller ID.[15]

As in intelligence work, analysis of the patterns of telephone calls can reveal the structures of organizations and the movements of people. Where billing records preserve such information, it can be employed after the fact, even though the need to do so was not anticipated.[16]

**Electronic Surveillance in Context**

To be understood correctly, electronic surveillance must be seen in the context of the use of technology by police.

Police have often been at the forefront of the use of new technologies. Scotland Yard was connected to the district police stations of London by telegraph in 1849, only 5 years after the telegraph was invented. In 1878 the Chicago police introduced telephone boxes along policemen's routes.

"Wirephoto," credited with the capture of a criminal as early as 1908, became widespread after World War I.

Some elements of today's police technology are entirely new; others have clearly recognizable roots but have changed so much that they are only barely recognizable in relation to their ancestral forms. The most basic of these are the technologies that shape the operations of a police organization: record keeping and what we will call by the military term "command and control."

Police records serve both a strategic and a tactical function. Strategically, they allow police to decide how to deploy their forces. Tactically, they provide information on persons, property, and events connected with the investigation of individual crimes. Police records were once local to cities or districts, and sharing of information between police was a slow, uncertain process. Today, however, a computerized National Crime Information Center provides information to federal, state, and local police forces throughout the United States. This source of information is augmented by police access to commercial credit databases, national telephone directories, and other online information services.

The utility of records is closely connected to another mainstay of police technology: communications. Today most on-duty officers, whether patrolling in cars or walking beats, are in immediate radio contact with their stations. Police cars in some cities carry data terminals that allow direct access to printed records; in other places, officers on patrol must make voice contact with a dispatcher who has access to databases. Police forces today not only have access to nationwide (and often worldwide) records, but much of that access is directly available to officers in the field.

Radio communication also gives the dispatcher immediate access to officers on patrol. To utilize this effectively, the dispatcher must have information about where the officers are and what they are doing. At regular intervals, officers report their locations and activities, and the information they provide is entered on maps and status boards. In the most advanced setups, tracking systems such as Teletrack automatically report the location of each patrol car and display it on the dispatcher's map. Coupled with databases of locations developed to support the 911 emergency system, this permits the dispatcher to recognize where a telephone call is coming from and identify the nearest available emergency personnel. Within a patrol car, it may provide automatic directions to the place the car has been told to go.

The same technologies that permit police forces to track their officers permit them to track and watch individuals and goods with unprecedented ease. Many truck, bus, and automobile fleets use tracking systems to monitor the movements of their vehicles. This allows vehicles to be tracked if they are stolen and makes it difficult for the drivers to use them for purposes other than those the employer intended. Surveillance is also facilitated by computerized road tolls, optical character recognition of license plates, and specialized networks for tracking "bumper-bugged" vehicles (Burnham 1996, p. 138).

Police track more than vehicles. It is a rare person in the modern world who can avoid being listed in numerous databases. From a police viewpoint, the process of identification is a process of matching a person with society's records about that person.[17] Until recently, fingerprints were of more use in confirming identity than establishing it. Even long after the availability of computers, the search of a large fingerprint file was a slow process requiring expert human labor.

Even though fingerprint records have been computerized, fingerprints are not an ideal way of tracking the movements of people, and they are rapidly being supplanted or augmented by other technologies.

Video cameras are now ubiquitous. It is popularly believed that such cameras run "tape loops" containing, for example, the last half-hour's view of people entering and leaving a bank. In fact, videotape is cheap, and many cameras record images for much longer periods. After the bombing of the Murrah federal building, the FBI collected videotapes from all over Oklahoma City, synchronized them using the shaking that resulted from the blast, and watched the movements of people before and after the explosion.[18] One developing technology allows automatic identification of people from their videotaped images (Busey 1994). Another new form of technology that allows "surreptitious fingerprinting" is infrared imaging of the veins in the face. Like fingerprints, these are unique to individuals. Unlike fingerprints, these veins can be detected by hidden infrared cameras installed in airports and other public places.

Today almost every American adult carries a driver's license and other forms of identification that are hard—and illegal—to counterfeit. The near ubiquity of identification cards has given them wide social acceptability. Many communities require hotel registrants to show identification, presumably as an anti-prostitution measure. The 1995 decision by the Federal Aviation Authority that air travelers may be required to show government-issued identification when checking in at airports has made anonymous travel slower and thus less practical. The Supreme Court ruling that the police cannot require a person to show identification (*Kolender, Chief of Police of San Diego, et al. v. Lawson* 461 US 352 (1983)) has brought no noticeable change in police practice.

Possibly the most important way of tracking individuals is through credit cards. Since credit cards are the easiest way of making most purchases and are essentially required of persons renting cars or checking into hotels, the databases used for billing and credit verification contain good pictures of most people's movements.

Material objects too are tracked; they are also examined. Fear of terrorism initiated the development of a broad range of devices intended to search for guns and bombs. The capabilities of the most recent equipment go far beyond that, however. Some baggage x-ray machines can be programmed to look for sharp things, for guns, for drugs, for precious metals, or for fruits and vegetables. Similar devices can look at an entire truck and detect drugs right through its aluminum skin. There are detectors based on magnetometry, on vapor analysis, on neutron activation analysis, and on nuclear magnetic resonance. Detection of mass concentrations from their gravitational effects is in an experimental stage.

Evaluating the numerous technologies that have appeared over the past 100 years for their law-enforcement potential versus their criminal potential produces a preponderance of cases that favor law enforcement. On the criminal side, chemistry has given us a variety of new drugs that have been condemned by society but enjoy good sales anyway. Improvements in manufacturing and competition in the international arms market have given us "Saturday night specials." Photography has contributed to blackmail. Computers and communications have brought us a new kind of crime—theft of computer and communication services—even while contributing to the operations of both criminals and police. It is hard to see much that microscopy, x-rays, database technology, microbiology, infrared imaging, MRI, or numerous other technologies have contributed to criminal enterprises; they have, however, given the police a host of techniques for tracking, identifying, and monitoring both people and physical objects. On balance, the impact of technology is so weighted on the side of law enforcement as to make it remarkable that crime has survived at all.

### Blurring the National Security/Law Enforcement Distinction

In general, "national security" refers to the government's operations outside the borders of the United States and "law enforcement" to its domestic operations. However, at times—most dramatically in the 1960s and the early 1970s—the distinction has been blurred.

In the mid 1970s, the Church Committee, a year-long Senate investigation of US intelligence operations, found evidence of "domestic intelligence activities [that] threaten to undermine our democratic society and fundamentally alter its nature" (USS 94d, p. 1). The Church Committee recommended that the CIA, NSA, the Defense Intelligence Agency, and the armed services be precluded, with narrow and specific exceptions, from conducting intelligence activities within the United States, and that their activities abroad be controlled so as to minimize impact on the rights of Americans (ibid., p. 297). Out of the Church Committee report grew a sharp delineation between laws governing (domestic) law-enforcement investigations and those governing (foreign) national-security ones. National-security investigators were allowed to operate with considerably more latitude outside the borders of the United States than within. This sharp delineation was in line with the 1878 Posse Comitatus Act, post-Civil War legislation that prohibited Army involvement in domestic arrests or searches and seizures.[19]

Within a decade of the Church Committee's recommendation, the line began to blur. In 1981 President Ronald Reagan declared that international drug trafficking posed a threat to national security (McGee 1996c), and the Military Cooperation with Civilian Law Enforcement Agencies Act sharply increased the Army's role in anti-drug efforts. The military's responsibilities in anti-drug efforts grew. The 1989 Defense Authorization Act put the Department of Defense in charge of applying US command, control, communications, and intelligence assets to monitor illegal drugs.

The National Guard does not face Posse Comitatus restrictions unless it is on federal duty, and it has been given a greater role in drug interdiction. In addition, Army Special Forces and the Marines patrol the Southwest and California for drug smugglers. Military intelligence officers also watch for gang and criminal activity in a number of US cities (McGee 1996b,c). Law enforcement and the military have become closely linked in their anti-drug activities. The scale of military participation is evident in the fact that since 1989 the military has spent over $7 billion on anti-drug operations (McGee 1996b).

Aside from drug trafficking, various international events have been cited as evidence of a need for closer coordination between national security and domestic law enforcement. One such event was the 1991 collapse of the Bank of Credit and Commerce International. According to a 1992 report by Senators John Kerry and Hank Brown, the CIA had discovered the essentials of the bank's criminal activities by 1985 but had never properly conveyed these facts to law-enforcement agencies.[20] Proponents of closer cooperation between intelligence and law-enforcement agencies maintain that globalization and the end of the Cold War make separation between national security and domestic law unrealistic.

A series of laws passed during the 1980s made various acts occurring outside the borders of the United States criminal acts prosecutable within the United States if they involved American citizens. These laws included the Omnibus Diplomatic Security and Antiterrorism Act of 1986 (Public Law 99-399), which established jurisdiction over violent terrorist acts against Americans overseas; the Act for the Prevention and Punishment of Hostage-Taking (18 USC §1203 (1988)); the Aircraft Sabotage Act (Public Law 98-473, 18 USC 63.2, 40 USC App. 1301, 1471 1972, (Supp. v. 1987)); and Public Law 101-519, which established US district court jurisdiction over suits to recover damages in international terrorism cases. The passage of these laws left unclear how they were to be implemented, and, in particular, what role national security should play in international law enforcement.

The Clinton administration initiated internal discussions on these issues. Then the 1997 Intelligence Authorization Act (§814) stated the following:

> ... elements of the Intelligence Community may, upon the request of a United States law enforcement agency collect information outside the United States about individuals who are not United States persons. Such elements may collect such information notwithstanding that the law enforcement agency intends to use the information collected for purposes of a law enforcement investigation or counterintelligence investigation.

This wording carefully steers clear of permitting the intelligence community to spy on Americans directly, but opens the way for unprecedented collaboration between the intelligence and law-enforcement communities.

# 6

## Privacy: Protections and Threats

Protecting the national security and enforcing the laws are basic societal values. Often they stand in competition with another basic societal value: privacy. The competition is hardly an equal contest. National security and law enforcement not only have political constituencies, they are represented by major societal organizations. Privacy has no such muscle behind it. As a result, although an attachment to privacy endures and at times grows, privacy is often violated.

### The Dimensions of Privacy

Our focus throughout this book is on privacy in communications. However, it is valuable to draw back and view privacy in a broader context.

Two hundred years ago, if you chose to speak to a colleague about private matters, you had to do it in person. Others might have seen the two of you walk off together, but to overhear your conversation an eavesdropper would have had to follow closely and would likely have been observed. Today, the very communication links that have made it possible to converse at a distance have the potential to destroy the privacy such conversations previously enjoyed.

From video cameras that record our entries into shops and buildings to supermarket checkout tapes that list every container of milk and package of cigarettes we buy, privacy is elusive in modern society. There are records of what we do, with whom we associate, where we go. Insurance companies know who our spouses are, how many children we have, how often we have our teeth cleaned. The increasing amount of transactional information—the electronic record of when you left the parking lot, the supermarket's record of your purchase—leaves a very large public footprint, and presents a far more detailed portrait of the individual than those recorded at any time in the past. Furthermore, information about individuals is no longer under the control of the person to whom the information pertains; such loss of control is loss of privacy.

### Privacy as a Fundamental Human Right

Privacy is at the very soul of being human. Legal rights to privacy appeared 2000 years ago in Jewish laws such as this: "[If one man builds a wall opposite his fellow's] windows, whether it is higher or lower than them ... it may not be within four cubits [If higher, it must be four cubits higher, for privacy's sake]." (Danby 1933, p. 367) The Talmud explains that a person's neighbor "should not peer and look into his house."

Privacy is the right to autonomy, and it includes the right to be let alone. Privacy encompasses the right to control information about ourselves, including the right to limit access to that information. The right to privacy embraces the right to keep confidences confidential and to share them in private conversation. Most important, the right to privacy means the right to enjoy solitude, intimacy, and anonymity (Flaherty 1989, p. 8).

Not all these rights can be attained in modern society. Some losses occur out of choice. (In the United States, for example, candidates for office make public much personal information, such as tax and medical records, that private citizens are allowed to keep private.) Some losses are matters of convenience. (Almost no one pays bills in cash anymore.) But the maintenance of some seclusion is fundamental to the human soul. Accordingly, privacy is recognized by the international community as a basic human right. Article 12 of the 1948 Universal Declaration of Human Rights states:

> No one shall be subjected to arbitrary interference with his privacy, family, home or correspondence, nor to attacks upon his honour and reputation. Everyone has the right to the protection of the law against such interference or attacks. (Academy on Human Rights 1993, p. 3)

The 1967 International Covenant on Human Rights makes the same point.[1]

The Soviet Union, East Germany, and other totalitarian states rarely respected the rights of individuals, and this includes the right to privacy. Those societies were permeated by informants,[2] telephones were assumed to be tapped and hotel rooms to be bugged: life was defined by police surveillance. Democratic societies are supposed to function differently.

### Privacy in American Society

Privacy is essential to political discourse. The fact is not immediately obvious, because the most familiar political discourse is public. History records political speeches, broadsides, pamphlets, and manifestos, not the quiet conversations among those who wrote them. Without the opportunity to discuss politics in private, however, the finished positions that appear in public might never be formulated.

Democracy requires a free press, confidential lawyer-client relations, and the right to a fair trial. The foundations of democracy rest upon privacy, but in various democratic societies the protection of privacy is interpreted in varying ways. Britain, for example, has much looser laws regarding wiretaps than the United States. A number of European nations extend more protection to individuals' data records than the US does.

Privacy is culture dependent. Citizens of crowded countries such as India and the Netherlands hold very different views of what constitutes privacy than citizens of the United States. The American concept developed in a land with a bountiful amount of physical space and in a culture woven from many disparate nationalities.

In the 1970s, as rapid computerization brought fear of a surveillance society, some nations sought to protect individuals from the misuse of personal data. Sweden, Germany, Canada, and France established data-protection boards to protect the privacy and the integrity of records on individual citizens. When the US Congress passed a Privacy Act with a similar goal,[3] President Gerald Ford objected to the creation of another federal bureaucracy, and no US data-protection commission was ever established (Flaherty 1989, p. 305). Ten states have data-protection laws, and California includes a right to privacy in its state constitution. New York is the only state that attempts any oversight (ibid.). It would, however, be a mistake to view the lack of a major regulatory apparatus in the United States as a lack of legal protection of privacy.

**Privacy Protection in the United States**

Most Americans believe that privacy is a basic right guaranteed by the Constitution. The belief has some truth to it, but not nearly as much as some believe. Nowhere is the word privacy mentioned in the Constitution, nor is a right to privacy explicit in any amendment. Privacy is nonetheless implicit to the Constitution.

The First Amendment protects the individual's freedoms of expression, religion, and association. The Third Amendment protects the private citizen against the state's harboring an army in his home, the Fourth against unreasonable search or seizure. The Fifth Amendment ensures that an individual cannot be compelled to provide testimony against himself. The Ninth Amendment reserves to "the people" those rights that are not enumerated in the Constitution. And "the Fourteenth Amendment's guarantee that no person can be deprived of life, liberty or property without due process of law, provides an additional bulwark against governmental interference with individual privacy" (USS 93c, p. ix).

**The Early Years**
Three hundred years ago, the colonists' portion of the North American continent consisted of farms, small towns, and a few small cities. Eavesdroppers were easily avoided by walking to a place where one could not be overheard. Although the colonists' application of English common law provided for the punishment of eavesdroppers (Friedman 1973, p. 254), more typically such crimes were handled by their discoverers (Flaherty 1989, p. 89).

The problem of the mail being less than private was less easily disposed of, for mail delivery entailed dependence on others. In colonial America mail delivery was haphazard; letters from Europe would be left by a ship's captain at a local tavern, awaiting pickup by their intended recipients but meanwhile open to inspection by all passersby. Within the colonies mail was delivered by travelers and merchants, or by special messengers, and privacy was likewise not assumed. In 1710, in creating a postal delivery system in the colonies, the British government established privacy protection similar to what existed in England; at least in law, the opening of letters and other forms of tampering was forbidden without authorization by the secretary of state (Seipp 1977, p. 11).[4]

Such protection, however, was incomplete. Before the establishment of the United States, Postmaster-General Benjamin Franklin believed that his own mail was being opened and read (Franklin 1907, pp. 461–462). Later, Thomas Jefferson held a similar concern.[5] In 1825 Congress addressed this problem with the Postal Act (4 Stat. 102, 109), which prohibited prying into another person's mail. Practice did not necessarily follow the law. During the 1850s there were complaints about the "greedy fingers" through which the mail passed,[6] and during the Civil War there were government attempts to open private civilian mail.[7] In 1878 the Supreme Court ruled that the government could not open first-class mail without a search warrant (*Ex Parte Jackson*, 96 US 727, p. 733).

The invention of the telegraph led to a new way of communicating and two new ways of eavesdropping: one could tap the wire[8] or one could read the messages later from copies kept by the telegraph companies. The latter was the search method preferred by the government.

At the beginning of the Civil War, the government took control of the telegraph wires and seized copies of all telegrams sent within the previous 12 months (Plum 1882, p. 69). For the duration of the war, the federal government censored all dispatches emanating from Washington (Randall 1951, pp. 482–483). But the War Department did not have full success in controlling the medium. In 1864, attempting to track down the source of a false newspaper story that the president planned to call up an additional 400,000 men, the government sought copies of all telegrams sent out from Washington, but company operators refused to cooperate. They were arrested and held for several days until Army investigators uncovered the perpetrator—a stock manipulator (Bates 1907, pp. 228–243).

Some of the complexity of the fight over the privacy protection afforded to telegraphs was due to the fact that, unlike the mails, this new communication medium was controlled by private enterprise. The government sought two seemingly contradictory goals: to protect privacy of communications from the prying eyes of operators (Seipp 1977, pp. 83–95) and to establish broad search privileges for itself.

Telegraph companies sought to assure the public that communications would be private (ibid., pp. 89–90). The government's determination to obtain copies of telegrams pressed against this, and the conflict came to a head in 1876 with the contested presidential election between Hayes and Tilden. During a fight over electoral votes from Louisiana and Oregon, a House committee questioned the manager of Western Union's New Orleans office about telegrams. Under orders from Western Union's president, the manager refused to reveal the contents of the disputed dispatches. The House held the manager in contempt. Another Western Union manager in Oregon faced a similar situation with the Senate. The company responded that it would henceforth destroy copies of telegrams as quickly as account keeping would allow (New York Tribune 1876). However, the policy was never carried out, and on January 20, 1877, with the manager of the New Orleans office in custody at the Capitol and the company's president ill, Western Union gave in to congressional pressure, and responded to the subpoena (Seipp 1977, p. 54). Western Union prepared a bill for Congress in which telegrams were provided the same legal protections as US mail (New York Tribune 1880). Although the bill was reported favorably out of committee, it was not heard of again.

Several court decisions put a partial closure on the issue. One of these involved a St. Louis grand jury investigation of a gambling ring that allegedly involved Missouri's governor and the police commissioner of St. Louis. When the manager of the Western Union office refused to hand over copies of telegrams (New York Times 1879), the company appealed and won a partial victory; the Missouri Supreme Court ruled that, although telegraph messages were not accorded the privacy protection the company sought (the same as for US mail), any request for copies of telegrams had to include both the date and the subject of the message (*Ex Parte Brown*, 72 Mo. 83 95 (1880), in Seipp, p. 58). A number of other decisions around that time reached the same conclusions (Seipp 1977, p. 59).[9]

After the Civil War the United States experienced rapid industrialization and urbanization. Small towns have never been much known as respecters of privacy, but in such locales the ubiquity of gossip was mitigated by the fact that news did not travel far. As the invention of rotary presses, linotypes, and automatic folders led to a sharp increase in the number of newspapers and to the advent of "yellow journalism," that ceased to be true. Against such a backdrop Samuel Warren, a socially prominent paper manufacturer, and his former law partner Louis Brandeis, later to become a Supreme Court Justice, wrote an article on privacy for the 1890 *Harvard Law Review*. Warren and Brandeis argued that the changes caused by technology called for a response in law:

> That the individual shall have full protection in person and in property is a principle as old as the common law; but it has been found necessary from time to time to define anew the exact nature and extent of such protection.... [I]n very early times, the law gave only for physical interference with life and property ... Later, there came a recognition of man's spiritual nature, of his feelings and his intellect. Gradually the scope of these legal rights broadened; and now the right to life has come to mean the right to enjoy life,—the right to be let alone.... (Warren and Brandeis 1890, p. 193)

> Instantaneous photographs and newspaper enterprise have invaded the sacred precincts of private and domestic life; and numerous mechanical devices threaten to make good the prediction that "what is whispered in the closet shall be proclaimed from the housetops." (ibid., p. 195)

## Privacy as a Principle of Law

Law review articles may shape legal philosophy, but statutes and court decisions actually determine it. In the first round between telephone technology and privacy, privacy lost.

In 1928 Prohibition was still in force and illegal liquor distribution was big business. Among the "businessmen" were Roy Olmstead and his partners, who had a large liquor importing and distribution operation in Seattle. The enterprise employed 50 people, including salesmen, dispatchers, deliverymen, bookkeepers, and even an attorney. Outside the city they had a ranch with an underground hideaway for storage, and throughout the city they had smaller caches. Their headquarters, in a large downtown office building, had three phone lines in the main office. In addition, Olmstead and several of his associates had office lines at home.

Federal agents installed wiretaps in the basement of the headquarters building and on lines in streets near the conspirators' homes. For months four prohibition officers eavesdropped on the conspirators as they ordered cases of liquor, arranged bribes for the Seattle police, and reported news of seized alcohol. The wiretap evidence played a crucial role in

Olmstead's conviction, but should the evidence have been admitted? No warrants were sought, but neither did the agents enter private homes or offices to place the taps (*Olmstead* 1928). Because the evidence had been obtained from warrantless wiretaps installed by the government, the defendants claimed that the wiretapped evidence had been obtained in violation of the Fourth Amendment. Use of the evidence also violated the Fifth Amendment, the defendants argued, because they had unwillingly become witnesses against themselves.

The US Supreme Court did not buy these arguments, and five of the justices voted to uphold a lower court's conviction. In an irony of history, the most famous opinion to come out of the case is Justice Louis Brandeis's dissent, which includes these passages:

> When the Fourth and Fifth Amendments were adopted, "the form that evil had heretofore taken" had been necessarily simple. Force and violence were then the only means known to man by which a Government could directly impel self-incrimination. It could compel the individual to testify—a compulsion effected, if need be, by torture. It could secure possession of his papers and other articles incident to his private life—a seizure effected, if need be, by breaking and entry. Protection against such invasion of "the sanctities of a man's home and the privacies of life" was provided in the Fourth and Fifth Amendment by specific language.... But "time works changes, brings into existence new conditions and purposes." Subtler and more far-reaching means of invading privacy have become available to the Government. Discovery and invention have made it possible for the Government, by means far more effective than stretching upon the rack, to obtain disclosure in court of what is whispered in the closet. (Brandeis 1928, p. 473)

> Unjustified search and seizure violates the Fourth Amendment.... [I]t follows necessarily that the Amendment is violated by the officer's reading the paper without a physical seizure, without his even touching it; and that use, in any criminal proceeding, of the contents of the paper so examined ... any such use constitutes a violation of the Fifth Amendment.
>
> The protection guaranteed by the Amendments is much broader in scope. The makers of our Constitution undertook to secure conditions favorable to the pursuit of happiness. They recognized the significance of man's spiritual nature, of his feelings and his intellect.... They sought to protect Americans in their beliefs, their thoughts, their emotions and their sensations. They conferred, as against the Government, the right to be let alone—the most comprehensive of rights and the right most valued by civilized man. To protect that right, every unjustifiable intrusion by the Government upon the privacy of the individual, whatever the means employed, must be deemed a

violation of the Fourth Amendment. And the use, of evidence in a criminal proceeding, of facts ascertained by such intrusion must be deemed a violation of the Fifth. (ibid., pp. 477–478)

A decade later, in the Nardone cases (*Nardone v. United States*, 302 US 379 (1937) and 308 US 338 (1939)), the Supreme Court avoided constitutional questions and used the Federal Communications Act as a basis for making warrantless wiretapping illegal. In effect, though not in law, this supported the principles Brandeis had espoused in *Olmstead*. In later rulings the Court outlawed the use of warrantless electronic surveillance of any type. Other cases before the Court further helped to define the parameters of privacy.

A 1958 ruling held that the First Amendment right to free association included the privacy of such association. In an effort to curb the political activities of the National Association for the Advancement of Colored People, Alabama filed suit against that organization, which had helped organize the Montgomery bus boycott and secure the admission of blacks to the segregated state university. The NAACP was ordered to produce a number of records, including its membership list. In the climate of the times, this would have been dangerous to the individuals named, and the NAACP refused to comply. The Court sided with the defendants:

> [O]n past occasions revelation of the identity of its rank-and-file members has exposed these members to economic reprisal, loss of employment, threat of physical coercion, and other manifestations of public hostility.... (*NAACP v. Alabama*. 357 US 449, 1958, p. 462)

> [I]mmunity from state scrutiny of membership lists that the Association claims on behalf of its members is here so related to the rights of the members to pursue their lawful private interests privately and to associate freely with others in so doing as to come within the protection of the Fourteenth Amendment.[10] (ibid., p. 466)

Seven years later, in *Griswold v. Connecticut*, the Supreme Court greatly expanded privacy protections by including rights that were not specifically enumerated within the Bill of Rights. Connecticut's Birth Control Act outlawed the sale and use of contraceptives, and the state had prosecuted the executive director of Planned Parenthood and a New Haven doctor who had given out contraceptive information. The Supreme Court ruled that the state had no business legislating on matters having to do with what goes on in the privacy of the bedroom. In so doing, it developed the theory that the protections afforded by the Bill of Rights cast wide shadows:

> This law ... operates directly on an intimate relation of husband and wife and their physician's role in one aspect of that relation.
> The association of people is not mentioned in the Constitution nor in the Bill of Rights. The right to educate a child in a school of the parents' choice —whether public or private or parochial—is also not mentioned. Nor is the right to study any particular subject or any foreign language. Yet the First Amendment has been construed to include certain of those rights. (*Griswold v. Connecticut*, 381 US 479, 1965, p. 482).

> In *NAACP v. Alabama*, 357 US 449, 462, we protected the "freedom to associate and privacy in one's associations.".... In other words the First Amendment has a penumbra where privacy is protected from governmental intrusion....
> [S]pecific guarantees in the Bill of Rights have penumbras, formed by emanations from those guarantees that help give them life and substance.... (ibid., p. 483)

Two years later, the Supreme Court ruled that telephone calls, including those made in public places, were private. Charles Katz had placed a $300 bet from a phone booth in Los Angeles. An FBI team investigating interstate gambling had, without benefit of a search warrant, installed an electronic bug in the phone booth and picked up Katz's portion of the conversation. The Court ruled:

> [T]he Fourth Amendment protects people, not places. What a person knowingly exposes to the public, even in his own home or office, is not a subject of Fourth Amendment protection.... But what he seeks to preserve as private, even in an area accessible to the public, may be constitutionally protected. (*Charles Katz v. United States*, 389 US 347, 1967, p. 311)

Katz's conviction was overturned. However, the Supreme Court was not heading down a one-way path to greater privacy protection, as Mitchell Miller, who used his checking account for an illegal moonshine business, discovered.

In December 1972, a deputy sheriff in Houston County, Georgia, stopped a suspicious van driven by Miller's business partners. The van was carrying materials for making a still. Several weeks later, during a fire at a warehouse Miller had rented, firemen and police discovered a distillery and whiskey, on which no taxes had been paid. The Bureau of Alcohol, Tobacco, and Firearms issued a subpoena to Miller's bank for his account records, which the bank gave to federal agents. A grand jury subsequently indicted Miller on various moonshining charges. Arguing that because the seized material constituted self-incriminating material the subpoena was an illegal search and seizure, Miller tried to suppress the account information. The Court did not support him:

> We find there is no intrusion into any area in which respondent had a protected Fourth Amendment interest.....
>
> On their face, the documents subpoenaed here are respondent's "private papers".... (*United States v. Miller*, 425 US 435, 1976, p. 440).

> [I]f we direct our attention to the original checks and deposit slips, rather than to the microfilm copies actually viewed and obtained through the subpoena, we perceive no legitimate "expectation of privacy" in their contents. The checks are not confidential communications, but negotiable instruments to be used in commercial transactions. All of the documents obtained, including financial statements and deposit slips, contain only information voluntarily conveyed to the banks and exposed to their employees in the ordinary course of business. (ibid., p. 442)

Here the Court deemed only that which has an "expectation of privacy" worthy of Fourth Amendment protection.

## Privacy Threatened

In the name of efficiency, the US government and many businesses have amassed huge databases containing profiles of their "customers." The gains in efficiency are accompanied by losses of privacy.

Credit cards leave a trail of where their holders travel, where they shop, and what they buy. Studying billing patterns, the European branch of American Express tailors the promotional material it sends its customers to their individual purchasing patterns, and plans are afoot to offer the same "service" in the United States. " 'A Northern Italian restaurant opens in midtown Manhattan,' [the CEO of American Express] says, by way of an example. 'We know from the spending of card members which of them have eaten in Northern Italian restaurants in New York, whether they live in New York or Los Angeles. We make the offer of a free or discounted meal available only to those card members.'" (Solomon 1995, p. 38) The long-distance telephone company MCI offers its users discounts on calls to the ten numbers they call most often, and the carrier identifies those numbers for the customers. These companies are not unique in the amount they know about their customers' purchasing patterns, though they are perhaps more public about it.

Although there has been no public protest of the two transactional data collections described above, there are periodic episodes in which the public says to a company "Leave us alone." Several years ago the software firm Lotus and the Equifax credit bureau were developing a CD-ROM that would contain the names, estimated incomes, and purchasing habits of 120 million Americans. The companies received 30,000 letters opposing the project, and it was killed (Piller 1993, p. 11). Similarly, for exactly 10 days Lexis-Nexis, a leading information broker, offered an online service that included access to Social Security numbers. An outpouring of objections from customers caused the company to discontinue the service (Flynn 1996).

On occasion the federal government has stepped in to safeguard privacy. In 1970 Congress passed the Fair Credit Reporting Act, which ensures that individuals have rights in connection with credit records maintained by private databases. The publicity surrounding Judge Robert Bork's rental habits[11] led to the Video Privacy Protection Act of 1988, which prohibits release of rental records. The Federal Privacy Act places limits on the types of information federal agencies may collect on individuals. California, Connecticut, the District of Columbia, Illinois, New Jersey, and Wisconsin all have laws that protect cable TV subscribers' records against release. Almost all states recognize the doctor-patient privilege (*Privacy Journal* 1992). Legislative protections of privacy are sparse but not unknown.

In the United States there are now over 500 commercial databases that buy and sell information (Piller 1993, p. 10). Despite this proliferation of private purveyors of information, US citizens fear their government more. A recent Harris survey showed that in response to the question "Which type of invasions of privacy worry you the most in America today—activities of government agencies or businesses?" 52% of the respondents answered that government agencies were their greater worry, while 40% said business (Center for Social and Legal Research, p. 7).

Luther King Jr. For a number of years the FBI had been investigating King's alleged ties to the Communist Party. King's closest connection to the Communist Party was through his friend and advisor Stanley Levison. But Levison had left the Party in 1954. The FBI was well aware of this: in 1960 it had attempted to recruit Levison in order to have him rejoin the Party as an FBI spy (Friedly and Gallen 1993, p. 24).

In 1963, during debates on a pending civil rights bill, Senator James Eastland of Mississippi, using information given to him by the FBI, charged that King and the SCLC were being advised by Communists. Attorney General Robert Kennedy authorized wiretaps on King (USS 93e, pp. 111–112). The FBI decided that the bugging of King was also authorized (ibid.). No evidence of Communist influence was discovered, but King remained a subject of wiretaps and bugs. The surveillance had uncovered other information too valuable for FBI Director J. Edgar Hoover, who hated King, to ignore.

Electronic surveillance in hotel rooms King stayed in when traveling picked up the minister telling bawdy stories and raucously partying (Darrow 1981, p. 109). Although this information had nothing to do with Communist activity in the civil rights movement, the FBI used the tapes in an attempt to discredit King. A version of the tapes was sent to his wife, and Hoover played the tapes for President Lyndon Johnson.

In a further attempt to discredit King, William Sullivan, Associate Director of the FBI, wrote a monograph on Communist influence in the civil rights movement that was then made available to the heads of intelligence agencies, the Department of State, the Department of Defense, and the United States Information Agency; it included a salacious section on King's personal life, apparently based on information from the bugs (USS 94e, pp. 173–174). The impetus for this siege was King's having received the Nobel Peace Prize. Enraged by this international honor, Hoover tried to spread the news of King's personal life anywhere honors for the civil rights leader were being contemplated.

There was also political espionage against King. At the request of the White House, the FBI sent 30 special agents to the 1964 Democratic National Convention in Atlantic City. Their job was to assist the Secret Service and to make sure that the convention was not disrupted by civil disturbances. The FBI interpreted the latter charge broadly enough to cover political activities. Johnson was especially concerned about a challenge to the seating of the regular Mississippi delegation by the Mississippi Freedom Democratic Party. From an FBI wiretap of King's hotel room in Atlantic City,[21] Johnson's staff discovered the efforts of King and his associates to unseat the Mississippi delegation. A Senate investigating committee later observed that "an unsigned White House memorandum disclosing Dr. King's strategy in connection with a meeting to be attended by President Johnson suggests there was political use of these FBI reports."[22]

The investigations of King were not based on national-security considerations. In the case of the Democratic National Convention, the purpose of the wiretap was to provide political intelligence for the president. As was well known to the FBI at the time, the other wiretaps and bugs had no legitimate purpose.

Where many saw peaceful dissent in the civil rights movement and in the protests against the Vietnam War, the FBI saw domestic upheaval and began a massive program of surveillance. Riots in Los Angeles and other cities in the summer of 1965 led to heavy FBI surveillance of black neighborhoods. In 1966, FBI field offices were told to begin preparing semimonthly summaries of "existing racial conditions" and of the activities of all civil rights organizations (USS 94d, p. 71). By 1972 the bureau had over 7400 informants in the ghettos, including, for example, "the proprietor of a candy store or barber shop" (ibid., p. 75). The informants were to attend meetings held by "extremists," to identify them when they came through the ghetto, and to identify persons distributing extremist literature (Moore 1972). Since the FBI's definition of extremists included such advocates of nonviolence as Martin Luther King and Ralph Abernathy,[23] it is not surprising that so many informants (one of every 3300 black Americans) were employed by the FBI during this period.

Fear of potential Communist infiltration led the FBI to investigate the anti-war movement (USS 94d, p. 49), and agents conducted their probes as if these apprehensions had a factual basis. For example, during the spring of 1968, the FBI sought to wiretap the National Mobilization Office, which was planning to hold demonstrations during the Democratic National Convention in Chicago. In this case, despite several requests by the FBI, Attorney General Ramsey Clark refused to give the bureau permission to wiretap (Clark 1968).

The FBI also investigated the women's liberation movement and various university, church and political groups opposed to the Vietnam War (USS 94d, p. 167). A woman whom the FBI had hired to report on the group Vietnam Veterans against the War later told a Senate committee: "I was to go to meetings, write up reports ... on what happened, who was there,... to try to totally identify the background of every person there what their relationships were, who they were living with, who they were sleeping with...." (USS 94c, p. 111)

A Senate subcommittee estimated that between 1967 and 1970 the US Army maintained files on at least 100,000 Americans (USS 92b, p. 96), including Joan Baez, Julian Bond, Rev. William Sloane Coffin Jr., Arlo Guthrie, Jesse Jackson, Martin Luther King Jr., Representative Abner Mikva, Dr. Benjamin Spock, and Senator Adlai Stevenson III.[24]

Much of the information contained in the Army's files was personal. "For example, the profile of a well-known local civil rights leader reported that he had four brothers, five sisters, and a widowed mother. An entertainer was recorded as married and the father of six children.... Another sketch stated that due to flat feet and torn ligaments, ___ failed to pass Selective Service physical examinations, and his draft board classified him 1-Y." (USS 93a, p. 56) Though these people had not served in the Army, the Army's files contained information about their financial affairs, sex lives, and psychiatric histories (USS 92b, p. 96).

The military also kept files on the American Friends Service Committee, Americans for Democratic Action, the Congress of Racial Equality, Clergy and Laymen Concerned about the War, the NAACP, the National Mobilization Committee to End the War in Vietnam, the SCLC, Veterans and Reservists to End the War, and Women's Strike for Peace, among others (USAINTC 1969). Army agents reported on such subversive activities as labor negotiations conducted by the sanitation workers' union in Atlanta and actions by Wisconsin welfare mothers who wanted higher payments (Stein 1971, p. 274). As a Senate subcommittee observed, "considerations of privacy, relevance, and self-restraint were cast to the winds" (USS 93a, p. 56).

The 1960s were also a time when President John Kennedy used national security as a pretext for FBI wiretaps on opponents of his administration's Sugar Bill (see chapter 6) and on several journalists,[25] and when the FBI kept President Johnson supplied with political intelligence through biweekly summaries of contacts between foreign officials and various senators and congressmen (USS 94d, pp. 119–120).

Despite his use of the King wiretaps and his reliance on the FBI for political surveillance of congressional opponents to the Vietnam War, President Johnson turned against the use of wiretaps.[26] Johnson called the Title III provisions for wiretapping undesirable even as he signed the Omnibus Crime Control and Safe Streets Act of 1968 (Congressional 1968b, p. 1842).[27] Richard Nixon took his oath of office as president 7 months later. In his first full day as president, Nixon told a reporter that his attorney general, John Mitchell, would govern wiretapping "with an iron hand" (White 1975, p. 125). Within 4 months, and without Mitchell's approval, Nixon's administration began wiretapping for political purposes.

The political wiretapping began after the *New York Times* reported that the United States had been bombing Cambodia for some time. Henry Kissinger, Nixon's national security advisor, asked J. Edgar Hoover to have the FBI find out who had leaked this information to the *Times*. Seventeen people, including several journalists, were wiretapped in this investigation.

Two of those tapped, John Sears and James McLane, were domestic-affairs advisors with no access to classified national-security material (USS 94e, p. 337). White House speechwriter William Safire was also wiretapped; he had been overheard on an existing tap promising a reporter background material pertaining to a presidential address on revenue sharing and welfare reform (USS 94e, p. 337). No national-security leaks were ever uncovered by this investigation.

Joseph Kraft, a columnist, was another target. Kraft had once been a favorite of Nixon's, having coined the term "Middle America" to describe Nixon's supporters. But in the spring of 1969 Kraft criticized Nixon's peace efforts, and in June John Ehrlichman, Nixon's counsel, arranged for Kraft's phone to be tapped. A "security consultant" to the Republican National Committee installed the warrantless wiretap (USHR 93b, p. 150). Kraft flew to Paris a week later to cover the Vietnam peace talks, and the tap was removed. But the Assistant Director of the FBI, William Sullivan, followed Kraft to Paris and arranged for further electronic surveillance (Sullivan 1969). The switching system of the hotel made it impossible to install a phone tap, so a microphone was placed in Kraft's room (USS 94e, p. 323). No evidence was ever found to support Ehrlichman's claim (Ehrlichman 1973) that Kraft was tapped for reasons of "national security." Indeed, in 1974, William Ruckelshaus, formerly a Deputy Attorney General and now Acting FBI Director, told Congress: "The justification would have been that [Kraft] was discussing with some—asking questions of some members of the North Vietnamese Government, representatives of the government. My own feeling is that this is just not an adequate national security justification for placing any kind of surveillance on an American citizen or newsman."[28] (Ruckelshaus 1974, pp. 320–321)

These wiretaps were ordered for national-security reasons, but summaries forwarded to the White House included such information as this:

> "meat was ordered [by the target's family] from a grocer," that the target's daughter had a toothache, that the target needed grass clippings for a compost heap he was building, that during a conversation between his wife and a friend, the two discussed "milk bills, hair, soap operas, and church" (FBI 1975b)

Although the FBI observed that this was "non-pertinent information" (USS 94e, p. 344), agents transcribed the conversations and faithfully sent the contents on to the White House. At least once the agents exercised some discretion. A wiretap on the home line of Henry Brandon, a *London Sunday Times* correspondent, picked up a conversation between the journalist's wife and her close friend Joan Kennedy, wife of Senator Ted Kennedy, in which Mrs. Kennedy discussed "problems with Teddy." The agent in charge said "I knew what those people would do with this stuff," and he destroyed the transcript (Hersh 1983, p. 324). President Nixon described the information he did receive as "gobs and gobs of stuff: gossip and bull" (USHR 93a, p. 1754).

Under Attorney General Mitchell, the FBI was empowered to collect political intelligence on the anti-war movement. On November 15, 1969, some 250,000 people marched on Washington in what the next day's *New York Times* described as "a great and peaceful army of dissent" (Herb 1969). Nine days earlier, Mitchell had approved an FBI request to wiretap the march's organizers.[29]

The excesses of the Nixon era were not limited to wiretaps. Tom

Huston, a White House staffer, had been put in charge of developing a report on the connection between domestic unrest and foreign movements and had devised a plan in which the resources of the Central Intelligence Agency, the Defense Intelligence Agency, the Federal Bureau of Investigation, and the National Security Agency were to be pooled to fight domestic unrest. NSA—contrary to law—would intercept communications of US citizens using international facilities. Rules regarding mail interception, electronic surveillance, and surreptitious entry would be relaxed. "Covert [mail] coverage is illegal, and there are serious risks involved," wrote Huston. "However, the advantages to be derived from its use outweigh the risks." (Huston 1970, p. 194) Regarding surreptitious entry, Huston wrote: "Use of this technique is clearly illegal: it amounts to burglary." (ibid., p. 195) Yet President Nixon approved the plan. Five days later—before it took effect—he rescinded his approval. That the Huston plan came within a hairsbreadth of being national policy shocked the nation when it was revealed several years later.

### The 1970s and the 1980s

The purpose of the FBI's Library Awareness Program, conducted between 1973 and 1988 at a number of public and university libraries,[30] was to investigate their use by foreigners. The FBI wanted to know about "Soviets [who] have come ... [with] unusual database requests" (Foerstal 1991, p. 56), about "computerized literature searches performed for library patrons," (ibid., p. 69), and about "reading habits of a visiting Russian student ... and anyone else 'similarly suspicious in nature'" (Robins 1988).

The FBI ran into trouble when it attempted to enlist librarians in surveillance. Librarians have a deep and abiding commitment to disseminating information, not protecting it. Librarians also strongly defend the privacy of their patrons. When the FBI sought to discover who was borrowing "unclassified, publicly available information relating more often than not to science and technical matters" (FBI 1987), many librarians would not comply with the informal requests and refused to release information about patrons without subpoenas. The American Library Association publicly opposed the Library Awareness Program. By 1989, most states had adopted laws making borrowers' records confidential (Foerstal 1991, p. 133).

When the Reagan administration came to power, a cornerstone of its foreign policy was support of the Duarte regime in El Salvador. The Committee in Solidarity with the People of El Salvador (CISPES) was a group of Americans who supported the opposition movement. In 1981 the FBI began an investigation of the Dallas chapter of CISPES to determine whether the group was in violation of the Foreign Agents Registration Act. It was not.

In 1983, using information supplied by an informant, the FBI began a second investigation of CISPES, this time focusing on the group's alleged connections with international terrorists. "The FBI undertook both photographic and visual surveillance of rallies, demonstrations, etc., in its investigations of CISPES," the bureau later reported. "This technique involved the taking of photographs during demonstrations, surveillance of rallies on college campuses, and attendance at a mass at a local university. The purpose of taking photographs during demonstrations was for use or future use in identifying CISPES leaders." (FBI 1989, p. 2) The bureau kept files on more than 2300 individuals and 1300 groups (ibid.). One source "provided the FBI a copy of another person's address list by gaining unconsented access to the desk where the address list was located." In another case, "FBI agents posing as potential home buyers toured the home of a subject of the investigation with a real estate agent" (ibid., pp. 5–6). The FBI expanded the investigation using long-distance telephone records of the Dallas chapter; agents added 13 CISPES offices to the list of those being probed, and the investigation grew.

There was no justification for these actions. The investigation was based on the words of an unreliable informant. CISPES was not a terrorist organization, nor was it allied with one. Testifying before Congress in 1988, FBI Director William Sessions said: "The broadening of the investigation in October 1983, in essence, directed all field offices to regard each CISPES chapter, wherever located, as a proper subject of investigation. Based on the documentation available to the FBI by October 1983, there was no reason ... to expand the investigation so widely." (Sessions, p. 122) Once again the privacy of Americans engaged in political protest had been violated.

The Senate investigating committee observed: "The CISPES case was a serious failure in FBI management, resulting in the investigation of domestic political activities that should not have come under governmental scrutiny. It raised issues that go to the heart of this country's commitments to the protection of constitutional rights. Unjustified investigations of political expression and dissent can have a debilitating effect upon our political system. When people see that this can happen, they become wary of associating with groups that disagree with the government and more wary of what they say or write. The impact is to undermine the effectiveness of popular self-government." (USS 101, p. 1)

## The 1990s

Other breaches of privacy have occurred despite safeguards. A recent government report noted that employees of the Internal Revenue Service's Data Retrieval System browsed the agency's database for information on accounts of "friends, neighbors, relatives and celebrities" (Edwards 1994).[31] Authorized users of the FBI's National Crime Information Center similarly misused that system (USGAO 1993a). These, of course, were only the activities that were discovered.

## Why Privacy?

Despite strictures to prevent abuses, the US government has invaded citizens' privacy many times over the last 50 years, in many different political situations, targeting individuals and political groups. Politicians have been wiretapped, and lawyers' confidential conversations with clients have been eavesdropped upon by FBI investigators.[32]

Sometimes invasion of privacy has been government policy; sometimes a breach has occurred because an individual within the government misappropriated collected information. The history of the last five decades shows that attacks on privacy are not an anomaly. When government has the power to invade privacy, abuses occur.

Conflict between protecting the security of the state and the privacy of its individuals is not new, but technology has given the state much more access to private information about individuals than it once had. As Justice Louis Brandeis so presciently observed in his dissenting opinion in *Olmstead*,

"in the application of a constitution, our contemplation cannot be only of what has been but of what may be." The progress of science in furnishing the government with means of espionage is not likely to stop with wiretapping. Ways may some day be developed by which the Government, without removing papers from secret drawers, can reproduce them in court, and by which it will be enabled to expose to a jury the most intimate occurrences of the home. Advances in the psychic and related sciences may bring means of exploring unexpressed beliefs, thoughts and emotions ... Can it be that the Constitution affords no protection against such invasions of individual security? (Brandeis 1928, p. 474)

Preservation of privacy is critical to a democratic political process. Change often begins most tentatively, and political discussion often starts in private. Journalists need to operate in private when cultivating sources. Attorneys cannot properly defend their clients if their communications are not privileged. As the Church Committee observed:

Personal privacy is protected because it is essential to liberty and the pursuit of happiness. Our Constitution checks the power of Government for the purpose of protecting the rights of individuals, in order that all our citizens may live in a free and decent society. Unlike totalitarian states, we do not believe that any government has a monopoly on truth.

When Government infringes those rights instead of nurturing and protecting them, the injury spreads far beyond the particular citizens targeted to untold numbers of other Americans who may be intimidated. (USS 94d, p. 290)

Persons most intimidated may well not be those at the extremes of the political spectrum, but rather those nearer the middle. Yet voices of moderation are vital to balance public debate and avoid polarization of our society (ibid., p. 291).

What type of society does the United States seek to be? The incarceration of Japanese-Americans during World War II began with an invasion of privacy and ended in the tyrannical disruption of many individual lives. Could the roundup of Japanese-Americans have occurred so easily if the Census Bureau's illegal cooperation had not made the process so efficient? The purpose of the Bill of Rights is to protect the rights of the people against the power of the government. In an era when technology makes the government ever more efficient, protection of these rights become ever more important.

Citizens of the former Eastern Bloc countries attest to the corruption of society that occurs when no thought or utterance is private. No one suggests that people living in the United States face imminent governmental infringements of this type, but in 1972 Congressional staffers wrote that "what separates military intelligence in the United States from its counterparts in totalitarian states, then, is not its capabilities, but its intentions" (USS 92b, p. 96). Electing officials we believe to be honest, trusting them to appoint officials who will be fair, and insulating the civil service from political abuse, we hope to fill the government with people of integrity. Recent history is replete with examples of abuse of power. Relying solely on intentions is dangerous for any society, and the Founding Fathers were careful to avoid it.

The right to be let alone is not realistic in modern society. But in a world that daily intrudes upon our personal space, privacy and confidentiality in discourse remain important to the human psyche. Thoughts and values still develop in the age-old traditions of talk, reflection, and argument, and trust and privacy are essential. Our conversations may be with people who are at a distance, and electronic media may transmit discussions that once might have occurred over a kitchen table or on a walk to work. But confidentiality—and the perception of confidentiality—are as necessary for the soul of mankind as bread is for the body.

# 7
# Wiretapping

*Wiretapping* is the traditional term for interception of telephone conversations. This should not be taken too literally. The word is no longer restricted to communications traveling by wire, and contemporary wiretaps are more commonly placed on radio links or inside telephone offices. The meaning has also broadened in that the thing being tapped need no longer be a telephone call in the classic sense; it may be some other form of electronic communication, such as fax or data.

Compared with the more precise but more general phrase "communications interception," the word "wiretapping" has two connotations. Much the stronger of these is that a wiretap is aimed at a particular target, in sharp contrast to the "vacuum cleaner" interception widely practiced by national intelligence agencies. The weaker connotation is that it is being done by the police.

The history of wiretapping in the United States is in fact two histories intertwined. It is a history of wiretapping per se—that is, a history of the installation and use of wiretaps by police, intelligence agencies, honest citizens, businesses, and criminals. It is also a history of society's legal response to wiretapping by these various groups.

The origins of wiretapping lie in two quite different practices: eavesdropping and letter opening. "Eavesdropping," although once more restricted in meaning,[1] has come to describe any attempt to overhear conversations without the knowledge of the participants. "Letter opening" takes in all acquisition, opening, reading, and copying of written messages, also without the knowledge of the sending and receiving parties. Telecommunication has unified and systematized these practices.

Before the electronic era, a conversation could only be carried on by people located within earshot of each other, typically a few feet apart. Neither advanced planning nor great effort on the part of the participants was required to ensure a high degree of security. Written communications were more vulnerable, but intercepting one was still a hit-or-miss affair. Messages traveled by a variety of postal services, couriers, travelers, and merchants. Politically sensitive messages, in particular, could not be counted on to go by predictable channels, so special couriers were sometimes employed.

And written messages enjoyed another sort of protection. Regardless of a spy's skill with flaps and seals, there was no guarantee that, if a letter was intercepted, opened, and read, the victim would not notice the intrusion. Since spying typically has to be done covertly in order to succeed, the chance of detection is a substantial deterrent.

Electronic communication has changed all this in three fundamental ways: it has made telecommunication too convenient to avoid; it has, despite appearances, reduced the diversity of channels by which written messages once traveled; and it has made the act of interception invisible to the target.

Conversation by telephone has achieved an almost equal footing with face-to-face conversation. It is impossible today to run a successful business without the telephone, and eccentric even to attempt to do without the telephone in private life. The telephone provides a means of communication so effective and convenient that even people who are aware of the danger of being overheard routinely put aside their caution and use it to convey sensitive information.

As the number of channels of communication has increased (there are now hundreds of communication companies, with myriad fibers, satellites, and microwave links), the diversity of communication paths has diminished. In the days of oxcart and sail, there was no registry of the thousands of people willing to carry a message in return for a tip from the recipient. Today, telecommunications carriers must be registered with national and local regulatory bodies and are well known to trade associations and industry watch groups. Thus, interception has become more systematic. Spies, no longer faced with a patchwork of ad hoc couriers, know better where to look for what they seek.

Perhaps more important, interception of telecommunications leaves no telltale "marks on the envelope." It is inherent in telecommunication—and inseparable from its virtues—that the sender and the receiver of a message have no way of telling who else may have recorded a copy.

Any discussion of wiretapping, particularly a legal discussion, is complicated by the fact that electronics has not only made interception of telecommunications possible; it has also made it easier to "bug" face-to-face conversations. Bugging would be nearly irrelevant to the central subject of this book—cryptography and secure telecommunications—were it not for the fact that bugs and wiretaps are inseparably intertwined in law and jurisprudence and named by one collective term: *electronic surveillance*.

Wiretaps and bugs are powerful investigative tools. They allow the eavesdropper to overhear conversations between politicians, criminals, lawyers, or lovers without the targets' knowing that their words are being shared with unwanted listeners. Electronic surveillance is a tool that can detect criminal conspiracies and provide prosecutors with strong evidence—the conspirators' incriminating statements in their own voices —all without danger to law-enforcement officers. On the other hand, the very invisibility on which electronic surveillance depends for its effectiveness makes it evasive of oversight and readily adaptable to malign uses.[2] Electronic surveillance can be and has been used by those in power to undermine the democratic process by spying on their political opponents. In light of this, it is not surprising that Congress and the courts have approached wiretapping and bugging with suspicion.

Today, communication enjoys a measure of protection under US law, and neither government agents nor private citizens are permitted to wiretap at will. This has not always been the case. The current view—that wiretaps are a kind of search—has evolved by fits and starts over a century and a half. The Supreme Court ruled in 1967 that the police may not employ wiretaps without court authorization. Congress has embraced this principle, limiting police use of wiretaps and setting standards for the granting of warrants. The same laws prohibit most wiretapping by private citizens.

The rules against unwarranted wiretapping are not absolute, however. For example, the courts ruled in 1992 (*United States v. David Lee Smith,*

978 F. 2nd 171, US App) that conversations over cordless phones were not protected and that police tapping of cordless phones did not require a search warrant. A 1994 statute (Communications Assistance for Law Enforcement Act of 1994, Public Law 103-414, §202) extended the warrant requirements of the earlier law to cover cordless phones. The law also makes some exceptions for businesses intercepting the communications of their own employees on company property.

### Constitutional Protection

Protection for the privacy of communications stems primarily from the Fourth Amendment to the US Constitution. Epitomizing the underlying principle of the Bill of Rights—that individual citizens need protection against the power of the state—the Fourth Amendment asserts "the right of the people to be secure in their persons, houses, papers, and effects, against unreasonable searches and seizures."

The Fourth Amendment was a response to the British writs of assistance, which empowered officers of the Crown to search "wherever they suspected uncustomed goods to be" and to "break open any receptacle or package falling under their suspecting eye" (Lassen 1937, p. 54). In framing the laws of the new nation, the founders sought to avoid creating such unrestricted governmental powers. However, they also recognized that since criminals try to hide the evidence of their crimes, law-enforcement officials must have the power to conduct searches. The Fourth Amendment thus allows searches, but restricts them, specifying that "no Warrants shall issue, but upon probable cause, supported by Oath or affirmation, and particularly describing the place to be searched and the persons or things to be seized."

As written, the Fourth Amendment, protects citizens against invasions of property. Although strongly suggested by the phrase "secure in their persons, houses, papers, and effects," the word 'privacy' is never used. The view that the Fourth Amendment protects things less tangible than property has taken more than a century to develop.

### Wiretaps of the Nineteenth Century

When the telegraph joined the covered wagon and the stagecoach as a channel of long-distance communication, wiretapping followed quickly.

During the Civil War, General Jeb Stuart traveled with his own tapper. In California in 1864, a former stockbroker obtained market information by intercepting telegraph messages; he was prosecuted for violating a surprisingly early California statute against wiretapping (Dash et al. 1959, p. 23).

The convenience of voice communication made it obvious that intercepted telephone calls would be a rich source of information. In 1899 the *San Francisco Call* accused a rival, the *San Francisco Examiner*, of wiretapping conversations between the *Call* and its reporters and stealing the *Call*'s exclusives. The 1905 California legislature, responded by extending an 1862 law prohibiting telegraph wiretapping to telephones (ibid., pp. 25–26).

The first tapping of telephones by police occurred in the early 1890s in New York City. An 1892 state law had made telephone tapping a felony, but New York policemen believed that the law did not apply to them and employed wiretaps anyway (ibid., p. 35). In 1916 the mayor of New York was found to have authorized wiretapping of some Catholic priests in connection with a charity-fraud investigation, despite the fact that none of the priests were suspected of participating in the illegal activity (New York Times 1916). The state legislature discovered that the police had the ability to tap any line of the New York Telephone Company. Using this power with abandon, the police had listened in on confidential conversations between lawyers and their clients, and between physicians and their patients. The *New York Times* reported that "in some cases the trunk lines of hotels were tapped and the conversations of all hotel guests listened to" (ibid.).

During this period, the federal government played no legislative role— except during World War I, when concern that enemy agents would tap phone lines led to a federal Anti-Wiretap Statute (40 Stat. 1017, 1918). After the war, law-enforcement agencies began to find wiretapping increasingly valuable. Wiretapping is said to have been the most frequently used tool for catching bootleggers during Prohibition (Dash et al. 1959, p. 28).

### The *Olmstead* Decision

As was mentioned in chapter 6, Roy Olmstead was caught running a $2 million-a-year bootlegging operation during Prohibition. Convicted partially on the basis of evidence obtained from warrantless wiretaps installed by federal agents, Olmstead appealed, and the case made its way to the US Supreme Court.

Though closely divided, the Court ruled that the evidence obtained by tapping the defendants' phone calls had not involved any trespass into their homes or offices. According to the Court: "There was no searching.... The evidence was secured by the use of ... hearing and that only...." (*Olmstead v. United States*, 277 US 438, 1928, p. 464) Five justices agreed that the Fourth Amendment protected tangibles alone, that conversation was an intangible, and that therefore using the evidence from the wiretaps did not constitute unreasonable search and seizure.

In his dissenting opinion in the *Olmstead* case (which has become one of the most quoted of judicial opinions), Justice Louis Brandeis argued that protections provided by the Bill of Rights should operate in a world of electronic communications. In 1928 the telephone was already necessary for commerce and was rapidly becoming an integral part of daily life. Brandeis described the threat that wiretapping posed to privacy:

> Whenever a telephone line is tapped, the privacy of the persons at both ends of the line is invaded, and all conversations between them upon any subject, and although proper, confidential and privileged, may be overheard. Moreover, the tapping of one man's telephone line involves the tapping of the telephone of every other person whom he may call, or who may call him. As a means of espionage, writs of assistance and general warrants are but puny instruments of tyranny and oppression when compared with wiretapping. (Brandeis 1928, pp. 475–476)

Despite his eloquence, Brandeis's viewpoint did not carry the Court. There was widespread consternation over the Court's ruling, but although there were several attempts to do so, Congress did not make wiretapping illegal.

### The *Nardone* Cases

In 1934, Congress passed the Federal Communications Act (FCA), which placed jurisdiction over radio and wire communications in the hands of the newly created Federal Communications Commission and established a regulatory framework that has dominated American telecommunications ever since. The FCA prohibited the "interception and divulgence" of wire communications. Although its wording was quite similar to that of the Radio Act of 1927 (the law in effect at the time of the *Olmstead* case), the Supreme Court used the FCA to reverse *Olmstead*.

In *Olmstead*, the Court had ruled on constitutional grounds and had found warrantless wiretaps legal. A decade later, it considered the case of Frank Carmine Nardone, another accused bootlegger. This time, the Court ruled on the basis of the new law and held that information from wiretaps placed by federal agents was not admissible as evidence (*Nardone v. United States*, 302 US 379, 1937).

Two years later Nardone was back. Having been convicted in a new trial that used evidence derived from the warrantless wiretaps, Nardone appealed, arguing that the evidence should not be admissible. The Court concurred and held that information even indirectly derived from wire-taps could not be used as evidence (*Nardone v. United States*, 308 US 338, 1939). The same day, in a different case, the Supreme Court ruled that the FCA applied to federal wiretapping of intrastate as well as interstate communications (*Weiss v. United States*, 302 US 321, 1939). In response to these decisions, Attorney General Robert Jackson ordered a halt to FBI wiretapping.

These decisions appeared to prohibit wiretapping by federal law-enforcement agencies, but the prohibition was overtaken by events and quickly eroded.

## Evidence versus Intelligence

With the start of World War II, FBI Director J. Edgar Hoover, citing the danger of spies and other subversives, pressed to have Attorney General Robert Jackson's anti-wiretapping order overturned (Morgenthau, May 21, 1940). In view of the Supreme Court's *Nardone* decisions, this would take some fancy footwork. But, under Jackson, the Department of Justice had interpreted the *Nardone* decisions to mean that it was unlawful to both "intercept" *and* "divulge" communications, and had decided that it was not unlawful to intercept communications as long as the contents were kept within the federal government (USS 94e, p. 278).

Hoover urged President Roosevelt to authorize wiretapping for what we have come to call national-security purposes. The president acceded to Hoover's request, but his order stopped short of giving the FBI blanket approval to wiretap:

> I am convinced that the Supreme Court never intended any dictum in the particular case which it decided to apply to grave matters involving the defense of the nation....
>
> You are therefore authorized and directed in such cases as you may approve, after investigation of the need in each case, to authorize the necessary investigative agencies that they are at liberty to secure information by listening devices ... of persons suspected of subversive activities against the government of the United States, including suspected spies. You are requested furthermore to limit these investigations so conducted to a minimum and to limit them insofar as possible to aliens. (Roosevelt 1940)

Jackson, who wanted no part in wiretapping, made a fateful decision in response to the presidential directive: he instructed Hoover to maintain the records of all wiretaps, listing times, places, and cases (Theoharis and Cox 1988, p. 171). In so doing, Jackson effectively permitted the FBI to use wiretapping, free of Department of Justice oversight.

In 1941, Francis Biddle, the succeeding Attorney General, wrested back control of wiretaps from Hoover and turned down applications he felt were unjustified (Biddle 1941; USS 94d, p. 37). In 1952, Attorney General J. Howard McGrath, in a letter to Hoover supporting the use of wiretaps "under the present highly restrictive basis," made explicit the requirement that all FBI wiretaps required the attorney general's prior approval (McGrath 1952). However, McGrath did not undo the custom that surveillance orders operated without time limits. Only in 1965, when Attorney General Nicholas Katzenbach recommended that authorizations be limited to 6 months (Hoover 1965), did the FBI change its practice.

In 1940 and 1941, several bills that attempted to establish a legal basis for electronic surveillance were introduced in Congress. One of these was endorsed by Roosevelt and Jackson (USS 94e, p. 280), but Hoover opposed any legislation requiring warrants for wiretapping (Hoover 1941) and no legislation passed.

When the war ended, Hoover sought and received continued wiretapping authority from President Harry Truman. Indeed, the power was broadened. In his reauthorization request to Attorney General Thomas

Clark, Hoover omitted the final sentence of Roosevelt's original memo, which had required that electronic surveillance be kept to a minimum and limited "insofar as possible to aliens" (Gentry 1991, p. 324). Clark forwarded the amended memo and urged Truman to approve wiretapping in cases "vitally affecting domestic security, or where human life is in jeopardy," and Truman apparently signed it without being aware of the shift from earlier policies (Clark 1946).

In time Truman's aides discovered the change. A 1950 memo to Truman from George Elsey, assistant counsel to the president, reported that "not only did Clark fail to inform the President that Mr. Roosevelt had directed the FBI to hold its wiretapping to a minimum ... he requested the President to approve very broad language [that was] a very far cry from the 1940 directive" (Elsey 1950). Truman, however, took no action to rescind the expanded authority. The new authorization meant that national security was no longer the sole justification for wiretaps (Clark 1946).

By adding "domestic security" to the list of reasons for which wiretapping could be employed, Clark's memo substantially broadened Roosevelt's directive. Developing intelligence is quite different from collecting evidence. In particular, intelligence investigations have less narrowly defined goals than criminal investigations. Developing intelligence is neither attempting to find evidence of a specific crime nor developing a case against a specific suspect. Rather, it is attempting to discern a pattern of behavior: What is the structure of an organization? What are its goals? What are its methods?

Those who work in intelligence emphasize the degree to which they operate under legal restraints intended to protect the rights of Americans. Yet the very character of intelligence work makes it unlikely that these restraints weigh as heavily on them as on criminal investigators. Intelligence officers don't go into court to face opposing attorneys. Criminal investigations are unsuccessful without convictions. Intelligence investigations— even in counterintelligence, where prosecution is sometimes appropriate —can be deemed successful even if no prosecutions occur. The changes Clark made were thus quite significant. They moved wiretap investigations into a shadowy area where, by and large, they were protected from public scrutiny.

Since the two *Nardone* rulings made both evidence from federal wire-taps and evidence tainted by federal wiretaps inadmissible in court, the Department of Justice believed that if wiretapping had been used in a case, it could not prosecute. This eventually gave rise to an elaborate FBI methodology for concealing evidence of wiretapping.

In 1949, Judith Coplon, a Department of Justice employee, was caught as she was about to hand over 28 confidential FBI documents to Valentin Gubitchev, a Soviet employed by the United Nations. Hoover sought to prevent the documents—which revealed FBI wiretapping of Coplon—from appearing at Coplon's trial, but the judge ruled that the government had to release copies to the court. Fearing public disclosure of the FBI's wiretapping practices, Hoover tried to persuade the attorney general to drop the charges against Coplon, but without success. Hoover responded with new procedures regarding wiretapping. FBI reports of "highly confidential" sources, including wiretaps, would not be included in the main case files; instead they would be kept in especially confidential files (FBI 1949).[3]

A second trial revealed that Coplon herself had been wiretapped, despite denials by an agent who turned out to have read the transcripts. Hoover then went to even greater lengths to hide the paper trail between wiretaps and their logs. Agents working on a case were kept in the dark about any associated wiretaps so that they could not even accidentally reveal wiretap information in court. Hoover accomplished this by disguising information derived from wiretaps when it appeared in the case files. He was largely successful in this strategy, but he hoped for looser rules regarding wiretaps.

In 1954, President Dwight Eisenhower's attorney general, Herbert Brownell, was pressing for legislation to permit warrantless wiretapping as an aid in prosecuting communists. "You can't trust a Communist to tell the truth on the witness stand," Brownell (1954a, p. 202) argued, "and you can't trust the courts not to leak information about wiretap applications." Brownell was frustrated because there was "evidence in the hands of the Department as a result of investigations conducted by the FBI which would prove espionage in certain ... cases." He argued that a change in the wiretap law would enable the Department of Justice to prosecute certain cases that it was currently prevented from pursuing (ibid., p. 203).

The House Judiciary Committee accepted Brownell's argument and recommended passage of legislation permitting warrantless wiretapping, but the full House of Representatives disagreed (USS 94e, p. 284). The legislation was amended to require a warrant, but this version did not receive support from the Department of Justice and died (ibid.). Although Congress periodically considered legislation on wiretapping, there were no new federal laws on the subject until the 1960s.

Meanwhile, as a result of the Federal Communications Act's prohibition against "interception and divulgence" of wired communications, wiretaps were useless as court evidence. As Attorney General Nicholas Katzenbach put it to Congress in 1965:

> I think perhaps the record ought to show that when you talk national security cases, they are not really cases, because as I have said repeatedly, once you put a wiretap on or an illegal device of any kind, the possibilities of prosecution are gone. It is just like a grant of immunity.... I have dismissed cases or failed to bring cases within that area because some of the information did come from wiretaps. But here we feel that the intelligence and the preventive aspect outweigh the desirability of prosecution in rare and exceptional circumstances. (USS 89, p. 1163)

In 1950, and again in 1953, presidential directives authorized the FBI to investigate "subversive activity" (USS 94d, p. 45). Since these directives failed to provide guidelines for such investigations, the FBI took a very broad view of what constituted subversive activity. Surveillance, often including wiretapping and electronic bugging, was not limited to those suspected of crimes or even to detecting suspected criminal activities.

Though many other types of domestic activities were the targets of surveillance, Hoover stressed the danger of Communist subversion, and the FBI collected intelligence about the influence of Communists in a variety of categories, including "political activities, Negro question, youth matters, women's matters, farmers' matters, veterans' matters" (FBI 1960a).

Believing that the growing civil rights movement was Communist inspired and would lead to violence, Hoover kept it under careful observation. In 1956 he briefed a cabinet meeting about the Communists' "efforts" and "plans" to influence the movement. This briefing demonstrates how far the FBI overreached its mandate in internal security investigations. Not limiting his discussion to the possibility of violence, Hoover went on to present to the cabinet the legislative strategy of the NAACP and "the activities of Southern Governors and Congressmen on behalf of groups opposing integration peacefully" (FBI 1956).

Permission to conduct investigations of domestic "subversive activity" without restraint gave the FBI free rein in collecting wide-ranging domestic intelligence. The FBI's choice of electronic surveillance as the means for doing this allowed it to keep its activities hidden and uncontrolled for a long time. An official of the Nation of Islam was wiretapped for 8 years without any efforts to prosecute him for illegal activities (Hoover 1956), and the Socialist Workers Party was the target of FBI wiretaps and bugs for 20 years.

The extent of the FBI's wiretapping under J. Edgar Hoover has never been clear.[4] Although Congress received annual testimony from Hoover, it was unable to discover how much wiretapping was actually occurring, since the figures Hoover gave did not include the taps installed by field agents on their own or the taps installed by local police at the FBI's request.

Hoover kept the transcripts of wiretaps—many of them hidden in obscure files—even when they revealed no evidence of criminal activity. Since wiretaps on suspected spies and organized crime figures sometimes picked up conversations with politicians or other influential people, Hoover developed a mass of material with great political value. This is how he ended up with transcripts of intimate conversations between John Kennedy and Inga Arvad, a Danish reporter and former Miss Europe who had visited Germany for social functions with high Third Reich officials, including Hitler. The FBI was investigating allegations that Arvad was a German spy (Anderson 1996a, pp. 48–52). The investigation itself may have been legitimate. The recordings were made during the World War II, while Kennedy was a Naval officer. Nonetheless, although the investigation produced no evidence of espionage, recordings of his pillow talk with Arvad were still in the FBI files when Kennedy became president nearly 20 years later.

It is believed that, without any pretense of investigating criminal activities, Hoover wiretapped senators and congressmen.[5] It is known that he wiretapped various Supreme Court justices.[6] The existence of extensive records on political figures was well known, and these files ensured that Hoover got much of what he wanted. Congress exercised little oversight of the FBI's affairs, wiretapping included.

One example is particularly illustrative of the way in which Hoover was able to use the FBI's investigative powers to protect its interests. In 1965, a Senate subcommittee undertook an investigation of electronic surveillance and mail covers. The FBI, a major focus of this review, was concerned. One FBI memo noted: "Senator Long ... has been taking testimony in connection with mail covers, wiretapping, and various snooping devices on the part of federal agencies. He cannot be trusted." (Jones 1965) Two high-ranking Bureau officials met with Edward Long (the chairman of the subcommittee) and a committee counsel. There is no indication that there were any briefings of other subcommittee members, nor is there any reason to believe that during the 90-minute meeting Long was told any details of FBI electronic surveillance, such as the bugging of a congressman's hotel room during the sugar lobby investigations (see below), the bugging and wiretapping of Martin Luther King, or the wiretapping of a congressional staffer, two newspaper reporters, and an editor of an anti-Communist newsletter (USS 94e, p. 309). The FBI men suggested that the senator issue a statement saying that he had held lengthy conferences with FBI officials and was now completely satisfied "that the FBI had never participated in uncontrolled usage of wiretaps or microphones and that FBI usage of such devices has been completely justified in all cases" (DeLoach 1966a). When Long said that he did not know how to write such a press release, the FBI officials said they would be happy to do so—and they did (ibid.).

The Long Subcommittee chose not to hold hearings on FBI electronic-surveillance practices. An internal FBI memo noted: "While we have neutralized the threat of being embarrassed by the Long Subcommittee, we have not eliminated certain dangers which might be created as a result of newspaper pressures on Long. We therefore must keep on top of this situation at all times." (DeLoach 1966b) The FBI's determination to control such investigations can be inferred from the fact that it maintained files on all members of the subcommittee (USS 94c, p. 477).

A year later Senator Long again took up the fight, introducing a bill to limit FBI electronic surveillance to national-security cases. Hoover was not pleased. Shortly afterwards *Life* broke a story that the senator had received $48,000 from Morris Shenker, Jimmy Hoffa's counsel (Lambert 1967). The article intimated that the money was a bribe to prevent or reverse charges against the Teamsters' leader. The senator's career ended, and his electronic-surveillance bill died.

Hoover remained firmly in power through eight presidencies and 48 years. His long tenure as director is now recognized as a period during which the FBI routinely engaged in the sort of widespread political surveillance usually associated with totalitarian regimes.

In part Hoover's control came about because of abdication of responsibility by other members of the government. Truman's 1946 authorization of wiretaps in investigating subversive activities required the attorney general to authorize their use. There were, however, many occasions on which an attorney general was informed of the wiretaps only after they had been installed (USS 94d, p. 63). In 1965, under a directive from President Johnson, Attorney General Katzenbach tightened requirements for electronic surveillance. By then Johnson opposed wiretapping except in cases of national security, and in a directive that went out to heads of agencies he wrote: "In my view, the invasion of privacy of communications is a highly offensive practice which should be engaged in only where the national security is at stake." (Johnson 1965) Installation of bugs now needed written approval from the attorney general, and both bugs and wiretaps were subject to 6-month time limits, after which new authorization from the attorney general was required (USS 94d, p. 105).

Even with the tightened restrictions, the Department of Justice did not feel that it controlled the FBI's use of wiretapping. In 1972, former Attorney General Ramsey Clark told a judge: "Reports by FBI agents on electronic surveillance had caused the Department [of Justice] 'deep embarrassment' many times. Often we would go to court and say that there had been no electronic surveillance and then we would find out we had been wrong. Often you could not find out what was going on ... frequently agents lost the facts." (Theoharis 1974, p. 342)

The FBI was not the only law-enforcement agency to engage in wire-tapping without regard for the views of legislators and judges. State police also wiretapped, sometimes legally, sometimes not.

Wiretapping was made illegal in Illinois in 1927, but Chicago's police intelligence unit ignored the law. The police saw no reason to try and change the legislation; the effort would only raise controversy. They merely continued wiretapping, aware that their actions were illegal (Dash et al. 1959, p. 222).

In California, wiretaps were similarly banned, but the police there took a different tack. When law-enforcement officers wanted to do a wiretap investigation, they would hire a private investigator, who was told to deny any official connections if caught in the act of tapping (ibid., pp. 164–165).

Even in states that permitted police wiretapping, numbers could be misleading. Official records in the State of New York showed fewer than 3000 wiretap orders for the period between 1950 and 1955. A careful study by Samuel Dash and his two co-authors led to different conclusions. They observed that the official figures omitted wiretaps installed by plain-clothesmen. Those numbers were surprisingly large. Dash et al. (ibid., p. 68) concluded that for every 10 wiretaps installed by plainclothesmen who had obtained court orders, another 90 taps were installed without court authorization. This interpretation would indicate that the New York police performed between 16,000 and 29,000 thousand wiretaps a year.

Oddly enough, in Massachusetts, a state with a particularly liberal wiretapping law that required only written permission from the attorney general or the district attorney, the Boston Police Department did not use wiretaps in criminal investigations. The public was opposed to it, and the police believed wiretapping was a "dirty business" to which "only a lazy police department" would resort (Dash et al. 1959, p. 147).

## Wiretaps versus Bugs

Microphone surveillance and wiretapping play similar investigative roles. But the Federal Communications Act said nothing about microphone surveillances, and the *Nardone* decisions therefore left such bugging legal.

Although ultimately the Supreme Court whittled away at the warrantless use of electronic bugs, its early decisions condoned the practice.

In 1942 the Supreme Court ruled that it was legally permissible for law-enforcement officers to plant a bugging device on a wall adjoining that of a suspect's office (*Goldman v. United States,* 316 US 129). In 1954 it upheld a state court conviction based on evidence obtained by microphones concealed in walls of the defendants' homes during warrantless break-ins by the police (*Irvine v. California,* 347 US 128).

In *Irvine,* in sharp contrast to later decisions, the Supreme Court ruled that, because the case in question had been a state prosecution within a state court, the conviction could stand. Members of the Court were disturbed, however, by violations of the Fourth and Fifth Amendments. The bug had been placed in a bedroom, and the justices were deeply offended by the invasion of privacy. Attorney General Herbert Brownell "clarified" policy for J. Edgar Hoover, warning that the language of the Court "indicates certain uses of microphones which it would be well to avoid" because "the Justices of the Supreme Court were outraged by what they regarded as the indecency of installing a microphone in the bedroom" (Brownell 1954b).

In 1961, in *Julius Silverman et al. v. United States* (365 US 505), the Supreme Court changed its direction, holding that a search occurred whenever a bug was used, even if the walls of the target's apartment had not been breached. The case arose when District of Columbia police, suspecting that gambling was taking place in a row house, pushed a foot-long "spike mike" into a space under the suspect's apartment from the vacant house next door. The spike hit a solid object (most likely a heating duct), which "became in effect a giant microphone" (ibid., p. 509). Telephone conversations were picked up from the room above, amplified, and taped. The Court held that, in the absence of a search warrant, the evidence was inadmissible. In the *Nardone* cases, the Court had ruled on the narrow basis of the FCA. In *Silverman,* it brushed away these technicalities ("In these circumstances we need not pause to consider whether or not there was a technical trespass under the local property law relating to party walls." (ibid., p. 511)) and ruled on the basis of the Fourth Amendment. With this decision, the Court began moving in the direction of constitutional protection against warrantless electronic surveillance.

In 1967, the Supreme Court established the doctrine of "legitimate expectation of privacy." In *Charles Katz v. United States*, (389 US 347) the Court determined that evidence obtained from a warrantless electronic bug placed in a public phone booth was inadmissible:

> ... [W]hat [Katz] sought to exclude when he entered the [telephone] booth was not the intruding eye—it was the uninvited ear.... No less than an individual in a business office, in a friend's apartment, or in a taxicab, a person in a telephone booth may rely upon the protection of the Fourth Amendment. One who occupies it, shuts the door behind him, and pays the toll that permits him to place a call is surely entitled to assume that the words he utters into the mouthpiece will not be broadcast to the world. To read the Constitution more narrowly is to ignore the vital role that the public telephone has come to play in private communication. (ibid., pp. 511–512)
>
> ... Wherever a man may be, he is entitled to know that he will remain free from unreasonable searches and seizures. (ibid., p. 515)

With this decision, the Supreme Court changed the doctrine underlying US wiretap law. Unlike the *Nardone* decisions, which relied on statutory interpretation, *Katz* is based on underlying principles of the Constitution. In ruling that electronic bugging was illegal without a search warrant, the Supreme Court arrived at the current view of bugs and wiretaps as a form of search: that they are permissible, but subject to the limitations and protections laid down in the Fourth Amendment.

## Wiretapping and Organized Crime

When asked to explain the need for wiretapping, police often cite organized crime as the principal application. In order to attack organized crime, police must find a way of penetrating the tightly knit organizations. This is not easy. The difficulty is compounded by the fact that "the core of organized crime activity is the supplying of illegal goods and services ... to countless numbers of citizen customers" (President's Commission on Law Enforcement 1967, p. 187), and the consensual nature of these crimes means that "law enforcement lacks its staunchest ally, the victim" (Duke and Gross 1993, p. 107). Organized crime is particularly effective in using the code of *omerta*—silence—to keep its participants and its victims from speaking to law-enforcement agents (ibid., p. 198). A common police response has been the use of electronic surveillance. The 1967 *Katz* decision took this tool from the police just as the visibility of organized crime was increasing.

Organized crime had been a force in American society for years. With the repeal of Prohibition, it had shifted its activities from bootlegging into gambling, loansharking, and control of legitimate businesses, including garbage disposal, garment manufacturing, real estate, restaurants, vending machines, and waterfront activities (ibid., p. 195). Yet between the 1930s and the 1950s the FBI pursued bank robbers, kidnappers, auto thieves, and the Communist Party, but not organized crime (although from time to time individual members of crime "families" made their way into the FBI's net).

There are various theories as to why J. Edgar Hoover ignored organized crime's very existence for some 30 years. It may be that any concerted federal effort would have involved the FBI in interagency cooperation, something that the turf-conscious Hoover abhorred. It may be that an investigation of organized crime would have been a drawn-out affair that would not have yielded the statistics on criminals caught and property recovered that were the "heart and soul" of Hoover's annual speech before the Senate Appropriations Committee (Sullivan 1979, pp. 117–118). It may be that investigating organized crime would have risked corruption of the investigators to a much greater extent than other types of criminal investigation.

### Organized Crime Becomes Visible

Sergeant Edgar Croswell, a New York State trooper, Robert Kennedy, Attorney General under his brother John, and Joseph Valachi, a 60-year-old "soldato" in the Genovese crime family, brought organized crime to the nation's attention in the late 1950s and the early 1960s.

On Saturday November 15, 1957, Sergeant Croswell was doing his morning rounds in Apalachin, a small village in the Southern Tier of New York State, near Pennsylvania, when he discovered limousine after black limousine turning into the country estate of Joseph Barbara, a bottler and distributor of soft drinks in nearby Endicott. His suspicion aroused, Croswell set up a roadblock near the estate to check for vehicle identification—a legal search under the state laws. Many of the crime bosses fled, but 67 of them were identified—some through the roadblock, others through various forms of carelessness, including registering under their own names at hotels in the area. The next day, the nation awoke to headlines like "Royal Clambake for Underworld Cooled by Police" and "Police Ponder NY Mob Meeting; All Claim They Were Visiting Sick Friend."

In 1961 Robert Kennedy became US attorney general. Five years earlier, while counsel to the Senate Select Committee on Improper Activities in the Labor or Management Field, Kennedy had investigated labor racketeering and had uncovered ties between the unions and organized crime. When he became attorney general, Kennedy made organized crime a priority (Lewis 1961). Congress soon passed legislation that Kennedy had requested to fight organized crime (New York Times 1961).

In 1963, Joseph Valachi broke the code of silence that had made investigations of organized crime so unrewarding. Imprisoned for heroin trafficking, Valachi killed a man whom he believed had been sent to assassinate him in jail. Soured by the belief that the "family" had tried to have him "hit" and facing murder charges for defending himself, Valachi turned government witness and began to talk. In the Senate's staid hearing rooms, Valachi laid out the complex system of bosses, soldiers, and international links that characterized organized crime. Charts describing the succession of gang control in the New York area graced the walls. The information was shocking to those who had been repeatedly told by the FBI's director that organized crime did not exist.

The combined effect was to transform organized crime from a myth to a priority in federal eyes. The government concluded that its involvement was crucial in working against organized crime because criminal networks flourished largely as a result of corruption in local police forces. In the words of Ramsey Clark, Kennedy's successor as attorney general: "The presence of any significant organized crime necessarily means that local criminal justice has been corrupted to some degree." (Clark 1970) Furthermore, because the criminal organizations spanned state borders, nationwide coordination of investigations was viewed as crucial.

By 1966, even J. Edgar Hoover had caught up on organized crime. Testifying before the House Subcommittee on Appropriations, Hoover said: "La Cosa Nostra is the largest organization of the criminal underworld in this country, very closely organized and strictly disciplined." (Carroll 1967)

### Title III: Wiretaps Made Legal

In their report on the Valachi hearings, members of the Senate Governmental Operations Committee called for legislation authorizing wiretapping. Their view was echoed by a presidential commission on law enforcement: "A majority of the members of the Commission believe that legislation should be enacted granting carefully circumscribed authority for electronic surveillance to law enforcement officers. . . ." (President's Commission on Law Enforcement 1967, p. 203)

Not all experts agreed with the commission's conclusions. Attorney General Clark prohibited all use of wiretaps by federal law-enforcement officers. He told Congress: "I know of no Federal conviction based upon any wiretapping or electronic surveillance, and there have been a lot of big ones. . . . I also think that we make cases effectively without wiretapping or electronic surveillance. I think it may well be that with the commitment of the same manpower to other techniques, even more convictions could be secured, because in terms of manpower, wiretapping, and electronic surveillance is very expensive." (Clark 1967, p. 320) Clark pointed out that in 1967, without using wiretaps, federal strike forces had obtained indictments against organized crime figures in nine states, and that "each strike force has obtained more indictments in its target city than all federal indictments in the nation against organized crime in as recent a year as 1960" (ibid., pp. 79–80).

In 1965, the Chief Judge of the US District Court in Northern Illinois, William Campbell, told Congress of his strong disapproval of wiretaps: "My experiences have produced in me a complete repugnance, opposition, and disapproval of wiretapping, regardless of circumstances. This invasion of privacy, too often an invasion of the privacy of innocent individuals, is not justified. In every case I know of where wiretapping has been used, the case could have been made without the use of the wiretap. Wiretapping in my opinion is mainly a crutch or shortcut used by inefficient or lazy investigators." (USS 90, p. 1495)

Detroit's police commissioner, Ray Girardin, was also opposed to wiretapping: "I feel that [wiretapping] is an outrageous tactic and that it is not necessary and has no place in law enforcement. . . . [T]he only exception to this that I would entertain at this time would be in a situation where

the security of the nation has to be protected against an outside power."
(Girardin)

At other times, in other places, other officials had denounced wiretapping. A 1961 congressional survey revealed that the attorneys general of California, Delaware, Missouri, and New Mexico opposed federal laws permitting wiretapping (USS 87, pp. 545, 547, 554, and 560). Daniel Ward, State's Attorney for Cook County, Illinois, testified in 1961: "I do not think that one can honestly say that wiretapping is a *sine qua non* of effective law enforcement." (Ward 1961)

Ramsey Clark's opposition was sustained by President Johnson, who proposed to Congress in 1967 that wiretapping be limited to national-security cases and that it be performed only by federal officials (*Congressional Quarterly Weekly* 1967, p. 222). But in the aftermath of the Crime Commission's report, and during a time of domestic unrest (riots in the ghettos, the Vietnam War protests, and several political assassinations), Congress saw the issues differently. Despite the lack of unanimity, even among police, Congress chose to legalize wiretapping as a tool for law-enforcement investigations in criminal cases. Title III of the Omnibus Crime Control and Safe Streets Act of 1968 (18 USC §2510–2521) established the basic law for interceptions performed in criminal investigations: wiretaps are limited to the crimes specified in the act—a list including murder, kidnapping, extortion, gambling, counterfeiting, and sale of marijuana. The Judiciary Committee made clear that organized crime was a central motivation for Title III.[7]

In order to conform to the standards of the Fourth Amendment, Congress required law enforcement to obtain a warrant before initiating a wiretap.[8] To receive a court order, an investigator draws up an affidavit showing that there is probable cause to believe that the targeted communication device—whether a phone, a fax, or a computer[9]—is being used to facilitate a crime. A government attorney prepares an application for a court order, and approval must be granted by a member of the Department of Justice at least at the level of Deputy Assistant Attorney General.

Observing that "wiretaps and eavesdrops are potentially more penetrating, less discriminating, and less visible than ordinary searches," Congress decided that review of the application by a federal district court judge was in order (National Commission 1976, p. 12). The judge must determine that (i) there is probable cause to believe that an individual is committing or is about to commit an indictable offense; (ii) there is probable cause to believe that communications about the offense will be obtained through the interception; (iii) normal investigative procedures have been tried and either have failed, appear unlikely to succeed, or are too dangerous; and (iv) there is probable cause to believe that the facilities subject to surveillance are being used or will be used in the commission of the crime. Only if all these criteria are satisfied will a judge approve a wiretap order.[10]

After a court order for electronic surveillance is approved, it is taken to a service provider (e.g., a telephone company) for execution. The provider is required to assist in placing the wiretap,[11] and is compensated for all expenses. Surveillances are approved for at most 30 days; any extension requires a new court order.

Thirty-seven states also passed statutes permitting wiretaps by state and local law enforcement officers for criminal investigations. Under Title III, state acts were required to be at least as restrictive in their requirements as the federal code, and many are more so.

In an effort to prevent repetition of the concealment practiced by J. Edgar Hoover, Congress required that records on electronic surveillance be available to the public. Each order, whether filed under Title III or under a state statute, must be reported, and every year the Administrative Office of the United States Courts issues a report detailing the duration of each order, the number of persons intercepted, the type of surveillance used, the outcome of the case, and other information.

### A New Wrinkle: "Domestic National Security"

There are different codes of conduct in wartime than in peacetime. Soldiers are permitted, under appropriate circumstances, to kill without the elaborate procedures required for a civil execution. The most common "appropriate circumstance" is, of course, war with a foreign power. Less commonly and more controversially, a country's military may be deployed against its own citizens in times of insurrection. Under these conditions, which constitute a threat to the state itself, it is generally felt that peacetime restraint would place the state at too great a disadvantage and permit the country to be conquered or the government to be overthrown.

Similar reasoning applies, even in peacetime, to the state's actions with respect to spies, subversives, and revolutionaries—people who are not, or do not consider themselves, bound by the country's laws. The state will, where possible and appropriate, treat such people as lawbreakers and prosecute, but it may also take other actions that are not taken against citizens in the normal course of events.

It is not surprising, therefore, that in matters affecting national security the legal requirements for the placement of wiretaps should be relaxed. This is the reasoning behind the 1940 authorization granted to J. Edgar Hoover by Franklin Roosevelt. In a more general sense, it is the reasoning under which all intelligence agencies conduct communications intercept operations against foreign targets.

The relaxed requirements for national-security wiretapping are an attractive target for abuse. A number of presidents, including Kennedy, Johnson, and Nixon, used "national security" as a pretext for employing wiretaps in domestic political intelligence.

Kennedy abused electronic surveillance only a month into his presidency. The Dominican Republic was pressing Congress to pass a bill that would allow more Dominican sugar to be imported. Kennedy opposed this legislation, and his administration suspected that congressmen were being bribed to support it. Such bribery would be a legitimate national-security concern. Attorney General Robert Kennedy requested that the FBI initiate an investigation to see what pressures the Dominican Republic was putting on Congress (Wannall 1966). The inquiry lasted 9 weeks. A dozen wiretaps and three microphone surveillances were involved. Three members of the Department of Agriculture and a Congressional staffer had their home phones tapped (Hoover 1961a,b). One lobbyist was wiretapped both at home and at the office (Hoover 1961b). No bribes were discovered, but the wiretaps provided the president with important political information. One FBI summary sent to the attorney general said that a lobbyist "mentioned he is working on the Senate and has the Republicans all lined up" (FBI 1962). The administration bill won, and the FBI concluded that its surveillance work had been a major factor (Wannall 1966).

Most of the wiretaps were taken off in April 1961, but two remained even after the administration's bill passed (USS 94e, p. 330).

President Lyndon Johnson was even more blatant in requesting for national-security wiretaps. During the 1968 election, Johnson (who was not a candidate for reelection) asked the FBI to conduct surveillance of Anna Chennault, a prominent Republican who, Johnson claimed, was attempting to undermine the US-Vietnam peace talks in Paris. The White House asked the FBI to institute physical coverage of Chennault and both physical and electronic coverage of South Vietnam's Embassy (USS 94e, p. 314). Summaries of the information obtained from the physical surveillance were later given to the White House (DeLoach 1968b; FBI 1968). Apparently the FBI was concerned about being involved in such a political case and eschewed electronic surveillance of Chennault. The electronic surveillance of the embassy was an indirect way of accomplishing the same goal (DeLoach 1968a; USS 94e, p. 315).

President Nixon went yet further, and ultimately the illegal electronic surveillance that started early in his administration played a pivotal role in toppling his presidency.

On May 9, 1969, a front-page story appeared in the *New York Times* reporting that the United States was bombing Cambodia and had been doing so for some time. By recording false coordinates for the sorties (placing them in South Vietnam), the Air Force had hidden the location of the attacks. News of the cover-up had been leaked to *Times* reporter William Beecher by someone in the government. Outraged, Henry Kissinger, Nixon's national security advisor, told J. Edgar Hoover to find the leaker(s). Within hours the FBI had focused on Morton Halperin, a Kissinger aide who "knew Beecher" and whom Hoover "considered part of the Harvard clique" (Hoover 1969a). Without written approval from the attorney general, a wiretap was installed on Halperin's home line that same afternoon. Seventeen people, some in the government and some in the news media, had their phones tapped during the investigation,[12] but no leakers were identified.

Some of the wiretaps were on for a matter of weeks, others for more than a year. The longest was the one on Morton Halperin, which remained active for 21 months, even though by September 1969 Halperin had left the White House. In February 1971, when the tap was finally removed, Halperin had been working for months for Edmund Muskie, a Democratic senator from Maine and a candidate for his party's presidential nomination (Halperin 1974, p. 296). Hoover was forwarding various tidbits of political information, such as the fact that former president Johnson "would not back Muskie" for the White House (Theoharis and Cox 1988, p. 415). By that time, information from the wiretaps was being sent directly to H. R. Haldeman, Nixon's political advisor (USS 93e, pp. 296 and 351).

Daniel Ellsberg's turn came next. Ellsberg had made copies of classified histories of US involvement in Vietnam—the 47-volume "Pentagon Papers"—available to *New York Times* reporter Neil Sheehan. On Sunday, June 13, 1971, portions of the papers, and articles based on them, began appearing in the *Times*. The government sued to block publication, but lost. Excerpts were printed in the *Times* and in the *Washington Post*.[13]

Although the Pentagon Papers were highly critical of the Democrats who had preceded him in the presidency, Nixon was infuriated by their publication. Ellsberg was indicted on charges of violating the Espionage Act, but the Nixon White House went further.

John Ehrlichman, Nixon's domestic affairs advisor, authorized a burglary of Ellsberg's psychiatrist, then covered it up in an attempt to keep Ellsberg's trial from ending in a dismissal of charges. Instead, as a result of the inquiries into the Watergate break-in, the burglary of the psychiatrist was discovered. Further inquiry revealed that Ellsberg's phone had been tapped by the government,[14] but the wiretap authorizations, logs, and other records could not be found. The judge declared a mistrial, and charges against Ellsberg were dismissed (*United States v. Susso*, CD Cal. 9373-WMB, 1973).

Charles Radford II, a Navy yeoman who was serving the Joint Chiefs of Staff, was wiretapped after a syndicated newspaper column by Jack Anderson described a conversation between Nixon and Kissinger concerning the administration's decision to "tilt" toward Pakistan in the India-Pakistan conflict—a column which was to contribute to Anderson's winning a Pulitzer Prize a few months later. Radford was a suspect in part because he and Anderson attended the same church (Smith 1973; Hersh 1983, p. 470). The FBI was asked to wiretap Radford, although the government did not plan any prosecution of the leak (Smith 1973).

Shortly afterward, Radford was transferred to the Naval Reserve Training Center near Portland, Oregon. He moved in with his stepfather until he could find permanent housing. A wiretap was put on the stepfather's phone. After Radford found a place of his own, a wiretap was placed on his new phone. The wiretap on the stepfather's phone remained for another 2 months. There were also wiretaps on the phones of two of Radford's friends, one a State Department employee and one a former Defense Attaché. None of the wiretaps were authorized by the attorney general, and at no time was prosecution planned (USS 94e, pp. 326–327).

### Wiretapping Requires a Court Order

Even after the Supreme Court's ruling in the *Katz* case and the passage of Title III, national security continued to serve as a cover for warrantless electronic surveillance in domestic political intelligence. In 1972 the Supreme Court ordered an end to warrantless wiretapping even for "national-security" purposes.

John Sinclair, Lawrence Plamondon, and John Waterhouse Forrest were charged with bombing a CIA office in Ann Arbor, Michigan. It turned out that the federal government had tapped Plamondon without prior judicial approval. Plamondon requested copies of the tapes to determine if the government's case had been tainted by the wiretaps. The District Court ordered the government to give Plamondon copies of the tapes.

The government refused and appealed. It argued before the Supreme Court that this was a matter of national security and that Title III requirements for a search warrant were not an attempt to limit surveillance in such cases. While the Supreme Court agreed that Title III was limited to criminal investigations, it did not buy the argument that domestic-security surveillance could justify departure from Fourth Amendment protections:

> ... These Fourth Amendment freedoms cannot be properly guaranteed if domestic security surveillances may be conducted solely within the discretion of the Executive Branch. ... (*United States v. United States District Court for the Eastern District of Michigan et al.*, 407 US 297, 1972, p. 316–317)

> Official surveillance, whether its purpose be criminal investigation or ongoing intelligence gathering, risks infringement of constitutionally protected privacy of speech. Security surveillances are especially sensitive because of the

inherent vagueness of the domestic security concept.... We recognize, as we have before, the constitutional basis of the President's domestic security role, but we think it must be exercised in a manner compatible with the Fourth Amendment....

We cannot accept the Government's argument that internal security matters are too subtle and complex for judicial evaluation. Courts regularly deal with the most difficult issues of our society.... If the threat is too subtle or complex for our senior law enforcement officers to convey its significance to a court, one may question whether there is probable cause for surveillance.... (ibid., p. 320)

Surveillance of domestic organizations now required a court order whether the national security was involved or not. The Court pointed to the absence of law on wiretapping for national-security purposes and invited Congress to fill the gap. Instead the country spent almost 2 years mesmerized by the president's illegal activities.

## Watergate

The Watergate affair began early on the morning of June 17, 1972, with a break-in at the Democratic National Committee's headquarters in the Watergate Office Building in Washington. The intruders were a group paid by the Committee to Re-Elect the President, Nixon's campaign committee. The burglary was the second attempt to install a bug on the phone of Lawrence O'Brien, the Democratic Party's chairman. A first attempt had only succeeded in placing a working bug in his secretary's phone. This provided information on the secretary's social life, but not on O'Brien's political plans.

The Watergate affair reached its climax on August 9, 1974, when Nixon, facing impeachment, became the first president to resign from office. Had he not done so, he could have expected to be impeached on counts that included the following:

[Nixon] misused the Federal Bureau of Investigation, the Secret Service, and other Executive Personnel ... by directing or authorizing such agencies or personnel to conduct or continue electronic surveillance or other investigations for purposes unrelated to national security, the enforcement of laws, or any other lawful function of his office; ... and he did direct the concealment of certain records made by the Federal Bureau of Investigation of electronic surveillance (USHR 93b, Book III, pp. 2255–2256, Article II, §2).

[Nixon] failed to take care that the laws were faithfully executed by failing to act when he knew or had reason to know that his close subordinates endeavored to impede and frustrate lawful inquiries ... concerning the electronic surveillance of private citizens.... (USHR 93b, Book III, pp. 2256–2258, Article II, §4)

### The Senate Investigates

The revelations of Watergate engendered a general distrust of government as high official after high official was implicated in the illegal actions of the Nixon presidency. There was deep concern about the involvement of intelligence agencies in many of the questionable proceedings of the Nixon administration. In January 1975 the Senate appointed an eleven-member special committee to investigate government intelligence operations to determine the extent to which "illegal, improper, or unethical activities" were engaged in by government agencies (USS 94a).

The Senate Select Committee to Study Governmental Operations with respect to Intelligence Activities (commonly known as the Church Committee, after its chairman, Senator Frank Church), began its study with the year 1936, which marked the reestablishment of domestic intelligence programs in the United States after a hiatus of about a decade. The committee uncovered a long history of presidential wiretapping, including Truman's wiretapping of the lobbyist Thomas Corcoran, Kennedy's "Sugar Lobby" taps, Johnson's surveillance of Anna Chennault, and Kennedy's and Johnson's wiretapping and bugging of Martin Luther King. It also examined the wiretap abuses of the Nixon era, including those enumerated above. The hearings revealed many illegal covert operations by the intelligence agencies, and the Church Committee concluded:

> Too many people have been spied upon by too many Government agencies and [too] much information has been collected. The Government has often undertaken the secret surveillance of citizens on the basis of their political beliefs, even when those beliefs posed no threat of violence or illegal acts on the behalf of a foreign power. The Government, operating primarily through secret informants, but also using other intrusive techniques such as wiretaps, microphone "bugs," surreptitious mail opening, and break-ins, has swept in vast amounts of information about the personal lives, views and associations of American citizens.... (USS 94d, p. 5)

Among these were "the interest of the wife of a US Senator in peace causes; a correspondent's report from Southeast Asia to his magazine in New York; an anti-war activist's request for a speaker in New York" (ibid., p. 108). The committee observed: "The surveillance which we investigated was not only vastly excessive in breadth . . . but was also often conducted by illegal or improper means." (ibid., p. 12)

Although much of this surveillance had occurred before Title III, the illegal activities of the Nixon administration had not. When Congress had regulated the use of electronic surveillance for criminal investigations under Title III, it had believed that the legislation would put tight restrictions on the use of wiretaps and electronic surveillance. Nonetheless, Title III had been circumvented by the Nixon administration, which had used the "national-security" justification for many investigations.

The Church Committee's inquiries emphasized not "Who did it?" but "How did it happen and what can be done to keep it from happening again?" (ibid., p. viii) The committee felt that Title III was appropriate as written, but set forth a list of recommendations for explicit laws on electronic surveillance in national-security investigations.[15]

The underlying premise of the Church Committee's recommendations was that Americans should be free of the type of surveillance the hearings had exposed. The CIA should refrain from electronic surveillances, unauthorized searches, or mail openings within the United States,[16] and NSA should not monitor communications from Americans, except in cases where the person is involved in terrorist activities or intelligence work, and then only when a search warrant has been obtained.[17] The committee also outlined the form a law permitting electronic surveillance for foreign intelligence might take.[18]

## The Foreign Intelligence Surveillance Act

In 1978 the Foreign Intelligence Surveillance Act (FISA), much of it based on the Church Committee's recommendations, became law. FISA (50 USC 1801 et seq.) governs wire and electronic communications with "United States persons"[19] who are within the country. It does not apply to those of US persons overseas, excepting communications with a US person resident in the United States. Under FISA, US persons in the US may be subject to surveillance if they are suspected of aiding and abetting international terrorism.

A court order is required for a FISA wiretap.[20] Such an order may be granted by the Foreign Intelligence Surveillance Court, which is made up of seven District Court judges specially appointed by the Chief Justice of the United States. The order must be applied for by a federal officer, and approved by the attorney general, who is required to inform the House and Senate Committees on Intelligence of all FISA wiretap activity twice a year.

The attorney general is required to furnish an annual report to the Administrative Office of the US Courts on the number of FISA applications and orders. All other information on FISA wiretaps is classified. Since 1979, there have been an average of slightly over 500 FISA wiretap orders per year.[21] As of 1995, more than 8000 requests had been made by the government for surveillance under FISA. None had been turned down. The reason for this is a matter of dispute. Proponents of FISA say it is because surveillance applications are carefully prepared and reviewed before being presented to the Foreign Intelligence Surveillance Court. Opponents argue that it is because the court is only a rubber stamp (Cinquegrana 1989, p. 815).

### The Electronic Communications Privacy Act

The next major federal wiretapping statute was the 1986 Electronic Communications Privacy Act (Public Law 99-508), which updated Title III to include digital and electronic communications. In recognition of new telecommunications switching technologies, ECPA allowed for approvals of "roving wiretaps"—wiretaps without specified locations—if there was demonstration of probable cause that the subject was attempting to evade surveillance by switching telephones. It required a warrant for wiretapping the non-radio portion of a cellular communication. The widespread availability of radio scanners makes the latter stronger in legal terms than it is in practice.

Under ECPA, pen registers and trap-and-trace devices require court orders. Any government attorney can file for such an order, and there is no requirement of probable cause for a search warrant to be issued.

The late 1980s witnessed two major changes in telecommunications. The breakup of the Bell System into a long-distance carrier and seven regional companies encouraged a proliferation of competitors in the industry; this made seeking a wiretap more complicated for law-enforcement agents, who now had to contend with a plethora of new companies instead of a monolithic "Ma Bell." The other change came when call forwarding, call waiting, cellular phones, and fax machines appeared on the market.

# 8

# Communications: The Current Scene

Briefings on the dangers of encryption by Raymond Kammer (the acting director of the National Institute of Standards and Technology) and Clinton Brooks (assistant to the director of the National Security Agency) gave rise to fear in the FBI that wiretaps would soon be rendered useless. In 1992 the FBI's Advanced Telephony Unit predicted that, because of encryption, by 1995 the FBI would have access to only 60% of intercepted communications.[1] Facing a technology it understood poorly, the FBI wanted a fast remedy. As a first step, it sought congressional action to protect wiretapping from technical encroachments. The idea was that, because wiretapping was a tool with accepted legal standing, new legislation could be presented as a matter of maintaining the status quo.

### Digital Telephony

Unless continued access to traffic is maintained, neither targeting nor analysis of electronic communications will be possible. The post-1982 breakup of AT&T presaged a period of tremendous growth in telecommunications products and businesses. For the FBI's wiretapping activities, it was a period of growing complexity. In executing wiretaps, agents could no longer deal with a single telephone company; they now had to deal with equipment supplied by a variety of companies and with service provided by numerous carriers.

In 1992 the FBI put forth what it called a Digital Telephony Proposal, which mandated the inclusion of provisions for authorized wiretapping in the design of telephone switching equipment. When the FBI approached Congress with that proposal, it was far from clear that the FBI was experiencing anything other than a crisis of confidence. The proposed bill required that all telecommunications providers, both public carriers and private branch exchanges (PBXs—the private switching centers typically used within large companies), design their systems to accommodate government interceptions. Common carriers had 18 months to comply; the PBXs had twice as long. All costs of redesign were to be borne by the companies (FBI 1992b). The FBI claimed that new switching technology and such improvements as cellular telephones and call forwarding had made it difficult to install court-authorized wiretaps.

Evidence to substantiate that claim was hard to find. On April 30, 1992, the *Washington Post* reported: "FBI officials said they have not yet fumbled a criminal probe due to the inability to tap a phone ..." (Mintz 1992). To this suggestion that it was not actually having any trouble, the FBI countered that, because of anticipated technological problems, court orders had not been sought, executed, or completely carried out (Denning et al. 1993, p. 26). Meanwhile, Freedom of Information Act litigation initiated by Computer Professionals for Social Responsibility found not a single example of wiretaps' being stymied by the new telecommunications technology.

Industry objected to the Digital Telephony Proposal, and major players in computers and communications protested. Among industry's concerns were the cost (estimated to be in the hundreds of millions of dollars[2]) and the effect on privacy. A built-in "back door" for government wiretapping could easily become a back door to illicit surreptitious surveillance.

The General Accounting Office briefed Congress, expressing concern that alternatives to the proposal had not been fully explored (USGAO 1992). The General Services Administration characterized the proposal as unnecessary and potentially harmful to the nation's competitiveness (USGSA 1992). In an internal government memo, the National Telecommunications and Information Agency observed that facilitating lawful government interception also facilitated unlawful interception by others, and described the bill as "highly regulatory and broad" (NTIA 1992).[3] There were no congressional sponsors for the proposal.

As internal memoranda show, the FBI had given the Digital Telephony Proposal only a 30% chance of passing (McNulty 1992, p. C-14). But the proposal established an FBI·beachhead.

## The Value of Wiretapping

The Digital Telephony Proposal took as given the proposition that wiretaps were essential to law enforcement. Wiretapping for that purpose has now been legal for 30 years, and, despite the fact that most Americans disapprove of it,[4] this surveillance has come to be an accepted tool of law enforcement.

Three decades of court-authorized wiretapping have provided a powerful analytic tool with which to assess its value: the reporting provision of Title III provides that the Administrative Office of the Federal Courts should annually publish a list of all wiretap orders issued under Title III and associated state statutes. This annual account is commonly known as the *Wiretap Report*, although, like Title III itself, it covers all forms of electronic surveillance, including microphone surveillance. Despite its value as an analytic tool, the *Wiretap Report* has severe limitations. In its statistical summaries it does not distinguish wiretaps from bugs. Another difficulty is establishing precise numbers. For example, in its statistical information on intercepts, the report uses the term "intercepts installed" to mean installed intercepts for which reports have been received. This probably results in a slight underestimate of those actually installed, since some are not subsequently reported upon. The 1988 report shows that there were 754 orders for electronic surveillance but indicates that 11 of these were never executed. Of the remaining 743 court orders, an additional 67 did not have an after-the-fact prosecutor's report.[5] Thus the report lists 676 "intercepts installed," although the actual number lies between 676 and 743. In our analysis, we have used the *Wiretap Report's* "intercepts installed" figure, as there is no way to ascertain the higher number.

### Limitations of the Data

From the *Wiretap Report* we can discern who the prosecutor was on a wiretap order, who the judge was, how long the order was for, and for what crime the order was authorized.[6] We can see how many arrests were made, and how many convictions occurred.[7] What we cannot discern from the *Wiretap Report* is what was said in the court hearings.

Court transcripts often reveal information that dry numbers hide. In

1972, law professor Herman Schwartz studied the 4½ years' worth of court-ordered wiretaps that had resulted from Title III. He observed:

> [T]here is an interesting item in the late J. Edgar Hoover's 1971 [FBI annual] report: right after a reference to the vital importance of electronic surveillance to the fight against organized crime, four major convictions are listed, including one of a Nicholas Ratteni. A check with counsel in the case disclosed that there was indeed a wiretap—against a co-defendant who was *acquitted*. (Schwartz 1974, pp. 186–187)

So the FBI dissembled. Schwartz uncovered a number of other results that undercut claims of wiretapping's usefulness:

> [I]n *United States versus Poeta*, the US Court of Appeals opened its opinion by observing that the tap-derived evidence was unnecessary to the conviction; in another case, *Uniformed Sanitation Men versus Commission of Sanitation*, the Court made the same observation. In a 1971 report, a Nevada prosecutor reported two indictments in a kidnapping case in which wiretapping was used ... but candidly added that the indictments were "not as a result of the interception." (Schwartz 1974, pp. 185–186)

The law requires that the number of interceptions, both incriminating and non-incriminating, be reported. Schwartz found that law-enforcement personnel were prone to exaggerate the number of incriminating intercepts:

> In *United States v. King*, the Government claimed that 80–85% of the conversations overheard in a drug case were incriminating, and so it reported in the 1971 report, Order #35. The Court, however, found that the contemporaneous reports showed that the percentages were really between 5 and 25%.[8]

Such anomalies continue, of course. Recently an enterprising New York lawyer used wiretaps made by police to argue that his client had been entrapped.[9] In a 1995 terrorist conspiracy case, the FBI worked hard to establish a connection between Sheik Omar Abdel Rahman, a blind Egyptian cleric living in Brooklyn, and Razmi Yousef, an alleged terrorist and bomb expert. The FBI emphasized the wiretap evidence. In fact the wiretap transcripts only revealed that there had been several calls between Rahman's phone and Yousef's (Fried 1995; McKinley 1995b)— something that could have been discovered by less intrusive investigative methods. Rahman and Yousef never spoke to each other on the tapped telephone. Wiretaps of Rahman's conversations were described in the above-cited *New York Times* stories as "not incriminat[ing]" and containing "no references to violence." In a situation reminiscent of the Ratteni case described by Schwartz, lawyers for the defense in the 1997 trial of Timothy McVeigh used wiretaps made by federal agents to demonstrate that a prosecution witness was unreliable (Brooke 1997b).[10] Such examples make clear that the data provided by the *Wiretap Report* give only a partial picture of wiretapping cases.

### Where Wiretaps Are Used

In 1968, wiretapping was seen as a tool for targeting gambling—the main source of income for organized crime. In the first 5 years after the "Title III" legislation, 64% of the 2362 reported intercepts were for investigations of gambling cases, 27% of the wiretaps were for narcotics cases, less than 5% for homicide and assault investigations, 2.5% for investigations into bribery, and under 1% for cases of "arson and explosives" (USAO 1977, p. xvi). (The *Wiretap Report* denotes as "narcotics" any case in which the most serious offense includes drugs of any sort, including marijuana.) With at least 38 states running lotteries, and gambling legalized from Connecticut to Nevada, it is difficult to recall that gambling was once targeted as a serious crime.

In 1977 the number of narcotics investigations employing electronic surveillance began increasing. In 1982 President Reagan declared a national "War on Drugs," and gambling investigations using electronic surveillance dropped while narcotics investigations rose. In 1994 narcotics investigations made up 77% of the cases using electronic surveillance, gambling investigations less than 8%. Cost is a limiting factor. The average cost of a wiretap has risen, from $1358 in 1968 to $49,478 in 1994; part of this increase was due to a doubling in the length of the average electronic surveillance, from approximately 20 days in 1969 to just under 40 in 1994. Drug investigations, which frequently involve wiretaps of several months' duration, are particularly costly.

Drug investigations are the major focus of wiretaps, and the seizure of major shipments of drugs is sometimes accomplished through their use. In a style similar to the Vietnam War's body counts, law-enforcement agencies set great store by the tonnage of drugs seized. However, not even the law-enforcement community is unanimous in believing that seizure is the best solution to the drug problem. Eliminating drug sources has had only limited success.[11] And money spent on drug busts may not be money well spent. A report prepared by a special committee of the American Bar Association concluded: "While law enforcement has had little effect on drug use, drug prosecutions have had a profound effect on the criminal justice system. In the cities the Committee visited, drug cases have overwhelmed the courts.... In light of the Committee's findings in the area of drugs, a simple but significant truth should be faced: conventional law enforcement methods are not controlling the drug problem." (American Bar Association 1988, pp. 46–47)

### Sample Data from the *Wiretap Report*

| Court-Authorized Electronic Surveillance, Title III, 1988–1994 | | | | | | | | (1994 Only) | |
|---|---|---|---|---|---|---|---|---|---|
| Year | 1988 | 1989 | 1990 | 1991 | 1992 | 1993 | 1994 | Federal | State |
| Orders Authorized | 738 | 763 | 872 | 856 | 919 | 976 | 1154 | 554 | 600 |
| Orders Denied | 2 | 0 | 0 | 0 | 0 | 0 | 0 | 0 | 0 |
| Orders Installed[1] | 678 | 720 | 812 | 802 | 846 | 938 | 1100 | 549 | 551 |
| Main Offense[2] | | | | | | | | | |
| Arson, Explosives, and Weapons | 3 | 0 | 0 | 0 | 0 | 0 | 0 | 0 | 0 |
| Gambling | 126 | 111 | 116 | 98 | 66 | 96 | 86 | 8 | 78 |
| Kidnapping | 1 | 3 | 2 | 5 | 9 | 1 | 11 | 7 | 4 |
| Narcotics | 435 | 471 | 520 | 536 | 634 | 679 | 876 | 435 | 441 |
| Racketeering | 80 | 89 | 90 | 114 | 90 | 101 | 88 | 68 | 20 |
| Telephone Wiretaps[3] | 549 | 621 | 591 | 591 | 632 | 679 | 768 | 397 | 371 |
| Electronic Bugs[4] | 61 | 65 | 62 | 62 | 38 | 55 | 52 | 42 | 10 |
| Average Number/Order | | | | | | | | | |
| Persons | 129 | 178 | 131 | 121 | 117 | 100 | 84 | 112 | 58 |
| Intercepts | 1251 | 1656 | 1487 | 1584 | 1861 | 1801 | 2139 | 2257 | 2030 |
| Incriminating Intercepts | 316 | 337 | 321 | 290 | 347 | 364 | 373 | 374 | 372 |

1. *The Wiretap Report* uses the term 'Intercepts Installed' to mean intercepts installed *and* reported upon. This is likely to be a slight underestimate of those actually installed, since some surveillances are not actually reported upon. We use the Administrative Office's terminology here.
2. As determined by judge issuing surveillance order.
3. This number does not include telephone wiretaps that were part of a "combination" tap involving more than one type of surveillance.
4. This number does not include electronic bugs that were part of a "combination" tap involving more than one type of surveillance.

While wiretaps may contribute to large drug busts (although we are not aware of any study that has compared spending comparable funds on other types of law-enforcement activities focusing on drugs), it is not clear that this effort makes any real difference in the underlying problem. Indeed, a 1994 RAND study observes that $34 million invested in drug treatment programs achieves the same consumption reduction as does $246 million spent for domestic law enforcement, $366 million spent for interdiction, or $783 million spent for source-country control.[12]

### Where Wiretaps Are Not Used

Although kidnappings are frequently touted as a reason for the need for electronic surveillance,[13] wiretapping does not seem to be useful in such cases. Between 1969 and 1994, wiretaps and microphone bugs were reported to have been used in 80 kidnapping cases; thus, on average, wiretapping played a role in two to three of those cases each year.[14] Though there is no reason to doubt that the court orders for surveillance were correctly made, there is some reason to doubt the necessity. Meanwhile, in recent years there have been approximately 500 kidnapping cases per year.[15]

It is not surprising that wiretaps rarely figure in kidnapping cases, since investigators are typically unaware of the kidnappers' location. But wiretapping's role is small for another reason: the interception of ransom calls from kidnappers does not require any court authorization if the recipient of the call consents—a form of interception called a "consensual overhear."[16]

Domestic terrorism is sometimes given as a reason for wiretap surveillance. There were 59 wiretapping cases between 1968 and 1994 involving arson, explosives, and weapons (explosives are the most frequent form of domestic terrorism), or about two a year. Unless there are ongoing investigations, which have yet to be reported, the period 1988–1994 saw no investigations of arson or explosives weapons using Title III wiretaps.[17] It is possible that no wiretaps were used in such cases. However, since intelligence wiretaps may also be used for investigating domestic terrorism if there is alleged foreign involvement, it seems more likely that federal authorities found it more expedient to employ the Foreign Intelligence Surveillance Act, under which nothing need be reported but the total annual number of surveillances.

## The States and Wiretapping

Thirty-seven of the states have their own wiretapping statutes, but not all of those states strongly support wiretapping. It took California more than 20 years to pass a wiretapping statute, and when the law finally did pass it was loaded with restrictions, including a limitation to drug investigations. The state of California performs few wiretaps a year—8 in 1994 compared to 71 federal wiretaps (USAO 1994, pp. A-2–A-7 and A-58). "If it's anything big, you should let the Feds do it," explained San Francisco Chief Assistant District Attorney Dick Iglehart, who was California's Chief Assistant Attorney General, Head of the Criminal Division, at the time of the passage of the California statute.[18] The states that do not permit state-police surveillance are generally those with few federal wiretaps; the exception is Michigan, which had 26 federal wiretaps in 1994.[19]

## Convictions from Wiretaps

How many convictions result from wiretaps?[20] In 1988 wiretaps were used in 609 investigations, including 45 in which both wiretaps and electronic bugs were employed. By the end of 1996, there were 279 court cases involving the 1988 phone wiretaps installed in criminal investigations and 1808 convictions. These convictions had cost $335 million for wiretapping alone.

Of course, it is impossible to know in how many of these cases wiretap evidence was crucial in obtaining a conviction or a guilty plea (whether directly or through evidence obtained as a result of the information gleaned from a wiretap). The numbers above provide only an upper bound on the potential effectiveness of wiretapping in law enforcement. It is essential to note that a wiretap is ordered only if there is already probable cause that the person being investigated is involved in a serious and indictable crime.

## Who Else Is Being Tapped?

Since Title III has been in force, the number of conversations intercepted has increased, the number of nonincriminating conversations intercepted has increased, and the number of incriminating conversations intercepted has remained the same. More specifically, according to data on the period 1968–1994 released by the Administrative Office of the US Courts, the average annual number of incriminating conversations intercepted remained between 200,000 and 400,000 per year, while the number of intercepted conversations increased steadily from about 400,000 in 1968 to over 2 million.[21] In 1994, for example, 1137 court orders for electronic surveillance resulted in the interception of 2.35 million conversations. Only 15% of the intercepted conversations were incriminating; the remainder of the wiretapped conversations were not related to illegal activities.[22]

Gambling accounted for 29% of the incriminating wiretap intercepts in 1994. Gambling skews the statistics, for it is an activity with a high number of incriminating intercepts. It is also low on convictions. If we look to the 1988 numbers now that there has been enough time for trials to have taken place, we see that gambling accounted for 27% of the incriminating wiretap intercepts but for less than 14% of the convictions (244 of 1808). It is not surprising that wiretaps authorized for a gambling investigation should yield incriminating calls, since there has to be probable cause for the authorization. Neither is the low level of convictions a surprise; if a bookmaking operation is tapped, the incriminating calls are likely to be people placing bets. Few, if any, of these low-level bettors are prosecuted.

Thus, from the raw data of the *Wiretap Report* we can observe that fewer than one-sixth of the intercepted calls resulted in anything of use to law enforcement.

### What Sways the Courts?

Citizens and legislators alike have generally accepted police claims of wiretapping's indispensability as a crime-fighting tool but have felt a sense of disquiet about the ease with which it lends itself to invasion of privacy and political spying. As a result, Congress gave with one hand and took away with the other, allowing wiretapping but hedging it about with stiff warrant requirements and a strict reporting regime.

It is impossible to be sure what determines a guilty verdict. It is possible to ask jurors why they voted as they did, but it is not clear that the jurors really know. Indeed, getting inside the mind of a jury is notoriously difficult. In trials with high-priced attorneys, a lot of time and energy is spent developing jury profiles. Much of this effort is guesswork.

The exacting standards for issuing wiretap warrants make it difficult to judge whether wiretaps were actually needed in the cases in which they have been used. The fact that we know of no definitive evidence for the value of wiretaps may mean that we are ignorant, that no one has ever tried to develop such evidence, or that there is none.

### Transactional Information

The Digital Telephony Proposal came along when electronic surveillance was on the rise. Title III phone wiretaps were up from approximately 620 per year in the late 1980s to an average of 870 five years later.[23] In 1987 some 1600 pen registers had been installed; by 1993 the annual number was 3400. In 1987 the FBI, the Drug Enforcement Agency, the Immigration and Naturalization Service, and the US Marshals Service requested a total of 91 trap-and-trace devices; in 1993, the number was over 2000.[24] Part of the reason for this expansion in obtaining transactional information undoubtedly lies in improvements in telephone signaling that have made the information easier to obtain.[25]

As we noted earlier, transactional information cuts both ways. As in the case of the World Trade Center bombing, it can be useful in determining the structure of a conspiracy. It can also be used to forage into people's private affairs. Probes of Hillary Clinton's involvement in the Whitewater affair included reconstructions of how the first lady spent the days immediately after Vincent Foster's death.[26] Long-distance phone records were used to expand the FBI's investigation of CISPES.

### Constraints on Wiretapping

Title III requires that there be a court order before a wiretap can be installed.[27] In contrast with what is done when examining bank records or phone logs, a law-enforcement investigator who wants to wiretap has to draw up an affidavit showing that there is probable cause to believe that the targeted communication device—whether a phone, a fax machine, or a computer—is being used to facilitate a crime. The crime must be serious and indictable. At the federal level, a wiretap request must be signed by a member of the Department of Justice at least at the level of Deputy Assistant Attorney General. Applications are decided upon by a federal

District Court judge. Taps are approved for at most 30 days; extensions require a new court order.

The law obliges agents to tap only what is relevant to the investigation. This is called "minimization," and it requires an investigator to stop listening if the suspects are discussing issues not related to a potential crime, then turn it on several minutes later to check if the conversation has returned to indictable actions. The expense of having investigators do this provides a practical limit on the use of wiretaps. For example, in the Illwind investigation of Pentagon fraud, which ultimately tapped 26 telephone lines, several hundred agents were needed just for monitoring (Pasztor 1995, p. 190).

Criminals, whether they be defense consultants, drug dealers, or anyone else involved in a complex business, speak cryptically, and wiretapped lines reveal only part of the puzzle. In a recent FBI case, a wiretap picked up a conversation in which a murder plot was being discussed. The agents could not understand the street slang and jargon employed by the criminals and were unable to prevent the crime (Dam and Lin 1996, p. 89).

If the criminal evidence being sought is obtained before the end of the 30-day period, the law requires that the interception be terminated immediately. The raw numerical data provided by the *Wiretap Report* are insufficient to establish how carefully this rule is followed. In 1994, 22% of the wiretaps ran for the full authorization period, but some wiretaps are terminated very quickly because there is a "pervasive pattern of innocence." In one case police discovered that one of their suspects had a very active telephone and moved to get a wiretap warrant. A brief period of monitoring revealed, however, that the calls were not evidence of an abundance of drug dealing, but only of a popular teenage daughter.[28]

These restrictions, like others on wiretapping, are artificial. Though built into the law, they can be changed.[29] Indeed, one important restriction, minimization, has exceptions. For example, if the suspects are speaking a language not understood by the agent who is listening, tapes can be made for later use when an agent who comprehends that language is available (Dam and Lin 1996, p. 400, note 17).

The FBI has consistently maintained that wiretapping is an expensive technique (Pasztor 1995, p. 186) and thus never likely to be put to broader use. A recent Australian investigation of telecommunications interception, however, reached quite different conclusions, estimating the cost of a day's wiretapping as $Aus570, as compared to $Aus1376 for a listening device and $Aus2772 for vehicle tracking (Barrett 1994). Most of the cost of American wiretaps appears to due to the requirement that, in most cases, someone must monitor the tap in real time, turning a recorder on and off as the conversation drifts from innocent to incriminating and back.

The essential question about the future costs of wiretapping under US law is whether the courts will hold that minimization can be done by machines in a legally satisfactory way. Since electronic evidence gathered using search warrants is already handled in this way,[30] it seems possible that the answer will be yes. Should this occur, it would pave the way for much broader surveillance by law-enforcement agencies in the fashion currently practiced by intelligence agencies.

**The FBI Makes a Case for Wiretapping**

Beginning with the 1992 Digital Telephony Proposal, the FBI began a massive lobbying effort for passage of a wiretapping bill, presenting facts and figures that made a case for the importance of electronic communications to law-enforcement investigations. In the period 1985–1991, court-ordered taps conducted by the FBI reportedly figured in 7324 convictions, almost $300 million in fines levied, and over $750 million in recoveries, restitutions, and court-ordered forfeitures (FBI 1992a). Since the FBI conducts fewer than one-third of the non-FISA wiretap investigations, it can be assumed that the numbers above would be substantially higher if all such surveillance were taken into account. In 1992, during the presidency of George Bush, some White House staffers objected to the way the FBI calculated the losses due to organized crime, and disputed the FBI's claim that all 7324 convictions were due to electronic surveillance: "[S]ome [of these] convictions could probably still be obtained absent surveillance." (Anderson and Buchholz 1992) The Treasury Department observed: "It is difficult to do a critical analysis of DOJ's cost benefit package without a full explanation of how DOJ arrived at its cost/benefit figures, and what costs and benefits were included in those figures. It is not clear that DOJ knows, or could know, all the costs and benefits involved, but this should be clearly stated." (Levy 1992) The vice-president's office also had trouble with the calculations, noting: "In several places in the analysis, figures are cited without reference to their sources or to how they were derived. For example, on p. 4 a figure of $1.8 billion is cited for potential economic loss. . . ." (McIntosh 1992) Despite the doubts cast upon these numbers, they appeared and reappeared in various briefings —most notably in 1993. Less than a month after President Bill Clinton took office, his senior director for intelligence programs received an FBI briefing paper on encryption, in which the FBI's questionable data were quoted (Sessions 1993b, p. 6).

## The Digital Telephony Proposal Reappears

In 1994 the FBI prepared a revised Digital Telephony Proposal that limited wiretapping to common carriers and allocated $500 million to cover their costs. Carriers would have 3 years "after the publication by the Attorney General of a notice of capacity requirements"[31] to comply; after that, failure to fulfill a wiretap order could result in a fine of up to $10,000 a day. The revised proposal, the "Digital Telephony and Communications Privacy Improvements Act of 1994," was submitted to Congress in March 1994.

FBI Director Louis Freeh pressed for the passage of the new bill. Again the FBI claimed that the new technology was impeding its wiretapping ability. In a February 17, 1994, in a speech to the Executives' Club of Chicago, Freeh said: "Development of technology is moving so rapidly that several hundred court-authorized surveillances already have been prevented by new technological impediments with advanced communications equipment." In March, testifying before Congress, Freeh presented a lower estimate, citing a 1993 informal survey of federal, state, and local law-enforcement agencies, which revealed 91 instances of recent court orders for electronic surveillance that could not be fully implemented (Freeh 1994b, p. 33). Even those numbers were not well substantiated.

Freeh's testimony had some curious gaps, the most serious of these was that, although Freeh was speaking in support of the Digital Telephony bill, his examples of electronic surveillance included electronic bugs.[32] Freeh himself seems confused about the distinction. When Senator Arlen

Spector congratulated Freeh on the timeliness of his appearance (the FBI had just arrested Philadelphia mobster John Stanfa), Freeh readily agreed. The tape used in the case had come from an electronic bug.[33]

In April 1994, under an agreement that the details not be publicly released, Freeh supplied to the House and Senate Judiciary Subcommittees details of 183 instances in which the FBI had encountered difficulties in conducting court-authorized interceptions (USHR 103c, p. 14). The General Accounting Office, which earlier had complained about the FBI's lack of specificity in its electronic surveillance requirements, confirmed that the FBI did face technical problems in wiretapping as a result of the use of new digital technologies, including call forwarding, optical fiber, and ISDN (ibid., pp. 14–15). Yet despite Freeh's efforts, by late fall the Digital Telephony bill was in trouble. Freeh returned to Congress in a "last-ditch lobbying effort," pushing hard for passage of the bill that he had made his agency's highest priority (Chartrand 1994). His work paid off, and the Digital Telephony bill became law under a new name: Communications Assistance for Law Enforcement Act (CALEA).[34]

CALEA put the government right in the middle of the process of designing telephone switches. It provided that, subject to federal appropriations to cover the costs of modification, telecommunications networks deployed after January 1, 1995 had to be configured to meet law-enforcement interception requirements,[35] whereas systems installed earlier did not have to be in compliance until the "equipment, facility, or service" was replaced or substantially upgraded (Communications Assistance for Law Enforcement Act, Public Law 103–414, §109). A cryptography provision was included in CALEA: "a telecommunications carrier shall not be responsible for decrypting, or ensuring the government's ability to decrypt ... unless the encryption was provided by the carrier and the carrier has the information necessary to decrypt the communication" (ibid., §103(b3)). The law authorized the expenditure of $500 million to cover costs of the modifications. It also empowered the attorney general to determine the appropriate level of surveillance standards the telephone companies would have to meet. Attorney General Janet Reno decided that the FBI, the agency that had written and lobbied for CALEA, would be in charge of determining those very standards.

Within a year, the attorney general was to publish notice of the maximum capacity required by law enforcement. In October 1995 the FBI announced its analysis, for purposes of which the United States was divided into three parts on the basis of previous rates of telecommunications surveillance. In Category I (the area with the highest-density locale for communications interceptions, which presumably included the New York metropolitan area and Dade County, Florida[36]) the phone companies were to "expeditiously" increase the capacity for monitoring until 1% of the "engineered capacity" could be intercepted. (Interceptions might mean pen registers, trap-and-trace devices, or actual wiretaps.) In Category II areas these numbers were halved, and in Category III areas the requirements for maximum surveillance were halved again. According to the FBI, "engineered capacity" is about 10% of the number of telephone lines, or some 15 million lines over the whole country.

These requirements translated to an extremely large number of simultaneous intercepts. There are approximately 160 million phone lines in the United States (FBI 1997b). Category I includes about 12.5% of these, or a bit under 2 million lines; Category II is another 12.5% of the lines. Category III covers the remaining 75% of telephone lines. Thus the FBI requirements would result in capacity to wiretap approximately 30,000 lines simultaneously (EPIC 1995b). That is over 4 times the *annual* number of phone surveillances (total number of trap-and-trace devices, pen registers, and FISA and Title III wiretaps) in 1993, and 20 times the *annual* number of FISA and Title III wiretaps. Were the telephone carriers' engineered capacity to increase, so would law enforcement's ability to wiretap and track transactional activity.

A few months later there were complaints about other FBI interpretations of CALEA. The FBI proposed that the cellular telecommunications group adopt a standard enabling law-enforcement agencies to determine the precise location of a wireless user within half a second (Markoff 1996). "In 1968 when they passed the original wiretap legislation, phones didn't move," said James Kallstrom.[37] "The notion that we in law enforcement should not be able to take advantage of the technology is a crazy notion." (Markoff 1996)

The industry objected. "The FBI is asking us to go beyond the legislation and ... turn all wireless phones into location beacons," fumed Ronald Nessen of the Cellular Telecommunications Industry Association

(McGee 1996a). The legislators had been explicit on this very point: "... such call-identifying information shall not include any information that may disclose the physical location of the subscriber (except as can be determined from the telephone number)" (CALEA, §103 a2B). In his congressional testimony, Louis Freeh had pledged that CALEA would not expand wiretapping powers.[38] In response to the industry objections, the FBI agreed to redraft its proposed cellular standards (McGee 1996a).

The FBI also reexamined the capacity issue. Scrutinizing surveillance activity county by county across the United States, in early 1997 the FBI proposed capacity numbers based on the maximum simultaneous surveillance that had occurred during the period from January 1993 to March 1995, defining "simultaneous surveillance" as surveillance that had occurred on the same day. Then the FBI added together all forms of telephone surveillance—wiretaps, penregisters, and trap-and-trace devices—to arrive at a baseline number. This was then multiplied by a growth factor to reflect the fact that the numbers were to apply in 1998.[39] The new regulations asked for the ability to conduct 39,767 "actual" simultaneous surveillances by 1998, and 57,749 in "maximal" ones.[40] The latter number is 8 times the total electronic surveillances (wiretap, electronic, combination (USAO 1993), pen register, and trap-and-trace devices) conducted in 1993. Some of the increase arises as a simple consequence of the county-by-county approach—if a county had no surveillance activity during the time period, the FBI gave it a baseline of one (FBI 1997b)—but this inflation of the total figure may not affect Americans' privacy as much as other aspects of the FBI's capacity requirements could.

The lines between wiretaps, pen registers, and trap-and-trace devices were blurred under the new proposals. The FBI's technique of combining the numbers for wiretaps, pen registers and trap-and-trace devices meant that it was requesting the capability to perform 57,000 simultaneous surveillances, which could mean 57,000 uses of trap-and-trace devices or 57,000 wiretaps.

Freeh made several other efforts to increase the wiretapping capabilities of law enforcement. In 1995, immediately after the bombing of the Murrah Federal Office Building in Oklahoma City, Freeh proposed new legislation that would permit law-enforcement agents to obtain roving wiretaps (taps on a suspect who moves from phone to phone) without having to get individual court orders for each tap (Purdom 1995). Before the Oklahoma bombing, the FBI had paid little attention to right-wing militia groups, and it is hard to imagine how expanded wiretapping capabilities could have prevented the act. Indeed, it was old-fashioned police work—including catching a speeder on a highway—that netted the suspects only a few days after the crime.

Responding to Oklahoma City, the White House sought expanded capabilities for electronic surveillance, including an expansion of Title III to cover *any* federal felony, the ability to use illegally obtained electronic surveillance information in court so long as the evidence had not been obtained in "bad faith," and the ability of the FBI to obtain long-distance telephone billing information without a court order. The White House also sought full funding for CALEA. Congress turned the president down on most of these requests; however, it approved funding for CALEA,[41] and it approved the use of subpoenas (as opposed to search warrants) to obtain local phone records (USC-104).

After the mysterious explosion of TWA Flight 800, in August 1996, Louis Freeh and James Kallstrom (the latter now an FBI Assistant Director) again urged an expansion of law enforcement's wiretap authority. President Clinton proposed that terrorist actions be included among the crimes for which electronic-surveillance orders could be obtained under Title III (terrorist actions were already included under FISA).[42] Clinton also recommended more liberal provisions for roving wiretaps, 48-hour emergency warrantless wiretapping, and profiling of airline passengers through electronic records (billing information and the like) to determine whose baggage should be the subject of careful searches for explosives.

The roving wiretaps were to be roughly akin to electronic writs of assistance. Whereas the Title III required judicial approval of each wiretap placed on a suspect, the government now sought the ability to wiretap any telephone the suspect might be using—at a bar, a coffee shop, a gym, or a pizza parlor—without specific prior judicial approval of the wiretap's location. These proposals did not pass. A year after the Flight 800 disaster, evidence points to mechanical failure rather than terrorist action.

**The International Connection**

In a behind-the-scenes effort, simultaneous with its domestic lobbying efforts for CALEA, the FBI worked the international front. Certain countries, including Britain, could be expected to be sympathetic to the FBI's viewpoint. In a worldwide context the British legal system appears similar to the American, but there are sharp differences in the area of communications interception. There have, for example, been numerous charges of wiretaps on British labor unions and on the British "green movement."[43] The lack of a constitution and the British experience with terrorism (Irish terrorism has been a constant in England for at least a century) has led to a wiretap law which is less restrictive than the American.[44]

The FBI briefed the international community on problems in communications interception at its research facility in Quantico, Virginia. Shortly afterward, the European Union (EU) opened discussions on interception.[45] The influence of the FBI was clear, although point 2 of the EU resolution lamely attempted to put some European control on the matter ("requirements of the member states will be conveyed ... in order to avoid a discussion based solely on the requirements of the FBI").

A little over a year later, and without any public debate, the European Council passed a resolution on "realtime" monitoring capabilities. Like CALEA, the EU resolution required telecommunications providers to give law-enforcement bodies access to transactional data and call content. But the EU resolution went farther; it required providers of mobile services to give the locations of their subscribers.

The origins of the European initiative were clarified by a Memorandum of Understanding (MOU),[46] which extended the agreement to non-EU nations that chose to sign. Nations interested in participating were told to contact the General Secretary of the EU Council or the Director of the FBI for further information.

The EU's resolution and memorandum were not publicized. Although the resolution had the force of law on EU members, it was not brought before various parliamentary bodies. When, in the British House of Lords, the chairman of the Select Committee on European Affairs sought information on the resolution and accompanying MOU, he was told that it was simply a "set of practical guidelines" and that it was not of parliamentary "significance."[47]

Standards bodies were kept informed, however. Service providers and manufacturers of telecommunications equipment were told that they would have to adhere to the standards of the resolution if they were to provide service or sell equipment to EU members or to signers of the MOU. In late 1996 the European Council began inviting non-EU members to participate in the MOU.[48] By early 1997 the FBI seemed to have made significant headway internationally in its attempt to develop law-enforcement access to telecommunications systems.

The FBI pressed for these surveillance technologies in a world where human rights guarantees are quite different from those of the United States. In the context of satellite-based communications systems, the European Union continued to look at surveillance issues. The EU Police Cooperation Working Group considered the possibility of "tagging" each subscriber "in view of a possibly necessary surveillance activity."[49] The United States may limit its use of wiretap surveillance to serious crimes and require a court order for such surveillance; however, as these excerpts from the US Department of State's Country Reports on Human Rights Practices for 1996 demonstrate, other countries do not.

- El Salvador: Wiretapping of telephone communications by the Government is illegal, but occurs.

- Colombia: Despite a law, various state authorities monitor telephone conversations without obtaining authorization.

- Spain: Investigation continues into allegations of wiretapping by the National Intelligence Agency of private conversations between the king, various ministers, and other prominent figures.

- Greece: On occasion the government placed international and domestic human rights activists under surveillance.

- Angola: The government maintained a sophisticated security apparatus dedicated to surveillance, monitoring, and wiretapping of certain groups, including journalists, opposition leaders, and diplomats.

- Nigeria: Human rights and prodemocracy leaders reported that security agents regularly cut off or monitored their organizations' phones.

- Singapore: The authorities have the capability to monitor telephone and other private conversations. While there were no proven allegations that they did so in 1996, it is widely believed that the authorities routinely conducted surveillance on some opposition politicians and other critics of the Government.

- China: All public dissent against party and government was effectively silenced. The 1982 constitution states that "freedom and privacy of correspondence of citizens are protected by law." In practice, however, authorities frequently record telephone conversations of foreign visitors, businessmen, diplomats, residents and journalists as well as Chinese dissidents and activists and others. Authorities also open and censor international mail.

- Indonesia: Security forces engaged in selective monitoring of local and international telephone calls without legal restraint. (USDoS 1997)

Hong Kong was an invited participant in these meetings from the beginning, despite the fact that in 1997 sovereignty of the British colony reverted to China, which has an abysmal record on human rights.

### Encryption and Wiretapping

The ability to wiretap is substantially less useful if the conversations under surveillance are encrypted, but the FBI sought to downplay CALEA's connections with encryption and, in particular, with escrowed encryption. After the introduction of the key-escrow program in 1993, many people raised questions about such connections. The government denied any ties between encryption and surveillance.[50]

Then in September of 1994, weeks before CALEA passed, FBI Director Freeh said otherwise. Asked how the FBI would respond should it encounter non-escrowed encrypted conversations in wiretapped communications, Freeh replied that he would go to Congress and ask for laws banning non-escrowed encryption.[51]

The White House disavowed the remarks, saying that Freeh tended to go his own way. In the following months, Freeh repeated his position, often quite strongly. (See e.g. Freeh 1996.) This did not surprise many of those who had opposed the original Digital Telephony Proposal. They had always expected such a response, and that expectation was borne out by documents obtained by the Electronic Privacy Information Center through Freedom of Information Act litigation.

A 1991 NIST Public Key Status Report mentioned that the "FBI [is] working on draft legislation to control and license all cryptography." (USDoC 1991c) A memo written by National Security Advisor Brent Scowcroft on January 17, 1992 said that two days earlier the president had approved that the Department of Justice "should go ahead now to seek a legislative fix to the digital telephony problem, and all parties should prepare to follow through on the encryption problem in about a year." The Scowcroft memo continued: "Success with digital telephony will lock in one major objective; we will have a beachhead we can exploit for the encryption fix, and the encryption access options can be developed more thoroughly in the meantime."[52] (Scowcroft 1992).

CALEA passed in 1994. One half of the fix was now in, ready to be exploited for the encryption "problem."

# 9
## Cryptography: The Current Scene

### Pretty Good Privacy

In 1990, a programmer from Boulder, Colorado, Philip Zimmermann, wrote Pretty Good Privacy (PGP), a program for protecting the privacy of email, and made it available over the Internet. Under the State Department's interpretation of the Arms Export Control Act, this constituted an illegal export.

Zimmermann might not have had any trouble had he not offended another vested interest. The PGP program was in blatant infringement of the Rivest-Shamir-Adleman patent, and it bore a remarkable resemblance to a program called Mailsafe (written by Ron Rivest) marketed in the mid 1980s by RSA Data Security. Zimmermann recalls receiving a visit from puzzled customs investigators, who told him they had received a complaint from RSA Data Security alleging the theft and international shipment of stolen intellectual property. The customs inspectors did not really understand what was at issue. Patent infringement wasn't their responsibility. Disks stolen out of warehouses and smuggled out of the country were, however, and this is how Zimmermann believed they had interpreted the complaint. A federal prosecutor in San Jose, California, began an investigation, and a grand jury in that city heard testimony on the subject for over a year. The experience was disquieting for all involved —not least the prosecutor and the grand jury, who were not used to investigating in a fish bowl. Many witnesses reported their experiences on the Internet and the cryptography community followed the events attentively.

Meanwhile, PGP spread out of anyone's control. Because the RSA patent held only in the United States, foreign users were not at risk of being sued for contributory infringement. A worldwide group of programmers began further development on the program and later versions were said to have been developed abroad and imported to the US. Midway through the course of criminal investigation, the patent-infringement aspect of the case became moot when RSA Data Security changed the license for its reference implementation of the RSA cryptosystem in a way that permitted a "legal" US version of PGP (PGP 2.6).

The investigation, of which the grand jury was only the most visible part, ended when the Department of Justice decided not to prosecute. The government's reasoning is not known. Quite independent of the central legal issue (whether posting code on the Internet, where foreigners can get at it, constitutes export under American law or is merely the exercise of a free-speech right to publish), the case was an evidential nightmare. Zimmermann had not actually posted the code himself; someone else had done it with his permission. More important than this, however, was an unquestioned act of publication. The MIT Press, with its thumb firmly on its nose, published the code of PGP as a 600-page hardbound book (Zimmermann 1995) printed in an OCR font, and sold it though its usual worldwide distribution channels. Had the government prosecuted Zimmermann and not gone after MIT, it would have invited scorn. But MIT is three times as old as NSA, just as well funded, and even more influential in the military-industrial complex. The Department of Justice let the case drop.

Free of the threat of prosecution, Zimmermann founded a company and began to expand his product line. Today, PGP has a worldwide following, and it has entered the mainstream by means of an easy-to-use interface to the popular Eudora email program. In writing PGP, Phil Zimmermann did something for cryptography that no technical paper could do: he gave people who were concerned with privacy but were not cryptographers (and not necessarily even programmers) a tool they could use to protect their communications.

**A National Encryption Policy**

In the period immediately following the 1989 NIST/NSA Memorandum of Understanding, from a public vantage point encryption policy seemed to be lurching along without direction. At the FBI's request, the chairman of the Senate Judiciary Committee, Joseph Biden, introduced a nonbinding sense-of-the-Congress resolution recommending that, under appropriate legal authorization, telephone companies provide the plaintext of encrypted messages they encountered while wiretapping. Biden later withdrew the resolution, which had been part of an anti-terrorism measure (Markoff 1991). Industry complaints about restrictive export controls on cryptography resulted in agreement on a slightly loosened export policy: seven-day approval for software employing RC2 and RC4, RSA Data Security algorithms that used 40-bit keys. Meanwhile DES continued to be restricted for export. The lack of clear direction complicated the situation for industry and thus vastly slowed the development of secure systems.

Various groups sought a clarification of federal encryption policy. The Computer System Security and Privacy Advisory Board, a NIST review committee created through the Computer Security Act, requested a national review of cryptography (Brooks 1992, p. C-13). A bill in Congress included a requirement for presidential analysis of aspects of encryption policy (ibid.).

The Brooks-Kammer briefings of the FBI had created a confluence of interest in law-enforcement and national-security circles. NSA urged discussion and adoption of a "national encryption policy." What NSA had in mind was a "national policy" that would "decree because of legitimate law enforcement needs in the US the US government will have to have a carefully controlled means of being able to decrypt information when legally authorized to do so" (ibid., p. C-12).

The FBI was pursuing passage of the Digital Telephony bill, and NSA was working on an algorithm to satisfy the FBI's need for strong but accessible cryptography. The Digital Telephony effort was known to the public; the encryption work was not. NSA opposed any public debate on cryptography.[1]

The US government's technique for attacking the spread of strong cryptography was also changing. The Clipper program attempted to use standardization and federal buying power to influence civilian use of cryptography. After the effective failure of this program, the government turned to the only other tool available without new legislation: export control. The most notable reason for this shift was that, as cryptography entered the mainstream market, exportability became essential for successful mass-market products.

NSA's work with NIST had been directed toward cryptography used in computers, so it was with some surprise that in 1992 the federal government faced the threat of deployment of strong, relatively inexpensive cryptography in telephones.[2]

### Cryptography and Telephony

In the past decade, secure telephones using advanced key management have become widespread in the national-security community. During the 1980s, approximately 10,000 second-generation (STU-II) secure telephones used by the US government were replaced with third-generation STU-IIIs. By now more than 300,000 STU-IIIs have been produced, and the price of one has dropped from several thousand dollars to about $1500. Each of the three current producers of STU-IIIs—AT&T, Motorola, and Lockheed-Martin[3]—also made commercial derivatives using DES and exportable versions using trade-secret algorithms. These versions are generally presumed to be less secure than STU-IIIs, and because of smaller production volumes they are more expensive. At least one, however, has a flexible key-management system that makes it more suitable to the commercial environment than a STU-III.[4]

The market is plagued by the existence of too many different kinds of secure telephones, most of which will not interoperate. (It has been jokingly said that the number of types of secure phones exceeds the number of instruments.) The US government now has at least three types[5] and is in the process of introducing more. The centerpiece of the new efforts is the Secure Terminal Equipment (STE) designed to operate with ISDN. The STE is interoperable with STU-III, but not with Clipper phones or any other Type II system.

**Figure 9.1**
The AT&T TSD 3600. (Photograph by Eric Neilsen.)

Voice-encryption systems for the commercial market have also been a staple of companies such as Gretag and Crypto Ag. in Switzerland and Datotek, Cylink, and TCC in the United States. It was only in 1992, however, that an attempt at selling a modern piece of equipment for secure telephony to a mass market occurred. AT&T announced the Telephone Security Device Model 3600 (TSD 3600) for an initial price of $1295.

In the fall of 1991, David Maher, an AT&T engineer who had been the chief architect of the AT&T STU-III, realized that it had become possible to design a secure phone using a single digital signal processing chip.[6] This permitted a piece of equipment for secure telephony to be built at a total cost of between $100 and $200. Like all modern secure telephones, it works by digitizing the voice signal and then encrypting the bitstream, using keys negotiated by public-key techniques. The beauty of the TSD 3600 is its size and simplicity: it is a 1½-pound box smaller than this book. After installing it in the cord between the handset and the body of a standard phone, the user has only to push a "go secure" button to operate it.

As the development of the TSD 3600 proceeded, the head of Maher's division, who had been hired in part for his excellent connections in the intelligence community, discussed AT&T's new security venture with NSA.

NSA was interested in using the TSD 3600 in government applications, but also expressed concern over the problems it might pose for law enforcement. The agency suggested a key-escrow scheme for the phones, promising to deliver the appropriate chips to AT&T by the fall of 1992 so as not to delay the project. AT&T agreed to incorporate the escrow algorithm in some models of the TSD.

The promised chips did not arrive on schedule, and sample TSD 3600s using DES were lent to prospective customers in the fall of 1992. At the time AT&T promised that the DES version would shortly be joined by another model containing a yet-to-be-announced federal encryption standard. The model with the new "Type IIE" encryption algorithm would enjoy the benefit of easy exportability and certification for use in government applications.

Bill Clinton became president on January 20, 1993. Six days after the inauguration, Clinton's Senior Advisor for Intelligence was briefed by the FBI on encryption and "the AT&T problem" (Sessions 1993a). The new administration agreed with the current plans. On April 16, 1993, the White House announced the Escrowed Encryption Initiative, a Federal Information Processing Standard intended to "improve security and privacy of telephone communications" (White House 1993).

## The Escrowed Encryption Standard

The Escrowed Encryption Standard (EES) was designed to fit a set of seemingly contradictory requirements: strong cryptography, yet readily exportable, with messages accessible to law enforcement under proper legal authorization. The trick was key escrow.

EES consisted of a classified algorithm (Skipjack) that was to be implemented on tamper-resistant chips (Clipper) with escrowed keys. The chips were to be fabricated in a secure facility (the original facility was run by Mykotronx), and escrow agents would be present during the process. Keys would be split into two components, with each piece stored at a secure facility under the control of a federal executive-branch agency. Each half of the key would be worthless without the other. Only under "proper legal authorization" would keys be released to law-enforcement agents. According to Senate testimony, the escrow agents would cost $14 million to set up and $16 million per year to run (USS 103a, p. 95).

When a Clipper chip prepares to encrypt a message, it generates a short preliminary signal called the Law Enforcement Access Field.[7] Before another Clipper chip will decrypt the message, this signal must be fed into it. The LEAF is tied to the key in use, and the two must match for decryption to be successful. The LEAF, when decrypted by a government-held key that is unique to the chip, will reveal the key used to encrypt the message.

The proposed standard was limited to encryption of voice, fax, and computer information transmitted over a telephone system (USDoC 1994b, p. 6003). At the initial Clipper announcement, the administration stated that it was neither prohibiting encryption outright, nor acknowledging Americans' right to unbreakable commercial encryption (White House 1993). In later briefings, the administration gave assurances that it would not seek legislation limiting the use of encryption products (USDoC 1994b, p. 5998; McConnell 1994, p. 102).

The key-escrow program provided a widely available form of cryptography of sufficient strength to satisfy the "Type II" requirement for protection of sensitive but unclassified government communications.[8]

This program has two essential elements: the algorithm is secret and is available to approved manufacturers in the form of tamper-resistant integrated circuits, and the cryptosystem contains a trap door that permits US authorities to exploit intercepted traffic when required.

Packaging cryptography in hardware provides the best security and has always been standard practice in the Type I systems used to protect classified information. In such environments, the restriction to isolated (separate chip) hardware implementations represents less additional cost, since the isolated implementation would be necessary for security reasons anyway.

## The Clipper Controversy

As required by law, NIST provided a period for public comments on the newly proposed Escrowed Encryption Standard.[9] The response was vociferous and loud. Supporters outside the government were few, while opponents were many and varied, ranging from the American Civil Liberties Union to Citicorp bankers to a large segment of the computer industry. During the public comment period NIST received 320 letters on the proposed standard. With the exception of letters from Motorola (a major manufacturer of secure telephones that may have been contemplating developing devices to meet the new standards), a professor of computer science at Georgetown University, and "no comment" statements from a number of government agencies, the remainder of the letters were negative—including several from government agencies.[10]

The major objection to key escrow was that the mechanism compromises an individual's privacy *even if the escrowed keys are never accessed.* The knowledge that the government has the technical ability to read all communications creates a perception that no communication is private, even if the vast majority of communications are never intercepted or read.

Concern with privacy was not, however, the only ground for objection. Escrowed keys represented a major step back from the encryption techniques that had been developed in the mid 1970s. One purpose of public-key cryptography is to facilitate secure communication in a diverse community by reducing the trust that must be placed in centralized resources. Another is to limit the lifetimes of keys; by extending these, escrow creates vulnerabilities both for society and for the individual.

The decision to escrow keys as part of the standard and to include the LEAF led naturally to the implementation of the algorithm in a tamper-resistant chip. But such a contrivance was most unusual for a Federal Information Processing Standard, and the implicit inclusion of classified portions in a Federal Information Processing Standard effectively changed it from a mechanism for promoting interoperability among communication products to one for exercising control over those products and the industry that produces them. Rather than being able to read the standard, implement conforming products, and submit samples for certification, companies would be required to purchase tamper-resistant chips from authorized suppliers. Both the diversity of sources and the availability lifetime of parts would be outside the company's control.

Formal government secrecy of a technology amounts to the most extreme form of regulation and to a great extent removes both the government and a segment of industry from accountability to the public. The EES stated that the government would regulate which companies would be allowed to include the new encryption product.[11] Companies would not only be beholden to the authorized suppliers of Clipper chips; they would be beholden to the government for permission to purchase them. The computer industry has been characterized by rapid and nimble developments; to many observers, this federal standard seemed to bode steep bureaucratic hurdles for any product that included security.

If the introduction of key-escrow technology is successful, we can expect that by early in the twenty-first century a vast body of traffic will have been transmitted under its "protection." Much of this will have been sent by radio or satellite, and we will have no way of estimating how much of it has been recorded and by whom. Under these circumstances, escrow agents will become an intelligence target of unprecedented proportions. Compromise them and all that has been recorded can be read.[12]

There is also a vulnerability that does not depend on even the continued existence of the escrow agents. Although the standard contains no statement as to the length of either the device-unique key or the family key, it has been stated elsewhere that, like the session keys, these will both be 80 bits. Under these circumstances, it appears that an opponent who knows the Skipjack algorithm, the LEAF creation method, and the escrow authenticator can recover the device-unique key in at most a small multiple of $2^{80}$ operations. A message so valuable that someone would attempt to perform $2^{80}$ operations to read it strains the imagination today. It is less of a strain to imagine a cipher chip whose history is such that a decade from now someone might perform a similar number of operations to acquire easy access to its lifetime traffic.[13]

Despite the strong protests, on February 9, 1994, NIST adopted the Escrowed Encryption Standard as a Federal Information Processing Standard (USDoC 1994b). To objections that the standard was a first step toward prohibition of non-escrowed encryption, NIST responded that the standard was voluntary. To concerns that the system might infringe on individual rights, NIST responded that decryption would occur only when legally authorized. To protests over the secrecy of the algorithm, NIST responded that there are no known trap doors or weaknesses in it. To objections that the standard would be ignored by people engaged in criminal activity, NIST responded that EES would make strong encryption widely available and that, to the degree that it was successful, non-escrowed encryption would become harder to obtain. Escrow agents remained undetermined, and NIST acknowledged that the standard lacked sufficient detail to function as an interoperability standard.

The standard was limited to voice, fax, and computer information communicated over a telephone system. But at the very last minute, NSA had attempted to scuttle that limitation. In memos between NIST and NSA days before EES was approved, NSA modified the standard to cover "telecommunications systems" instead of "telephone communications." NSA also expanded the coverage of the standard to include PCMCIA (Personal Computer Memory Card International Association) cards (US-DoD 1994). Apprised of the changes, NIST scientists objected, and the modifications disappeared. Had they remained, EES would have become a standard for both voice and data communications. In addition, EES would have given Fortezza—a PCMCIA card that performs key exchange, computes digital signatures, and encrypts using Skipjack—a free pass around the laborious exception-approval process.[14]

AT&T ultimately developed half a dozen models of the TSD 3600, only some of which could interoperate. These included the D model, which used DES with a 768-bit modulus for Diffie-Hellman key exchange. D models were able to interoperate only with other D models. There were exportable F models that used a Datotek algorithm with a 512-bit modulus, and non-exportable P models running an algorithm developed by the Swiss company Gretag A.G. The S models had Clipper, P, and F algorithms, so they could interoperate with the F model, the P model, and the government G model (equipped with Clipper).

AT&T anticipated a large market for these devices, expecting them to appeal to executives in businesses facing aggressive international competition. The original TSD 3600 with DES encryption might have achieved its market objectives. The "improved" Clipper model saw disappointing sales.

By the fall of 1995, total sales of all TSD 3600s were about 17,000. The largest single block were the 9000 Clipper models bought by the FBI in an attempt to seed the market. Most of the remainder were an exportable version exported to buyers in Venezuela and several Middle Eastern countries.[15] According to the government, the Escrowed Encryption Standard was developed to "make strong encryption broadly available and affordable" (USDoC 1994b, p. 6000). The immediate effect of EES, however, was to kill off the first secure phone device targeted at a mass market. By 1997 no secure phone product had come along to take the TSD's place, and telephone conversations remained unencrypted and unprotected. A National Research Council panel cited the lack of encryption between cellular telephones and base stations as a serious problem[16] and recommended it be fixed forthwith (Dam and Lin 1996, p. 327).

**The Larger Plan: Capstone et al.**
Far from being the whole of the key-escrow plan, Clipper was only the beginning. Paralleling its development, and perhaps started earlier,[17] was the data-oriented Capstone program.

Like the Clipper chip, the Capstone chip implemented the Skipjack algorithm and key escrow. It also provided key management via the Key Exchange Algorithm (KEA). It has been claimed that this name is merely NSA's way of concealing use of Diffie-Hellman key exchange. The claim in made plausible by Capstone's third major capability: performing the NIST Digital Signature Algorithm, which uses the same arithmetic mechanism as Diffie-Hellman.

The major use for the Capstone chip was as the heart of a PCMCIA card originally called Tessera[18] and later renamed Fortezza. The initial use of the Fortezza card to provide security for the Military Messaging System (a form of email used by the Department of Defense) was expected to "bootstrap" the use of Fortezza cards for a wide range of computer applications.

**Clipper II, III, IV**

By the fall of 1995, it was clear that the Clipper chip was not popular. Only the AT&T product was using it, and only a few thousand of these had been sold. During the previous year, joint work between NIST, Georgetown University, and Trusted Information Systems (a small security company with headquarters in Maryland) had produced a software mechanism remarkably similar in function to the Clipper chip, using public-key cryptography where the Clipper chip had used physical tamper resistance. NIST issued a set of ten principles for software key escrow and scheduled two meetings to discuss the idea with industry representatives.

The project had a certain oddity to it. The promise was that systems complying with the ten principles would be exportable, but the meetings were hosted by an organization (NIST) without any role in the export process, and even its parent, the Department of Commerce, plays a role secondary to the Department of State in the issue of cryptography export. (Everyone in the game knows that if the Department of State agrees to "Commerce jurisdiction" for a product, export permission follows.) There was talk of a Federal Information Processing Standard for key escrow, but this too was odd. Each of the two extant cryptographic FIPS says, in effect, "This system is good enough for some category of government traffic." The proposal for software key escrow said nothing about cryptographic quality; indeed, it only specified a particular type of weakness. In the end no FIPS was ever proposed.

The essence of the "Ten Commandments," as they came to be known, was to limit the keys of exportable cryptosystems to 64 bits. Such systems must allow recovery of the key from traffic in either direction. They must not interoperate with unescrowed versions of the same systems.[19] Most important, the escrow agents would have to be in the United States[20] or in countries having bilateral agreements with the United States that guaranteed the US government access to the keys.

In 1996, derivatives of the software key escrow proposal evolved and eventually became part of the export regime. Technical developments included dropping the key-length restriction and relaxing the non-interoperability requirements, but the real developments were in marketing.

Intentionally blurring the distinction between communication and storage, proponents of key escrow have pushed the notion that key escrow is something that users need in order to be able to recover their data if they lose their keys. Along with this notion goes a new name, "key recovery," and a claim that key recovery is substantively different from key escrow. In respect to stored data, there is much to be said for this view. If you have encrypted all the copies of a file, then the keys are as valuable as the information the file contained. If you lose the keys, you lose the information. Under these circumstances, spare keys are more than a good idea; they are essential. On the other hand, the same is not true of communication. There is no reason to want to decrypt the ciphertext of a secure phone call after the call has ended. If either of the callers wanted a recording of the call, the right thing would be to record the plain text at one end of the line; that does not require escrowing any keys. Some forms of communication, such as email, do blur the distinction between key escrow and key recovery. Encrypted email is sometimes decrypted and reencrypted in a local storage key and sometimes left encrypted in the transit key (which is retained).

The other marketing angle was to present key recovery as an essential capability of the key-management infrastructure.[21] The message here is that users won't trust cryptographic systems unless they are sure that they can always get their data back.

These notions were set forth in the late spring of 1996 in the report of an interagency committee assembled to study cryptographic policy (White House 1996). In the fall, a proposed set of regulations containing a new sort of incentive followed. For two years, beginning on January 1, 1997, the government would allow export of unescrowed systems with 56-bit keys (mostly DES systems, presumably) in return for promises from the exporters that they would implement key-recovery systems in their products. Essentially simultaneously, IBM formed a coalition with other companies to implement key-recovery technology and announced what it claimed were fundamentally new and secure techniques for satisfying everybody. For nearly a year, IBM treated its new techniques as trade secrets, but in September 1997 they were made public in a technical report (Gennaro et al. 1997).

### The Multi-level Information Systems Security Initiative

After the success of the STU-III project, NSA broadened its objectives and began a project that was originally called the Future Secure Data System (paralleling Future Secure Voice System, the developmental name of STU-III) and later the Secure Data Network System (SDNS). The SDNS project developed protocols for security at several levels of network architecture, addressing such issues as network layer encryption and key management.

The Secure Data Network System has evolved into a substantial program called the Multi-level Information System Security Initiative (MISSI), the main goal of which is to solve a much broader range of computer security problems using encryption embodied in individually carried PCMCIA cards. A user sitting down at a workstation on the Defense Message System inserts a PCMCIA card that encrypts and decrypts email, for example. The Type II portion of the program uses the Fortezza card from the Capstone program and is entirely tied to key escrow.[22] After a brief flirtation with a Fortezza+ card, the Type I portion evolved a new PCMCIA card (called Krypton) with much higher performance.

The Computer Security Act of 1987 appeared to have put NSA out of the mass-market cryptography business in the late 1980s, but MISSI certainly looked like an attempt to get back in.

### The National Research Council Report

The Clipper controversy convinced Congress that an independent study was needed. In 1994 the National Research Council (NRC) was asked to conduct a "comprehensive independent review of national encryption policy" (PL 103-160, Sec. 267). Everything was to be considered, including the effect of cryptography on the national-security, the law-enforcement, commercial, and privacy interests of the United States, and the effect of export controls on US commercial interests.

The NRC put together a panel of 16 experts from government, industry, and science, 13 of whom had received security clearances.[23] The chairman, Kenneth Dam, had been Deputy Secretary of State under President Reagan; other panelists included General William Smith (former Deputy Commander in Chief of the European Command, and President Emeritus of the Institute for Defense Analyses), Ann Caracristi (former Deputy Director of NSA), and Benjamin Civiletti (Attorney General under President Carter).[24] Many opponents of the government's policies anticipated that such a group would support the Clinton administration's conservative directions in cryptography policy, but in its 1996 report it did not. Arguably its most important finding was that "the debate over national cryptography policy can be carried out in a reasonable manner on an unclassified basis" (Dam and Lin 1996, p. 298). The NRC panelists declared that, although classified information was often important in operational decisions, it was not essential to deciding how cryptography policy should evolve. This ran counter to the long-standing position of the intelligence community, and it was a striking conclusion to have come from a panel that included so many members of the national-security establishment.

The panel argued for broader use of cryptography ("on balance, the advantages of more widespread use of cryptography outweigh the disadvantages") and emphasized that there should be "broad availability of cryptography to all legitimate elements of US society." Current US policy, they said, was inadequate for the security requirements of an information society (ibid., p. 300–301), and current export policy hampered the domestic use of strong cryptosystems.[25] The panel urged that the market be allowed to decide the development and use of commercial cryptography.

Panelists urged an immediate loosening of export-control regulations. They recommended that products using DES for confidentiality purposes immediately be made easily exportable (ibid., p. 312). Observing that escrowed encryption was a new technology, and that new technologies come with potential flaws, the panel urged the US government to go slow with escrowed encryption—to experiment with the technique, but not to aggressively promote the concept until it had experimented with it on a small scale and knew how to adapt it for large-scale practice (ibid., pp. 328–329). Echoing the First Amendment and contradicting FBI Director Louis Freeh, the panel said that "no law should bar the manufacture, sale, or use of any form of encryption within the United States" (ibid., p. 303).

The panelists recognized that some of their recommendations would complicate law enforcement, and they urged that the government take steps to assist those responsible for law enforcement and national security in adjusting to the new technical realities (ibid., p. 322). In an analogy to the statute that criminalizes the use of the mails in commission of a crime, they suggested that the government consider legislation that would criminalize the use of encryption in interstate commerce with criminal intent. They also urged that law-enforcement agencies be given resources to help them handle the challenges posed by new technologies.

The short message of the report was that the United States would be better off with widespread use of cryptography than without it (ibid., p. 299). This was not a message the Clinton administration wanted to hear.

## International Lobbying

When the Clipper effort ran into problems at home, US government officials began lobbying for it—quietly—in other countries. In 1994, under the influence of such lobbying, the Australian government reported that the biggest *current* threats to telecommunications interception were digital telephony and encryption (Barrett 1994, p. 4). This was at a time when the only mass-market telephone encryption device available was the TSD 3600, most examples of which were either Clipper models bought by the FBI or export models with weak encryption.

The US lobbying had more profound success in Great Britain.[26] Beginning shortly after the announcement of the Clipper program in the United States, the Department of Trade and Industry began to sponsor research on public-key based escrow schemes at the Cryptologic Research Unit of the University of London. At the same time, development was going on behind the scenes on a draconian legal framework that would effectively outlaw the use of non-escrowed cryptography.[27]

Bilateral agreements on key escrow did not materialize, and the White House took a more public route through the Organization for Economic Cooperation and Development. The OECD is an association of industrialized democracies[28] that seeks to foster—not impede—international trade.

Cryptography was a natural topic for the OECD, which had a distinguished history in privacy policy.[29] Having developed policy guidelines for transborder data flows in 1980 and for information security in 1992, the OECD tackled encryption in early 1996.

The Clinton administration saw the OECD's efforts as a chance to get an international stamp of approval on its key-escrow plans and sent a delegation glaringly different from those usually seen at meetings of international economic-development organizations. Most often, Scott Charney, head of the Department of Justice's Computer Crime Unit, acted as chairman of this delegation. Also included were current and former members of the security establishment, such as Stewart Baker, former general counsel of NSA (who at one point took minutes for the OECD Secretariat), and Edward Appel of the National Security Council staff. With members representing the White House viewpoint, the US delegation pressed for adoption of key escrow. Initial reactions by the other delegates ranged from skepticism (the Japanese delegation wanted to know what would prevent criminals from using their own cryptography systems—see Baker 1997) to mild support for the US position (most notably from the British delegation).

In the economic-development setting of the OECD, key escrow was difficult to sell. Unlike law enforcement, business has little need for real-time access to communications, encrypted or otherwise. Other nations did not see the issues as the United States did. The Danish government's Information Technology panel recommended that no limits be placed on a citizen's right to use encryption (ITSC 1996). The Dutch delegate spoke in opposition (Rotenberg 1996, p. 7). The Nordic countries argued for strong cryptography without trap doors.[30] Meanwhile, German companies, taking advantage of the restrictions on their US competitors, were selling strong cryptography, and the German government had little interest in restricting such sales.[31] Behind the scenes, and kept very much in the background, was Phil Reitinger, a member of the US Department of Justice Computer Crime Division, who was seconded to the OECD to write a draft policy. Yet even this influence was insufficient to convince OECD member nations to support the US policy.

In late March of 1997 the OECD issued its cryptography guidelines, which sidestepped key escrow and emphasized the importance of trust in cryptographic products ("Principle 1: Market forces should serve to build trust in reliable systems"). The OECD recommended that cryptography be developed in response to the needs of "individuals, businesses, and [lastly] governments," and urged that "the development and provision of cryptographic methods should be determined by the market in an open and competitive environment, and that the development of international technical standards, criteria and protocols for cryptographic methods should also be market driven" (OECD 1997). Despite the intense lobbying efforts by the Clinton administration, mandatory key escrow did not make it into the OECD's cryptography guidelines.

Seven months later the European Commission dealt a further blow to the US position. In a policy paper on a European framework for digital signatures and encryption, the commission was cool to key escrow. It observed that such schemes are easily circumvented and that the involvement of a third party increases the likelihood of message exposure (European Commission 1997, pp. 16–17). The Commission expressed concern about the difficulty of key escrow across national borders. The report said that any such scheme should be limited to what is "absolutely necessary" (ibid., p. 18)—hardly the ringing endorsement the US was seeking.

### The US Congress' Response

Congress entered the fray in March of 1996 when Senator Patrick Leahy introduced the Encrypted Communications Privacy Act of 1996 (S 1587), a compromise bill that allowed for a relaxation of export controls, affirmed the right to use any form of encryption domestically, created a legal framework for escrow agents, and criminalized the use of encryption in the furtherance of a crime. Less than a month later, Senator Conrad Burns proposed the more strongly pro-cryptography Promotion of Commerce On-Line in the Digital Era (PRO-CODE) Act (S 1726). Burns's bill prohibited mandatory key escrow, enshrined the freedom to sell and use any type of encryption domestically, and liberalized export rules. But 1996 was a presidential-election year, and the complex legislation did not go forward.

Burns reintroduced PRO-CODE in 1997 (S 377). In the House, Representative Bob Goodlatte proposed the Security and Freedom through Encryption Act (SAFE) Act (HR 695). Under both bills, the freedom to sell and use any type of encryption would be unconstrained, and mandatory key escrow would be prohibited. Export of cryptography would be under the control of the Department of Commerce, and export of strong encryption would be permitted if similar products were available overseas. The SAFE bill would criminalize the use of encryption in the furtherance of a crime; the PRO-CODE bill did not address that issue.

In his trademark cowboy hat, Montana Senator Burns seemed like an unusual legislator to be pressing for liberalization of laws on high technology. Burns saw PRO-CODE as having a significant impact on rural areas, where distances preclude face-to-face communication, and where substantial economic growth in recent years has occurred exactly in activities that would greatly benefit from secure electronic communications (Carney 1997).

When Congress reconvened at the end of the summer, the tables turned again. At a Senate Commerce Committee markup, the PRO-CODE bill was sidetracked and replaced by one introduced by Senators Bob Kerrey and John McCain. The Secure Public Networks Act (S. 909), tightened rather than loosened control over the export of encryption products and created incentives for many organizations to introduce key escrow.

Cryptography was also in trouble in the House of Representatives. Despite repeated assurances from the Clinton administration that it would not move for domestic regulation of cryptography, FBI Director Louis Freeh pressed Congress for restrictive laws. The House International Relations and Judiciary Committees had reported the SAFE bill out positively, but the House National Security Committee listened closely to Freeh's requests, and accepted an "amendment in the nature of a substitute," introduced by Representatives Porter J. Goss and Norman D. Dicks, which turned Goodlatte's measure around completely. It not only tightened controls on export, but proposed legal controls on the use of cryptography. With various versions of the SAFE bill in the House, and different measure pending in the Senate, it was far from clear what direction Congress would take.

# 10
# Conclusion

Telecommunication, barely a century and a half old, has so transformed society that, for most people in industrialized countries, it is a necessity, not an option. People move thousands of miles from friends and family, knowing that they can keep in touch by phone and email. People telecommute to work or, having commuted to the office, spend the day on the phone talking to distant offices or customers. People order goods from dealers on the other side of the continent by dialing 800 numbers. For a remarkable range and an increasing number of activities, telecommunication stands on an equal footing with physical communication.

Side by side with the growth of telecommunication there has grown up a major "industry" of spying on telecommunications. Communications interception has played a crucial role in intelligence since World War I, and despite improvements in communication security it continues to grow. The growth of interception is a consequence of the essential fact that the most important effect of the improvements in communications technology on communications intelligence has been to draw more and more valuable traffic into telecommunications channels. As a result, spying on such channels becomes more and more rewarding for governments, businesses, and criminals.

Consider two sets of imaginary events, one taking place in 1945 and the other in 1995. Both take place within major companies with physically separated facilities. The 1945 call is brief, a minute or two. It invites you to an end-of-year project review. You must take a two-day trip to the Pfister Hotel in Milwaukee. It is a nuisance just before Christmas, but there is no alternative. Half a century later, the project review might very well be conducted by conference call, and the associated final report might be sent to all the participants by fax or email.

Now consider the impact of a competitor's intercepting the communications. The 1945 spy has learned only that interesting information will be available at the Pfister Hotel in Milwaukee a few days hence. He knows where to go to get the information he wants, but is still separated from the information by substantial work and risk. On the other hand, the 1995 spy will have all the information handed to her on the same circuit through which she learned about the meeting. All she has to do is keep listening.

The potential impact on privacy is profound. Telecommunications are intrinsically interceptable, and this interceptability has by and large been enhanced by digital technology. Communications designed to be sorted and switched by digital computers can be sorted and recorded by digital computers. Common-channel signaling, broadcast networks, and communication satellites facilitate interception on a grand scale previously unknown. Laws will not change these facts.

It may not be possible to prevent communications from being intercepted, but it is possible to protect them. The technology for protecting telecommunications is cryptography, which, despite its ancient origins, is largely a product of the twentieth century. For the first 50 years after radio brought cryptography to the fore in World War I, the field was dominated by the military. Then, in the late 1960s and the early 1970s, a combination of the declining cost of digital computation and foreseeable civilian needs brought a surge of academic and commercial interest in the field.

The work of the civilian cryptographers revealed two things. One was that cryptography was not a field that could effectively be kept secret.[1] In the 1930s and the 1950s—both formative periods in American military cryptography—computational capabilities lagged so far behind requirements that building secure cryptosystems took a lot of cleverness and used techniques not applicable elsewhere. By comparison, in a world in which inexpensive digital computing is ubiquitous, cryptography does not usually represent a large fraction of the computing budget.[2]

Today, constructing cryptographic devices and programs is regarded as easy. Developing sophisticated cryptographic hardware is within the abilities of a talented engineer or a small startup company.[3] Developing cryptographic programs is far easier; it is within the means of any competent programmer who possesses a copy of, for example, Bruce Schneier's book *Applied Cryptography*.

Independent cryptographers startled the cryptographic world by demonstrating that privacy can be manufactured "end to end" without the help of any centralized resources. Diffie-Hellman key exchange allows two parties to derive a secret from negotiations in which every bid and every response is public. This changed the basic power relationships in cryptography. Before public-key technology, cryptography always required centralized facilities to manufacture and distribute equipment and keys, a feature particularly compatible with the top-down organization of the military. By contrast, public-key cryptography was developed to support the interactions of businesses in a community of equals.

Privacy is the best-known benefit of cryptography; however, it is not the only one, and it may not be the most valuable one. Cryptography also provides authenticity, which enables communicators to be sure of the identities of the people they are communicating with.[4] In a business transaction, authentication verifies that the person acting in one instance is the same person who acted in another—that the person who is writing a check, for example, is the same person who opened the account and put the money in it.

The US military responded to the rise of private cryptography by attempting to reestablish control over the technology through Atomic Energy Act-like prior restraint of research and publication.[5] When this effort appeared to have failed (largely as a result of its obvious unconstitutionality), the government attempted to control cryptographic products directly, first through standardization and later through regulation of exports. In 1993, it unveiled the concept of key escrow—cryptography that would provide protection against everyone except the US government. Although the notion was not well received, its proponents (most of them in the government) have kept pushing, constantly giving ground to business objections but holding firmly to the view that it is the government's right to take measures to guarantee that citizens cannot encode things so that the government cannot read them.

Over roughly a century there evolved in the United States the concept of wiretapping as a form of search that should be controlled by court-issued warrants similar to those required for searches of physical premises. Although law-enforcement agencies had been intercepting communications since the 1890s, it was not until 1968 that Congress put law-enforcement wiretaps on a solid legal footing. The Omnibus Safe Streets and Crime Control Act, which limited the use of wiretaps to certain crimes and established stringent warrant requirements, was upheld by the courts. As a result, wiretapping has become a generally accepted, if not widely employed, police practice. Law enforcement speaks freely of its "right to use court-ordered wiretaps" and appears to think of the use of cryptography as a threat to this right.

There is a clearly discernible difference, however, between the right to listen and the right to understand what one has heard. The doctrine of wiretapping as a type of search takes for granted the government's ability to practice wiretapping, just as the Fourth Amendment to the Constitution takes for granted the government's ability to break down doors and look under floorboards. It recognizes the power to intercept telecommunication, like the ability to search houses, as having such potential for abuse as to require stringent judicial control. It regulates the right to listen.

Guaranteeing the right to understand is different. To do that, you must regulate the individual to prevent him from taking actions that would otherwise be within his power to protect his communications from being understood. This seems analogous to the ludicrous notion that the government's right to search your house entails a right to find what it is looking for and a power to forbid people to hide things.

There is another problem with the notion of wiretaps as searches. Searches are, by legal intention and usually by physical fact, obvious. It is difficult to search a property and be sure that the search will not be detected. Furthermore, in a tradition dating back to English common law, secret searches were forbidden; where possible, the searchers were expected to knock and to confront the householder.[6] Wiretaps, in contrast, are invisible. Although it behooves anyone who takes the privacy of communication seriously to assume that every word is being recorded, obtaining confirmation of that fact in any individual instance is usually impossible. Treating wiretaps as searches thus leaves open the possibility that wiretapping may be rampant, may be used as a mechanism of political and social control far beyond the bounds of proper law enforcement, and yet may go unchecked because of public ignorance. Under the "Title III" law of 1968, Congress sought to preclude this possibility by means of stringent reporting requirements. Individuals must be notified that they have been wiretapped, even if they are not prosecuted, and details of all legal wiretapping activity are collected and published in the annual *Wiretap Report*. Ten years later, however, Congress created new authority to wiretap, primarily for counterintelligence purposes. Under the Foreign Intelligence Surveillance Act of 1978, only the total numbers of wiretaps are reported. Details need never be made public.[7]

The government's attempts to control the citizens' access to technology for protecting their communications (and thereby guarantee its ability to understand what it intercepts) have been accompanied by a dramatic expansion of the basic ability to wiretap. The Communications Assistance for Law Enforcement Act of 1994 (CALEA) requires telephone companies make their networks "wiretap ready" so that new features in communications do not interfere with government wiretapping.

The government is attempting to expand its powers of search despite the gradual acceptance of a basic human right to privacy. Although it was already recognized in ancient times, privacy has come into its own as a legal entity only in recent centuries. In large part this has been a response to the developments of the technological age. Through a series of court decisions (including *NAACP v. Alabama*, *Griswold*, and *Katz*), the US Supreme Court expanded the notion of privacy that is implicit, but never given that name, in the Constitution. Though private businesses often intrude upon individual privacy, their intrusions pale beside those of the government. Over the past 50 years, government has invaded individuals' privacy on myriad occasions. Citizens engaged in peaceful political activity (including the Socialist Workers Party, the civil rights movement, and protests against the Vietnam War in the 1950s and the 1960s and the Committee in Solidarity with the People of El Salvador in the 1980s), journalists and editors, and political leaders (including Supreme Court justices) all have been wiretapped. Members of Congress who disagreed with the president's policies during the Vietnam era were subjects of biweekly FBI reports. Even politically uninvolved citizens who happened to use mail or telegraph to communicate internationally have had their communications intercepted.[8] Information obtained by the government for use in one venue has often been used in another. Census data were used to locate Japanese-Americans so they could be interned during World War II. Some "national-security" wiretaps under various presidents were actually investigations aimed at domestic politics.[9]

The government's record of privacy violations means that any broadening of its snooping powers must be viewed with the gravest concern. CALEA is the basis for a vast expansion of government surveillance powers. As even the government will admit, its efforts have succeeded in slowing down cryptography's progress and its use in the public sector. Even were the government's record of using its powers not strewn with tales of abuse, there would be reason to worry.

Intentions can change far more quickly than capabilities. Today the authority of most government officials to use wiretaps is tightly regulated by law. Laws, however, can change. Were Congress to decide that wiretaps should be usable by any police department without court supervision— much as the police are free to employ stool pigeons without court supervision—the situation could change overnight. The capacity of the telephone system to support wiretaps, by contrast, would not. Although the present-day phone system is quite capable of supporting the 1500 or so wiretaps that now occur each year, it would not be capable of supporting 10 or 100 times as many. But if the FBI has its way, in a decade or two, after the impact of CALEA has been felt, this may no longer be the case. The way will have been paved for a vast expansion in government surveillance, and only an act of Congress will be required to bring it about.

The push to expand the interception of communications comes at a time when police have experienced an unprecedented expansion of their powers of surveillance in almost every area. Advances in electronics permit subminiature bugs that are hard to detect electronically or physically. Video cameras watch streets, shops, subways, and public buildings. Vast databases keep tabs on the credit, the possessions, and the criminal records of most of the population. Many of these facilities play far greater roles in criminal investigations than wiretaps, and any loss of investigative power that results from changes in communications technology seems minuscule in comparison.

## The Government's Case

Throughout its history, the National Security Agency has sought to prevent the development of cryptography in the public world. In the 1960s, NSA tried to prevent the publication of David Kahn's popular book *The Codebreakers* (Bamford 1982, pp. 125–126). In the 1970s, its director, Bobby Ray Inman, threatened the academic community with prior restraint. In the early 1980s, it tried to halt other government funding of academic research in cryptography, and it also tried to prevent the publication of James Bamford's history of NSA, *The Puzzle Palace*. In the mid 1980s it succeeded in getting the Reagan administration to promulgate NSDD-145, a directive that sought to expand NSA's authority to include control over the technology for handling "sensitive but unclassified information."

The NSDD-145 effort backfired, and instead increased the National Institute of Standards and Technology's responsibilities for computer security standards (including those for civilian cryptography). Unfortunately, the Computer Security Act of 1987, which conferred this responsibility on NIST, was not accompanied by sufficient funding to enable NIST to do the job. The NSA, which had vastly greater resources, forced NIST into a Memorandum of Understanding that shackled NIST's attempt to develop its own cryptography standardization program. The dismal record of the Digital Signature Standard is one example. The Clipper episode, an even more striking example of the misuse of the standards process to further NSA's aims rather than the goals of the law, resulted in the demise of the AT&T TSD 3600, the first mass-market telephone-security device. For over a decade, cryptography policy in the Commerce Department has been dictated by NSA.[10]

Despite its apparent ability to control NIST, NSA has acted like an agency under fire ever since the passage of the Computer Security Act. The law, after all, is quite clear about where responsibilities lie, and a different Congress or a new president might decide that US interests are best served by a liberal policy regarding the use of cryptography. NSA's decision to involve the FBI in the cryptography wars proved astute.

The end of the Cold War had diminished the heft that national-security arguments carried, and even that weight had proved insufficient to guarantee NSA the role it sought under the Computer Security Act. It was one thing to bend everything to the will of an intelligence agency in a world where the United States had an enemy that could annihilate it on a day's notice. It was quite another in a world where people were talking about the degree to which intelligence could assist US industry.

In the post-Cold War world, law enforcement was playing a more significant role in national-security issues than ever before. Involvement of the FBI in cryptography policy had the potential to result in a rewriting of the government equation on encryption. In the late 1980s, when the FBI learned about encryption, it asked the Senate Judiciary Committee for a resolution calling on telephone companies to provide the plaintext of any encrypted messages that were encountered during court-authorized wiretapping. The FBI also submitted "digital telephony" bills to Congress.

The FBI's Advanced Telephony Unit studied encryption. In 1992 it warned that by 1995 no more that 40% of Title III wiretaps would be intelligible and that in worst case all might be rendered useless (Advanced Telephony Unit 1992). In 1994, when he testified before Congress in support of the "Digital Telephony" bill (later passed as CALEA), FBI Director Louis Freeh emphasized the importance of wiretaps in solving kidnappings and in preventing terrorist actions (Freeh 1994b).[11] Freeh claimed that the FBI sought only to maintain the status quo given to law enforcement by Title III and to keep up with the new technology. Whatever truth there may be in these statements is hard to find. In 1994 Assistant Attorney General Jo Ann Harris admitted that, a year after the introduction of the Clipper proposal, the FBI had yet to encounter a single instance of encrypted voice communications (Harris 1994).[12] Two years later, the National Research Council panel was also unable to find any FBI Title III surveillances that had encountered problems due to encryption (Dam 1997, p. 3). Freeh had claimed in February 1994 that hundreds of wiretaps had been rendered useless by advanced switching technology, but he cited only 93 instances when he testified to Congress a month later. Even then, not all of the instances Freeh cited were wiretaps; some were electronic bugs, which are not affected by encryption.

FBI Directors have always emphasized the use of wiretaps in kidnapping investigations, and Louis Freeh was no exception. In fact wiretaps were used on average in only two to three kidnapping cases a year in the period 1968–1993.[13] Terrorist actions were likewise cited as an important reason for wiretaps, despite the fact that there were no Title III wiretaps in terrorist cases in the period 1988–1994.

In pressing for various new wiretapping capabilities, FBI Assistant Director James Kallstrom argued: "... just for the FBI alone, we have used court-authorized electronic surveillance to capture terrorists intent on blowing up buildings and tunnels in New York, to detect and capture pedophiles who intended to brutally murder their intended victim, to arrest and convict various organized crime leaders like John Gotti, and to successfully investigate a spy whose espionage cost many their lives" (Kallstrom 1997). However, the Rahman case ("terrorists intent on blowing up buildings and tunnels in New York") turned not on wiretaps, but on other forms of electronic surveillance, including a body wire (which does not require a warrant); the valuable evidence in the Gotti case came from an electronic bug;[14] and the wiretap in the Ames case ("a spy whose espionage cost many their lives") served in a tangential fashion, enabling the government to pressure Ames to reveal information in order that his wife—whose knowledge of his spying activities was revealed on the wiretaps—receive a reduced sentence.[15]

Immediately after the Oklahoma City bombing and the TWA 800 explosion, the FBI called for expanded wiretapping capabilities, even though wiretapping would not have prevented Oklahoma City and the FBI has now acknowledged that TWA 800 appears to have been the result of mechanical failure. The FBI's interpretations of CALEA have included substantial expansions of wiretapping capabilities, and some of the FBI's requests (e.g. in regard to locations of cell phones) were actually in direct contradiction to the law.

NSA was fighting a turf battle with NIST, and was using the cloak of national security to make its arguments. The FBI, on the other hand, stretched the truth and distorted the facts. Few of the government's arguments regarding the criticality of wiretaps in criminal investigations hold up under scrutiny. It seems fair to conclude that the government has not made its case regarding encryption.

### Prospects for Intelligence

For thousands of years, a country could strictly limit what other nations could learn about it. The past century and a half, however, brought the camera, the airplane, and the spy satellite. The interiors of countries are no longer closed to view. They are visible to all the major powers, and with every passing year they are more visible to smaller countries, news media, and commercial interests.

In recent years, the development of space technology has served communications intelligence just as it served photographic intelligence, allowing giant antennas to be put in orbit where they can catch signals from any nation. However, the growth of technology bodes another change: the development of encryption may cause a steady decline in the amount of intercepted traffic that can be understood.

As we have stated before, the principal effect of advancing communication technology on communications intelligence is to bring more and more valuable traffic into telecommunications channels. By comparison with the explosive expansion in the use of telecommunications, the application of protective measures will turn out to lie somewhere between "less important" and "insignificant." Losses due to encryption will be mitigated by many factors, and communications intelligence will be with us for as long as people communicate.

That is not so say that communications intelligence will be untouched or unchanged by the spread of cryptography. It seems likely, indeed, that the character of the COMINT product will change, improving in some respects and declining in others. Because people are often prone to mourn the loss of something on which they have come to depend and slow to see the possibilities of the unfamiliar, it will not be surprising if the change is perceived as decline by many COMINT professionals.

One area in particular in which COMINT has surpassed all other forms of intelligence, with the possible exception of HUMINT, is the discovery of opponents' intentions. Listening to people's communications—particularly when they are speaking or writing candidly out of misplaced faith in their security—can reveal their real objectives and the unspoken desires that underlie their public negotiating positions. This coveted capability is one that COMINT may have to surrender, and a replacement for it seems hard to find.

On the other hand, improvements in communications and increasing human dependence on communications will open new areas of intelligence. Network-penetration techniques will make it possible to capture information that is being stored rather than communicated, and such information is less likely to be encrypted. Even more exciting is the prospect that, in a world with hundreds of countries and thousands of other centers of authority, there will be innumerable agencies responsible for issuing credentials and authorizing acceptance of other agencies' credentials. We will no doubt see numerous cases in which information is leaked to opponents because they are not recognized as opponents. Active network intelligence measures will become the HUMINT of the next century and it will interact extensively with traditional HUMINT.

In the United States, and perhaps elsewhere, communications intelligence plays less of a role in industrial espionage than in national espionage. Businesses often have a better means of acquiring information: hiring workers away from their competitors. In the world of the Cold War, a world of open hostility between two major coalitions, changing sides was difficult. It did happen, and some people[16] made a big success of it, but it was a risky business and hard to do more than once. In a world of shifting alliances in which international competition is more commercial than military, defection may become as big a feature of national intelligence as of industrial intelligence.

Tactical communications intelligence will probably improve despite the prevalence of encryption. Cryptography is much less successful at concealing patterns of communication than at concealing the contents of messages. In many environments, addresses (and, equally important, precedences) must be left in clear so that routers will know how packets are to be forwarded. In most environments, the lengths and timings of messages are difficult to conceal. SIGINT organizations are already adept at extracting intelligence from traffic patterns and will adapt to extract more. The resulting intelligence product, abetted by increases in computer power, may not give as detailed a picture in some places but will give a more comprehensive overview.

Some improvements in SIGINT technology cannot easily be categorized as tactical or strategic. They take the form of increased speed and flexibility of the sort that has changed many organizations over the past decades. The current intelligence cycle in SIGINT is a slow one that can be summarized as follows:

- Intelligence consumers formulate requirements.

- The requirements are translated into guidelines about what to intercept.

- Intercepted material is acquired "in the field" and shipped home for analysis and interpretation.[17]

- On the basis of cryptanalysis, interpretation, and political analysis, the information is judged, as are the guidelines under which it is acquired.

- The guidelines are either continued or modified. New intercept facilities may be assigned to a project, new facilities may be built, new instructions on traffic characteristics may be issued, or the project may be dropped.

This process may take weeks, months, or years. Often, significant information will not be acquired simply because it was not being looked for.

Increasing automation and decreasing size and cost of electronic equipment will make for vast improvements in this cycle, resulting in a tighter "target, intercept, analyze" loop. This will be aided by the development of tamper-resistance technology. The secrecy of many SIGINT processes makes intelligence organizations reluctant to use them anywhere but in the most secure areas of their own headquarters. Tamper-resistant chips allow intercept equipment in the field to perform such sensitive operations as cryptanalysis. This permits them to search the contents of ciphertext messages just as they would the contents of plaintext messages.[18]

An example of a SIGINT technology with unfathomed potential is emitter identification. The vanishing cost of signal processors has reduced the cost of this technology and so expanded the range of possible uses.[19] In many cases, emitter identification will counter the concealment of addressing by link encryption.

Not all the growth that can be expected in SIGINT will result from SIGINT technologies. A fast-growing portion of the telecommunications market all over the world is *fixed position cellular telephony*. The cost of radio technology has dropped to the point where, in many rural areas, it is cheaper to have a cellular telephone in each house than to run wire. The result is that a whole segment of the telecommunications market that was once effectively out of reach of intelligence organizations is now coming, at least partly, within its grasp.

From a practical viewpoint, it is important to note that nothing will happen overnight. The vast legacy of equipment, services, experience, and investments in communications from the twentieth century will guarantee the future of much of communications intelligence well into the twenty-first.

## Prospects for Law Enforcement

The dramatic growth of technology in the twentieth century has given law enforcement a wide variety of technical capabilities, one of which is wire-tapping. At present, law-enforcement personnel are worried that advances in communications technology, particularly in cryptography, will lead to a decline in the usefulness of wiretaps. Should this happen, its effect on law enforcement is likely to be modest. Even among tools of electronic surveillance, wiretaps are generally overshadowed by the many kinds of bugging devices used to intercept face-to-face conversations. Electronic surveillance, furthermore, plays a minor role in police investigation by comparison with record keeping, photography, and a broad spectrum of forensic techniques.

Yet wiretapping would appear to have gained more than it has lost (and perhaps more than it stands to lose) from modern technology. At one time a wiretap was, literally a pair of wires attached somewhere between the target's telephone and the telephone office. Its placement and its use entailed a risk of discovery and brought the listeners only disembodied voices. Today, even without the vast wiretapping capacity envisioned by CALEA, wiretaps are "installed" in the software of digital telephone switches. Knowledge about installed wiretaps can be kept to a few telephone-company employees. More important, the taps carry with them extensive call-status information that often makes the identities of the talkers or their locations immediately available.[20]

Law enforcement's gains from advances in technology are not, however, limited to investigation. The police are a mechanism of social control (Manning 1977, p. 23), and their work goes hand in hand with other mechanisms of social control. Improving communication is enhancing "employee supervision" throughout society. In the past, ambassadors and senior military commanders were sent off to the other side of the world with general mission statements and no opportunity to report their successes and failures—let alone ask for advice—for months or years. Today, the president can reach his senior emissaries at a moment's notice anywhere on Earth. At lower levels, employees in many jobs are now monitored by machines. Workers who once had substantial autonomy, such as truck drivers, find that they are subject to the same sort of close monitoring that might have been expected on a factory floor.[21]

Society is also gaining an ability to keep close track of individuals' interests and expertise. Online uses of information resources are intrinsically less private than paper ones. For example, monitoring which documents visitors to libraries consult or what pages they copy would be expensive and, despite the FBI's Library Awareness Program, is probably rare. When people consult sources of information on the Internet, however, monitoring is inexpensive and hard to separate from services the users value. Commercial Web pages record IP addresses and other available information about the "callers" and use it for marketing. Exchange of information among Web sites presents the prospect of a comprehensive profile of each Web user.

### What Kind of Society Do We Want?

In deciding that the Constitution protected Charles Katz against electronic surveillance even though there was no intrusion onto Katz's property, the Supreme Court looked through the propertarian technicality of the Fourth Amendment to its essential objective. As human society changes from one dominated by physical contact to one dominated by digital communication, we will have many opportunities to choose between preserving the older forms of social interaction and asking ourselves what those forms were intended to achieve.

In the societies that have dominated human culture for most of its existence, a general awareness of the pattern of contacts among people was an essential feature of life. In a society dominated by telecommunication, a pattern of contacts is far less visible to the ordinary person and far more susceptible to monitoring by police and intelligence organizations. This produces a fundamental shift of power away from the general population and into the hands of those organizations.

Technology seems to make some losses of privacy inevitable. The capacity to build databases and feed them the details of every credit-card transaction exists, and the result is an excruciatingly detailed portrait of the shopping, traveling, and trysting habits of hundreds of millions of people. Yet, since such databases are an essential component of today's commerce and millions of people work in the industry they support, it seems realistic to accept them. The best we can hope to do is to regulate their use in a way that protects individual privacy.

On the other hand, perhaps the compilation of databases—born of the need for billing and credit verification, but later put to numerous intrusive marketing uses—can be avoided by means of another technology. One strong theme in electronic commerce is a return to the anonymity of money. If you have funds in your electronic wallet, you can spend them, and merchants have no need to know who you are or how good your credit is. In such an environment, the desire of marketers to keep records on customers could well give way to the customers' desire for privacy.

The area in which technology can most clearly make a positive contribution to privacy is encryption. If we assert the individual's right to private conversation and take measures in the construction of our communication systems to protect that right, we may remove the danger that surveillance will grow to unprecedented proportions and become an oppressive mechanism of social control. Fortunately, the fight for cryptographic freedom, unlike the fight against credit databases, is a fight in which privacy and commerce are on the same side.

The great vision of electronic commerce is an orgy of buying and selling over the Internet, and the vastness of the Internet is essential to this vision.

This vastness is less a function of the tens of thousands of miles over which it spreads or of the millions of computers connected to it (though this comes closer) than of the diversity of those computers—a diversity of hardware, a diversity of protocols, a diversity of tasks, a diversity of ownership, a diversity of businesses, a diversity of regulatory environments, and a diversity of objectives.[22] What is required in this environment is what public-key cryptography has made possible: secure communication between parties with minimal trust. Requiring key escrow, which came to seem natural to the military mind as a result of decades of a key management system that amounted to escrow, would cripple cryptography's contribution to secure worldwide communication.

### Cryptography in Context

The words of the Supreme Court's *Katz* opinion have an importance that transcends the development of American wiretap law. They echo in concrete form Louis Brandeis's view that "time works changes." If there is a right to use cryptography, it must grow from the historical fact of private conversation. Since many conversations today can take place only by telephone, stepping away from other people is no longer a universally applicable security measure. It is not realistic to say to someone "If you don't like the possibility of being tapped, you have the choice of not using the telephone." Stepping away from other people is the expression of a right to keep conversation private in a face-to-face world; use of cryptography is an expression of that right in an electronic world.

The discussion of which this book is part has focused on whether cryptography should be allowed to develop in response to commercial and technical influences or whether it should be regulated by governments. This narrow question excludes consideration of many possibilities —technical and otherwise—that address the larger social issues on which communications privacy bears.

In a sense, it is curious that the Constitution regulates the power of the police to search (and, derivatively, their power to conduct electronic surveillance) but leaves activities that are at least as dangerous and disruptive, such as the use of undercover agents and the mounting of sting operations, up to individual detectives or their chiefs.[23]

In light of the curiously small number of prosecutions in which wiretap evidence plays a significant role, it appears that wiretapping is far more valuable as an intelligence tool than as a way of gathering evidence. This utility, however, is not recognized by US law, under which wiretap warrants must name particular suspects and crimes. Police who wish to use wiretaps in the gathering of intelligence are therefore forced into the duplicitous position of representing any wiretap as an attempt to gather evidence. A reform of wiretap law might plausibly recognize the police intelligence applications of wiretapping and give courts the means to supervise it.

Technology might also be applied to streamline the courts' oversight of law-enforcement activities, just as it has made so many improvements in the activities themselves. It seems certain that at some time in the future courts will choose to accept applications and issue warrants electronically, using digitally signed messages. This would reduce law enforcement's logistic overhead and would permit warrants to be more carefully focused. Police might, for example, be more readily granted a warrant limited to communications between two people than a warrant encompassing all the communications of one person. Quick turnaround would permit police to base such warrant requests on the calling patterns of suspects and to get a new warrant promptly when a new link in a conspiracy was identified. Such an arrangement would respond to Brandeis's concern that "whenever a telephone line is tapped, the privacy of the persons at both ends of the line is invaded" (Brandeis 1928, pp. 475–476) by making an effort to target only calls in which both participants were suspects.

Of course, if the utility of wiretaps is no greater than the publicly available evidence suggests,[24] perhaps they should be dropped from police methodology altogether—not because they are an invasion of anyone's privacy, but merely because they are a waste of tax money.

## What Is Possible?

Cryptography, once an arcane art, is now inseparable from mainstream computing technology. Cryptographic equipment is neither difficult to build nor demanding in its computing requirements. Any attempt to control the deployment of cryptography must contend with this fact. Attempting to control cryptography is more like the notoriously unsuccessful attempt to outlaw alcohol than it is like the control of guns, the manufacture of which is beyond the capabilities of the typical home shop.

Furthermore, antisocial uses of cryptography are less demanding than socially beneficial uses. A group of conspirators trying to rob a bank, blow up a building, or commit fraud is typically small, rarely more than a dozen people. On the other hand, the use of cryptography in electronic commerce will require providing millions of people with interoperable cryptographic devices and a steady supply of supporting electronic credentials. In short, the latter is probably controllable; the former probably is not. In pursuing policies that limit the use of cryptography for business purposes, out of fear that it will be used for criminal ones, we deny ourselves one benefit without achieving the other.

It has been argued that it is important to prevent the ubiquitous use of cryptography in order not to lose the ability to monitor communications between criminals and non-criminals. Arranging any substantial crime, from a bank heist to a bombing, is likely to entail commonplace actions such as renting cars, booking hotel rooms, or buying airplane tickets. If the police can monitor the phone calls in which criminals transact the ordinary part of their business, they will have a very good idea of what the criminals are up to, even if all the calls from criminal to criminal are encrypted. On the other hand, since the signaling information will tell the police what legitimate businesses the suspects are calling, the police will be able to approach the businesses and make enquiries.

Another area in which cryptography is said to be interfering with police work is the protection of stored data. One view holds that searches and seizures of computer media are far more important to police than wiretaps, and that cryptography may make them ineffective. The precise importance of seized computer media is hard to judge. The FBI has a central laboratory for processing those that cannot be adequately examined by field offices.[25] This lab handled about 400 cases in 1994, of which it estimated that 2% involved cryptography. This does not mean that the FBI was unable to read the files; in any case, it is probably a generous estimate that counts anything that could possibly be called cryptography.[26]

The protection of storage—particularly as it might be applied to protecting the records of a criminal group—appears to be a less complex phenomenon than the protection of communications. In the former case the decrypting can be done by the person who did the encrypting, reducing problems of key management. In view of the fact that the desire to protect the information in readily stealable laptop computers provides widespread motivation to use encrypted storage, it appears unlikely that any law would be effective in preventing the encryption of stored data in non-escrowed systems.

It is also appropriate to ask what is legally sustainable. The Constitution has a strong principle of freedom of speech that is generally interpreted as encompassing the freedom to write and publish. It is the US government's current position that publication of programs on the Internet is not protected free speech and can legitimately be regulated as export. This view has been challenged by the mathematician Daniel Bernstein, who has asserted a free-speech right to publish the code of a cryptographic algorithm electronically. Bernstein has won the first round. In June 1996, US District Court Judge Marilyn Hall Patel ruled that computer programs are a form of speech and thus subject to First Amendment protection.[27] In a stinging opinion issued later that year (*Daniel Bernstein v. United States Department of State*, 945 F. Supp. 1279. (N.D. Cal. 1996)), Patel held that the government's action was an unconstitutional prior restraint on free speech, but the issue will not be effectively decided until the case makes its way to the Supreme Court.[28] If free speech prevails, export control may be entirely bypassed. This will likely be true even if the government's narrower position—that executable computer programs are not protected—is upheld. If technical papers and standards and other non-executable information can circulate freely, compatible cryptographic systems can simply be implemented locally, and no exports or imports need actually occur.

## Suppose We Were to Make a Mistake?

Suppose we were to allow the unfettered development of cryptography and later decide that government access to communications is necessary?

Suppose we were to build surveillance into our communications although none is needed? Which would be the more serious error?

It is generally accepted that rights are not absolute. If private access to high-grade encryption presented a clear and present danger to society, there would be little political opposition to controlling it. The reason there is so much disagreement is that there is so little evidence of a problem.

If allowing or even encouraging wide dissemination of high-grade cryptography proves to be a mistake, it will be a correctable mistake. Generations of electronic equipment follow one another very quickly. If cryptography comes to present such a problem that there is popular consensus for regulating it, regulation will be just as possible in a decade as it is today. The laws will change, strong cryptography will not be made part of new products, and the ready availability that government claims to fear will decline quite quickly. If, on the other hand, we set the precedent of building government surveillance capabilities into our security equipment, we risk the very survival of democracy.

Control of cryptography is being promoted on the grounds that it will protect our sources of foreign intelligence and protect the ability of police to use wiretaps to investigate criminals. None of the current plans seems to offer much hope in either direction.

Key escrow would protect our ability to collect intelligence against other countries only if we could persuade them to escrow their keys in the United States. Had the Clipper system had any chance of achieving worldwide deployment, it might have served this function; its escrow agents appear capable of providing keys in real time,[29] which would allow intercept equipment to make use of them in deciding whether traffic was worth recording. More recent proposals appear to recognize the infeasibility of persuading countries to accept extra-territorial escrow and to acknowledge that key escrow will function under the laws of the countries in which it operates. We have argued that cryptography can be implemented by a startup programmer. It can probably be implemented by any industrialized nation. If the United States is to have any hope of selling crypto-capable systems outside its own borders, it will have to accept the national sovereignty of the countries with which it trades.

There may be more hope of controlling the use of cryptography within a national population, but even here it seems difficult to achieve any worthwhile result. If cryptography is regulated by law, most businesses and most citizens will comply and will thereby be deprived of some of their ability to protect their privacy. Anyone who is engaged in serious criminal activity and who believes that cryptography would further that activity is unlikely to be deterred from using home-grown or underground products. One class of criminals in particular, state-sponsored terrorists, can be expected to be able to turn to foreign supporters for cryptographic support.

The availability of cryptography for criminal uses may not turn out to matter all that much. Cryptography is a tool well suited to legitimate activities of people who can openly say "I have secrets and I have a right to keep them private." It is not well suited to an activity that will be unable to defend itself if discovered and is trying to remain invisible. Criminals today make far more use of covert means of communication (most notably cloned cell phones) rather than of overtly secure means. Expanding bandwidth offers plenty of opportunity for covert communication (Anderson 1996b), and, this, rather than cryptography, will probably prove to be the major communications-related concern of police in the future.

Whatever the truth of the arguments, government efforts to keep honest citizens from using cryptography to protect their privacy continue. Such efforts are unlikely to achieve what governments claim to want, but very likely to cause serious damage to both business and democracy in the process.

# Notes

1. (p. 11) In the text we have been careful to distinguish this from a true wiretap. It is closely related to what we call a "consensual overhear."

2. (p. 13) The prototype was funded by John Gilmore, one of EFF's founders, and was primarily designed by Paul Kocher. It was constructed by Advanced Wireless technologies of Santa Clara. (EFF 1998, Markoff 1998)

## Chapter 1. Introduction

1. (p. 4) The Watergate scandal, which forced the resignation of President Richard Nixon in 1974, was initiated by the installation of electronic surveillance in the Watergate offices of the Democratic National Committee. Watergate is only one of a number of cases in which electronic eavesdropping was used by the party in power for *political* purposes and was justified on grounds of "national security."

2. (p. 5) There is one major exception: radio and television are used to deliver a product to consumers.

3. (p. 6) At a 1995 talk in Brisbane, Australia, Ross Anderson of Cambridge University estimated the commercial market at over a billion dollars a year and likely to be augmented by another billion a year from developing industries (Anderson 1995), but the dollar figures do not appear in the printed paper.

4. (p. 6) The exact fraction is difficult to determine, partly because the budget is secret and partly because the most expensive items in the budget are spy satellites (some of which both listen to communications and take photographs).

5. (p. 8) This is one aspect in which telecommunications may forever remain less satisfactory than physical meetings.

## Chapter 2. Cryptography

1. (p. 12) A signal sent by satellite can typically be received in an area thousands of miles across. One sent by microwave is hard to pick up more than a few miles from the "line of sight" between the towers. An intriguing approach to secure communication is used in some military satellite systems. Signals are transmitted from one satellite to another at frequencies that are absorbed by oxygen and cannot travel far enough through the Earth's atmosphere to be received on the ground. This forces an eavesdropper to put up a satellite to spy on other satellites —an expensive proposition.

2. (p. 12) What it means to know someone in this sense is not straightforward. Essentially it means that your expectations about the person you are dealing with are correct. Those expectations may or may not include such identifying information as a name and address. There are some interactions, such as discussing your marital troubles with a stranger in a bar, in which what you are depending on is simply that the other party is, true to appearance, a sympathetic stranger who does not know your spouse and will not carry your tale back home.

3. (p. 13) The principle, alas, is often honored more in the breach than in the observance. For reasons discussed in the chapter 3, there is a tradition of secrecy about cryptographic systems, both governmental and commercial. There is, however, a sense in which Kerckhoffs's principle holds, even in regard to secret systems. For example US government cryptographic systems that are used to protect TOP SECRET information are only classified SECRET and the equipment that embodies them is rarely classified higher than CONFIDENTIAL.

4. (p. 14) It is not made any clearer by the practice of using the terms "code" and "coding" for numerous transformations in modern computing and communication that have nothing to do with security.

5. (p. 15) You may also attempt to conceal the fact that what you are conveying is an encrypted message at all. This strategy—called steganography or covert communication—will be touched on from time to time in the text.

6. (p. 16) The police will recognize that they have a plausible candidate for a time-and-place message because the various positions in which only some digits are possible will all assume acceptable values.

7. (p. 17) A mask file is the digital input to a "fab line" that produces a computer chip. It can represent millions of dollars of engineering effort. Furthermore, semiconductors are often fabricated far from where they are designed and so, whether on a disk or over a phone line, the mask file must be transmitted from one to the other.

8. (p. 17) A one-part code is one in which the plaintext phrases and the code groups are simultaneously in alphabetical (or numerical) order so that the same book can be used for both encoding and decoding.

9. (p. 19) The Venona messages are available from the National Security Agency Web page: http://www.nsa.gov:8080/docs/venona/venona.html

10. (p. 21) The alphabets used in the first Vigenère table are in fact related. They were generated algorithmically by starting with a standard alphabet and using the GNU Emacs pseudo-random number generator to pick pairs of letters to be swapped. One thousand swaps were used to produce each alphabet. This process was intended only to produce such examples and is far from secure. The set of alphabets given can probably be cryptanalyzed to find the parameters of the underlying pseudo-random number source.

11. (p. 21) The classical Caesar Cipher, in which every character is moved forward in the alphabet by three places, is the most famous example of a direct standard alphabet.

12. (p. 24) This is usually called a *combiner* if it accepts several bits as inputs and produces one output and an *S-box* if its output is more than one bit.

13. (p. 25) The vast number of keys was offered as an argument for the unbreakability of ciphers during the Renaissance (Kahn 1967, p. 145) and probably earlier. Modern theories, including the theory of *non-deterministic polynomial time* or *NP* computing, (Aho et al. 1974) are far more mathematical but little more satisfactory.

14. (p. 25) In fact the cryptanalyst must also know enough about the plaintext to be able to recognize it; otherwise a correct solution to the problem cannot be distinguished from an incorrect one.

15. (p. 26) Chosen plaintext can arise in the real world in several ways. Suppose for example that the US Department of State delivers a diplomatique communiqué to a foreign embassy. The embassy must transmit the message home to its own government and is therefore likely to encrypt a message whose contents are known to the US government. Chosen plaintext may also be available to an organization that shares an encrypted channel—for example, a high-bandwidth satellite channel encrypted by the provider—with another organization.

16. (p. 26) This is popularly known as Moore's Law, and has held for the past several decades.

17. (p. 26) This doesn't work the other way around, because a large part of the cost of a computer is in such housekeeping aspects as its case and power supply, whose costs change less quickly.

18. (p. 27) In the US a typical TOP SECRET document is downgraded to UNCLASSIFIED in between 20 and 30 years.

19. (p. 28) An announcement in the *Federal Register* of January 2, 1997 (pp. 93–94) asked for comments on proposed criteria for a replacement. NIST, an agency of the Department of Commerce, is responsible for setting civilian cryptographic standards (Computer Security Act, 1987, Public Law 100-235.).

20. (p. 28) Double DES allows a 112-bit key and appears at first to be adequate,

but it is subject to an attack called "meet-in-the-middle." First discussed by David Snow at a National Bureau of Standards meeting in September 1976, this attack exploits a matching plaintext-and-ciphertext pair by encrypting the plaintext under all possible keys, decrypting the ciphertext under all possible keys, sorting the results, and looking for a match. Refinements of this technique are applicable in a surprising number of cryptanalytic circumstances.

21. (p. 28) The lifetimes of public-key cryptosystems are harder to quantify because terms such as RSA and Diffie-Hellman denote general techniques; they do not fix key lengths or register sizes.

22. (p. 28) For example, various forms of the German Enigma system were in use from the 1920s until well after World War II and are probably still in use today.

23. (p. 30) As the name suggests, material under two-person control is never handled by one person alone. It would thus require a conspiracy of two people to, for example, make an unauthorized copy. Two-person control is supported by such things as safes with two combinations and areas called *no lone zones* in which at least two people must be present if anyone is present at all. "COMSEC" is short for "communications security."

24. (p. 30) Some keys used in the STU-III secure telephone, for example, have editions. Unless understood in the context of codebooks, the terminology seems peculiar for keys that never exist in any form other than an electronic one.

25. (p. 31) The term usually used for the system about to be described is *key distribution center* (KDC). Because more modern systems do not always distribute keys, the more general term KMF has come into use; we will use it throughout.

26. (p. 31) In fact, sharing a key with the KMF defines membership in the network.

27. (p. 32) The STU-II, an obsolete US military secure phone system was said to suffer from KDC congestion at busy times of the day.

28. (p. 35) Celebrated examples of this are to be found in the cases of Boyce and Lee (Lindsey 1979) and Whitworth (Blum 1987, pp. 280–326). In both cases, keys were saved rather than destroyed after use and were later sold to Soviet intelligence officers.

29. (p. 36) This technique of signing, which might be called a *primitive digital signature* has the disadvantage that in order to maintain the evidence of authorship, the recipient must store the ciphertext and must therefore either store the plaintext as well or decrypt the ciphertext again each time the plaintext is needed. In practice, what is done is to generate a *message digest* using one of several message-digest algorithms (Schneier 1996, pp. 435–455) and compute a primitive digital signature of that.

30. (p. 37) It would be more accurate to call this *key agreement*. Unfortunately, the original name was generally accepted before it was observed that the things exchanged were not keys.

31. (p. 40) This is a codeword of obscure origin, not an acronym.

32. (p. 42) The recent lawsuit between General Motors and Volkswagen illustrates how valuable information about manufacturing design can be (Meredith 1997).

33. (p. 42) Consider, for example, the 1987 testimony of Cheryl Helsing, chairman of the Data Security Committee for the American Bankers Association, before Congress, "[I]f I were in charge of the Social Security system and concerned about getting those checks out every month, I would be much more concerned about whether those checks were in the correct amounts, made out to the right people, and that they did get out on time, than I would be concerned about an intruder gaining unauthorized access and looking at the files."

34. (p. 42) For example, all transactions over ten thousand dollars must be reported to the Internal Revenue Service. In *United States v. Miller* (425 US 435, 1976, p. 442), the Supreme Court ruled that deposit information does not have an "expectation of privacy" and may be subpoenaed. (A search warrant requires a higher standard of proof.)

35. (p. 42) A Citicorp electronic banking system used directly by corporate customers for funds transfer was penetrated. Posing as a corporate customer, a user from St. Petersburg, Russia, transferred funds to an account in Finland; the money was withdrawn from the bank the next day. The falsified transaction was accomplished with a personal computer and the phone lines. Over the next several months, this scenario was repeated, with the user's locale changing to Rotterdam, San Francisco, St. Petersburg, and Tel Aviv. Citicorp became aware of the thefts after several customers complained of irregularities in their accounts. By August, $12 million had actually been moved, and $400,000 had been stolen. Relative to the amount that Citicorp transfers daily (about $500 billion) this is relatively little, but of course banks' business is providing security, and in that sense the theft loomed large. Access to the system required a customer's authorization code; it is believed that the perpetrator (allegedly one Vladimir Levin) had an accomplice within the system who supplied these. The bank has now changed its security to using one-time passwords (Carley 1995; Hansell 1995).

36. (p. 43) An Alaskan oil company investigated why it had been losing leasing bids by small amounts to a competitor and discovered that a line between a computer in its Alaska office and one at its home base in Texas were being wiretapped. A competitor was intercepting pricing advice being sent from the Texas office (Parker 1983, p. 322).

37. (p. 43) *Annual Report to Congress on Foreign Economic Collection and Industrial Espionage,* National Counterintelligence Center, Washington, D.C., July 1995, as reported in (Dam and Lin 1996, p. 33).

38. (p. 43) Command 9438, para 10, as cited in Fitzgerald and Leopold 1987, p. 148.

39. (p. 46) One example occurred in the 1970s, when thousands of phone con-

versations between IBM executives conducted on the company's private microwave network were systematically eavesdropped on by Soviet intelligence agents. NSA informed IBM of the eavesdropping (Landau et al. 1994, p. 1). A similar incident occurred in the 1980s with a different US corporation (Dam and Lin 1996, p. 68).

40. (p. 47) Electronic commerce is still a loosely defined term. At present, examples range from individuals' purchasing physical objects over the Internet by sending electronic mail to businesses' making automatic purchases from their suppliers using Electronic Data Interchange protocols. The grand conception is of large-scale purchase and sale of information over the network using a combination of digital credit cards (which would sign digital sales slips with digital signatures) and electronic cash (which would be anonymous and have many of the properties of physical money).

## Chapter 3. Cryptography and Public Policy

1. (p. 49) "Probabilistic cryptography," as put forth by Goldwasser and Micali (1984), is a formalization of the long-standing method of using *message indicators* to guarantee that a cryptosystem starts each message in a unique state.

2. (p. 52) For quite some time, communications security was poor in parts of the US government (particularly the Department of State) that lacked access to the services of the military cryptographers.

3. (p. 54) A 2400-bit-per-second mode of operation is one of the *Minimum Essential Requirements* of the third generation secure telephone unit (STU-III), which went into use in 1987.

4. (p. 55) There appear to have been rotor-based voice systems, but these were probably analog scramblers that filtered the signal into several bands employed rotors to shuffle the bands in a constantly changing pattern.

5. (p. 56) A small number of serious books were published in Europe, in particular Eyraud 1959.

6. (p. 56) Papers on points pure of mathematics whose cryptographic inspiration is clearly visible to people familiar with the subject were written by Andrew Gleason, Marshall Hall, W. H. Mills, and presumably others.

7. (p. 56) Kennedy's orders do not mention cryptography, but require that US nuclear weapons be put under *positive control* of the National Command Authority, wherever in the world they may be located. What this came down to was that they could not be armed by anyone unable to send them properly encrypted messages. The key component in this program is the *permissive action link*, which, in effect, issues an encrypted order to a nuclear weapon. Earlier PALs used conventional cryptography; more recent ones use public-key techniques.

8. (p. 57) Source: private conversations between Diffie and Feistel.

9. (p. 57) Eventually, in the late 1960s, the cryptographic system Feistel's group designed was bundled together with the existing modes of operation of the Mark X IFF. The result was called the Mark XII (there never was an XI), and its cryptographic mode was Mode 4. The Mark XII is employed extensively by the military aircraft of the US and its allies.

10. (p. 57) Source: private conversations between Diffie and Carl Engelman of Mitre in the 1970s and between Diffie and Horst Feistel circa 1990.

11. (p. 58) The importance of the Federal Information Processing standards is illustrated by FIPS 1, the American Standard Code for Information Interchange or ASCII. The government's adoption of this code, which is ubiquitous today, made it dominant over the rival EBCDIC encoding used by IBM, then the world's largest computer manufacturer.

12. (p. 59) The one in the 2984 is now called the Alternate Encryption Technique. At least two other IBM systems were also called Lucifer. One designed by John Lynn Smith, but never developed into a product, presents the fullest exposition of Feistel's techniques (Smith 1971). Another system called Lucifer was used only as a tutorial device (Feistel 1973).

13. (p. 59) At NSA, Howard Rosenblum, Deputy Director for Communication Security, and Doug Hogan; at NBS, Ruth Davis, Seymour Jeffery, and Dennis Branstad.

14. (p. 59) NOFORN means "No foreign dissemination allowed." This is an odd designation for many NSA algorithms, since several of the most important are NATO standards.

15. (p. 60) In testimony to congress, NSA Director Bobby Ray Inman asserted that public key cryptography had been discovered at NSA 10 years earlier. The work in question appears to be that of three GCHQ employees done about 1972. The precise scope of the British discoveries has yet to come out, but in the words of one of the three "You did much more with it than we did." It appears that Inman preferred to give credit to three Brits with clearances than three Yanks without.

16. (p. 61) The term is a misnomer because the items exchanged are not actually keys. In contemporary literature, the more precise terms *key negotiation* or *key agreement* are preferred, but the original terminology persists.

17. (p. 62) In the early 1970s, for example, secrecy orders were placed on some of the inventions of Horst Feistel, nucleus of the cryptographic research group at IBM.

18. (p. 62) Secrecy orders are often helpful to a company because they delay the granting (and thus expiration) of its patents until a time when the invention is more appropriate to the market. In 1939 the famous actress Hedy Lamarr filed for the first patent on frequency hopping radio (Markey 1942). Had this application

been kept secret until the 1970s, when spread spectrum technology emerged from military into civilian applications, Hedy Lamarr would be enjoying a much more comfortable retirement.

19. (p. 63) Uriel Feige, Amos Fiat, and Adi Shamir had discovered a practical implementation of "Zero-Knowledge" protocols (Feige et al. 1987). They submitted a US patent application even as Shamir lectured worldwide on the algorithm. The Army requested a secrecy order be placed on the invention. This was classic shut-the-barn-door-after-the-horse-has-fled; for several months the researchers had been giving lectures about the work. Since secrecy orders forbade the discussion of the research with the foreign nationals, and Feige, Fiat, and Shamir were all Israeli citizens, what American law could do in this situation was unclear. Fearing to present the work at an American research conference under the circumstances, Shamir let various colleagues know about the problem. Help came. Shamir's lawyer got an anonymous call from Dr. Richard A. Leibler, retired head of R5, telling him precisely whom to call to get the secrecy order lifted. Shamir publicly thanked "the NSA ... who were extremely helpful behind the scenes ..." (Landau 1988, p. 12)

20. (p. 64) It was rumored that DES was used by the Argentines in the Falklands War and had seriously hampered British SIGINT.

21. (p. 64) CCEP was modeled on the earlier Industrial Tempest Program, begun in the 1970s, which encouraged industry to build electromagnetically shielded versions of their products.

22. (p. 64) The government also appeared to be laying legal framework for broadened availability of cryptographic equipment. For as long as anyone could remember, all cryptographic devices approved for protection of classified traffic had been owned by the government. Now with NSA's COMSEC Instruction 6002 it provided two ways that government contractors could own the equipment and charge the costs back to government contracts in the same way they did with buildings, computers, or safes.

23. (p. 65) Type I equipment is managed through COMSEC accounts and is basically available only to organizations with government contracts. Under the new rules, owners of Type II equipment would not have COMSEC accounts but would need to have the equipment supplied to them by government sponsors. From the point of view of the user, the distinction between having a government sponsor and having a government agency as customer was minor.

24. (p. 65) Development of the STU-III was paid for directly by NSA, beginning by funding five competitors to prepare proposals.

25. (p. 66) Only a year late, and about 50% over the target price.

26. (p. 66) The Type II version, affected by the same fluctuation of availability rules as other Type II equipment, was not a success. In a move incomprehensible to marketing people everywhere, the Type II STU-III, though advertised from the beginning as inferior to the Type I, was always priced higher. This is at least partly

because the Type II never achieved the volume of production originally planned and did not benefit from the same economy of scale as the Type I.

27. (p. 66) Perhaps to help NSA avoid the need to pay royalties for public key technology, just as it used secrecy to avoid paying Hebern.

28. (p. 66) "This policy assigns to the heads of Federal Government Departments and Agencies the responsibility to determine what information is sensitive, but unclassified and to provide systems protection of such information which is electronically communicated, transferred, processed, or stored on telecommunications and automated information systems." (Poindexter 1986, p. 542)

29. (p. 67) Ten years later, DES remains a Federal Information Processing Standard.

30. (p. 68) By this time Poindexter was deep in the middle of the Iran-Contra controversy, and the administration was loath to have him appear at any congressional hearing lest the questioning veer to Iran-Contra. Thus Poindexter did not appear when first requested, and the House committee then subpoenaed him (USHR 100a, p. 381). A discussion ensued between the White House and the committee, and the committee delayed hearings an additional two weeks, while the White House withdrew Poindexter's directive (Carlucci 1987), hoping to avoid Poindexter's appearance in Congress.

The committee insisted that the former Presidential National Security Advisor appear, which he did, accompanied by counsel. Despite the fact that Representative Jack Brooks, chair of the Committee, promised that questions would be limited to issues related to the NSDD-145 and the Poindexter Directive (USHR 100a, p. 399), Poindexter declined to answer any questions and pleaded the Fifth Amendment. The congressmen, having achieved the withdrawal of the Poindexter directive, did not pursue the matter further.

31. (p. 68) "The development of standards requires interaction with many segments of our society, i.e. government agencies, computer and communications industry, international organizations, etc. [NIST] has performed this kind of activity very well over the last 22 years. NSA, on the other hand, is unfamiliar with it." (USHR 100b, p. 26)

32. (p. 68) The Committee on Governmental Operations was the subject of a similar attempt by NSA. "In January 1981, the Director of the NSA even went so far as to write this Committee and complain that the Committee had not forwarded to NSA a copy of its investigative report, 'The Government's Classification of Private Ideas,' *prior* to its issuance. As pointed out by Chairman Brooks in reply to NSA, Congress does not submit its reports to Executive Branch agencies for prereview." (USHR 100b, pp. 21–22)

33. (p. 70) The Budget Office also noted that the Act would result in savings due to the elimination of fraud and other financial losses (USHR 100b, p. 43).

34. (p. 70) Officially known as the Balanced Budget and Emergency Deficit Act of

1985, the act set annual deficit targets for five years, aiming for a balanced budget in 1991. It was never fully implemented.

35. (p. 70) There was an additional $800,000 of 'reimbursable' funds from other agencies; such funds are typically for help in deploying advanced technologies.

36. (p. 70) One example of such deference to NSA was NBS's failure to support its own standard in the International Standards Organization. About 1985 ISO took up consideration of DES as an international standard and approached the American National Standards Institute, which in turn approached its cryptographic committee X3T1, on which NBS sat. NBS cast its vote in X3T1 against recommending DES; ANSI abstained in the international committee, and ultimately ISO did not adopt DES. Another example is Raymond Kammer's decision that NIST would support NSA's decision that NIST abandon RSA as a choice for a public-key signature standard (Source: private conversation between Landau and Kammer, December 19, 1996.)

37. (p. 71) Source: private conversation between Landau and McNulty, December 2, 1996.

38. (p. 73) Source: private conversation between Landau and McNulty, December 2, 1996.

39. (p. 73) Schnorr applied through the EEC for a patent, thus obtaining patents in Germany, United Kingdom, France, the Netherlands, Italy, Spain, Belgium, Switzerland, Sweden, Liechtenstein, and Austria; see Schnorr 1989, Schnorr 1990, and Schnorr 1991.

40. (p. 73) NIST countered this last point by noting that the Kravitz algorithm was roughly 25 times faster than the RSA algorithm in signing (USDoC 1991a).

For most applications speed of verification is more important than speed of signing, since a signature is signed only once and may be verified many times. In some applications such as signing software to protect against the introduction of viruses, the signature may literally be checked billions of times over the lifetime of the product. On the other hand, there is something to be said for making the signing operation more economical, because it is the one that uses the secret information and is best done in an isolated environment like a smart card. At the time, such cards had limited computational power.

41. (p. 74) "The key question during the hearings was: Should a military intelligence agency, NSA, or a civilian agency, [NIST], be in charge of the government's computer standards program?" (USHR 100b, p. 19)

42. (p. 74) "Observers—including OTA—consider that [the MOU] appears to cede to NSA much more authority than the act itself had granted or envisioned, especially considering the House report accompanying the legislation." (USC-OTA 1994, pp. 13–14)

The General Accounting Office said: "[T]his Memorandum of Understanding made NSA appear to more influential in NIST's standard-setting procedure relative to cryptographic systems than was intended by the Congress in the Computer Security Act of 1987." (USGAO 1993a, p. 16)

43. (p. 74) Claus Schnorr's patent was licensed from him by RSA Data Security, which provides DSS code in its cryptographic toolkits. On the other hand, many people have studied Schnorr's patent and maintain that it does not cover DSS. To date the issue of the patent's validity has yet to be litigated.

44. (p. 75) Source: private conversation between Landau and Brooks, January, 17, 1997.

45. (p. 75) Source: private conversation between Landau and Kammer, December 19, 1996.

46. (p. 75) Source: private conversation between Landau and Kallstrom, January 16, 1997.

47. (p. 75) New York City's District Attorney of the fifties, Frank Hogan, was a strong proponent of wiretapping, and in 1955 he testified to Congress: "In these and in many other important prosecutions, the investigative technique of wiretapping was invaluable. In a substantial number I may say, gentlemen, it is indispensable." (USHR 84, p. 322)

48. (p. 75) There were 419 electronic surveillances conducted in New York in 1994 (USAO 1994, pp. A26–A33, and p. A90) (USAO 1995, pp. 54–60 and pp. 126–140).

49. (p. 75) There were 53 court-ordered surveillances in California during 1994 (USAO 1994, pp. A2–A7 and p. A8), (USAO 1995, pp. 34–38 and p. 94).

50. (p. 76) Source: private conversation between Landau and Kallstrom, January 16, 1997.

51. (p. 76) Source: private conversation between Landau and Brooks, January 17, 1997.

## Chapter 4. National Security

1. (p. 78) On October 24, 1969, President Nixon announced a decision to make narcotics a matter of foreign policy. The CIA was asked to "contribute to the maximum extent possible in the collection of foreign intelligence related to traffic in opium and heroin" (USDoJ 1976, pp. 46–47). President Ford later called the smuggling of opium to the United States a "national-security" issue (ibid., p. 59).

2. (p. 78) In a speech in the Spring of 1997, President Bill Clinton invoked the name of national security in support of education.

3. (p. 79) The CIA Foreign Broadcast Information Service publishes transcripts of numerous foreign radio shows.

4. (p. 79) A similar inference might simply have been drawn from looking at the

number of cars in the parking lot or the number of lighted windows. The significance of the pizza story lies in showing how difficult operations intelligence is to counter. Security officers may well have thought to hold meetings in inner offices, or to take measures to avoid having the parking lot look full. Any large scale operation, however, leaves many telltale traces and it is hard to anticipate and cover up all of them. Keeping the kitchens open all night might stem the flow of pizza orders only to create other signs of activity: the amount of raw food being ordered, the quantity of garbage put out for collection, or the hours of the kitchen staff. In many organizations where all professional staff members are required to have security clearances, employees such as cooks, whose activities can be confined to daytime hours and a small part of the building, are not.

5. (p. 79) An amusing example of the CIA's aggressive interest in using travelers as spies is given by the Hemingway scholar Michael Reynolds. In 1975, Reynolds made persistent attempts to get a visa to Cuba in order to study Hemingway's library. In the process, the CIA contacted him on the chance that if he got to Cuba, he might get to meet Fidel Castro—who was known for surprise visits with tourists. Reynolds also gives plausible evidence that the CIA's enthusiasm for his trip to Cuba went so far that they had his phone bugged (Source: Michael S. Reynolds, *Hemingway's Reading*, 1910–1940, Princeton University Press, 1981.)

6. (p. 81) These, however, have created embarrassments of their own. Consider the shooting down of an American U2 spy plane over the Soviet Union in 1960 or the capture of the American spy ship *Pueblo* by North Korea in early 1968.

7. (p. 82) This appears to have been a longer-range, and higher-altitude version of the mechanism that seagulls use to detect an impending storm and fly inland. It is an eerie commentary on the success of secrecy in the intelligence community that this project, which is supposed to have been abandoned, was kept secret for nearly 50 years. In 1995 it was offered as the explanation for the Roswell Incident of 1947, which is, despite official denials, believed by many people to have been the crash of an alien spaceship (Thomas 1995).

8. (p. 82) Distinguishing nuclear explosions from other events, such as large lightning bolts or explosions of meteors in the atmosphere, is not easy. The satellite reacts less to the total energy of the blast than to the form of the flash. Nuclear explosions have a characteristic two-humped flash caused by gamma ray induced formation of nitrogen pentoxide ($N_2O_5$). The time between the humps is called the *bhang metre* and is characteristic of the type of weapon.

9. (p. 83) For example, the Krasnoyarsk radar, which was alleged to violate the ABM treaty, was photographed from space only after its location had been reported by a human source (Richelson 1987, p. 79).

10. (p. 83) The study of radar signals sometimes involves elaborate provocations designed to create the impression that an attack is in progress and thereby to fool an enemy into using radars that are not meant to "come to life" except under battle conditions. A persistent theory of the strange movements of Korean Airlines

007, which led to its being shot down, is that its purpose was to provoke the radars of the Kamchatka Peninsula air defense system into action so that other aircraft —RC-135's designated Cobra Ball—could observe them (Johnson 1978).

11. (p. 84) It has long been known that, unless a radio is specifically designed to conceal the information, one can discover what station is being received by measuring the frequency of the local oscillator. This, however, depends on knowing the intermediate frequency, and that information may not be available about a radio of unknown type. Around 1960, it was discovered that many radios had a frequency shift in the local oscillator, resulting from an effect of the automatic gain control on the high-voltage supply, that was proportional to the frequency of the received signal. That discovery portended vastly expanded exploitation of unintentional signals emitted by receivers (Wright 1987, p. 93).

12. (p. 84) One function of the US Argos satellites was to monitor telemetry from Soviet missile tests. This fact is believed to have come to Soviet attention as a result of the activities of Christopher Boyce, who was subsequently convicted of spying on CIA projects at a contractor, TRW, in Southern California (Lindsey 1979).

13. (p. 84) In order to prevent tampering with the satellite, control link transmissions are often encrypted. The device used for this purpose by the military, the KI-23, is the main product of Mykotronx, now a maker of Clipper and Capstone chips.

14. (p. 84) In the 1950s, British counterintelligence employed a corps of "watchers" to follow hostile diplomats. The watchers communicated with MI5 by radio, and in an attempt to conceal the their activities, they tried communicating in code. Peter Wright recalls in his autobiography *Spycatcher* that this was of little use; the mere occurrence of the traffic was sufficient to reveal to the Russians where the watchers were operating (Wright 1987, pp. 52–53). In a much more recent example of the same phenomenon, Tsutomu Shimomura (1996, 1997, p. 76) reports that in tracking Kevin Mitnick, who had broken into Shimomura's computer, Mitnick's use of cryptography "didn't slow them down at all." Quite a different example came to light in conjunction with the Yom Kippur war of 1973: it was said that the Israelis should have been alerted that something was up by the improved communication security on the part of the Egyptians.

15. (p. 85) A remarkable example of this occurred shortly before the Normandy invasion in World War II. The Japanese military attache in Germany demanded a tour of German defenses in Normandy and reported what he had seen to Tokyo. That transmission, presumably encrypted in Purple, was read by the Allies and supplied them with an expert assessment of German channel defenses (Kahn 1967, p. 508; Boyd 1993). Another example is provided by the Gamma Guppy intercepts of the early 1960s, in which the US embassy in Moscow monitored mobile phone traffic from the limousines of Soviet officials (Bamford 1982, p. 283).

16. (p. 85) Physical taps on lines do have a role, however, and not just in counterintelligence work. In the 1980s a former NSA employee named Ronald Pelton

was recruited by the Soviets. One of the things he allegedly told them was that the United States had placed a tap on a cable running under the Sea of Okhatsk. According to a Soviet publication, the tap, which weighed 12 tons, was powered by plutonium and serviced by US submarines.

17. (p. 86) The largest Soviet intercept station outside the USSR was at Lourdes, Cuba. It could pick up satellite transmissions intended for receivers in Washington, New York, and other eastern cities.

18. (p. 87) On the face of it, this incident, in which the Israelis attacked and nearly sank the *Liberty*, is inexplicable. It was claimed that the *Liberty* should actually have been hundreds of miles away, in the waters off Cyprus, but that its orders got delayed. If the *Liberty* was, as publicly claimed, spying on the Arabs, there is no reason for the Israelis to have attacked it. On the other hand, the Israelis' claim that they mistook the *Liberty* for an Egyptian freighter hardly seems credible. Loftus and Aarons (1994) have produced an explanation that, although not supported by overwhelming evidence, is at least sensible. It is their thesis that the *Liberty* was actually listening to traffic from Israeli tanks and manpack radios as part of a secret deal to report weaknesses in the Israeli southern front to Egypt. To do this, it would have to have been quite close.

19. (p. 90) During the shootdown of KAL 007 in September 1983, for example, signals intelligence was severely hampered by the fact that only the transmissions of the interceptor pilots and not those of their ground controllers could be intercepted (Hersh 1986, p. 70).

20. (p. 90) Multiplexing takes three common forms. Two of these are well illustrated by broadcast radio. *Frequency division multiplexing* is the phenomenon by which different stations have different frequencies. To select a station you tune to its frequency. *Time division multiplexing* is the phenomenon that distinguishes programs. Within the frequency of a given station, you listen at a particular time to find the right program. The third form is called *code division multiplexing*. Code division multiplexing is one of the benefits of *spread spectrum communication*, in which a transmitter uses a wide range of frequencies, often by hopping rapidly from one to another. Using code division multiplexing, multiple transmitters can avoid interference with little prior coordination. The more advanced cordless telephones are perhaps the most common items that use code division multiplexing.

21. (p. 92) The cryptanalysis of World War II systems is discussed in detail in Deavours and Kruh 1985 and in Welchman 1982. Cryptanalysis of classical systems makes up much of the content of *Cryptologia*, the journal of cryptographic history. Cryptanalysis of contemporary cryptosystems can be found in the *Journal of Cryptology* and in the proceedings of numerous annual and biannual conferences, such as Crypto (held in late August in Santa Barbara, California), Eurocrypt (held at a different location in Europe each spring), and Asiacrypt (held

somewhere in the Asia Pacific region about every other year). A particularly note-worthy book on the subject is Biham and Shamir 1993.

22. (p. 92) Most books on the breaking of the German Enigma cryptosystem dur-ing World War II focus on the researchers, especially Alan Turing, at Bletchley Park. The actual reading of most of the traffic, however, was done with several hundred special purpose computing machines, called *bombes*, which were oper-ated 24 hours a day by women from the Women's Reserve Navy Service (Welch-man 1982, pp. 138–148).

23. (p. 92) Many systems in use today have either 40-bit keys (which can be searched easily) or 56-bit keys (which can be searched with difficulty). *Dragging key* (looking through all possible keys) thus has a role to play in contemporary cryptanalysis. A far more subtle, but also universal, cryptanalytic method is the Berlekamp-Massey algorithm (Berlekamp 1968; Massey 1969). It is a fact that any sequence of bits (keystream) whatsoever can be generated by a linear shift register of sufficient length. The Berlekamp-Massey algorithm automatically pro-duces the right register. A major design criterion in modern cryptography is that the "right register" be too long for this approach to be practical.

24. (p. 92) Traffic analysis is fundamentally a matter of discovering the relation-ships among a number of "address spaces," some observable and others inferred. The call signs, like phone numbers, are the name space of the communications network. Direction finding, emitter identification, and collateral intelligence al-low these to be correlated with physical positions, individual pieces of equipment, or command functions.

25. (p. 93) Sanitization goes hand in hand with the desire of intelligence officers to keep raw intelligence out of the hands of their customers. The British learned this lesson in a particularly blunt fashion at the Battle of Jutland in World War I. Before the battle, a British officer of the line walked into the intelligence cen-ter and asked the location of the radio callsign of the admiral commanding the German fleet. He was told, correctly, that it was located in the Jade River. What the officer actually wanted to know was the location of the admiral, who had switched call signs when the fleet had set sail precisely in order to fool the British about his location. British intelligence was not fooled; it knew the German ad-miral's new location and new callsign. Nonetheless, as a result of the intelligence center's releasing raw intelligence on call-signs, rather than finished intelligence on the locations of forces, the Germans achieved their purpose. The British fleet delayed sailing and the battle, which might have been a major British victory, was indecisive (Beesley 1977).

26. (p. 93) In 1961, William Martin and Bernan Mitchell, two NSA cryptanalysts, defected to Moscow and gave a press conference in which they revealed intercep-tion by the US of its allies' communications. According to David Kahn, the loss of intelligence was felt immediately (Kahn 1967, p. 694).

27. (p. 94) In the mid 1970s a panel headed by Nelson Rockefeller concluded

that the Soviets were intercepting conversations on microwave telephone channels from Capitol Hill. Even though congressmen were not supposed to discuss classified information over their telephones, the intercepted information, when taken in aggregate, has tremendous intelligence potential. It has been speculated that the Soviet activity was detected because the volume of traffic intercepted was sufficient to permit correlations between fluctuation in the Capitol Hill traffic and communications from the Soviet Embassy to Moscow to be observed.

28. (p. 94) Bobby Inman remarked in an informal discussion after his talk at AFCEA West in Anaheim, California on January 8, 1981 that NSA's product had never been better.

29. (p. 94) Speaking in 1980 at the IEEE Wescon conference in San Francisco, Robert Morris (then at Bell Labs and later Chief Scientist of the National Computer Security Center) said: "We are just leaving a period of relative sanity in cryptography that began shortly after the First World War. During that time people spoke of cryptosystems that were secure for hours, days, weeks, months, and sometimes, years. Before it and after it, they spoke of cryptosystems that were unbreakable."

30. (p. 94) In the 1980s, for example, NSA built two new operations buildings, a new research and engineering building, a chip fabrication facility, and two advanced laboratories away from Fort Meade to be operated by a contractor.

31. (p. 95) Kim Philby is believed to have had access to information on the Venona program; the Soviets would thus have learned about it soon after it began.

32. (p. 95) This laboratory is the subject of Aleksandr Solzhenitsyn's novel *The First Circle* (1968) and of a later memoir by Lev Kopelev (who was Rubin in the novel). It is Kopelev (1983, pp. 52–55) who discusses the remarkable technique of assessing the security of *mosaic* or *two-dimensional* (time and frequency) voice scramblers they were developing by printing out a sonogram (a plot of energy and frequency over time) and measuring the time it took to solve the sonogram as though it were a jigsaw puzzle and reassemble it into one representing human voice.

In *The First Circle*, which takes place around Christmas 1948, Solzhenitsyn and his fellow workers are under the gun from Stalin to deliver "secret telephony" within about six months. The year I read it was 1974. That year, digitized speech (pre-requisite to high-quality secret telephony or as we call it "secure voice") was the main topic at the ARPA Principal Investigators' Conference.—WD

33. (p. 97) In the 1980s, US companies were not permitted to export optical-fiber communications systems to the USSR, presumably on the ground that communications carried by fiber would replace radio communications and could not be intercepted.

34. (p. 98) The raw data rate of the V.fast standard is 28 kilobits-per-second, but it incorporates real-time data compression and can often achieve effective throughput of 200 kbps—far more that is available on many current leased line networks.

35. (p. 98) The difficulty of separating the two signals in the communication of autocancelling modems is a function of the size of the *constellation*, the number of combinations of amplitude and phase used in communication. V26ter uses four points, V32bis uses 32 and the newly introduced V.fast uses 64.

36. (p. 98) Much of dynamic routing technology was developed for another purpose: it increases the survivability of networks against direct attack, a phenomenon that occurs primarily, though not entirely, during open hostilities.

37. (p. 99) AT&T developed a specialized cryptographic device for protecting signaling channels (Myers 1979; Brickell and Simmons 1983, pp. 4–5).

38. (p. 99) The US government successor to the STU-III, the Secure Terminal Equipment (STE), is primarily an ISDN phone, but is compatible with STU-III. The STE is being manufactured by Lockheed-Martin and Motorola and is available in sample quantities.

39. (p. 100) A precise figure is made difficult to obtain by the problem of deciding what counts as encrypted. For example, most of the world's encrypted traffic consists of scrambled pay-tv broadcasts, a good example of the sort of encrypted traffic that either does not interest intelligence agencies or can be accessed without resorting to cryptanalysis.

40. (p. 101) The bombing of communication facilities in France forced the Germans to use radio for their communications with Berlin. The traffic that thereby became available for interception was encrypted with the Siemens and Halske T52 cipher machine. This was especially fortunate because the principles of operation of the T52 are similar to those of the Lorenz SZ40 (an online cipher machine that had earlier been used with radios), and cryptanalytic methods developed to attack the SZ40 proved applicable to the T52. It was to attack these machines, not the Enigma, that the Colossus—arguably the first computer—was built.

41. (p. 101) Photographs of the destruction of a bridge in Baghdad were repeatedly shown during the early days of the attack. The bridge was destroyed, not for its capacity to carry cars and trucks, but to destroy the optical fiber that ran underneath.

42. (p. 101) One development has been the *HARM* or *High-Speed Antiradiation Missile* which is launched from aircraft to home in on the fire-control radars of anti-aircraft weapons and destroy them.

43. (p. 101) The destructive effects of the *Electromagnetic Pulse* or *EMP* was first observed by the United States in a high altitude nuclear test above Johnson Island in the South Pacific. The test damaged electronic equipment as far away as Hawaii. The technique, which has since been refined and can be produced by non-nuclear means, goes under the name *High Energy Microwave* (Van Keuren 1991; Schwartau 1994; AWST 1997a).

44. (p. 101) Jamming describes transmissions intended to interfere with an opponent's communications or other signals such as radar. This is not always a wartime

phenomenon. In the mid-eighties HBO was briefly pushed off the air by a more powerful beam carrying a message critical of HBO activities.

45. (p. 102) Communications deceptions are classified as *imitative* if they mimic the communications of an opponent. More subtle communications deceptions are *manipulative*: they do not misrepresent the allegiance of the sender, but convey a false impression of its activities. In the months leading up to the invasion of Normandy in 1944, General George Patton commanded a division, stationed in southern England, that was pretending—by its communications and other activities—to be an entire army.

46. (p. 102) The distinction between viruses and worms (which might better have been called bacteria) is biologically based. Biological viruses are combinations of genetic material with protective protein coats. They function by invading the genetic material of cells and instructing the cell to produce more viruses. In a similar way, computer viruses incorporate themselves into computer programs. When the program is executed, the virus is executed and exploits the occasion to copy itself into other available programs. A worm, by comparison, is a "free-living" program that invades a computer or a network and tricks its host into running it as a separate process.

47. (p. 102) Viruses first became visible in the 1980s. Their origin is unclear. (I recall discussing the notion of viruses—though not what term was used—with my colleague Jack Holloway in 1970. When I mentioned this to Oliver Selfridge, member of the Baker committee and a longtime advisor to NSA, he told me that the notion had been about in the late 1950s.—WD)

48. (p. 102) Although the claim that viruses were employed against the Iraqis in the Gulf War appears to be groundless, there are repeated discussions of their development for military applications (AWST 1993; Richardson 1991; Robinson 1993b).

49. (p. 103) A cut out of this sort that prevents the tracing of phone calls is called a *cheese box*.

50. (p. 104) Even introducing a small number of errors makes the analysis of data far more difficult, and an error rate of just over 11% reduces the information content of a channel by half. In the mid-1980s, the notion of having the DoD give out false information about weapons developments was publicly mooted (North 1986).

51. (p. 105) Motorola manufactured a device called Ladner to encrypt analog telephone lines. Linkabit, California Microwave, Racal Datacom, and Cylink made high-speed DES-based encryptors to protect the digital ones.

52. (p. 105) AT&T developed DES and public-key-based encryption devices that were subsequently applied to securing common channel interoffice signaling (Myers 1979).

53. (p. 106) As we will see later, this is no longer entirely true.

54. (p. 107) People often refer to high grade cryptographic systems as being "unexportable." In fact, much of the best US cryptographic equipment—for example, the KG-84, general purpose data encrypter—is sold to the governments of NATO countries and other American allies and in some cases even "co-manufactured" in foreign countries.

55. (p. 107) Precisely what the capabilities of intercept equipment are is hard to tell. Under a deal between NSA and the Software Publisher's Association, some cryptographic systems with 40-bit keys can be rather freely exported when embodied in "mass market software." Since modern computer workstations can execute $2^{40}$ instructions in an hour, 40-bit keys do not represent very much security from a commercial viewpoint. On the other hand, it is unlikely that intercept devices, which are comparable in price to high-end workstations, can do any better. Since decisions about intercept must be made not in hours, but in fractions of a second, it is prudent to presume that NSA knows how to break the ciphers in question with a workfactor substantially less than $2^{40}$.

56. (p. 108) That the true mission of NSA's export-control office is intelligence and not administration is revealed by its organizational designation: G033 (recently changed to Z033) rather than Q or D—arguably a failure of operational security.

57. (p. 108) Aside from electronic funds transfers between banks, businesses use telecommunications for a variety of other high value communications. Oil companies routinely prospect at locations scattered around the world. Their analyses of core samples and other data form the basis for bids on drilling rights. Bids by multinational corporations on contracts distant from their headquarters require communication of information that is sometimes valuable enough to affect the company's survival. Internal transfers of equipment and supplies, can rival actual funds transfers in value.

## Chapter 5. Law Enforcement

1. (p. 110) Fingerprints serve two related but distinct functions in police work: identifying available people uniquely and identifying unavailable people via *latent* fingerprints on objects at crime scenes. The former function was not new—fingerprints impressed in clay had been used by the Babylonians for identification of written tablets—but before fingerprinting Europeans used the Bertillion system of body measurements. Fingerprints were an improvement both in being more precise and in having a forensic as well as identificational function (Kelling 1991, p. 960).

2. (p. 111) Earlier *stipendiary police*, like bounty hunters and some sheriffs, were paid at least in part through a share of collected fines—a mechanism whose corrupting potential is obvious. In some measure this system has been reintroduced

via forfeiture laws that reward police departments, thought not their members directly, with a share of the proceeds derived from selling property confiscated from criminals.

3. (p. 112) The British scholar Sydney Fowler Wright (1929), commented that so great was the influence of the police over the magistrates' courts that they had come popularly to be called "police courts."

4. (p. 112) The police commonly express the sentiment "We don't make the laws, we merely enforce them." Although it is technically true that laws are made by legislatures, the law-enforcement community exercises substantial influence over the process. Not only do senior law-enforcement officials ranging from the assistant directors of the FBI to the attorney general frequently testify before Congress on pending bills; many bills are first seen by Congress and its staff in the form of drafts prepared by law-enforcement agencies.

5. (p. 114) Even circumspect statements on a wiretapped phone can be quite useful. Fat Ange Ruggerio of the Gambino crime family was not aware his phone was being wiretapped when he told a colleague, "[I'm handling some] H." The FBI was listening, and agents photographed Ruggerio as he made deliveries to three different drug traffickers (Blum 1993, p. 83).

6. (p. 114) Gravano read the government transcripts. He saw the strength of the Federal case and learned that Gotti was angry with him for being too greedy (Blum 1993, pp. 255–257 and pp. 317–318). Fearing that Gotti was developing a strategy to blame him for various crimes, the underboss turned the tables, and testified against Gotti (Blum 1993, pp. 319–326).

7. (p. 114) Although US agents learned of meetings, they never succeeded in tracking Ames to one (Weiner et al. 1995, pp. 229–230, pp. 245–246).

8. (p. 115) A tap of this kind is often called a bug and not clearly distinguished from a microphone listening to the room. Such devices are inexpensive and easy to install. A radio bug built into an RJ11 "octopus plug" has been advertised in *Popular Electronics* by a company called Seymore-Radix. Its price is about $30.

9. (p. 115) For a more detailed exploration of the ways a line can be tapped see Dash et al. 1959 and Fitzgerald and Leopold 1987.

10. (p. 115) On his first visit to Democratic National Committee Headquarters in the Watergate Building, James McCord succeeded in placing a bug in the phone of the chair's secretary. But this elicited very little useful information, so McCord returned a few weeks later for a second—and fateful—try.

11. (p. 117) Apparently because the results were written down with a pen.

12. (p. 117) In Europe this has not been the case. Long-distance bills were instead compiled by means of a tone-based message-unit system that did not reveal the called number.

13. (p. 117) Signaling System 7 (SS7), introduced to support ISDN in the 1980s,

passes the identity of the called phone from switch to switch throughout the whole length of the call.

14. (p. 117) Clifford Stoll (1989, p. 68) gives a dramatic account of such an exercise that took place as late as the mid 1980s.

15. (p. 117) Privacy blocking will prevent the ID information from being given to the receiving telephone but will not conceal it from either a telephone company switch or private branch exchange attached to the network by a DS1 connection.

16. (p. 117) Analysis of billing information during their investigation of World Trade Center bombing led the FBI from the initial suspect to his co-conspirators (Mashberg 1993; Bernstein 1994).

17. (p. 119) Another conspirator in the World Trade Center bombing, Eyad Ismoil, was picked up through a matching of telephone records with airline manifests; he was later convicted (McKinley 1995a).

18. (p. 119) Investigators also used photos from several days before the explosion to prove that Timothy McVeigh was the "Robert D. Kling" who, on the afternoon of April 17, 1995, in Junction City, Kansas, rented the Ryder truck used in the bombing. Days and weeks after the bombing investigators meticulously reconstructed McVeigh's movements on April 17. Surveillance photos taken at a McDonald's about a mile from the Ryder agency showed McVeigh at the restaurant at 3:49 and 3:57 PM on that day. Shortly afterward, "Kling" rented the truck. When prosecutors claimed that the McDonald's photo was of McVeigh, his lawyer did not dispute the point. The photo was taken several days before there was any hint it would be useful in a criminal case—and *then the evidence was available when needed* (Brooke 1997a).

19. (p. 121) The provisions were later extended to the other armed forces.

20. (p. 122) Other investigators have reached different conclusions (Burnham 1996, p. 218).

## Chapter 6. Privacy: Protections and Threats

1. (p. 126) Article 17 1. No one shall be subjected to arbitrary or unlawful interference with his privacy, family, home or correspondence, nor to unlawful attacks on his honour and reputation. 2. Everyone has the right to the protection of the law against such interference or attacks (United Nations 1985, p. 149).

2. (p. 127) In East Germany clergymen and other religious workers were informants; siblings informed on one another, and there were even husbands who informed on their wives (Kinzer 1992).

3. (p. 127) The main purpose of the Privacy Act of 1974 (Public Law 93-579) was to ensure that federal records on individuals were accurate, timely, complete, and relevant (US-PPSC 1977, p. 17).

4. (p. 129) The term "Secretary of State" must have designated an office more like that of the secretary of state of California (whose duties include certifying election returns) than like that of the US secretary of state, whose position in Britain is called "foreign secretary."

5. (p. 129) "You will know from whom this comes without a signature: the omission of which as rendered almost by the curiosity of the post office. Indeed a period is now approaching during which I shall discontinue writing letters as much as possible, knowing every snare will be used to get hold of what may be perverted in the eyes of the public." (Thomas Jefferson, in a letter to James Thomas Callender, October 6, 1799; see Jefferson, *Works*, Federal Edition, Vol. 9, p. 488).

6. (p. 129) The complaints centered on theft rather than lack of confidentiality.

7. (p. 129) Mail from prisoners of war, and between the Union and the Confederacy, was a different matter; it was routinely opened and censored (Scheele 1970, p. 88).

8. (p. 129) Wiretapping appears to have been rare.

9. (p. 130) See, e.g., *State v. Litchfield* 58 Me. 267 (1870), *National Bank v. National Bank* 7 W. Va. 544 (1874), *United States v. Babcock* 3 Dill 567 (1880), *United States v. Hunter* 15 Fed. 712 (1882), *Ex Parte Jaynes* 70 Cal. 638 (1886), *Re Storrer* 63 Fed. 564 (1894), *Western Union Telegraph Co. v. Bierhaus* 8 Ind. App. 563 (1894), as reported in (Seipp 1977, p. 59).

10. (p. 133) Under the Fourteenth Amendment the citizens are protected from intrusions by the states.

11. (p. 136) Bork was a candidate for the Supreme Court. During his confirmation hearings, the press reported his video-rental habits, which tended to run to Hitchcock and Cary Grant.

12. (p. 137) For example, the Social Security Administration matches its Supplemental Security Income Benefit with the Internal Revenue Service's tax data so as to avoid paying duplicate benefits (USGAO 1990, p. 24)

13. (p. 137) Thus, for example, the doings of the Mississippi Sovereignty Commission, in which, the state, from 1956 to 1977, authorized spying, harrassment and intimidation of civil-rights workers in order to delay or halt desegregation, only became public in 1998 (Kettle 1998).

14. (p. 138) Act of June 18, 1929, ch. 28, sec., 11, 46 Stat. 25.

15. (p. 138) Thomas Clark, who later became US Attorney General, was assigned to the Western Command. He recalled that a Census Bureau member had shown him files detailing exactly where Japanese-Americans lived (reported in (Okamura 1981, pp. 112–113)).

16. (p. 138) Postal workers are permitted to open first-class mail, but only with the explicit permission of the addressee or if the employee is trying to determine an address to which to send the mail (39 U.S.C. 3623(d)). Otherwise, a warrant

is needed; that has been US law since at least 1878 (*Ex Parte Jackson*, 96 US 727, 1878, p. 733).

17. (p. 140) See Chapter 2 of Charns 1992, for a fuller discussion of this incident.

18. (p. 140) "Evidence indicates that the FBI did not believe that the Communist Party [constituted] as serious a threat as it had in the 1940s" (USS 94d, p. 66).

19. (p. 140) These are from the following FBI memos: Memo from FBI Headquarters to New York Field Office, July 11, 1960; Memo from FBI Headquarters to New York Field Office, December 16, 1960; Memo from FBI Headquarters to New York Field Office, November 3, 1961, as reported in (USS 94e, pp. 363–364).

20. (p. 140) $42,500 for disruption activities by the FBI, $96,500 for surreptitious entries by the FBI, and $125,000 for the FBI's use of informants (*Socialist Workers Party v. Attorney General of the United States*, 73 Civ. 3160, 1986).

21. (p. 142) The justification was "Martin Luther King, Jr., head of the Southern Christian Leadership Conference (SCLC), an organization set up to promote integration which we are investigating to determine the extent of Communist Party (CP) influence on King and the SCLC, plans to attend and possibly may indulge in a hunger fast as a means of protest." (Sullivan 1964)

22. (p. 142) The memo is reproduced on p. 713 of USS 94b.

23. (p. 142) In a letter from the FBI to Vice President Agnew, Ralph Abernathy, President of the SCLC, is characterized as a man "who, although he advocates nonviolence, has invited violence by some of his statements." (USS 94c, p. 494, Exhibit 38-3.) In 1970 the FBI forwarded information on Abernathy's private life to Vice President Agnew. The Church Committee hearing exhibits include a letter the FBI [signature blanked out] to the Vice President, "... In response to your request, there is attached information regarding ... Ralph David Abernathy ... The material also includes information about [his private life] (sic) ..." Exhibit 38-3, in (USS 94c, p. 494).

24. (p. 143) Bond, a Georgia state legislator, and Jackson, executive director of SCLC Operation Breadbasket, were active in the civil rights movement. Baez and Guthrie (son of the legendary Woody Guthrie) were folk singers, Coffin, chaplain at Yale, Spock, a physician and the author of the well-known *Baby and Child Care*, that had been the bible of American parents in the post-war years, were all active in the anti-war movement. Stevenson made it into the files because of his association with Jackson (O'Brien 1971, p. 127). Mikva, a member of the House active in the anti-war movement, said that he learned from Senator John Tunney "how I became eligible for the files. Jesse Jackson is a constituent of mine; Adlai Stevenson is a friend of mine; and my wife used to work for the American Civil Liberties Union." (Mikva 1971, p. 130). Ralph Stein, formerly with US Army, Counterintelligence, in (Stein 1971, p. 266) told of the surveillance of Baez, Bond, Coffin, Guthrie, Jackson, King, and Spock. Stein did not mention Mikva or Stevenson,

but Mikva testified to the existence of Army surveillance files on both, as did O'Brien. (Mikva 1971, p. 136; O'Brien 1971, p. 120 and p. 127)

25. (p. 143) This included Lloyd Norman, a *Newsweek* reporter writing on US military plans in Germany, and Hanson Baldwin, a *New York Times* reporter and military historian who had written on Soviet missile sites (USS 94d, p. 63).

26. (p. 144) During Johnson's administration Attorney General Nicholas deB. Katzenbach had wrested control of electronic surveillance back from the FBI and imposed certain limitations on its use (USS 94d, p. 105).

27. (p. 144) As he signed the bill, Johnson said: "Title III of this legislation deals with wiretapping and eavesdropping.

My views on this subject are clear. In a special message to Congress in 1967 and again this year, I called—in the Right to Privacy Act—for an end to the bugging and snooping that invade the privacy of citizens.

I urged that the Congress outlaw 'all wiretapping and electronic eavesdropping, public and private, wherever and whenever it occurs.' The only exceptions would be those instances where 'the security of the Nation itself was at stake—and then only under the strictest safeguards.'

In the bill I sign today, Congress has moved part of the way by

— banning all wiretapping and eavesdropping by private parties;

— prohibiting the sale and distribution of 'listening-in' devices in interstate commerce.

But the Congress, in my judgement, has taken an unwise and potentially dangerous step by sanctioning eavesdropping and wiretapping by Federal, State, and local law officials in an almost unlimited variety of situations.

If we are very careful and cautious in our planning, these legislative provisions could result in producing a nation of snoopers bending through the keyholes of the homes and offices of America, spying on our neighbors. No conversation in the sanctity of the bedroom or relayed over a copper telephone wire would be free of eavesdropping by those who say they want to ferret out crime." [Johnson 1968]

28. (p. 145) Attorney General Edward Levi later wrote Kraft that the FBI's file "did not indicate that [Kraft's] activities posed any risk to the national interest" (Pincus 1976).

29. (p. 145) "This demonstration could possibly attract the largest number of demonstrators ever to assemble in Washington, D.C. The large number is cause for major concern should violence of any type break out. It is necessary for this Bureau to keep abreast of events as they occur, and we feel in this instance advance knowledge of plans ... would be most advantageous to our coverage and the safety of individuals and property." (Hoover 1969b)

30. (p. 146) These included Columbia University's Mathematics and Science Li-

brary, the New York Public Library, the Lockwood Memorial Library at the State University of New York at Buffalo, the Courant Institute of Mathematical Sciences Library, the University of Maryland at College Park Engineering and Physical Sciences Library, the University of Houston Library, and the Engineering and Mathematical Sciences Library at the University of California at Los Angeles (Foerstal 1991, pp. 54–69).

31. (p. 148) Despite repeated warnings from the General Accounting Office, these browsings continued. There were 449 unauthorized file searches in 1994, 774 in 1995, 797 in 1996 (USGAO 1997; Richardson 1997).

32. (p. 148) During the investigation of the "sugar lobby" in 1962, ten phone lines of a Washington law firm were wiretapped. Several advisors to Martin Luther King who were lawyers were wiretapped (USS 94e, p. 340).

## Chapter 7. Wiretapping

1. (p. 151) "Eavesdrop" does not, as it might appear, mean to hang from the eaves and listen to what is going on in an adjacent room. The eavesdrop is the area within the eaves of a house, what we would today call, the footprint of the house, and to eavesdrop is to trespass within the eavesdrop in order to look or listen.

2. (p. 153) In 1998 it was revealed that the Los Angeles Police Department had routinely used information gleaned from ongoing — and legal — wiretaps to open new investigations in which, in direct contravention of the law, suspects were never informed of the role that wiretaps had played in their case, even during trial (Krikorian 1998).

3. (p. 160) Hoover went to extraordinary lengths to hide the wiretap logs as well as records that would reveal wiretapping had occurred; the FBI Director even hid the name of the filing system in which wiretap records were stored. After the Coplon case, wiretap information went into the "June" files, June being Hoover's codeword for "Top Secret." See Theoharis and Cox 1988, pp. 256–261 for a discussion of Hoover's methods.

4. (p. 162) For many years stories circulated that before Hoover's annual testimony to Congress the FBI Director had wiretaps removed, and then had the taps reinstated afterwards. This way Hoover could minimize the number of active wiretaps reported to Congress. The Church Committee carefully examined the number of wiretaps for the dates in question and concluded this story was apocryphal (USS 94e, p. 302).

5. (p. 163) He certainly had no objection to doing so when the president made such requests (FBI 1975a; USS 94e, p. 313–314).

6. (p. 163) The wiretapped justices include Hugo Black, Stanley Reed, William O. Douglas, Abe Fortas, and Potter Stewart (Charns 1992, pp. 17, 25, 87); (Hoover 1970).

7. (p. 171) The Judiciary Committee Report on the act said that "each offense was chosen because it was intrinsically serious or because it is characteristic of the operations of organized crime," (USS 90, p. 97) and that "the last provision [interstate transport of stolen goods] is included to make it possible to strike at organized crime fencing" (USS 90, p. 98).

8. (p. 171) In an emergency, a wiretap may be placed without a warrant; however, if a warrant is not obtained within 48 hours, the information produced—like any electronic communication intercepted in violation of Title III—may not be received in evidence or even divulged (Omnibus Crime Control Act 1968 §515).

9. (p. 171) The fax and computer provisions were added by the Electronic Communications Privacy Act.

10. (p. 172) The stringent requirements for obtaining a wiretap order do not, however, mean that such surveillance may only be done as a "last resort." (*United States v. David Smith.* 893 F. 2nd 1573 (9th cir. 1990))

11. (p. 172) This requirement was codified in a supplementary law enacted in 1970 (Omnibus Crime Control and Safe Streets Act §2518(4)).

12. (p. 174) Aside from Morton Halperin, there were:

- National Security Council members Helmut Sonnenfeldt, Daniel Davidson, Richard Sneider, Winston Lord, and Tony Lake;

- State Department members Richard Pedersen and Richard Moose, Ambassador William Sullivan;

- Department of Defense member Colonel Robert Pursley;

- White House staff John Sears, William Safire, and James McLane, and;

- correspondents Henry Brandon (*London Sunday Times*), Hedrick Smith (*New York Times*), and Marvin Kalb (CBS News).

13. (p. 175) The *Post* began to publish the papers after the *Times* was served with an injunction barring publication.

14. (p. 175) Ellsberg had also been picked up on the Halperin wiretaps; during the 21 months, Ellsberg had been overheard on 15 occasions (Hersh 1983, p. 325). Halperin was circumspect in his conversation, but Ellsberg was not; he talked about taking "trips" and carrying "stuff" to a friend's house—clear allusions to drugs. The wiretap transcripts, including these comments, went to the White House.

When Ellsberg's role in leaking the Pentagon Papers was discovered, Kissinger, who had earlier hired Ellsberg as a consultant to the National Security Council, tried to distance himself from the leaker. He disparaged Ellsberg to the president by calling him a drug abuser. When Nixon queried Kissinger about this, the National Security Advisor replied "There is no doubt about it." (Hersh 1983, p. 384) Thus we see the insidiousness of wiretaps; the Halperin-Ellsberg wiretapped conversations, *which had never showed any evidence of national-security leaks* (ibid.,

p. 397), were forwarded to the White House, where the private discussions between two colleagues became ammunition for character assassination and worse.

15. (p. 179) The Church Committee observed that certain types of surveillance carried out by the intelligence agencies had been illegal at the time (USS 94d, pp. 12–13). The members recommended legislation to regulate "domestic security activities of the Federal Government" (ibid., p. 295).

16. (p. 179) *Recommendation 6.*—The CIA should not conduct electronic surveillance, unauthorized entry, or mail opening within the United States for any purpose (USS 94d, p. 302).

17. (p. 179) *Recommendation 15.*—NSA should take all practicable measures consistent with its foreign intelligence mission to eliminate or minimize the interception, selection, and monitoring of communications of Americans from the foreign communications.

*Recommendation 16.*—NSA should not be permitted to select for monitoring any communication to, from, or about an American without his consent, except for the purpose of obtaining information about hostile foreign intelligence or terrorist activities, and then only if a warrant approving such monitoring is obtained in accordance with procedures similar to those contained in Title III of the Omnibus Crime Control and Safe Streets Act of 1968 (USS 94d, p. 309).

18. (p. 179) *Recommendation 52.*—All non-consensual electronic surveillance should be conducted to judicial warrants issued under authority of Title III of the Omnibus Crime Control and Safe Streets Act of 1968.

The Act should be amended to provide, with respect to electronic surveillance of foreigners in the United States, that a warrant may issue if:

(a) There is probable cause that the target is an officer, employee, or conscious agent of a foreign power.

(b) The Attorney General has certified that the surveillance is likely to reveal information necessary to the protection of the nation against actual or potential attack or other hostile acts of force of a foreign power; to obtain foreign intelligence deemed essential to the security of the United States; or to protect national security information against hostile foreign intelligence activity.

(c) With respect to any such electronic surveillance, the judge should adopt procedures to minimize the acquisition and retention of non-foreign intelligence information about Americans.

(d) Such electronic surveillance should be exempt from the disclosure requirements of Title III of the 1968 Act as to foreigners generally and as to Americans if they are involved in hostile foreign intelligence activity (except where disclosure is called for in connection with the defense in the case of criminal prosecution) (USS 94d, pp. 327–328).

19. (p. 179) For the purposes of FISA, a "United States person" is a citizen, a permanent resident alien, a group of such people, or a US corporation.

20. (p. 179) There are two exceptions to this rule. After a declaration of war, the president, through the attorney general, can authorize a wiretap for foreign intelligence purposes for up to 15 days without a court order. A court order is also unnecessary if communications are exclusively between foreign powers or involve intelligence other than spoken communications from a location under the exclusive control of a foreign power.

21. (p. 180) An approved application may result in several wiretap orders, since the target may be using several communication devices.

## Chapter 8. Communications: The Current Scene

1. (p. 183) This was the best-case scenario; the worst-case showed no access to intercepted communications by 1995 (Advanced Telephony Unit 1992).

2. (p. 184) In 1994 the US Telephone Association estimated that the costs for call forwarding information alone would come to as much as $1.8 billion (Neel 1994b, p. 101). New equipment and software for wiretapping were estimated to be another $450 million (Neel 1994a, p. 60).

3. (p. 184) In particular, by 1991 virtually all mid-size and large companies were using PBXs, with more than 25 million lines (NTIA 1992).

4. (p. 185) "Everything considered, would you say that you approve or disapprove of wiretapping?" In 1994 76% of Americans said they disapprove (USDoJ 1994b, p. 173).

5. (p. 185) All the missing reports occurred in state electronic surveillance cases.

6. (p. 185) In the case of multiple crimes, the *Wiretap Report* lists only the most serious crime as the reason for the order.

7. (p. 185) Since a case takes several years to wend its way through the courts, convictions are usually reported several years later.

8. (p. 186) 355 F. Supp. 523, 542 (S.D. Calif. 1971), cited in Schwartz 1974, p. 194.

9. (p. 186) The case involved bid-rigging in the window-replacement industry. Lawyer Benjamin Brafman argued that his client had been entrapped, "Others on the tapes would refer to my client as 'the kid.'" The defendant was acquitted (Marks 1995).

10. (p. 187) "In attacking Mr. Fortier today, the defense played recordings of a series of his telephone conversations that were wiretapped by Federal agents in the weeks immediately after the bombing, when Mr. Fortier himself was considered a possible suspect. In those recordings, turned over to the defense as part of a pretrial process, he boasted that he could mislead Federal agents and make a million dollars through book rights from his connection to Mr. McVeigh."

(Brooke 1997b) Fortier was the lead witness against McVeigh, who was charged with bombing the federal building in Oklahoma City.

11. (p. 188) Elimination of supplies from one area leads to increased cultivation elsewhere (Reuter 1985, pp. 90–93). Increased law enforcement in northern California led to marijuana growing shifting to Kentucky (Kleiman 1993, p. 284). The success of the "French Connection" case caused a significant reduction in the flow of heroin into the United States from Turkey, but within three years this was replaced by heroin from Mexico and Southeast Asia (Moore 1990, p. 136). When US efforts eliminated Mexican marijuana, the drug was replaced almost instantly by hemp from Colombia that turned out to be significantly more potent than the Central American variety (Reuter 1985, pp. 91–92).

Simple arithmetic makes clear an additional reason for the failure of interdiction: drugs that are valued at $2000 per pound where they are grown end up costing well over $100,000 per pound on American streets (Rydell 1994, p. 11). The profit margin is sufficiently high and the demand by addicts sufficiently inelastic that seizures have little effect on the commerce in drugs.

12. (p. 189) This is to achieve a 1% reduction in current annual consumption (Rydell, p. xiii). Treating all heavy users once each year would reduce US consumption of cocaine by half in fifteen years, and by less than half in earlier years (Rydell, p. xix).

13. (p. 189) Over the years, FBI Directors and Attorneys General have been eloquent in their appeals for electronic surveillance.

"I dare say that the most violent critic of the FBI would urge the use of wire tapping techniques if his child were kidnapped, and held in custody," [Hoover 1950, p. 230].

"[E]very Attorney General over the last twenty-two years has favored and authorized wire tapping by Federal officials in security cases and other heinous crimes such as kidnapping . . . ," Attorney General Herbert Brownell, in [Brownell 1954a, p. 201].

"By way of background, telecommunications systems and networks are often used to further organized crime, racketeering, extortion, kidnapping . . ." wrote Assistant Attorney General Lee Rawls to Speaker of the House Thomas Foley in 1992 [Rawls 1992].

"Wiretapping is used in the most important life and death cases—terrorism, espionage, drug trafficking, organized crime, kidnapping, and a variety of other crimes," FBI Director Louis Freeh testified to Congress in hearings on the digital telephony bill [USS 103b, p. 6].

Freeh was speaking of digital telephony and wiretapping when he told the committee, "I sat last week with Polly Klaas' father [Polly Klaas was the victim of a kidnapper], who came from California to talk to me, and he said to me, "Mr. Freeh, the FBI did everything in that case to find my little girl." I do not want to be in a position where I am going to tell some father I could not do everything I would normally do because I could not get the access that I have today." [USS 103b, p. 13]

In fact, as the Director well knew, wiretapping would not have prevented Klaas's murder.

14. (p. 189) Approximately at the time that the FBI began its hard push on CALEA, the use of electronic surveillance in kidnapping cases saw a sharp increase. During the period 1968–1993, there were a total of 69 court orders for electronic surveillance. In 1994 the number jumped to 11 kidnapping cases using electronic surveillance, and in 1995, to 25. Much is heard about how carefully the court reviews electronic surveillance applications, but it is striking to note that of the 11 court orders in kidnapping cases, 2 surveillances that were never installed, and two that were installed but yielded no incriminating intercepts. Furthermore, 2 of the kidnapping cases (one of which did not have an intercept installed) were related to other cases investigated through wiretaps.

The 1995 kidnapping cases show the same pattern: 1 intercept was not installed, 10 had no incriminating intercepts, and 2 of the cases (1 installed, 1 not) were related to gambling cases already being investigated through wiretaps. Thus of the 25 so-called kidnapping electronic surveillances, at most 13 yielded any information in a kidnapping case. Installed surveillances that yield no incriminating intercepts are rare, and the kidnapping cases before 1994 do not show this pattern.

15. (p. 189) According to the FBI, the precise numbers are 1990:624; 1991:481; 1992:495; 1993:401; 1994:418 (source: Michael Kortan, Unit Chief, FBI National Press Office, private communication to Susan Landau, August 7, 1995).

16. (p. 189) This is an area in which improvements in telecommunications have made investigation easier and kidnappers' lives riskier. The familiar process of trying to keep the caller talking long enough that the line can be traced is often made unnecessary by caller-ID mechanisms that reveal the calling number immediately. When this is coupled with *911 databases* that give police information about the locations of phone numbers, it means that even a kidnapper who calls from a phone booth must talk fast and leave quickly.

17. (p. 189) Administrative Office of the United States Courts, *Report on Applications for Orders Authorizing or Approving the Interception of Wire, Oral, or Electronic Communications (Wiretap Report)*, 1988–1993.

18. (p. 190) Source: private conversation between Landau and Iglehart, January 16, 1997.

19. (p. 190) The *Wiretap Report* reports 41 jurisdictions that permit wiretapping: the Federal, Puerto Rico, the Virgin Islands, Washington, D.C., and thirty-seven states. In addition, 5 states permit state police tapping of consensual overhears (Alaska, North Carolina, Tennessee, Washington, and West Virginia).

20. (p. 190) The Administrative Office of the US Courts release annual reports

on wiretaps. In late spring of each year, data is available on the electronic surveillances of the previous year (except for those still in use) as well as new information on previous surveillances. It typically takes about four years for cases involving wiretaps to wend their way through the court system; thus we have picked 1988 as a year to study, since that leaves a sufficiently long window.

21. (p. 191) These statistics are based on the raw data provided in the 1994 *Wiretap Report*. Although the "Reports by Judges on Court Authorized Intercepts" are supposed to be exact data, some of the reports appear instead to be estimates (presumably supplied by the prosecutors). For example, on pages A36–A37, cases A.O. 471*, 472*, 473*, and 474*, list 2000, 1500, 300, and 1000 intercepts and 100, 300, 200, and 200 incriminating intercepts respectively. This seems unlikely. On pages A38–A39, A.O. 475* lists 2000 intercepts, of which 500 are recorded as being incriminating. Similarly, on pages A90–A91, cases A.O. 13, 14 and 15 list 6200, 1200, and 200 intercepts, and 180, 80, and 60 incriminating intercepts respectively. There are a number of other such anomalous figures in the *Wiretap Report*.

22. (p. 191) For this statistic, we are including court authorizations that are solely for wiretaps, and not for combination wiretap and electronic bug surveillance.

23. (p. 192) Table 6 in the appropriate *Wiretap Report*. In using the summary tables of the *Wiretap Report*s one loses specificity; the numbers cited are the sum of all surveillances (phone, electronic, and combination) that are not purely microphone.

24. (p. 192) Annual Department of Justice letter to the Chair of the House Judiciary Committee, as reported in (Burnham 1996, p. 159.)

25. (p. 192) Most calls, regardless of distance, now "arrive" with indication of the calling number. This information is often blocked from going to the subscriber, but it is available to the local telephone switch and thus to law enforcement.

26. (p. 192) At the time of Foster's death, Clinton's friends and advisors had been scattered across the continent. Had they instead been down the hallway, these conversations—five-minute discussions—might have disappeared into dust. But with hard records of when phone conversations took place, political Washington drew all sorts of conclusions.

27. (p. 192) An exception occurs if there is an emergency; in that case, a court order authorizing the tap must be approved within 48 hours, or all oral and wire communication intercepted in violation of Title III, and cannot be used in evidence—or even divulged. However, electronic communications intercepted in violation of Title III may not be received in evidence. (Omnibus Crime Control and Safe Streets Act, §2515)

28. (p. 193) Source: private conversation between Diffie and Charney, 1975.

29. (p. 193) One possibility is to relax the minimization requirement but increase the reporting requirement by requiring recording of all conversation on a tapped

line and making the entire body of material available to the wiretap victims at the close of the investigation, whether or not that investigation leads to a prosecution.

30. (p. 194) Source: private conversation between Diffie and Charney, 1975.

31. (p. 195) Communications Assistance for Law Enforcement Act, Public Law 103-414.

32. (p. 195) One such example is Freeh's reference to the Tina Isa murder (Bryant 1993), which had been recorded by an FBI bug—not wiretap.

33. (p. 196) "Coincidentally, Director Freeh, with your testimony today the *Philadelphia Inquirer* has a major story on 'FBI Nets Stanfa in Mob Sweep,' and the subheadline is 'FBI's Rich Harvest is a Tale of the Tape,' which could not come at a more opportune time to underscore the kind of need of which you are testifying," Spector said (USS 103b, p. 46).

But the Stanfa case is described in detail in several newspaper articles, and the surveillance used is microphone bugs, including one planted in Stanfa's lawyer's office in Camden, New Jersey (Anastasia 1994; Hinds 1994). The case corresponds to A.O. number 230 in the 1993 *Wiretap Report*; the surveillance is explicitly listed as a microphone bug.

34. (p. 196) CALEA applied only to telecommunications carriers, and did not affect companies supplying information services, including electronic mail, and Internet services.

35. (p. 196) This includes not only wiretaps, but also dialing and signaling information, including "redirection numbers" (call forwarding, call transfers), and call attempts (including unanswered calls).

36. (p. 197) The FBI did not release information indicating which geographic areas corresponded to which categories.

37. (p. 197) Of course, in 1968, you could not typically trace a call in less than several minutes. Furthermore, tracing a call only tells you the calling phone number. The location of the phone is now available to law enforcement from the databases constructed to support the 911 service, but these did not exist in 1968.

38. (p. 198) "The proposed legislation does not seek to expand the current laws." (Freeh 1994b, p. 29)

39. (p. 198) The growth factor varies depending on whether the number is "actual" or "maximal" and whether the interception is for wired or wireless communications. For "actual" wired communications the growth factor is 1.259, for "actual" wireless is 1.707, for "maximal" wired communications is 1.303, and for "maximal" wired communications is 1.621 (FBI 1997b).

40. (p. 198) "Actual" means the number of simultaneous communications intercepts, pen registers, and trap-and-trace devices, that the Attorney General anticipates will be simultaneously conducted in 1998, "maximal" means the maximum number (FBI 1997b).

41. (p. 199)  The funding was approved in the "Omnibus Consolidated Appropriations Act," and it provided for funding through a combination of money supplied by various intelligence agencies, as well as $60 million in direct funding. An additional $12 million was provided through unspent Department of Justice funds.

42. (p. 199)  The 1996 Antiterrorist and Effective Death Penalty Act (PL 104-32) empowered the Attorney General to determine whether a group constituted a foreign terrorist group and made this designation immune to subsequent judicial review.

43. (p. 200)  Some of the evidence was merely circumstantial, as when demonstrators, who used only a telephone to communicate the particulars, appeared at a march or rally and discovered a police presence, or when members of the government knew about tactics that union officials had decided on a short time earlier (Fitzgerald and Leopold 1987, pp. 27–28). But the ubiquity of such wiretapping was confirmed by the General Treasurer of the Post Office Engineering Union—until 1980 the British Post Office ran the telephone system—who in 1980 said there was much evidence to confirm that the Security Services monitored the calls of union officials during work actions (ibid., p. 29). The activities that have come to light occurred before 1985, when Britain codified the procedure for obtaining a wiretap. However, currently the British green movement, whose most disruptive tactics consist of blocking road-building projects, is being investigated by the Anti-Terrorist Squad. Like labor activists before them, environmental protestors have found police waiting for them at demonstrations whose venues had been relayed only by telephone (Monbiot 1996).

44. (p. 200)  It was only in 1985, in response to a European Court ruling that objected to the lack of a clear warrant procedure for wiretaps, that Britain adopted wiretap legislation. Before that wiretaps proceeded through a combination of warrants, executive orders, and even informal requests.

Malone challenged the legality of the wiretap, arguing that (i) telephone users had privacy rights, (ii) the wiretapping violated the European Convention on Human Rights, and (iii) in the absence of a specific wiretap law, the interception was illegal (Fitzgerald and Leopold 1987, pp. 134–135). The British High Court rejected Malone's arguments, but the European Convention on Human Rights, after determining the case was admissible, referred it to the European Court on Human Rights, whose rulings can require governments to correct deficiencies in the law. The European Court ruled that British wiretap law "cannot be said with any reasonable certainty what elements of the powers to intercept are incorporated in legal rules and what elements remain within the discretion of the executive ... the minimum degree of legal protection to which citizens are entitled under the rule of law in a democratic society is lacking ..." (Bailey et al. 1991, p. 803)

Current British wiretap law is significantly less specific than US law governing wiretaps and permits the interception of lines not specified in the warrant if it is believed these are *likely* to make contact with lines that are specified in a warrant (Fitzgerald and Leopold 1987, p. 146). In a surprisingly broad view of circumstances that can justify wiretap surveillance, the 1985 British law allows interception in cases that the Foreign Secretary deems to be necessary "to safeguard the economic wellbeing of the country." (Command 9438, paragraph 10, as cited in (ibid., p. 148))

45. (p. 200) See "Interception of Communications," Report to COREPER, ENFOCO 40, 10090/93, Confidential, Brussels, 16.11.93, as reported in "European Union and FBI Launch Global Surveillance System," (Statewatch, London).

46. (p. 200) "Memorandum of Understanding concerning the lawful interception of telecommunications," ENFOPOL 112, 10037/95, Limite, Brussels, in "EU and FBI" (see preceding note).

47. (p. 200) Correspondence with Ministers, 9th Session 1995–1996, HL 74, pp. 26–29, in "EU and FBI."

48. (p. 201) Draft letter to non-EU participants in the informal international Law Enforcement Telecommunications Seminar regarding the Council Resolution, ENFOPOL 180, 11282/96, Limite 6.11.96, in "EU and FBI."

49. (p. 201) "Legally permitted surveillance of telecommunications systems provided from a point outside the national territory," Report from the UK delegation to the Working Group on Police Cooperation, ENFOPOL 1, 4118/95, Restricted, 9.1.95, Report from the Presidency to the Working Group on Police Cooperation, ENFOPOL 1, 4118/2/95 REV 2, Limite, 2.6.95, in "EU and FBI."

50. (p. 202) For example, Louis Freeh testified to Congress on May 19, 1994 that "The proposed [Digital Telephony] legislation relates solely to advanced technology, not legal authority or privacy. It has nothing to do with the separate, but important, 'Clipper Chip' technology." (Freeh 1994c)

51. (p. 202) This took place at a conference on Global Cryptography in Washington, D.C.

52. (p. 203) The memo is dated January 17, 1991, but from context it is clear that the correct date is January 17, 1992.

## Chapter 9. Cryptography: The Current Scene

1. (p. 207) For example, the NSA Director wrote to Dr. Willis Ware, chair of NIST's Computer System Security and Privacy Advisory Board that, "The National Security Agency has serious reservations about a public debate on cryptography." (McConnell 1992)

2. (p. 208) According to one of the NSA "flag badges," NSA's Deputy Director for Operations went looking for the Deputy Director of Information Security with a TSD (telephone security device) in hand. At an encounter in the hall, he rammed

the TSD firmly into his opposite number's stomach as though he were passing a football and said: "What are you trying to do to me?"

3. (p. 208) The original producer was RCA's COMSEC division in Camden, New Jersey, which was bought by GTE and later absorbed into Lockheed-Martin.

4. (p. 208) Use of the STU-III in secure mode is controlled by an "ignition key," a 64-kilobit storage device packaged in the form of a small plastic key. One key may authorize its holder to use as many as 8 different phones, and as many as 32 distinct keys may be used in any one phone.

5. (p. 208) Far the most numerous are the STU-IIIs, but some STU-IIs remain in use, and Clipper phones have official status. STU-IIs are also used in parts of NATO, but STU-IIIs have limited availability to US allies.

6. (p. 209) In fact it had a second signal processor dedicated as a modem, but this was a big improvement on earlier secure phones, some of which had seven.

7. (p. 211) Originally, this was more candidly entitled the Law Enforcement Exploitation Field (LEEF), a phrase consistent with standard SIGINT terminology. The less accurate term "access" was adopted for marketing reasons.

8. (p. 211) The natural question arises: Why not escrow Type I keys? Such a proposal is in line with the standard command and control objective, so carefully sought in the nuclear field, of denying the use of captured weapons to an opponent and may ultimately be undertaken. At present, however, there are hundreds of thousands of Type I devices in the field and any prompt conversion is out of the question. All known forms of key-escrow, moreover, harbor potential vulnerabilities. Introducing key escrow technology first in Type II equipment provides a less sensitive environment in which to refine the techniques.

9. (p. 212) Although the standard was announced on April 16, 1993, it was first-published in the *Federal Register* on July 30. The public comment period was through September 28 (USDoC 1993).

10. (p. 212) The Department of Energy, the US Agency for International Development, and the Nuclear Regulatory Commission all submitted letters opposing the adoption of the Clipper standard.

11. (p. 213) "Authorized implementations may be procured by authorized organizations for integration into security equipment." (USDoC 1994b, p. 6004)

12. (p. 213) There will also be a vulnerability associated with each individual chip. No tamper-resistant technology seems likely to be immortal. At some point, recovery of the device unique key from an individual chip may become economical, rendering each device a threat to all the past traffic it was used to transmit.

13. (p. 213) NSA, however, doesn't seem worried. In early 1996, Fortezza cards were authorized for SECRET traffic and NSA officials have used the TSD3600 to stay in touch with their offices while traveling.

14. (p. 214) Federal procurement practices generally combine a standard with a process for approving exceptional requirements. The object is to lower costs

through volume purchases resulting from conformance to the standards. Getting approval for exceptions can therefore be very tedious.

15. (p. 215) Source: private conversation between Diffie and AT&T personnel.

16. (p. 215) This lack of confidentiality led to the embarrassing problem Speaker of the House of Representatives Newton Gingrich faced in January 1997 (Lacey 1997).

17. (p. 215) By the early fall of 1992, industry groups working on secure computing had been promised a "Type IIE" cryptosystem—a system with an 80-bit key that would be certified for protecting sensitive government information, but would also be exportable—and had been told the names Skipjack and Capstone. This appears to have been the main program and was probably planned to handle voice traffic among other things. The more limited Clipper program seems to have been pushed forward to accommodate the needs of AT&T's new secure telephone.

18. (p. 215) The name Tessera was taken from a form of "ID" used by the Roman empire to identify subject peoples. Many people considered this a fitting name, but it seems to have been dropped due to an unforeseen trademark infringement.

19. (p. 216) These two principles, taken together, were widely regarded as a show stopper, because a receiving email agent does not transmit and thus has no way of making up for the sender's failure to include an escrow field.

20. (p. 216) The Department of Justice representative even said they would probably have to have SECRET facility clearances.

21. (p. 217) This idea was first put forth by Silvio Micali at Eurocrypt '94 in Italy. His point was that if you want to get something from the user (the escrowing of his key) you have to demand it at a point where the user is getting something he cannot do for himself. Since privacy can be manufactured on an end-to-end basis by a pair of users and authenticity cannot, the service that provides users with letters of introduction, the key management infrastructure, is an appropriate place to attach the string.

22. (p. 218) There was an announcement in early 1997, however, that the earlier form of key escrow was being removed and replaced with the commercially oriented "key recovery" techniques (O'Hara 1997).

23. (p. 218) These were Top Secret Special Intelligence or TS/SI clearances. The three who chose not to go through the process were Colin Crook, Leslie Gelb, and Raymond Ozzie.

24. (p. 218) The other panelists were Lee Bollinger, Colin Crook, Samuel Fuller, Leslie Gelb, Ronald Graham, Martin Hellman, Julius Katz, Peter Neumann, Raymond Ozzie, Edward Schmults, Elliot Stone, and Willis Ware.

25. (p. 219) Even opponents of publicly available strong unescrowed encryption agreed that this was the case. The FBI testified to the NRC panel "the use of

export controls may well have slowed the speed, proliferation, and volume of encryption products sold in the US" (Dam and Lin 1996, p. 138).

26. (p. 220) The degree of success that the US lobbying has achieved in Britain should not be surprising. Cryptologic cooperation between the two countries which began during World War II and was later codified into the UK-USA Treaty (Richelson and Ball 1985).

27. (p. 220) The hostility to privacy in British law has spread beyond cryptography. A recent law vastly expands police powers of search and virtually removes judicial oversight.

28. (p. 220) Members of the OECD are: Austria, Australia, Belgium, Canada, the Czech Republic, Denmark, Finland, France, Germany, Greece, Hungary, Iceland, Ireland, Italy, Japan, South Korea, Luxembourg, Mexico, New Zealand, the Netherlands, Norway, Poland, Portugal, Spain, Sweden, Switzerland, Turkey, the United Kingdom, and the United States.

29. (p. 220) OECD recommendations form the basis for privacy laws in more than a dozen European and Pacific Rim nations (Rotenberg 1996, p. 5).

30. (p. 221) Source: private conversation between Landau and Deborah Hurley, April 3, 1997.

31. (p. 221) In an ironic twist, in early 1997 the German company Brokat Informationssysteme proposed that it ship its strong cryptography systems to the United States, where they would be embedded in products to be exported. Arguing that the shipment from the United States would simply constitute returning the strong encryption to its original markets, Brokat sought to circumvent the restrictive export controls imposed by the US government (Andrews 1997).

## Chapter 10. Conclusion

1. (p. 226) At the first of the American public cryptographic conferences, Crypto '81, which was held at the University of California at Santa Barbara, one of the NSA people said to me: "It's not that we haven't seen this territory before, but you are covering it very quickly."—WD

2. (p. 226) In the AT&T TSD3600, for example, encryption represents approximately 1–2% of the computation. It is 3% of the cycles of the main processor, but this is assisted by a dedicated modem chip. In short, the TSD spends almost all of its effort either preparing the speech to be encrypted or preparing the cipher text to be sent over the phone line. The rest goes to encrypting it.

3. (p. 226) For example, the GSP8191 secure telephone, which has recently appeared on the market, was designed by one person, Eric Blossom, in a little more than 2 years.

4. (p. 227) Establishing that the person you are communicating with now is the

same person you were communicating with at some previous time is socially fundamental; it is the way acquaintances develop. The ability to assume a persona and to sign email provides a mechanism by which people can meet on the Internet and have some confidence that they are communicating with the same person each time, without exchanging any absolute information about their identities.

5. (p. 227) The Atomic Energy Act of 1954 created the notion that ideas in atomic energy were "born secret" and were to remain secret unless the government said they could be disclosed.

6. (p. 228) This doctrine has been eroded in US law, at first by judicial tolerance and later by congressional action. In the 1970s courts began allowing federal agents to make secret entries into private property in order to plant bugs (Burnham 1996, p. 133). As an outgrowth of the Aldrich Ames case—in which a secret search was conducted, but the legitimacy of the evidence so obtained never enjoyed court scrutiny—the Foreign Intelligence Surveillance Court was given the power to order secret searches.

7. (p. 229) This is a point that Congress might do well to consider amending.

8. (p. 229) Mail covers operated from the 1940s til the early 1970s; copies of telegrams were also sent to NSA during that period. See Chapter 6.

9. (p. 230) See chapter 6, and discussions on Kennedy, Johnson, and Nixon.

10. (p. 231) For example, William Reinsch, the Undersecretary of Commerce, recently testified in Congress that the Administration's policy is to "promote" key recovery in the marketplace (Reinsch 1997).

11. (p. 232) At the time of Freeh's testimony (1994b), Title III was just turning twenty-five years old. If wiretaps are an important tool of law enforcement, there should be enough clear-cut cases in twenty-five years to allow a persuasive case to be made. Freeh's account of the value of wiretapping, is remarkably vague. He refers to numerous convictions, including:

| page | 14 | line | 14: | conviction of two federal district court judges |
|------|----|------|-----|---------------------------------------------------|
| page | 14 | line | 16: | four [Florida state judges] convicted |
| page | 14 | line | 17: | five attorneys ... convicted |
| page | 15 | line | 5: | 65 [ILL-WIND] convictions |
| page | 15 | line | 22: | 79 individuals ... convicted |
| page | 16 | line | 19: | 4 convictions |
| page | 17 | line | 8: | conviction of the principals |
| page | 18 | line | 7: | conviction of two individuals |
| page | 19 | line | 23: | found guilty of racketeering |
| page | 20 | line | 4: | ... and a conviction obtained ... |

without mentioning the name of a single defendant, court, presiding judge, case name, or docket number. This makes the information difficult to verify or explore. It is one thing to say that you can't give the details of ongoing investigations or that cases ended in plea bargains or that crimes were prevented without any trials resulting; it is another to fail to identify cases that must be the results of public trials.

Credence is further strained by the inclusion of at least one identifiable case —The Tina Isa case—in which the surveillance was a microphone planted in the living room in which a teenage girl was murdered [Bryant 1993].

12. (p. 232) Harris said: "The fact is that at this particular point in time law enforcement has not been frustrated by, or significantly frustrated by voice band encryption." Senator Leahy sought a clarification and asked for a precise number, "Did many of these involve encrypted conversations?" "The short answer," Harris replied, "is no." (Harris 1994, pp. 7–8)

13. (p. 233) Oddly enough, just at the time that the FBI began pushing for the Digital Telephony bill, the number of kidnapping cases in which wiretap orders were requested shot upwards. From an average of 2–3 kidnapping cases a year in which wiretapping is used, 1994 saw 11 such cases, 1995 saw 25. Those years were anomalous in other ways as well. Half of the wiretaps in 1994 and 1995 either were not installed or were installed and produced no incriminating intercepts.

An additional difference between the kidnapping investigations of 1994 and 1995 and previous years is that in several of the 1994 and 1995 cases for which wiretaps were used were associated with racketeering, narcotics and gambling investigations in which law enforcement was also using wiretaps or other forms of electronic surveillance. In other words, the kidnapping was part of a larger conspiracy investigation. Thus these cases were not what would be considered traditional kidnapping cases.

14. (p. 233) Less than eight months after Kallstrom's remarks, FBI Director Louis Freeh testified to a Senate Judiciary committee: "John Gotti never implicated himself on a telephone conversation with one of his confederates." (USS 105d)

15. (p. 233) The value of the wiretap in the Ames investigation should be placed in context: a recent Department of Justice (USDoJ 1997) report severely castigated the FBI for inadequately investigating the FBI and CIA spy losses years earlier and thus allowing Ames to inflict further damage on US intelligence.

16. (p. 235) A good example is Anatoli Golitsin, a Soviet defector who initiated a decade long search for "moles" in the CIA.

17. (p. 236) A common division of responsibility in this respect has been that field stations do signal processing on received material, but leave all cryptanalytic operations to be done by headquarters.

18. (p. 236) One fascinating possibility is that the cryptanalysis of some popular cryptographic algorithm such as DES or 40-bit RC4 might be achieved and embedded in a tamper-resistant chip. Intercept equipment with explicit "counter-DES capability" or "counter-RC4 capability" might thereby become available.

19. (p. 236) Some of the uses are commercial. Emitter identification is being used to detect cloned cellular phones (AWST 1997b).

20. (p. 238) The technology that makes this available is the same as that of caller ID.

21. (p. 238) Systems such as *Teletrack* keep track of the locations of fleet vehicles and report this information automatically to a dispatcher. They may even have profiling capabilities that allow them to warn the dispatcher when a vehicle is out of its expected area, behind schedule, etc.

22. (p. 240) It is an irony that, while the Internet provides a venue for those living under repressive regimes to work for political change, the denial of confidentiality by US export control on crypto undermines their ability to do so.

23. (p. 240) French law requires the police to consult the courts when initiating any investigation of a citizen (Kelling 1991, p. 965).

24. (p. 241) Textbooks on criminal investigation devote approximately 1% of their pages to the subject.

25. (p. 242) Quite independent of cryptography, disks often contain far too much material to be read by humans, and programs are written to look for incriminating information.

26. (p. 242) Source: private conversation between Diffie and Charney, 1975.

27. (p. 243) *Daniel Bernstein v. US Department of State*, 922 F. Supp. 1426, 1428–30 (N.D. Cal. 1996). Judge Patel ruled that source code constituted speech. She did not rule on so-called object code, the strings of 0s and 1s that the program is translated into before it is executed.

28. (p. 243) The documents for the Bernstein case, together with various commentaries, can be found on the EPIC web page: http://www.epic.org.

29. (p. 244) Except for the division of keys between two escrow agents, the process would be very similar to that described for a "pre-public-key" secure telephone in chapter 2.

# Glossary

AES — Advanced Encryption Standard — A NIST project to provide a replacement for the Data Encryption Standard.

ANSI — American National Standards Institute.

asymmetric cryptography — See: public key cryptography.

CCEP — Commercial COMSEC Endorsement Program — A program set up in the mid 1980s by NSA in an attempt to get industry to invest in building a new generation of communication security equipment.

cipher text — Unintelligible text or signal produced by a cryptographic system. (adj.: ciphertext)

Clipper — name of a chip implementing the Skipjack encryption algorithm with key recovery.

COMINT — Communications intelligence — the extraction of information for opponents communications.

COMSEC — Communications security — protection of communications against communications intelligence.

Diffie-Hellman key exchange — a process using exponentiation in modular arithmetic for negotiating a shared secret key between two parties without concealing any of the messages from opponents.

DS1 — Telephone communication standard for transmitting 24 voice channels, together with signaling information, simultaneously at a rate of 1.544 megabits per second.

ISDN — Integrated Services Digital Network — ongoing replacement of existing 'analog' telephone service by digital service.

KMF — Key Management Facility — a network resource that assists users in acquiring keys needed to establish secure communications.

LEAF — Law Enforcement Access Field; the law-enforcement access to the keys of the Clipper system.

MI5 — Military Intelligence 5, more accurately known as the Security Service — the British counterintelligence organization. The closest US cognate is the counterintelligence function of the FBI.

MI6 — Military Intelligence 6, more accurately known as the Secret Intelligence Service — the British foreign intelligence service. The US cognate is the CIA.

MOU — Memorandum of Understanding — a legal contract determining the obligations of two govermental entities (or between the government and a contractor) regarding joint work.

NBS — National Bureau of Standards — US government research laboratory whose responsibilities included the development of civilian computer security standards; renamed National Institute of Standards and Technology in 1988.

NIST — National Institute of Standards and Technology — US government research laboratory whose responsibilities include the development of civilian computer security standards.

NRC — National Research Council — research arm of the National Academy of Sciences and the National Academy of Engineering.

NSA — National Security Agency — the US government agency responsible for spying on foreign communications and for protecting military, diplomatic, and intelligence communications of the US government and its contractors.

NSDD — National Security Decision Directive — a directive issued by the president (usually classified) on military, intelligence, and security matters. Such directives, unlike Executive Orders, often change name from one administration to the next and in recent decades have also been called "national security directives," "presidential directives," and "national security action memoranda."

PBX — Private Branch Exchange — a telephone switch belonging to a business or other organization rather than the phone company.

PCMCIA — Personal Computer Memory Card International Association.

PGP — Pretty Good Privacy — A program originally written by Philip Zimmerman for encrypting computer files and email and the name of the company formed to develop and market the program.

plain text — Intelligible text or signals — text or signals that have not been encrypted. (adj.: plaintext)

public-key cryptography — cryptography in which communications are controlled by two keys, one of which can be made public without revealing the other. Public key cryptography makes it possible to separate the capabilities for encrypting and decrypting.

RC2 — a block cipher designed by Ron Rivest of MIT and marketed by RSA Data Security as an exportable replacement for DES.

RC4 — a fast stream cipher designed by Ron Rivest of MIT and marketed by RSA Data Security.

realtime — something operating in 'real time' i.e., without the opportunity to calculate for as long as needed.

RSA — the Rivest, Shamir, and Adelman public-key cryptosystem. The security of the RSA system is based on the difficulty of factoring large numbers.

STU-III — third-generation secure telephone unit — US Government secure telephone system constructed during the 1980s and using public key cryptography.

symmetric cryptography — cryptography in which the capability to encrypt and the capability to decrypt are inseparable, in contrast to asymmetric cryptography.

TSD — Telephone security device — a device that is not a complete telephone but provides encryption when installed in conjunction with a telephone. Especially, the AT&T TSD-3600.

TWG — Technical Working Group set up between NIST and NSA to implement joint work on cryptography.

Venona — a long running project by NSA (along with other organizations such as the British Government Communications Headquarters [GCHQ] and MI5) to exploit a set of Soviet messages sent in the 1940s and early 1950s. The messages, made vulnerable by the reuse of 'one-time' keying material revealed much information about Soviet spies working against Britain and the United States.

# Bibliography

In this book, congressional documents are often cited as sources of memoranda, of previously published articles, and of other materials. Besides making the bibliographic scheme more efficient, and revealing where materials that otherwise would be nearly unobtainable can more easily be found, this illuminates how the original materials have been used in congressional investigations of privacy-related matters. *Data on the original materials can be found in the cited documents.*

Some sources are cited by abbreviations—for example, "USDoC" means United States Department of Commerce, and "USS" stands for United States Senate. (Note that in an abbreviation citing a congressional document the number refers to the Congress—for example, "USS 94c" cites a Senate document from the 94th Congress.)

— A —

Academy on Human Rights, *Handbook of Human Rights*.

Advanced Telephony Unit, Federal Bureau of Investigation. (1992). "Telecommunications Overview" briefing.

Aho, Alfred V., John E. Hopcroft, Jeffrey D. Ullman. (1974). *The Design and Analysis of Computer Algorithms*, Addison-Wesley, Reading, Massachusetts.

American Bar Association. (1988). Special Committee on Criminal Justice in a Free Society of the American Bar Association Criminal Justice Section, Samuel Dash, chair, *Criminal Justice in Crisis: A Report to the American People and the American Bar on Criminal Justice in the United States: Some Myths, Some Realities, and Some Questions for the Future*.

American Council on Education, Public Cryptography Study Group. (1981). *Report of the Public Cryptography Study Group*, February 1981.

Agee, Philip. (1975). *Inside the Company: CIA Diary*, New York: Stonehill.

American National Standards Institute, Committee X9, Financial Services, Working Group X9.E.9. (1984). "Financial Institution Key Management (Wholesale)" American National Standard X9.17.

Anastasia, George. (1994). "FBI Tapes Provide Information Overflow on Mob," *Bergen Record*, July 31, 1994, p. N04.

Anderson, Betsy and Todd Buchholz. (1992). Memo for Jim Jukes, May 22, in EPIC 1994.

Anderson, Christopher. (1996a). *Jack and Jackie, Portrait of an American Marriage*. New York: William Morrow.

Anderson, Ross. (1995). "Crypto in Europe—Markets, Law and Policy" *Cryptography Policy and Algorithms Conference*, July 3–5, 1995, Brisbane, Australia, pp. 41–54.

Anderson, Ross. (1996b). *Information Hiding*, Proceedings of the First International Workshop, Cambridge, U.K., May/June 1996. Springer Lecture Notes in Computer Science No. 1174.

Andrews, Edmund. (1997). "U.S. Restrictions on Exports Aid German Software Maker," *New York Times*, April 7, 1997, p. D1.

*AWST*. (1986). "Contractors Ready Low-Cost, Secure Telephone for 1987 Service Start" *Aviation Week and Space Technology*, January 20, 1986, pp. 114–115.

*AWST*. (1993b). "Infectious Electronics," *Aviation Week and Space Technology*, 18 October 1993, page 29.

*AWST*. (1997a). "Put Out Their Lights," *Aviation Week and Space Technology*, March 31, 1997, p. 19.

*AWST*. (1997b). "Not Your Average Calliope," *Aviation Week and Space Technology*, March 31, 1997, p. 19.

— B —

Bailey, S. H., D. J. Harris, and B. L. Jones. (1991). *Civil Liberties: Cases and Materials*, Butterworths, London.

Baker, Stewart. (1997). "Summary Report on the OECD Ad Hoc Meeting of Experts in Cryptography," http://www.steptoe.com/276908.htm, March 1997, to appear, *International Lawyer*.

Bamford, James. (1982). *The Puzzle Palace*, Houghton Mifflin.

Banisar, David. (1993). Statistical Analysis of Electronic Surveillance, presentation at the National Institute of Standards and Technology, Computer System Security and Privacy Advisory Board, June 3, 1993.

Banks, William, and Peter Raven-Hansen. (1994). *National Security Law and the Power of the Purse*, Oxford University Press, New York and Oxford.

Barrett, P. J. (1994). "Review of the Long Term Cost Effectiveness of Telecommunications Interception," Draft report to the Security Committee of Cabinet (Australia), March 1.

Bates, David. (1907). *Lincoln in the Telegraph Office*, Century Company, New York.

Baumgardner, Frederick. (1964). Memorandum to William Sullivan, King FBI File, January 28, 1964.

Bayh, Birch. (1978). "Unclassified Summary: Involvement of NSA in the Development of the Data Encryption Standard," (United States Senate Select Committee on Intelligence), *IEEE Communication Society Magazine*, Vol. 16, No. 6, November 1978, pp. 53–55.

Beesley, Patrick. (1977). *Very Special Intelligence: The Story of the Admiralty's Operational Intelligence Center*, Hamilton, London.

Berlekamp, Elwyn R. (1968). *Algebraic Coding Theory*, McGraw Hill.

Bernstein, Richard. (1994). "Testimony in Bomb Case Links Loose Ends," in *New York Times,* January 19, 1994, p. B2.

Beth, Th., M. Frisch and G. J. Simmons, editors. (1992). *Public Key Cryptography: State of the Art and Future Directions*, Lecture Notes in Computer Science No. 578, Springer-Verlag.

Biddle, Francis. (1941). Confidential Memorandum for Mr. Hoover, October 9, 1941 in USS 94e, p. 281.

Biham, Eli, and Adi Shamir. (1993). *Differential Cryptanalysis of the Data Encryption Standard*, Springer-Verlag.

Blaze, Matt. (1994). "Protocol Failure in the Escrowed Encryption Standard," May 31, 1994.

Blaze, Matt, Whitfield Diffie, Ronald Rivest, Bruce Schneier, Tsutomu Shimomura, Eric Thompson, and Michael Wiener. (1996). "Minimal Key Lengths Symmetric Ciphers to Provide Adequate Commercial Security: A Report by an Ad Hoc Group of Cryptographers and Computer Scientists," Business Software Alliance. See also (http://www.bsa.org/policy/encryption/cryptographers.html).

Blum, Howard. (1987). *I Pledge Allegiance...*, Simon & Schuster, New York.

Blum, Howard. (1993). *Gangland: How the FBI Broke the Mob*, Simon & Schuster, New York.

Boyd, Carl. (1993). *Hitler's Japanese Confidant*, University Press of Kansas.

Brandeis, Louis. (1928). Dissenting opinion in (*Olmstead v. United States*, 277 U.S. 438, 1928.)

Brickell, Ernest F., and Gustavus J. Simmons. (1983). "A Status Report on Knapsack Based Public Key Cryptosystems" Congressus Numerantium, Vol. 7, pp. 3–72.

Brickell, Ernest, Dorothy Denning, Stephen Kent, David Maher, and Walter Tuchman. (1993). "SKIPJACK Review: Interim Report, The SKIPJACK Algorithm," July 28, 1993, available electronically from http://www.cpsr.org.

Broad, William. (1982). "Evading the Soviet Ear at Glen Cove," *Science*, Vol. 217 (3), September, pp. 910–911.

Brooke, James. (1997a). "Prosecutors in Bomb Trial Focus on Time Span and Truck Rental," *New York Times*, May 10, 1997, p. A1 and A10.

Brooke, James. (1997b). "McVeigh Lawyers Rest his Defense in Bombing Trial," *New York Times*, May 29, 1997, p. A1.

Brooks, Clinton C. (1992). Memo, April 28, 1992, in EPIC 1996, pp. C8–C13.

Brooks, Jack. (1987). Opening Statement, in USHR 100a, pp. 1–2

Brownell, Herbert. (1954a). "The Public Security and Wire Tapping," in *Cornell Law Quarterly*, pp. 195–212.

Brownell, Herbert. (1954b). Memo to J. Hoover, May 20, 1954, in USS 94e, pp. 296–297.

Bryant, Tim. (1993). "4 Indicted Here as Terrorists; FBI: Tina Isa Killing Part of Conspiracy" *St. Louis Post-Dispatch,* April 2, 1993, p. 1A.

Burnham, David. (1980). *The Rise of the Computer State*, Random House, New York.

Burnham, David. (1996). *Above the Law*, Scribners, New York.

Burrows, William E. (1987). *Deep Black*, Random House.

Busey IV, James B. (1994). Imaging Advances Impact Criminal Detection *Signal* June 1994, p. 13.

— C —

Caba, S. (1994). "FBI Nets Stanfa in Mob Sweep," *Philadelphia Inquirer*, March 18, 1994, Sec. A.

Campen, Alan D., editor. (1993a). *The First Information War,* AFCEA International Press.

Carley, William, and Timothy O'Brien. (1995). "Cyber Caper: How Citicorp System was Raided and Funds Moved Across the World," *Wall Street Journal*, September 12, 1995, p. 1.

Carlucci, Frank. (1987). Letter to Chairman Jack Brooks, March 12, 1987, in USHR 100a, p. 386.

Carney, Dan. (1997). "Promoting Technology in America's Rural Areas," *New York Times*, January 20, 1997, p. D5.

Carroll, Maurice. (1967). "Federal Agencies Open Unified Drive to Control Mafia," *New York Times*, February 22, 1967, p. 1.

Center for Social and Legal Research, *Privacy and American Business*, Volume 1(3), Hackensack, New Jersey, 1994.

Charns, Alexander. (1992). *Cloak and Gavel; FBI Wiretaps, Bugs, Informers, and the Supreme Court*, University of Illinois Press, 1992.

Chartrand, Sabra. (1994). "Clinton Gets a Wiretapping Bill That Covers New Technologies," *New York Times*, October 9, 1994, p. A27.

Cinquegrana, Amerigo. (1978). "The Walls (and Wires) Have Ears: The Background and First Ten Years of the Foreign Intelligence Surveillance Act of 1978," 137 *University of Pennsylvania Law Review* 793 (1989), pp. 814–815.

Clark, Tom. (1946). Letter to the President, July 17, 1946, as reported in USS 94e, p. 282.

Clark, Ramsey. (1967). in USHR 90, pp. 285–321.

Clark, Ramsey. (1968). Communications between Clark and J. Edgar Hoover, footnote 372 in USS 94e, p. 349

Clark, Ramsey. (1970). *Crime in America*, Simon and Schuster, 1970.

Clark, Ronald W. (1977). *The Man Who Broke Purple*, Boston: Little Brown and Company, 1977.

Clark, Tom. (1981). Recollections in "Japanese-American Relocation Reviewed,"

Earl Warren Oral History Project, Bancroft Library, University of California, Berkeley as cited in Okamura, p. 113.

Clark, David Earl. (1986). Testimony in *United States vs. Jerry Alfred Whitworth*, No. CR 85–552 JPV, in the United States District Court, Northern District of California, March 25, 1986. Reporter's transcript of proceedings, Volume 11, page 1345.

Computer Professionals for Social Responsibility, David Banisar and Marc Rotenberg, editors. (1993). *1993 Cryptography and Privacy Sourcebook: Primary Documents on U.S. Encryption Policy, the Clipper Chip, the Digital Telephony Proposal and Export Controls*, 1993.

Congressional Quarterly Weekly, Vol. 25, Washington, D.C., February 10, 1967.

Congressional Quarterly Weekly. (1968a). Vol. 26, Washington, D.C., June 28.

Congressional Quarterly Weekly. (1968b). Vol. 26, Washington, D.C., July 19.

Corson, William R. and Robert T. Crowley. (1989). *The New KGB*, New York: William Morrow and Company, 1985.

Corson, William R., Susan B. Trento, and Joseph J. Trento. (1989). *Widows*, New York: Crown Publishers, 1989.

Gersho, Allen, editor. (1982). "Crypto '81," U.C. Santa Barbara Dept. of Elec. and Computer Eng., Tech Report 82-04, 1982.

— D —

Dam, Kenneth. (1997). Letter to Orrin Hatch, in (USS 105c).

Dam, Kenneth and Herbert Lin, editors. (1996). National Research Council, Commission on Physical Sciences, Mathematics, and Applications, Computer Science and Telecommunications Board, Committee to Study National Cryptography Policy, *Cryptography's Role in Securing the Information Society*, National Academy Press, 1996.

Danby, Herbert. (1933). *The Mishnah*, Oxford University Press, Oxford, 1933.

Darrow, David. (1981). *The FBI and Martin Luther King Jr.*, W. W. Norton, New York, 1981.

Dash, Samuel, Richard Schwartz, and Robert Knowlton. (1959). *The Eavesdroppers*, Rutgers University Press, 1959.

Davis, Robert. (1973). "Confidentiality and the Census, 1790–1929" in USHEW.

Deavours, Cipher A. and Louis Kruh. (1985). *Machine Cryptography and Modern Cryptanalysis, Artech House, 1985.*

Delaney, Donald, Dorothy Denning, John Kaye, and Alan McDonald. (1993). "Wiretap Laws and Procedures: What Happens When the U.S. Government Taps A Line," September 23, 1993, available electronically from http://www.cpsr.org.

DeLoach, Cartha. (1966a). Memorandum to Clive Tolson, January 10, 1966, as reported in USS 94e, p. 308.

DeLoach, Cartha. (1966b). Memorandum to Clive Tolson, January 21, 1966, as reported in USS 94e, p. 310.

DeLoach, Cartha. (1968a). Memorandum to Clive Tolson, October 30, 1968, as reported in USS 94e, p. 315.

DeLoach, Cartha. (1968b). Memorandum to Clive Tolson, November 4, 1968, as reported in USS 94e, p. 314.

Denning, Dorothy, Mike Godwin, William Bayse, Marc Rotenberg, Lewis Branscomb, Anne Branscomb, Ronald Rivest, Andrew Grosso, and Gary Marx. (1996). "To Tap or Not to Tap," in *Communications of the ACM*, Vol. 36 (3), March 1993, pp. 24–44.

Denning, Dorothy. (1994). "Encryption and Law Enforcement." February 21, 1994. Available electronically from http://www.cpsr.org.

Diffie, Whitfield and Martin E. Hellman. (1976). "New Directions in Cryptography," *IEEE Transactions on Information Theory*, Vol. IT-22, pp. 644–654, Nov. 1976.

Diffie, Whitfield. (1982). "Cryptographic Technology: Fifteen Year Forecast," in Simmons 1982

Diffie, Whitfield, Leo Strawczynski, Brian O'Higgins, and David Steer. (1987). "An ISDN Secure Telephone Unit" in *Proc. National Communications Forum 1987*, pp. 473–477.

Diffie, Whitfield. (1988). "The First Ten Years of Public Key Cryptography," *Proceedings of the IEEE*, Vol. 76 No. 5, May 1988, pp. 560–577.

Diffie, Whitfield, Paul van Oorschot, and Michael Wiener. (1992) "Authentication and Authenticated Key Exchanges," in *Designs, Codes, and Cryptography*, Volume 2, Number 2, 1992, pp. 107–125.

Duke, Steven B., and Albert C. Gross. (1993). *America's Longest War: Rethinking Our Tragic Crusade Against Drugs.* Putnam.

— E —

Eberle, Hans. (1992). "A High-speed DES Implementation for Network Applications," DEC SRC Research Report 90, September 23, 1992.

Edwards, Hazel. (1994). As reported in USC-OTA 1994, p. 3.

Ehrlichman, John. (1973). Testimony in USS 93b, p. 2535

Electronic Frontier Foundation. (1998) *Cracking DES: Secrets of Encryption Research, Wiretap Politics, and Chip Design*, O'Reilly & Associates, 1998.

Electronic Industries Association. (1992). "Dual Mode Cellular System" TR45.3 IS-54 Rev. B, Appendix A, "Authentication, Message Encryption, Vice Privacy Mask Generation, Shared Secret Data Generation, A-Key Verification, and Test Data," February 1992.

Electronic Privacy Information Center, David Banisar, editor. (1994). *1994 Cryptography and Privacy Sourcebook: Primary Documents on U.S. Encryption Policy, the Clipper Chip, the Digital Telephony Proposal and Export Controls*, Diane Publishing, Upland, Pennsylvania, 1994.

Electronic Privacy Information Center. (1995a). *1995 EPIC Cryptography and Privacy Sourcebook: Documents on Wiretapping, Cryptography, the Clipper Chip, Key Escrow and Export Controls*, Diane Publishing Co., Upland, PA, 1995.

EPIC. (1995b). Letter to Telecommunications Industry Liaison Unit, Federal Bureau of Investigation, November 13, 1995, in EPIC 1996 pp. B14–B20.

Electronic Privacy Information Center. (1996). *1996 EPIC Cryptography and Privacy Sourcebook: Documents on Wiretapping, Cryptography, the Clipper Chip, Key Escrow and Export Controls*, Diane Publishing Co., Upland, PA, 1996.

ElGamal, Taher. (1985). "A Public-Key Cryptosystem and a Signature Scheme Based on Discrete Logarithms," *IEEE Transactions on Information Theory*, IT-31 (1985), pp. 469–472.

Elsey, G. (1950). Memorandum to the President, February 2, 1950, as reported in USS 94e, pp. 282–283.

European Commission, *Towards a European Framework for Digital Signatures and Encryption*.

Eyraud, Charles. (1959). *Precis de Cryptographie Moderne*, Editions Raoul Tari, Paris, 1959. This was the second edition; an earlier one appeared in 1953.

— F —

Federal Bureau of Investigation. (1949). SAC Letter No. 69, Ser. 1949, June 29, 1949, FBI 66-1372-1, as reported in Theoharis, pp. 460–461.

Federal Bureau of Investigation. (1956). "Racial Tensions and Civil Rights," March 1, 1956, statement used by the FBI Director at Cabinet briefing, March 9, 1956, as reported in USS 94d, p. 50.

Federal Bureau of Investigation. (1960a). FBI Manual Section 87, pp. 5–11, as reported in USS 94d, p. 48.

Federal Bureau of Investigation. (1960b). Memo from FBI Headquarters to New York Field Office, July 11, 1960, as reported in USS 94e, pp. 363.

Federal Bureau of Investigation. (1960c). Memo from FBI Headquarters to New York Field Office, December 16, 1960, as reported in USS 94e, p. 364.

Federal Bureau of Investigation. (1961a). FBI Summary Memo, February 15, 1961, as reported in USS 94e, p. 329.

Federal Bureau of Investigation. (1961b). Memo from FBI Headquarters to New York Field Office, November 3, 1961, as reported in USS 94e, p. 364.

Federal Bureau of Investigation. (1962). FBI Summary Memo, June 15, 1962, as reported in USS 94e, p. 346.

Federal Bureau of Investigation. (1968). Teletypes from the FBI to the White House Situation Room, 30 October 1968, October 31, 1968, November 1, 1968, November 2, 1968, November 3, 1968, and November 4, 1968 in USS 94e, p. 314.

Federal Bureau of Investigation. (1975b). FBI Summary Memo, February 3, 1975, as reported in USS 94e, pp. 313–314.

Federal Bureau of Investigation. (1975c). Staff summary of FBI Review, August 22, 1975, as reported in USS 94e, p. 344.

Federal Bureau of Investigation. (1987). Memo from FBI New York to FBI Headquarters, September 21, 1987, as reported in Foerstal 1991, p. 55.

Federal Bureau of Investigation. (1989). *FBI Inspection Division Report*, as reported in USS 101, pp. 2–6.

Federal Bureau of Investigation. (1992a). "Benefits and Costs of Legislation to Ensure the Government's Continued Capability to Investigate Crime with the Implementation of New Telecommunications Technologies," in EPIC 1994.

Federal Bureau of Investigation. (1992b). "Digital Telephony Proposal," in CPSR 1993.

Federal Bureau of Investigation. (1995). Federal Bureau of Investigation, "Implementation of the Communications Assistance for Law Enforcement Act," in *Federal Register* Vol. 60, No. 199, October 16, 1995, pp. 53643–53646.

Federal Bureau of Investigation. (1997a). FBI, "Electronic Surveillance—Report on the FBI Publication of the Second Notice of Capacity," Press Release, January 14, 1997.

Federal Bureau of Investigation. (1997b). FBI, "Implications of Section 104 of the Communications Act for Law Enforcement," in *Federal Register*, Vol. 62, Number 9, January 14, 1997, pp. 192–1911.

Federal Communications Commission, Industry Analysis Division, Common Carrier Bureau, "Telephone Lines and Offices," in EPIC 1996, p. B-19.

Federal Communications Commission (1998a). "Memorandum Opinion and Order," September 10, 1998.

Federal Communications Commission (1998b). "Engineering and Technology Action: FCC Proposes Rules to Meet Technical Requirements of CALEA (CC Docket 97-213)," October 22, 1998.

Feige, Uriel, Amos Fiat, and Adi Shamir, "Zero Knowledge Proofs of Identity," in proceedings *19th ACM Symposium on Theory of Computing*, May 1987, pp. 210–217.

Feistel, Horst. (1973). "Cryptography and Computer Privacy," *Scientific American*, Vol. 228, No. 5, May 1973, pp. 15–23.

Fisher, David. (1995). *Hard Evidence*, Simon and Schuster, 1995.

Fitzgerald, Patrick and Mark Leopold. (1987). *Stranger on the Line: the Secret History of Phone Tapping*, Bodley Head, London, 1987.

Flaherty, David. (1989). *Protecting Privacy in Surveillance Societies: the Federal Republic of Germany, Sweden, France, Canada, and the United States*, University of North Carolina Press, 1989.

Flynn, Laurie. (1996). "Company Stops On-Line Access to Key Social Security Numbers," in *New York Times*, June 13, 1996, p. B11.

Foerstal, Herbert. (1991). *Surveillance in the Stacks: the FBI's Library Awareness Program*, Greenwood Press, New York, 1991.

Franklin, Benjamin. (1907). *Writings*, ed. Albert H. Smyth, Volume 5, New York, 1907.

Freeh, Louis. (1994a). Speech to the Executives' Club of Chicago, 17 February, 1994.

Freeh, Louis. (1994b). Testimony in USS 103b, pp. 5–51.

Freeh, Louis. (1994c). Speech to American Law Institute, May 19, 1994, in EPIC 1994, p. 6 of speech.

Freeh, Louis. (1996). Statement to Committee on Commerce, Science, and Transportation, U.S. Senate, July 25, 1996.

Fried, Joseph. (1995). "In Conspiracy Case, Much Evidence that Egyptian Sheik Has a Healthy Ego, at Least," *New York Times*, April 30, 1995, p. A38.

Friedly, Michael and David Gallen. (1993). *Martin Luther King, Jr. The FBI File*, Carroll and Graf Publishers, Inc., New York, 1993.

Friedman, Lawrence. (1973). *A History of American Law*, Simon and Schuster, New York, 1973.

Froomkin, A. Michael. (1995). "The Metaphor Is the Key: Cryptography, the Clipper Chip, and the Constitution," *University of Pennsylvania Law Review*, Vol. 143 (1995) p. 709–897.

Frost, Mike. (1994). *Spyworld: Inside the Canadian and American Intelligence Establishments*, Doubleday, Canada, 1994.

— G —

Gardner, Martin. (1977). "A New Kind of Cipher That Would Take Millions of Years to Break," Scientific American, Vol. 237, No. 2, Aug 1977, pp. 120–124.

Gennaro, Rosario, Paul Karger, Stephen Matyas, Mohammad Peyravian, Allen Roginsky, David Safford, Michael Willett, and Nev Zunic. (1997). "Secure Key Recovery" IBM TR 29.2273.

Gentry, Curt. (1991). *J. Edgar Hoover. The Man and the Secrets*, Norton, New York, 1991.

Girardin, Ray. Letter to Herman Schwartz, as reported in USHR 90, p. 1013.

Goldwasser, S. and S. Micali. (1984) "Probabilistic Encryption," *Journal of Computer and System Sciences*, Vol. 28, No. 2, April 1984, pp. 270–299.

Gombossy, George. (1989). "Wiretapping Scandal Mushrooms; Congressional Hearings Scheduled," *National Law Journal*, December 25, 1989–January 1, 1990, p. 3.

Gotti, John. (1992). *The Gotti Tapes*, Times Books, 1992, p. 26.

— H —

Halperin, Morton. (1974). in USS 93e, pp. 295–311.

Hansell, Saul. (1995). "Citibank Fraud Case Raises Computer Security Questions," *New York Times*. August 19, 1995, p. 31.

Jo Ann Harris, Testimony in USS 103a.

Headrick, Daniel R. (1991). *The Invisible Weapon, Telecommunications and International Politics, 1851–1945*, Oxford University Press.

Helsing, Cheryl. (1987). Chair, Data Security Committee, American Bankers Association, and Vice President for Corporate Preparedness and Information Security, Bank of America, Testimony in USHR 100a, pp. 112–123.

Herb, John. (1969). "250,000 War Protesters Stage Peaceful Rally in Washington; Militants Stir Clashes Later," *New York Times*, November 16, 1969, p. 1.

Hersh, Seymour. (1983). *The Price of Power, Kissinger in the Nixon White House*, Summit Books, 1983.

Hersh, Seymour. (1986). *"The Target is Destroyed": What Really Happened to Flight 007 and What America Knew About It,* Random House, 1986.

Hersh, Seymour. (1987). "Was Castro Out of Control in 1962?," in *Washington Post*, October 11, 1987, p. H1.

Hinds, Michael De Courcy. (1994). "FBI Arrests Reputed Leader of Philadelphia Mob and 23 Others," *New York Times*, March 8, 1994, p. A16.

Hoover, J. Edgar. (1941). Memo to the Attorney General, January 27, 1941, as reported in USS 94e, pp. 280–281.

Hoover, J. Edgar. (1950). Testimony in USHR 81, pp. 205–244.

Hoover, J. Edgar (1956). Memo to Attorney General Brownell, December 31, 1956, as reported in USS 94d, p. 63.

Hoover, J. Edgar. (1961a). Memo to Attorney General Robert Kennedy, February 14, 1961, as reported in USS 94e, p. 329.

Hoover, J. Edgar. (1961b). Memo to Attorney General Robert Kennedy, February 16, 1961, as reported in USS 94e, p. 329.

Hoover, J. Edgar. (1965). Memo to Attorney General Nicholas Katzenbach, March 30, 1965, as reported in USS 94e, p. 286.

Hoover, J. Edgar. (1969a). Memo to Clive Tolson, Cartha DeLoach, William Sullivan, and Mr. Bishop, May 9, 1969, 5:05 p.m., as reported in USS 94e, p. 324.

Hoover, J. Edgar. (1969b). Memo to the Attorney General, November 5, 1969, as reported in USS 94e, p. 338.

Hoover, J. Edgar. (1970). Letter to H. R. Haldeman, June 25, 1970, in USS 94e, p. 345.

Huston, Tom. (1970). Attachment to memo, p. 2, in USS 94b, p. 194.

— I —

Information Technology Security Council, Ministry of Research and Information Technology (Denmark). (1996). "The Right to Encryption," June 11, 1996.

— J —

Johnson, Lyndon. (1965). "Directive to Heads of Agencies," June 30, 1965, in USS 94e, p. 286.

Johnson, Lyndon B. (1968). Speech, as cited in Congressional 1968a, p. 1632.

Johnson, Brian. (1978). *The Secret War*, New York: Methuen, 1978.

Jones, M. A. (1965). Memorandum to Cartha DeLoach, August 2, 1965, as reported in USS 94e, p. 308.

Jones, R. V. (1939). *The Wizard War—British Scientific Intelligence 1939–1945*, Coward, McCann, & Geoghegan, 1978.

Jupp, M. J., (1989). "Monolog—A Single-Line Call Logging Device," *British Telecommunications Engineering*, Vo. 8, April 1989.

— K —

Kahn, David. (1967). *The Codebreakers, The Story of Secret Writing*, New York: The Macmillan Company, 1967.

Kallstrom, James. (1997). Statement of FBI Assistant Director James Kallstrom Concerning the Second Notice of Capacity, January 14, 1997.

Kammer, Raymond. (1989). Testimony in USHR 101, pp. 219–220.

Katzenbach, Nicholas. (1965). Memo to J. Edgar Hoover, September 27, 1965, as reported in USS 94e, p. 287.

Kelling, George L. (1991). "Police," *Encyclopaedia Britannica*, 15th Edition, 1991, pp. 957–973.

Kent, Steven T. (1977). "Some Thoughts on TCP and Communication Security," MIT, Laboratory for Computer Science, Local Network Note No. 6, May 4, 1977.

Kerckhoffs, Auguste. (1883). *La Cryptographie militaire*, 1883, as cited in Kahn 1967, pp. 230.

Kerry, John and Hank Brown. (1992). "The BCCI Affair: A Report to the Committee on Foreign Relations, United States Senate," Report 102-140, One Hundred and Second Congress, Second Session, 1992.

Kessler, Ronald. (1993). *The FBI*, New York: Pocket Books, 1993.

Kettle, Martin. (1998). "State-wide Informer and Secret Policing Network," *The Guardian*, March 19, 1998, p. 11.

Kinzer, Stephen. (1992). "East Germans Face their Accusers," *New York Times*, April 12, 1992, p. 24–52.

Kleiman, Mark. (1993). *Against Excess: Drug Policy for Results*, Basic Books, 1993.

Kopelev, Lev. (1983). *Ease My Sorrows*, Random House, 1983.

Kravitz, David. (1991). Digital Signature Algorithm, US Patent Number 5231668, applied for July 26, 1991, received July 27, 1993.

Krikorian, Greg. (1998). "D.A., Police Challenged on Wiretap Procedures," *Los Angeles Times*, April 22, 1998, p. B1.

— L —

Lacey, Mark. (1997). "Florida Couple say They Recorded Gingrich's Call," *Los Angeles Times*, January 14, 1997, p. A1.

LaMacchia, Brian and Andrew Odlyzko. (1991). "Computation of Discrete Logarithms in Prime Fields," *Design, Codes, and Cryptography*, Vol. 1, 1991, pp. 47–62.

Lambert, William. (1967). "Strange Help—Hoffa Campaign of the U.S. Senator from Missouri," *Life Magazine*, May 26, 1967.

Landau, Susan. (1988). "Zero Knowledge and the Department of Defense," *Notices of the American Mathematical Society (Special Article Series)*, Vol. 35, No. 1 (1988), pp. 5–12.

Landau, Susan, Stephen Kent, Clinton Brooks, Scott Charney, Dorothy Denning, Whitfield Diffie, Anthony Lauck, Douglas Miller, Peter Neumann, and David Sobel. (1994). *Codes, Keys and Conflicts: Issues in U.S. Crypto Policy*, ACM Press, 1994.

Lassen, Nelson. (1937). "The History and Development of the Fourth Amendment to the United States Constitution," *The Johns Hopkins University Studies in Historical and Political Science*, Series LV, 1937.

Levy, Ron. (1992). Memo for Doug Steiger, May 26, in EPIC 1994.

Lewis, Anthony. (1961). "Robert Kennedy Vows in Georgia to Act on Rights, *New York Times*, May 7, 1961, p. 1.

Lindsey, Robert. (1979). *The Falcon and the Snowman*, Simon and Schuster, 1979.

Loftus, John and Mark Aarons. (1994). *The Secret War Against the Jews, How Western Espionage Betrayed the Jewish People*, St. Martins Press, 1994.

Lyons, John. (1992). Testimony in USHR 102, pp. 163–176.

— M —

Manning, Peter K. (1977). *Police Work: The Social Organization of Policing*, MIT Press, June 1977.

Markey, Hedy Keisler and George Antheil. (1942) "Secret Communications System," US Patent Number 2,292,387, August 11, 1942. (Hedy Lamarr was the stage name of Hedy Markey.)

Markoff, John. (1991). "Move on Unscrambling of Messages is Assailed," *New York Times*, April 17, 1991, p. A16.

Markoff, John. (1993). "Electronics Plan Aims to Balance Government Access with Privacy," *New York Times*, April 16, 1993, p. A1.

Markoff, John. (1996). "Cellular Industry Rejects U.S. Plan for Surveillance," *New York Times*, September 20, 1996, p. A1.

Markoff, John. (1998). "U.S. Data-Scrambling Code Cracked With Homemade Equipment," *New York Times*, July 17, 1998.

Marks, Peter. (1995). "When the Best Defense is the Prosecution's Own Tapes," *New York Times*, June 30, 1995, p. D20.

Martin, David. (1980). *Wilderness of Mirrors*, Harper and Row, New York, 1980.

Mashberg, Tom. (1993). "N.J. Engineer Held in Blast in N.Y. Tower," *Boston Globe*, March 11, 1993, p. 1.

Massey, James L. (1969). "Shift-register synthesis and BCH decoding," IEEE Transactions on Information Theory, IT-15, 1969, pp. 122–127.

McConnell, John M. (1992). Letter to Willis Ware, July 23, 1992, in EPIC 1995a, p. C-14.

McConnell, John M. (1994) Testimony in USS 103a, pp. 95–106.

McGee, Jim. (1996a). "Tension Rises Over Digital Taps," *Washington Post*, October 27, 1996, p. H1.

McGee, Jim. (1996b). "Military Goes to War on Narcotics," *Manchester Guardian Weekly*, December 29, 1996, p. 12.

McGee, Jim. (1996c). "How Drugs Sucked in the Army," *Manchester Guardian Weekly*, December 29, 1996, p. 12.

McGrath, J. Howard. (1952). Memorandum to J. Edgar Hoover, February 26, 1952, in USS 94e, p. 283.

McIntosh, David and James Gattuso. (1992). Memo for Jim Jukes, May 22, 1992, in EPIC 1994.

McKinley, James, Jr. (1995a). "Suspect is Said to be Longtime Friend of Bombing Mastermind," *New York Times*, August 4, 1995, p. B5.

McKinley, James. (1995b). "The Terror Conspiracy: The Verdict," *New York Times*, October 2, 1995, p. B5.

McNulty, Lynn. (1992). Memo for the Record, August 18, 1992, in EPIC 1996, pp. C14–C19.

Meredith, Robyn. (1997). "VW Agrees to Pay G.M. $100 Million in Espionage Suit," *New York Times*, January 10, 1997, p. A1.

Merkle, Ralph C. (1978). "Secure Communications Over Insecure Channels," Communications of the ACM, Vol. 21, No. 4, April 1978, pp. 294–299.

Mikva, Abner. (1971). Testimony in USS 92a, pp. 130–146.

Mintz, John. (1992). "Intelligence Community in Breach with Business," *Washington Post*, April 30, 1992, p. A8.

Monbiot, George. (1996). "Heavy Hand of the Law Keeps Tabs on the 'Enemy Within'," *Manchester Guardian Weekly*, September 8, 1996, p. 23.

Moore, G. C. (1972). Memo to E. S. Miller, September 27, 1972, as reported in USS 94d, p. 75.

Moore, Mark. (1990). "Supply Reduction and Drug Law Enforcement," in Tonry 1990, 109–157.

Morgenthau, Henry. *The Presidential Diaries of Henry Morgenthau Jr. 1938–1945*, University Publications of America, Frederick, Maryland. (The name is mistakenly spelled 'Morganthau' on the title page.)

Myers, F. (1979). "A Data Link Encryption System," *National Telecommunications Conference*, Washington, D.C., November 27–29, 1979, pp. 43.5.1–43.5.8.

— N —

National Research Council, Commission on Physical Sciences, Mathematics, and its Applications, Computer Science and Telecommunications Board, Committee on Maintaining Privacy and Security in Health Care Applications of the National Information Infrastructure. (1997). *For the Record: Protecting Electronic Health Information.*

National Commission for the Review of Federal and State Laws relating to Wiretapping and Electronic Surveillance. (1976). *Commission Studies*, Washington, D.C.

National Security Decision Directive 145, September 17, 1984, in USHR 100a, pp. 528–537.

National Telecommunications and Information Agency. (1992). "Technological, Competitiveness, and Policy Concerns." in EPIC 1994.

Needham, Roger M. and Michael D. Schroeder, "Using Encryption for Authentication in Large Networks of Computers" (1978). *Communications of the ACM*, Vol. 21, No. 12, pp. 993–999.

Neel, Roy. (1994a). President of the U.S. Telephone Association, in USS 103b, pp. 53–64.

Neel, Roy. (1994b). President of the U.S. Telephone Association, in USHR 103b, pp. 101–115.

Neumann, Peter. (1994). *Computer-Related Risks*, ACM Press (Addison-Wesley).

*New York Times*. (1879). "The Privacy of the Telegraph," (1879). March 21, p. 1, col. 3.

*New York Times*. (1916). "Priests Deny the Mayor's Charges; His Tapped Wire Records Falsified to Justify Himself, they Declare," May 27, 1916. p. 1.

*New York Times*. (1961). "Anti-Crime Bill is Passed," September 20, 1961, p. 3.

*New York Times*. (1971). "Vietnam Archive: Pentagon Study Traces 3 Decades of Growing U.S. Involvement," June 13, 1971, p. 1.

*New York Tribune*. (1876). "The Privacy of Telegrams," December 26, 1876, p. 1, col. 4.

*New York Tribune*. (1880). "Inviolability of Telegrams," January 11, 1880, p. 5, col. 3.

*New York Tribune.* (1880). "They Will Probably Answer Now," June 10, 1890, p. 3, col. 6.

North, David. (1986). "U.S. Using Disinformation Policy to Impede Technical Data Flow." *Aviation Week and Space Technology,* March 17, 1986, pp. 16–17.

— O —

O'Brien, John. (1971). Testimony in USS 92a, pp. 100–130.

O'Hara, Colleen and Heather Harreld. (1997). "DOD sinks the Clipper," *Federal Computer Week,* February 17.

Odom, Lt. Genl. William. (1987). Testimony in USHR 100a, pp. 276–297.

Organization for Economic Cooperation and Development, "Cryptography Policy Guidelines," March 27, 1997.

Okamura, Raymond. (1981). "The Myth of Census Confidentiality," *Amerasia,* pp. 111–120.

Ostrovsky, Victor and Claire Hoy. (1990). *By Way of Deception, the Making and Unmaking of a Mossad Officer,* St. Martins Press, New York.

— P —

Parker, Donn. (1983). *Fighting Computer Crime,* Charles Scribner's, New York.

Pasztor, Andy. (1995). *When the Pentagon Was for Sale,* Charles Scribner's, New York.

Peterson, A. Padgett. (1993). "Tactical Computers Vulnerable to Malicious Software Attacks." *SIGNAL,* November, pp. 74–75.

Piller, Charles. (1993). "Privacy in Peril," *MacWorld,* July, pp. 8–14.

Pincus, Walter. (1976). "Data to be Destroyed," *Washington Post,* March 31, p. 1.

Plum, William. (1882). *The Military Telegraph During the Civil War,* Volume 1 Chicago.

Poindexter, John. (1986). "National Policy on the Protection of Sensitive, but Unclassified Information in Federal Government Telecommunications and Automated Systems," October 29, in USHR 100a, pp. 541–545.

Polis, Richard. (1987). "European Needs and Attitudes Towards Information Security," *Fifteenth Annual Telecommunications Policy Research Conference,* September 27–30.

The President's Commission on Law Enforcement and the Administration of Justice, *The Challenge of Crime in a Free Society*, United States Government Printing Office, 1967.

*Privacy Journal*. (1992). *Compilation of State and Federal Privacy Laws*, Washington, D.C.

Purdom, Todd. (1995). "Clinton Assails Effort to Change His Anti-Terrorism Plan," *New York Times*, May 27, p. 24.

— R —

Raber, Ellen and Michael O. Riley. (1989). "Protective Coatings for Secure Integrated Circuits, *Energy and Technology Review*, May–June pp. 13–20.

Randall, James. (1951). *Constitutional Problems Under Lincoln*, University of Illinois Press.

Rawls, W. Lee. (1992). Assistant Attorney General, letter to Speaker of the House Thomas S. Foley, September 14.

Reinsch, William. (1985). in USS 105a.

Reuter, Peter. (1985). "Eternal Hope: America's International Narcotics Efforts," *Public Interest*, Spring, pp. 79–85.

Richardson, Doug. (1991). "More Pernicious Computer Viruses Menace, Germinate." *SIGNAL*, December, p. 64.

Richardson, Margaret. (1997). "Disposition of Unauthorized Access Cases, 1994–1997" in USS 105b.

Richelson, Jeffrey T. and Desmond Ball. (1985). *The Ties That Bind, Intelligence Cooperation between the UKUSA countries—the United Kingdom, the United States of America, Canada, Australia and New Zealand* Allen & Unwin.

Richelson, Jeffrey. (1987). *American Espionage and the Soviet Target*, New York: William Morrow and Company.

Richelson, Jeffrey T. (1990). *America's Secret Eyes in Space—The U.S. Keyhole Spy Satellite Program*, Harper & Row.

Rivest, R., A. Shamir, and L. Adleman, (1978). "A Method for Obtaining Digital Signatures and Public Key Cryptosystems," *Communications of the ACM*, Vol. 21 (2), pp. 120–126, February.

Rivest, Ronald. (1992). "Responses to NIST's Proposal," *Communications of the ACM*, Vol. 35 (7), July, pp. 41–47.

Robins, Natalie. (1988). "The FBI's Invasion of Libraries," *The Nation*, April 9, p. 499.

Robinson, Clarence A. Jr. (1993a). "Wireless Era Dawns—Tests extend voice and data via seamless networks to follow subscribers automatically, wherever they are located." *SIGNAL*, Volume 47 Number 7, March, pp. 19–23.

Robinson, Clarence A. Jr. (1993b). "Information Warfare Avoids Army Virus Contamination." *SIGNAL*, November, p. 75.

Rogers, Herbert L. (1987). "An Overview of the Caneware Program" paper 31, in proc. *3rd Annual Symposium on Physical / Electronic Security*, Armed Forces Communications and Electronics Association, Philadelphia Chapter, August.

Roosevelt, Franklin Delano. (1940). Memo to Attorney General Jackson, May 21, as cited in USS 94e, p. 279.

Rosenblum, Howard E. (1980). "Secure communication system with remote key setting—uses automatic iterative replacement of working variables of system subscribers" US Patent No. 4182933, January 8.

Rotenberg, Marc. (1996). "U.S. Lobbies OECD to Adopt Key Escrow," in *The International Privacy Bulletin*, Vol. 4, No. 2. Spring, pp. 4–7.

Ruckelshaus, William. (1974). in USS 93d, pp. 310–378.

Rydell, C. Peter and Susan Everingham. (1994). *Controlling Cocaine: Supply Versus Demand Program*, Drug Policy Research Center, RAND.

— S —

Sanger, David. (1987). "Rise and Fall of Data Directive," *New York Times*, March 19.

Scheele, Carl. (1970). *Neither Snow nor Rain . . . ; The Story of the United States Mails*, Smithsonian Institutional Press.

Schneier, Bruce. (1996). *Applied Cryptography: Protocols, Algorithms, and Source Code in C*, Addison-Wesley. (The first edition appeared in 1993.)

Schnorr, Claus. (1989). Procedures for the Identification of Participants as well as the Generation and Verification of Electronic Signatures in a Digital Exchange System, German Patent Number 9010348.1, patent applied for February 24, patent received August 29, 1990.

Schnorr, Claus. (1990). "Efficient Identification and Signatures for Smart Cards," in *Advances in Cryptology—Crypto '89*, Springer-Verlag, New York, pp. 239–251.

Schnorr, Claus. (1991). "Method for Identifying Subscribers and for Generating and Verifying Electronic Signatures in a Data Exchange System," US Patent Number 4995082, patent applied for February 23, 1990, patent received February 19, 1991.

Schrage, Michael. (1986). "U.S. Seeking to Limit Access of Soviets to Computer Data," *Washington Post*, May 27, p. A1.

Schwartau, Winn. (1994). *Information Warfare: Chaos on the Electronic Superhighway*, Thunder's Mouth Press.

Schwartz, Herman. (1972). "A Report on the Costs and Benefits of Electronic Surveillance—," American Civil Liberties Union Reports, 1972, in USS 93e, pp. 102–209.

Schwartz, Herman. (1974). Testimony in USS 93e, pp. 95–214.

Schweizer, Peter. (1993). *Friendly Spies, How America's Allies are using Economic Espionage to Steal Our Secrets*, Atlantic Monthly Press.

Scowcroft, Brent. (1992). Memorandum to Secretary of Defense Dick Cheney, Attorney General William Barr, and Director of Central Intelligence Robert Gates, January 17.

Seipp, David. (1977). *The Right to Privacy in American History*, Program in Information Resources Policy, Harvard University, Cambridge, Massachusetts, June.

Sessions, William. (1988). Testimony in USS 100, pp. 119–156.

Sessions, William. (1993a). Letter to Mr. George Tenet, February 9, in EPIC 1996, p. C-24.

Sessions, William. (1993b). Letter to George Tenet and Briefing Document, "Encryption: The Threat, Applications, and Potential Solutions," February 19, in EPIC 1996, pp. C44–C61.

Shackelford. (1976). as reported in USS 94e, p. 251, February 2.

Shane, Scott and Tom Bowman. (1995). "America's Fortress of Spies" *Baltimore Sun*, a series of 6 articles, December 3–15, 1995.

Shapley, Deborah and Gina Kolata. (1977). "Cryptology: Scientists Puzzle over Threat to Open Research, Publication," *Science*, September 30, pp. 1345–1349.

Shimomura, Tsutomu and John Markoff. (1996). *Takedown: The Pursuit and Capture of Kevin Mitnick, America's Most Wanted Computer Outlaw—By the Man Who Did It*, Hyperion.

Shimomura, Tsutomu. (1997). Testimony in USHR 105.

Simmons, Gustavus J., editor. (1982). *Secure Communications and Asymmetric Cryptosystems*, AAAS Selected Symposium No. 69, Westview Press.

Simmons, Gustavus J. (1986). "Cryptology," *Encyclopaedia Britannica*, 16th Edition, pp. 913–924B.

Simpson, Jack. (1988). Testimony in USHR 100a, pp. 324–344.

Smith, Bradley F. (1993). *The Ultra-Magic Deals and the Most Secret Special Relationship, 1940–1946*, Presidio, Novato, California.

Smith, John Lynn. (1971). "The Design of Lucifer, A Cryptographic Device for Data Communications," IBM White Plains, N. Y., RC 3326.

Smith, T. J. (1973). Memo to E. Miller, February 26, in USS 94e, p. 326.

Smith, William W. Jr. (1991). "Passive Location of Mobile Cellular Telephone Terminals" *Proceedings of the International Carnahan Conference on Security Technology*, October 1–3, Taipei, Taiwan, pp. 221–225.

Socolar, Milton. (1989). Testimony of in USHR 101, pp. 36–49.

Solomon, Stephen. (1995). "American Express Applies for a New Line of Credit," *New York Times Magazine*, July 30, p. 38.

Solzhenitsyn, Aleksandr I. (1968). *The First Circle* (Translated by Thomas P. Whitney.) Harper & Row.

Statewatch (1997). "European Union and FBI Launch Global Surveillance System," Statewatch, P.O. Box 1516, London N16 OEW, England.

Stein, Ralph. (1971). Testimony in USS 92a, pp. 244–277.

Stoll, Clifford. (1989). *The Cuckoo's Egg, Tracking a Spy Through the Maze of Computer Espionage*, New York: Doubleday.

Sullivan, William. (1964). Memo to A. Belmont, August 21, as reported in USS 94d, p. 118.

Sullivan, William. (1969). Letter to J. Edgar Hoover, July 2, as reported in USS 94e, p. 323.

Sullivan, William. (1979). *The Bureau: My Thirty Years in Hoover's FBI*, W. W. Norton and Co.

— T —

Theoharis, Athan. (1974). Testimony in USS 93e, pp. 337–348.

Theoharis, Athan and John Cox. (1988). *The Boss. J. Edgar Hoover and the Great American Inquisition*, Temple University Press.

Thomas, Dave "The Roswell Incident and Project Mogul, Skeptical Inquirer Vol. 19, No. 4, July–August, 1995: pp. 15–18.

Tonry, Michael and James Wilson, editors. (1990). *Drugs and Crime*, University of Chicago Press.

— U —

United Nations. (1985). *International Covenants on Civil and Political Rights: Human Rights Commission, Selected Decisions under the Optional Protocol, Second to Sixteenth Sessions*, United Nations Office of Public Information, New York.

USAINTC. (1969). Information Collection Plan, April 23, 1969, as reported in USS 93a, pp. 41–42.

United States, Administrative Office of the United States Courts. (1971). *Report on Applications for Orders Authorizing or Approving the Interception of Wire, Oral, or Electronic Communications (Wiretap Report).*

United States, Administrative Office of the United States Courts. (1977) *Report on Applications for Orders Authorizing or Approving the Interception of Wire, Oral, or Electronic Communications (Wiretap Report).*

United States, Administrative Office of the United States Courts. (1988). *Report on Applications for Orders Authorizing or Approving the Interception of Wire, Oral, or Electronic Communications (Wiretap Report).*

United States, Administrative Office of the United States Courts. (1988). *Report on Applications for Orders Authorizing or Approving the Interception of Wire, Oral, or Electronic Communications (Wiretap Report).*

United States, Administrative Office of the United States Courts. (1990). *Report on Applications for Orders Authorizing or Approving the Interception of Wire, Oral, or Electronic Communications (Wiretap Report).*

United States, Administrative Office of the United States Courts. (1991). *Report on Applications for Orders Authorizing or Approving the Interception of Wire, Oral, or Electronic Communications (Wiretap Report).*

United States, Administrative Office of the United States Courts. (1992). *Report on Applications for Orders Authorizing or Approving the Interception of Wire, Oral, or Electronic Communications (Wiretap Report).*

United States, Administrative Office of the United States Courts. (1993). *Report on Applications for Orders Authorizing or Approving the Interception of Wire, Oral, or Electronic Communications (Wiretap Report).*

United States, Administrative Office of the United States Courts. (1994) *Report on Applications for Orders Authorizing or Approving the Interception of Wire, Oral, or Electronic Communications (Wiretap Report).*

United States, Administrative Office of the United States Courts. (1995). *Report on Applications for Orders Authorizing or Approving the Interception of Wire, Oral, or Electronic Communications (Wiretap Report).*

United States Congress, Office of Technology Assessment. (1987). *Defending Secrets, Sharing Data: New Locks and Keys for Electronic Information,* OTA-CIT-310, Washington, D.C.: Government Printing Office, Washington, D.C.

United States Congress, Office of Technology Assessment. (1994). *Information Security and Privacy in Network Environments,* OTA-TCT-606.

United States Department of Commerce, National Bureau of Standards. (1973). "Cryptographic algorithms for protection of computer data during transmission and dormant storage: solicitation of proposals." *Federal Register* Vol. 38, No. 93, p. 12763, May 15, 1973.

United States Department of Commerce, National Bureau Standards. (1974). "Encryption algorithms for computer data protection: reopening of solicitation." *Federal Register* Vol. 39, No. 167, p. 30961, August 27, 1974.

United States Department of Commerce, National Bureau of Standards. (1977). "Data Encryption Standard," Federal Information Processing Standard Publication No. 46.

United States Department of Commerce, National Bureau of Standards. (1980). "DES Modes of Operation," Federal Information Processing Standard 81.

United States Department of Commerce, National Bureau of Standards. (1982). "Solicitation for Public Key Cryptographic Algorithms," *Federal Register,* Vol. 47, No. 126, p. 28445, June 30, 1982.

United States Department of Commerce, National Institute of Standards and Technology. (1989). "Comments of NSA Changes to NIST MOU of March 8," March 13, 1989 in USHR 101, p. 270.

United States Department of Commerce, National Institute of Standards and Technology. (1990a). "Memorandum for the Record, January 31, 1990," in CPSR 1993.

United States Department of Commerce, National Institute for Standards and

Technology. (1990b). "Memorandum for the Record, March 26, 1990," in CPSR 1993.

United States Department of Commerce, National Institute of Standards and Technology. (1991a). "Memorandum for the Record, Twenty-Seventh Meeting of the Technical Working Group," May 28, 1991, in CPSR 1993.

United States Department of Commerce, National Institute of Standards and Technology. (1991b). *Publication XX: Announcement and Specifications for a Digital Signature Standard (DSS)*, August 19, 1991.

United States Department of Commerce, National Institute of Standards and Technology. (1991c). "Public Key Status Report," in EPIC 1996, p. C-3.

United States Department of Commerce, National Institute of Standards and Technology. (1993). "A Proposed Federal Information Processing Standard for an Escrowed Encryption Standard (EES)," *Federal Register*, Vol. 58, July 30, 1993, pp. 40791–40793.

United States Department of Commerce. (1994a). "Briefing re Escrowed Encryption Standard, Department of Commerce, February, 4, 1994."

United States Department of Commerce, National Institute of Standards and Technology. (1994b). "Approval of Federal Information Processing Standards Publication 185, Escrowed Encryption Standard," *Federal Register*, Vol. 59, No. 27, February 9, 1994.

United States Department of Commerce, National Institute of Standards and Technology. (1994c). *Federal Information Processing Standards Publication 186: Digital Signature Standard (DSS)*, May 19, 1994.

United States Department of Commerce, National Institute of Standards and Technology, (1997). "Announcing Development of a Federal Information Processing Standard for Advanced Encryption Standard," *Federal Register*, Vol. 62, No. 1, January 2, 1997, pp. 93–94.

United States Department of Commerce, National Institute of Standards and Technology, and United States Department of Defense, National Security Agency, (1989). "Memorandum of Understanding between the Director of the National Institute of Standards and Technology and the Director of the National Security Agency concerning the Implementation of Public Law 100–235," March 24, 1989.

United States Department of Defense, National Security Agency, Office of General Counsel. (1994). "Proposed Changes to Escrow Encryption Standard," 12 January 1994.

United States Department of Justice. (1976). *Report on Enquiry into CIA-Related Electronic Surveillance Activities*, SC-05078-76, June 30.

United States Department of Justice. (1994a). "Briefing re Escrowed Encryption Standard, Department of Commerce," February 4, 1994.

U.S. Department of Justice. (1994b). *Sourcebook of Criminal Justice Statistics.*

United States Department of Justice, Office of the Inspector General, Michael Bromwich. (1997). "A Review of the FBI's Performance in Uncovering the Espionage of Aldrich Hazen Ames (April 1997)," (unclassified version).

United States Department of State. (1997). Country Reports on Human Rights Practices for 1996.

United States Department of War. (1943). Wartime Civil Control Administration, Western Defense Command and Fourth Army, Press Release No. 1, *Final Report: Japanese Evacuation from the West Coast 1942*, March 14, 1942, Washington 1943.

United States General Accounting Office. (1990). *Computers and Power: How the Government Obtains, Verifies, Uses and Protects Personal Data*, Briefing to the Chairman, Subcommittee of Telecommunications and Finance, Committees on Energy and Commerce, House of Representatives, August 3, 1990.

United States General Accounting Office. (1992). *Advanced Communications Technologies Pose Wiretapping Challenges*, Briefing Report to the Chairman, Subcommittee on Telecommunications and Finance, Committee on Energy and Commerce, House of Representatives, July 1992.

U.S. General Accounting Office. (1993a). *National Crime Information Center: Legislation Needed to Deter Misuse of Criminal Justice Information*, GAO/T-GGD-93-41, Washington, D.C., U.S. Government Printing Office, July 1993.

United States General Accounting Office. (1993b). *Communications Privacy: Federal Policy and Actions*, (Letter Report, 11/04/93, GAO/OSI-94-2).

United States General Accounting Office. (1997). *IRS Systems Security: Tax Processing and Data Still at Risk due to Serious Weaknesses*, (Letter Report, 4/8/97, GAO/AIMD-97-49).

United States General Services Administration. (1992). "Attachment to May 5, 1992 GSA memo, p. 2," in CPSR 1993.

United States House of Representatives, Committee on Appropriations, *Department of Justice Appropriations for 1951*, Eighty-First Congress, Second Session, 1950.

United States House of Representatives, Committee on Appropriations, Subcommittee on Commerce, Justice, State, and the Judiciary, *FY 99 Appropriations for the Department of Justice*, One Hundred and Fifth Congress, Second Session, 1998.

United States House of Representatives, Committee on the Judiciary, Subcommittee No. 5, *Wiretapping*, Hearings on HR 762, Eighty-Fourth Congress, First Session, 1955.

United States House of Representatives, Committee on the Judiciary, Subcommittee No. 5, *Anti-Crime Program*, Hearings on HR 5037, 5038, 5384, 5385 and 5386, March 15, 16, 22, 23, April 5, 7, 10, 12, 19, 20, 26 and 27, 1967, Ninetieth Congress, First Session, 1967.

United States House of Representatives, Committee on Judiciary, *Statement of Information, Book VII, Part 4,* Ninety-Third Congress, Second Session, 1974.

United States House of Representatives, Committee of the Judiciary, *Impeachment Inquiry*, Hearings, Ninety-Third Congress, Second Session, 1974.

United States House of Representatives, Committee on Government Operations, Subcommittee, *Computer Security Act of 1987*, Hearings on HR 145, February 25, 26, and March 17, 1987, One Hundredth Congress, First Session, 1987.

United States House of Representatives, Committee on Government Operations, House Report 100-153, Part 2, *Report on the Computer Security Act of 1987*, One Hundredth Congress, First Session, Washington, D.C.

United States House of Representatives, Committee of Government Operations, Legislative and National Security Subcommittee, *Military and Civilian Control of Computer Security Issues*, Hearings on May 4 1989, One Hundred First Congress, First Session, 1989.

United States House of Representatives, Committee on the Judiciary, Subcommittee on Economic and Commercial Law, *The Threat of Foreign Economic Espionage to U.S. Corporations*, Hearings on April 29 and May 7, 1992, One Hundred Second Congress, Second Session.

United States House of Representatives, Committee on Foreign Affairs, Subcommittee on Economic Policy, Trade, and the Environment, *Export Controls on Mass Market Software*, Hearings on October 12, 1993, One Hundred Third Congress, First Session.

United States House of Representatives, Committee on Energy and Commerce, Subcommittee on Telecommunications and Finance, *Network Wiretapping Capabilities*, Hearings on September 13, 1994, One Hundred Third Congress, Second Session.

United States House of Representatives, Committee on the Judiciary, *Report on*

'*Telecommunications Carrier Assistance to the Government,*' HR103-827, One Hundred Third Congress, Second Session.

United States House of Representatives, Committee on Science, Subcommittee on Technology. *Secure Communications.* One Hundred Fifth Congress, First Session. February 11, 1997.

United States, Privacy Protection Study Commission, *Personal Privacy in an Information Society*, U.S. Government Printing Office, Washington, D.C., 1977.

United States Senate, Committee on the Judiciary, Subcommittee on Constitutional Rights. *Wiretapping and Eavesdropping Legislation*, Hearings on S. 1086, S. 1221, S. 1495, and S. 1822, May 9, 10, 11 and 12, 1961, Eighty-Seventh Congress, First Session.

United States Senate, Committee of the Judiciary, Subcommittee on Administrative Practice and Procedure. *Invasions of Privacy*, Hearings Pursuant to Senate Resolution 39, Eighty-Ninth Congress, First Session, 1965.

United States Senate. *Senate Judiciary Committee Report, together with Minority, Individual, and Additional Views, on Omnibus Crime Control and Safe Streets Act of 1967*, Report No. 1097, *Senate Miscellaneous Reports on Public Bills*, Serial Set 12972-1, Ninetieth Congress, Second Session, April 29, 1968.

United States Senate, Committee of the Judiciary, Subcommittee on Constitutional Rights, *Federal Data Banks, Computers, and the Bill of Rights*, Hearings on February 23, 24, 25, March 2, 3, 4, 9, 10, 11, 15, 17, 1971, Part 1, Ninety-Second Congress, First Session.

United States Senate, Committee on the Judiciary, Staff of the Subcommittee on Constitutional Rights, *Army Surveillance of Civilians: A Documentary Analysis*, Ninety-Second Congress, Second Session, 1972.

United States Senate, Committee of the Judiciary, Subcommittee on Constitutional Rights, *Military Surveillance of Civilian Politics*, U.S. Government Printing Office, Washington, D.C., Ninety-Third Congress, First Session, 1973.

United States Senate, Select Committee on Presidential Campaign Activities, *Hearings, Phase 1: Watergate Investigation,* Ninety-Third Congress, First Session, 1973.

United States Senate, Committee on the Judiciary, Subcommittee on Constitutional Rights, *Federal Data Banks and Constitutional Rights*, Vol. I, Ninety-third Congress, Second Session, 1974.

United States Senate, Committee on the Judiciary, Subcommittee on Administrative Practice and Procedure, and Committee on Foreign Relations, Subcommittee on Surveillance, *Warrantless Wiretapping and Electronic Surveillance*, Hearings on April 3, 8, May 8, 9, 10, and 23, 1974, Ninety-Third Congress, Second Session.

United States Senate, Committee on the Judiciary, Subcommittee on Criminal Laws and Procedures and Constitutional Rights, *Electronic Surveillance for National Security Purposes*, Hearings, October 1–3, 1974, Ninety-Third Congress, Second Session, 1974.

United States Senate, "A Resolution to Establish a Committee to Study Government Operations with Respect to Intelligence," Senate Resolution 21, Ninety-Fourth Congress, First Session, January 27, 1975.

United States Senate, Select Committee to Study Governmental Operations with Respect to Intelligence Activities, *Intelligence Activities. Senate Resolution 21. Volume 2: Huston Plan*, Hearings, September 23, 24, and 25, 1975, Ninety-Fourth Congress, First Session, 1975.

United States Senate, Select Committee to Study Governmental Operations with respect to Intelligence Activities, *Intelligence Activities. Senate Resolution 21. Volume 6: Federal Bureau of Investigation*, Hearings, November 18, 19, December 2, 3, 9, 10, 11, 1975, Ninety-Fourth Congress, First Session, 1975.

United States, Senate Select Committee to Study Governmental Operations with respect to Intelligence Activities, *Intelligence Activities and the Rights of Americans, Final Report, Book II*, Report 94-755, Ninety-fourth Congress, Second Session, April 23, 1976.

United States, Senate Select Committee to Study Governmental Operations with respect to Intelligence Activities, *Supplementary Staff Reports on Intelligence Activities and the Rights of Americans, Final Report, Book III*, Report 94-755, Ninety-fourth Congress, Second Session, April 23, 1976.

United States Senate, Select Committee on Intelligence, *Senate Select Committee on Intelligence Inquiry into the FBI Investigation of the Committee in Solidarity with the People of El Salvador*, Hearings on February 23, April 13, September 14 and 29, 1988, One Hundredth Congress, Second Session.

United States Senate, Select Committee on Intelligence, *The FBI and CISPES*, Report 101-46, One Hundred First Congress, First Session, July, 1989.

United States Senate, Committee on the Judiciary, Subcommittee on Technology and the Law, *Administration's Clipper Chip Key Escrow Encryption Program*, Hearings, May 3, 1994, One Hundred Third Congress, Second Session.

United States Senate, Committee on the Judiciary, Subcommittee on Technology and the Law (Senate), and United States House of Representatives, Committee on the Judiciary, Subcommittee on Civil and Constitutional Rights, *Digital Telephony and Law Enforcement Access to Advanced Telecommunications Technologies and Services*, Joint Hearings on HR 4922 and S. 2375, March 18 and August 11, 1994, One Hundred Third Congress, Second Session.

United States Senate, Committee on Commerce, Science, and Transportation, *S377, Promotion of Commerce Online in the Digital Era (PROCODE) Act of 1997,* March 19, 1997, One Hundred Fifth Congress, First Session.

United States Senate, Appropriations Committee, Subcommittee on Treasury and General Government, *Overview of Internal Revenue Service Employees Misuse of Taxpayers' Files,* Hearings on April 15, 1997, One Hundred Fifth Congress, First Session.

United States Senate, Judiciary Committee, *Encryption, Key Recovery, and Privacy Protection in the Information Age,* Hearings on July 9, 1997, One Hundred Fifth Congress, First Session.

United States Senate, Judiciary Committee, Subcommittee on Technology, Terrorism, and Government Information, *The Encryption Debate: Criminals, Terrorists, and the Security Needs of Business and Industry,* Hearings on September 3, 1997, One Hundred Fifth Congress, First Session.

— V —

Van Keuren, Edgar. (1991). "Utilization of the high power microwave sources in electronics sabotage and terrorism," *Proc. International Carnahan Conference on Security Technology*, October 1–3, 1991, Taipei, Taiwan, pp. 16–20.

— W —

Wannall, W. (1966). Memo to W. Sullivan, December 22 as reported in USS 94e, p. 328 and p. 346.

Ward, Daniel. (1961). State's Attorney, Cook County, Illinois, in USS 87, p. 400.

Warren, Samuel and Louis Brandeis. (1890). "The Right to Privacy," *Harvard Law Review*, pp. 193–220.

Weiner, Tim, David Johnston, and Neil Lewis. (1995). *Betrayal: The Story of Aldrich Ames, an American Spy*, Random House, New York.

Weingarten, Fred. (1997). "Cryptography: Who Holds the Key?," *SIAM News*, January/February, p. 2.

Welchman, Gordon. (1982). *The Hut Six Story*, McGraw Hill.

White, Theodore H. (1975). *Breach of Faith*, Atheneum Publishers.

The White House, Office of the Press Secretary. (1993). "Statement on the Clipper Chip Initiative," in EPIC 1994 April 16, Washington, D.C.

The White House, Office of the Press Secretary. (1998). "Administration Updates Encryption Policy," September 16, 1998.

Executive Office of the President, Office of Management and Budget, Interagency Working Group on Cryptography Policy, Bruce W. McConnell and Edward J. Appel, Co-Chairs. (1996). *Enabling Privacy, Commerce, Security and Public Safety in the Global Information Infrastructure (draft)*, May 20, 1996.

Wiener, Michael. (1993). "Efficient DES Key Search," presented at the Rump Session of CRYPTO, TR-244, School of Computer Science, Carleton University, May 1994.

Wilk, Charles K. and Donald E. Kraft. (1979). "Protected Government Telecommunications: The National Issues" National Telecommunications Conference, Washington, D.C., November 27–29, pp. 43.1.1–43.1.4.

Wilk, Charles K. and Donald E. Kraft. (1980). "The Passive Security Risk in Telecommunications" Security Management, August, pp. 52–54, 67–68.

Williams, Robert H. (1992). "Economic Spying by Foes, Friends Gains Momentum." *SIGNAL*, July, pp. 56–57.

Wines, Michael. (1990). "Security Agency Debates New Role: Economic Spying," *New York Times*, June 18, p. 1.

Wright, Carroll D. and William C. Hunt. (1900). *The History and Growth of the United States Senate*, Government Printing Office, Washington.

Wright, S. Fowler. (1929). "Police and Public" Second Revised Edition, Fowler Wright Ltd., 240, High Holborn, London W.C.1.

Wright, Peter. (1987). *Spy Catcher, The Candid Autobiography of a Senior Intelligence Officer*, Viking.

— Y —

Yardley, Herbert O. (1931). *The American Black Chamber*, Indianapolis, Bobbs-Merrill.

— Z —

Zimmermann, Philip. (1995). *PGP: Source Code and Internals*, MIT Press.

# Index

Demodulating modem signals, 91–92, 263

Denmark, encryption policy in, 221

Department of Energy
opposition to EES, 281

Department of Justice, 277

Department of State
Early weakness of COMSEC in, 252

Depth in Vigenère systems, 22

DES. *See* Data Encryption Standard

Detection of interception, 46

Deterrence in crime prevention, 111–112

Diagnosis
of cryptosystems, 100
of signals, 90–92

Dicks, Norman D., 223

Diffie, Whitfield, 60–61, 262, 264, 278, 282, 283, 286

Diffie-Hellman key exchange, 37–38
for business, 227
development of, 61
in Key Exchange Algorithm, 215
in TSD 3600, 214

Digital signal processing, 285
in secure telephones, 281

Digital Signature Algorithm, 215

Digital Signature Standard, 72–74, 231
speed of, 256

Digital signatures, 36, 60, 71–74, 250
primitive, 250

Digital Telephony Proposal, 183–184.
*See also* CALEA
Clipper chip and, 280
costs of, 274
FBI support for, 194–195, 232
and kidnapping cases, 285
revised, 195–199
and transactional information, 192
wiretapping value asserted in, 185

Digital telephone switches, 116

Direct standard alphabets in Vigenère systems, 21

Direction finding, 261

Disinformation, 102, 264

Disks
automated searching of, 286

Distribution of keys, 30–32

Dobrynin, Anatoly, 96

Domestic organizations, privacy violations against, 140, 143, 146–148

Domestic security, wiretapping for, 159, 172–176

Domestic terrorism, wiretapping targeting of, 189, 233

Dominican Republic sugar case, 173

Double DES. *See* triple DES

Double Vigenère systems, 22

Douglas, William O., 139

Downgrading schedule for classified information, 249

Dragging key, 261

Drug Enforcement Agency, 277

Drug trafficking
military involvement against, 121–122
wiretapping targeting of, 188–189

Drugs
market inelasticity of, 275
as a national security issue, 257
reducing consumption of, 275

Dual-use items, 106

Dynamic key distribution, 31–32

Dynamic routing, 98, 263

E-mail, cryptography for, 205–206

ESS series telephone switches, 116

Eastland, James, 141

Eavesdropping
meaning of, 151
punishment of, 128

Economic espionage, 43–44

Editions of code books, 250

Editions of cryptographic keys, 30, 250

Hemingway, Ernest, 258
Hersh, Seymour, 96
High energy microwave, 263
High-Speed Anti-radiation Missile, 263
Hogan, Doug, 253
Hogan, Frank, 257
Holloway, Jack, 264
Home Box Office, 263–264
Hong Kong, 202
Hoover, J. Edgar, 275–276. *See also* Federal Bureau of Investigation
journalists bugged by, 270
and Martin Luther King, Jr., 141
on organized crime, 168–169
Hops for messages, 90
House Judiciary Committee, 277
Human intelligence (HUMINT), 79, 234–235
Hurley, Deborah, 283
Huston, Tom, 145

IBM2984 banking system, 59
Identification Friend or Foe (IFF) devices, 56
Identification, technology for, 119–120
Identities
absolute vs. consistent, 283–284
Iglehart, Dick, 190, 276
ILL-WIND, 284–285
Imitative communications deception, 264
Immigration and Naturalization Service, 277
Improvements in telecommunications
impact on crime of, 276
Incriminating conversations
overheard in wiretapping, 274
Indonesia, surveillance in, 202
Industrial espionage, 251, 251
foreign, 251
by governments, 43–44
Industrial Tempest Program

CCEP modeled on, 254
Infiltration, 113
Informants, 127, 142, 267, 269
Information theory, 264
Information warfare, 101–102, 103
Infrared imaging, 119, 120
Inman, Bobby Ray, 63, 231, 253, 262
Insurrections and wiretapping, 172–173
ISDN. *See* Integrated Services Digital Network (ISDN)
Integrated Services Digital Network (ISDN), 99
secure telephones for, 263
Integrity of messages, 12
Intellectual property, 5
Intelligence Authorization Act, 123
Intelligence collection
embarrassments in, 258
Intelligence communications, *See* Communications intelligence (COMINT)
prospects for, 233–237
security from, 103–105
spectrum of, 78–83
from wiretapping, 157–165
Intercept equipment
capabilities of, 265
cryptanalysis in, 285
Interception
in communications intelligence, 85–93
impediments to, 97–99
national policies on, 200–202
one-sided, 260
signal processing problems of, 263
Interdiction of crimes, 111
Internal Revenue Service, 148
browsing of citizen files by, 271
International Business Machines, 253
telephone security of, 251–252
Alternate Encryption Technique of, 253

## DATE DUE